War in the Shadow of
Auschwitz

Religion, Theology, and the Holocaust
Alan L. Berger, *Series Editor*

War in the Shadow of
AUSCHWITZ

Memoirs of a Polish Resistance Fighter
and Survivor of the Death Camps

John Wiernicki

SYRACUSE UNIVERSITY PRESS

The paper used in this publication meets the ~~~~~~~ ~~~~~~~~~~ ~~ ~~~~~~~ ~~~~ ~~~ ~~~~~~~~ ~~~ ~~~~~~~~
Information Sciences—Permanence of Paper for Printed Library Materials, ANSI Z39.48–1984. ∞™

Library of Congress Cataloging-in-Publication Data
Wiernicki, John.
War in the shadow of Auschwitz : memoirs of a Polish resistance fighter and survivor
of the death camps / John Wiernicki.
  p. cm. — (Religion, theology, and the Holocaust)
  Includes bibliographical references and index.
  ISBN 0-8156-0722-9 (alk. paper)
  1. Wiernicki, John. 2. World War, 1939–1945—Personal narratives, Polish. 3.
  Guerrillas—Poland—Biography. 4. Prisoners of war—Poland—Biography. 5. Auschwitz
  (Concentration camp) I. Title. II. Series.
D811.W4827 2001
940.54'7243'094386—dc21   2001034168

Manufactured in the United States of America

This book is dedicated to my grandchildren,
Sarah, Anna, Caitlin, Caroline, and John,
with my hope that in their lifetime
they will not experience the anguish
of my generation.

As a seventeen-year-old boy, John Wiernicki fought with the Polish partisans against German aggressors. He was arrested by the Gestapo and imprisoned in the German concentration camp Auschwitz-Birkenau. After a daring escape, he joined the Allied Forces in Italy and after the war returned to civilian life. He eventually married, emigrated to the United States, raised two sons, and became a successful architect. In 1995, he was decorated by Lech Wałęsa, the president of Poland, for his military services during the war.

Contents

Illustrations   ix

Acknowledgments   xi

Introduction   xiii

CHAPTER ONE   Dry September   3

CHAPTER TWO   Uneven Struggle   18

CHAPTER THREE   Freedom Fighters   47

CHAPTER FOUR   Devil's Empire   77

CHAPTER FIVE   Auschwitz-Birkenau   88

CHAPTER SIX   Men's Camp BIId   114

CHAPTER SEVEN   Dr. Thilo's Hospital   141

CHAPTER EIGHT   *Desinfektionskommando*   162

CHAPTER NINE   Buchenwald-Ohrdruf   209

CHAPTER TEN   Death March   236

CHAPTER ELEVEN   White Stars   246

Epilogue   252

Appendix: Table of Military Ranks   261

Glossary of Camp Terms   263

Bibliography   267

Index   269

Illustrations

Plan of Auschwitz   2

Following page 140

First day as a cadet

Manor house in Matczyn

Working in Potoczek

Lieutenant Czarnota-Szaruga and his staff

Czarnota-Szaruga partisans

Central watchtower and main entrance to Birkenau

Central bathhouse in Birkenau

Steam room in the bathhouse

List of functional prisoners who received bonuses

Preparation for selection of Jewish transport

Dr. H. Thilo selecting Jews at the railroad platform

Prisoner transfer list to Buchenwald, page 1

Prisoner transfer list to Buchenwald, page 7

Ovens in Buchenwald crematorium

Entrance to tunnels at Jonastal Valley

General Eisenhower's visit to Ohrdruf camp

SS atrocities in Ohrdruf camp

Acknowledgments

THIS BOOK REFLECTS on the important, exciting and sometimes painful history of the early years in my life. The events that I describe took place more than a half-century ago. After the end of the war in 1945, I tried to summarize some of the highlights of my involvement with the Polish Underground and my subsequent imprisonment, but I couldn't reconstruct all of them without the help and assistance of many people in the United States, Poland, and Germany.

Apart from my early childhood, most of my story takes place in the secret world of the underground and the murky, impersonal, and barbaric world of the extermination camps. At that time, I knew only "code names" of fellow freedom fighters and "numbers" of inmates at the concentration camps. It took many hours of extensive search and the detailed review of existing records to identify and verify names of victims and oppressors. However, some of the names of survivors have been changed to protect their privacy and to respect their preference for anonymity. Other names could not be found and verified. The real challenge was to confirm the facts and identify the heroes who lived, fought, suffered, and died as the victims of Nazi persecution. Many people helped me to meet this challenge.

I wish to acknowledge the contribution of Dr. Ireneusz Caban from Lublin, Poland, and Dr. Jerzy Krzyżanowski from Ohio State University for helping me to identify the chronology of underground activities in the Lublin district of the Polish Home Army.

I appreciate the support and data received from the Archives and the staff members of the State Museum Oświęcim-Brzezinka in Poland. I am also grateful to the researchers of the United States Holocaust Memorial Museum in Washington, D.C. and archivists of the Gedenkstatte Buchenwald in Germany.

I am thankful to my daughters-in-law, Joan, for her perseverance and patience in typing my manuscript, and Kathy, for her support and encouragement. Especially, I am grateful to my sons, Christopher and Peter, for their analysis, constructive comments, and editorial help.

Last but not least, I wish to acknowledge the contribution of my wife Anne, my lifetime companion and partner, whose encouragement, patience, research, editing, and endless retyping were invaluable in the completion of the final text.

John Wiernicki

"Strzemię" and "Shutzhäftling 150302"
Bethesda, Maryland, 2000

Introduction

SOME OF THE EVENTS that shaped my early days and influenced many important decisions in my life I remember distinctly. Other activities seem blurred and easily forgotten. Years of turmoil in war-torn Poland are intermingled with days of underground resistance, partisan warfare, and the horrors of Auschwitz-Birkenau.

My military service with the Polish Home Army and imprisonment in the German concentration camps represent a past that overshadows all other experiences in my life. This memorable period lives with utmost clarity in my mind.

I remember long days with the partisans, and the endless marching, hiding, waiting, and marching again. I recall days of high expectations and sudden disappointments, full of secret codes and assumed names. Above all, I remember days of daring encounters with Germans and hope for final victory. I also remember another world of pain and despair in Auschwitz-Birkenau. Although it is impossible to adequately describe the tragedy of all who were imprisoned in this infamous concentration camp, I particularly remember watching helplessly as long lines of Jews—men, women, and children—waited to enter the crematoria.

These events took place many years ago. The passage of time, including the life span of almost two generations, has allowed me to reflect on my wartime experiences in a more mature and perhaps less emotional way.

Immediately after my escape from the Ohrdruf Concentration Camp in 1945, and during a short stay with the American Guard Battalion, I used all of my available time to recall and record my most memorable experiences from Auschwitz-Birkenau and other concentration camps. These included names, dates, SS identities, inmates' numbers, and their behavior. As a witness to the massive genocide of innocent people, I had a strong desire and determination to document the history and share the "unthinkable" with others.Fifty years ago I felt deeply that the incredible events in Auschwitz-Birkenau must not be forgotten, both for the sake of the victims and as a warning to future oppressors. Today my desire to share my war experiences is even stronger than it was a half century ago. The hard facts are still the same, but extensive research over the past few years, recently available documentation, and testimonies of survivors have enriched my understanding of history and allowed me to reconstruct more accurately what I witnessed. Indeed, the passage of time has opened the door wider for assessing the truth about life and death in the German concentration and extermination camps.

The prisoners' general knowledge of camp events during the war was limited, because the SS Kommandant and his staff purposely suppressed the facts. The inmates concentrated on survival of the daily camp routine, which included avoidance of SS personnel and the brutal camp functionaries. Surviving each day was a victory. As a nonprivileged and nonfunctionary prisoner, I was on the bottom of the camp's social structure. Awareness of international politics and the outside events, including the war itself, was severely limited at that time, and thus such matters did not seriously affect the prisoners' struggle for everyday existence. Life span expectations were limited to days, perhaps weeks, certainly not years. The dream of the victorious ending of the war was constantly on everybody's mind. Surviving from morning "roll call" to evening "lights out" was a necessity to make this dream viable.

As time moves on, the continuous political, social, and economic changes in the world generate new issues with new concerns and create a frightening turmoil around peoples' lives. Yesterday's atrocities are easily forgotten in view of today's new disasters and the uncertainties of tomorrow.

My story covers a broad range of human experiences. The growing-up years in prewar Poland and the dignity of armed resistance under German occupation are overshadowed by the misery of human indifference and the tragedy of the senseless killings of Jews and others in Auschwitz-Birkenau. The deliberate, cold, premeditated murder of innocent people, condemned by birth to the gas chambers, must be engraved in our memories as a living reminder of the capability for cruelty and cold indifference on the part of the human race.

It did happen. The extermination camp in Auschwitz-Birkenau did exist. The SS doctors: Thilo and Mengele were real people, selecting Jews and other innocent victims for gassing. The SS guards did carry out their mission of providing and dispensing Zyklon B canisters to the crematoria chambers. I know this because I was there. A half century after it happened, the truth is well known. I want to add this testimony to the existing evidence so it will be available to others for a long time after the last survivor from Auschwitz-Birkenau departs from this world.

The purpose of my story is to encourage new generations to preserve our painful past and cherish the promises of a brighter future. The existence of Auschwitz-Birkenau and all other camps brought the dark side of humanity into sharp focus. This experience should serve as a sole reminder in our never-ending effort to practice tolerance, respect, and compassion in order to build a just and better world.

War in the Shadow of
Auschwitz

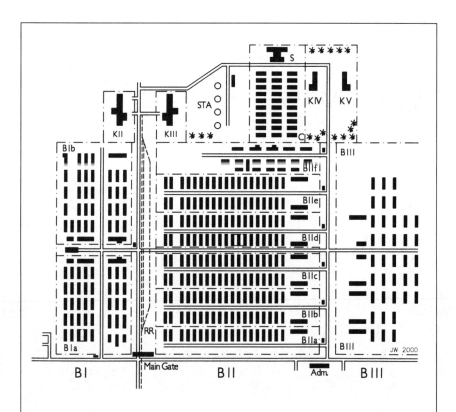

PLAN OF AUSCHWITZ II (BIRKENAU)
As of 1944

BIa	Women's Camp	KIII	Gas Chamber and Crematorium III
BIb	Women's Camp	KIV	Gas Chamber and Crematorium IV
BIIa	Men's Quarantine Camp	KV	Gas Chamber and Crematorium V
BIIb	Theresienstadt Jewish Family Camp	MG	Main Gate and Guard House
BIIc	Hungarian Jewish Women's Camp	RR	Railway Ramp
BIId	Men's Camp	S	"Sauna"-Central Bath House
BIIe	Gypsy Family Camp	C	"Canada"-Personal Effects Depot
BIIf	Men's Hospital	ADM	SS Barracks and Administration
BIII	"Mexico"-Jewish Transit Camp	STA	Sewage Treatment Area
KII	Gas Chamber and Crematorium II	-..-..	Electrified Barbed Wire Fence

Plan is based on the aerial photograph taken by the U.S. Air Force in May 1944 and revised by the author.

Plan of Auschwitz

CHAPTER ONE

Dry September

THE RAILROAD STATION was full of people. Volunteers and soldiers mixed with the crowds of ordinary travelers who formed endless lines waiting for trains, tickets, taxis, and arriving families. A bright August sun penetrated the glazed roof of the railroad station canopy, as people boarded two long trains on both sides of the platform. I could see the sweaty faces of soldiers behind closed windows of the waiting trains. I could hear the sound of a military band stationed at the entrance to the waiting room competing with the cheering of the enthusiastic crowd. Soldiers of the First Battalion of the Fortieth Infantry Regiment from Lwów, the largest city in southeast Poland, were going west to join their comrades for the impending war with Germany.

Detached from the noise and excitement, deep in my own thoughts, I was trying to sort out my personal problems. I was slowly hobbling toward one of the trains. Relying heavily on a strong wooden cane and without a shoe on my swollen left foot, I was carefully making my way through the excited crowd.

The summer of 1939 had been full of surprises. After completing my freshman year at the Military Academy in Lwów, I passed all of my examinations and was formally accepted into the academy's senior class. Next year, as a sign of my growing military competence, I was going to receive a rifle and join the cadet training battalion. This unit consisted of upperclassmen, fourteen to eighteen years old, who would be given extensive military training with knowledge of all kinds of modern weapons. I looked forward to my remaining four years at the Academy. On June 1, I had left for a summer vacation with my Aunt Helena at her estate in Potoczek near Lublin. However, in late July, I experienced severe pains in my left foot and since country doctors in the area could not arrive at a reasonable diagnosis, I left my aunt's estate to get medical advice from the military doctors in Lwów. The painful swelling of my foot also puzzled the doctors in Lwów. All X rays were inconclusive. Out of frustration, the doctors finally decided to apply ointments to the infected area and to monitor the healing progress.

Meanwhile the cadet training battalion was to be mobilized at the beginning of August. When I reported to the Military Academy, the company commander gave me a surprised look.

"Janusz, you are too young to be attached to a rifle company and with your sick foot, I can't even use you as a runner. The best thing for you is to go on sick leave until you fully recover. Perhaps you could leave town."

"Captain, sir," I tried to argue. "My foot is getting better. In a few days, I will be healthy and fit."

"Janusz." I sensed a little annoyance in Captain Bielak's voice. "We can't take any chances. When you are ready, you can always come back and I will have a job for you."

"Yes, sir," I saluted smartly. Half-resigned and half-disappointed, I decided to return to my aunt's home in Potoczek.

Walking slowly through the city's streets, I sensed a high degree of war fever. Everywhere there were people in uniform. On Main Street, a military band, surrounded by young boys, was marching to the sounds of the Polish national anthem and leading columns of volunteers to the recruiting station. In my pocket, I carried a permit from Captain Bielak, which allowed me to board the first military train going north. The stationmaster whistled and signaled the departure to the conductor, and the steaming locomotive pierced the air with two sharp whistles. I had hardly managed to board the train when the wheels started to move. There were last-minute handshakes, kisses, and tearful good-byes. Men were running to jump aboard the moving train, as it slowly increased its speed. Soon the station disappeared behind the last carriage.

The train was packed with military personnel. Soldiers, nurses, and draftees and volunteers in civilian clothes filled all compartments and corridors. Unexpected mobilization and the possibility of a war with Germany made people anxiously aware that the situation was dangerous. I looked with envy upon young and healthy men and listened as they discussed anticipated wartime adventures. They all expected a sudden and decisive victory. Sitting near the window, lost in the crowd of strangers, I closed my eyes and reflected upon the last few days. The rumors of war were both disturbing and exhilarating.

My "sick" foot had made me an invalid at the most inappropriate time. I listened to the exuberant and highly spirited discussions around me about the unquestionable Polish victory. The self-assurance and confidence of my fellow travelers made me proud as a soldier yet sad because of my personal circumstances. My dreams of actively participating in the defense of my country faded away as the increasing pain in my foot constantly reminded me about my untimely injury. "Why me and why now?" I silently muttered the usual questions and searched for answers, which were not there.

The train gradually reached full speed. Images of sleepy villages tucked away among the trees on both sides of the railroad flickered fast in reflections on the compartment's windows. After we passed the city of Przemyśl, the train turned north toward the flat, rolling fields and isolated farms of the Lublin district. As the landscape changed from the industrial environment of Przemyśl to the farming fields of eastern Poland, my thoughts wandered back to my life in my hometown of Lwów.

Life in Lwów had been pleasant and carefree. My family's apartment, on the sixth floor, was small but elegant. It consisted of four rooms, an entrance hall, bathroom, kitchen, and two balconies. My room adjoined a small balcony, and the master bedroom was located at the end of the entrance hall, separated from my quarters by an imposing dining room and my father's study, which faced a large balcony. The maid slept in the kitchen on a bed recessed behind a curtain. Every morning a young soldier, Stach Lis, arrived from the regiment to take care of my father's military uniform, shoes and equipment.

My father was a professional soldier, a major in the cavalry in the Fourteenth Lancers Regiment, stationed in Łyczaków, a suburb of Lwów. My parents led a busy life. As the quartermaster and deputy commander of the regiment, my father was well known in Lwów. Twice a week, in the evening, he played bridge with his friends at the George, a downtown hotel. Occasionally, he took me with him to a popular *"kawiarnia,"* a coffeehouse for an ice cream where I met many of his friends. My mother spent most of her time working with many charitable organizations in the city and was a volunteer nurse in the military hospital.

Most of my summer vacations were spent with my mother's relatives in Potoczek. Her sister, my aunt Helena, had married a young landowner before the First World War. His name was Wojciech Przanowski and he inherited a large and industrialized estate, Potoczek, from his childless uncle. Wojciech expanded his holdings and his investments and became one of the more successful landowners in the area. Life in Potoczek was typical of that of the Polish gentry at that time. It was elegant and exclusive, with many servants, chambermaids and grooms. Helena and her husband were well known for their traditional Polish hospitality. They were gracious and generous hosts. During one of my summer visits, I was given a white pony as a present from my aunt and uncle. After few lessons, I learned many equestrian skills from my cousins. It was a family tradition that Helena's sisters and their children would spend part of each summer together on the estate in Potoczek. This summer had been no different. I vacationed on the estate from June until July when I was forced to seek medical attention and prepare for the August mobilization of the cadets.

The sudden whistle of a locomotive interrupted my reveries about the past and brought me back to reality. I opened my eyes when the conductor touched my shoulder. "Wake up, young man. Time to get ready. Take your cane and I will help you with your luggage. Zaklików is the next station."

I was very grateful. "Thank you for your help, conductor."

My school day memories almost made me miss my destination. Zaklików was a small station and trains stopped only when requested to discharge passengers. I slowly climbed down from the carriage. The conductor left the luggage on the ground.

"Good luck. I hope that you will feel better soon," he called from the departing train.

"Thank you again," I waved from the distance.

It was dark and the platform was deserted except for one lonely figure standing in front of the stationmaster's office. I knew it was Jan Patosz waiting to take me to Potoczek. As long as I can remember, Jan was an inseparable part of my uncle's estate. His father had worked all his life at Potoczek and after his father retired as the estate's head coachman, Jan inherited his position. With two sons, Józef and Janek, as his helpers, he was responsible for the maintenance of several horse drawn carriages and the care of sixteen horses. My uncle and his family used the horses exclusively for business, social visits, excursions, hunting and trips to traditional Sunday mass in local church. Jan had spent all his life working in Potoczek, first as a groom and subsequently as the head coachman. His dedication to my uncle's family was well known and sometimes even discouraged and criticized by the other servants.

"Good evening, Jan." I greeted him warmly as I slowly stepped from the train. He and I were old friends. He had known me since my childhood.

"Good evening, Mr. Janusz. How was your trip?"

"Too many people and too much talk about the war. How is life in Potoczek?"

"Fine. We are all getting ready for the war. My older son, Józef, was called by his regiment yesterday and he is leaving tomorrow."

I looked at the horses and carriage waiting in front of the station. "Jan, I see you have new horses?"

"Yes, Mr. Michał decided to try some young ones. It is working fine."

Quickly, he packed my suitcase under the seat of the black landau and we were on our way to Potoczek. It took about an hour to reach our destination. All the houses in the village were dark, but a few lights flickered in the windows of the big manor house. As we stopped in front of the main entrance, under an impressive portico supported by four columns, a young and fresh voice greeted me from the porch.

"Good morning, Mr. Janusz. Nice to have you back."

"Hello, Anna. How are you?"

Anna was one of the kitchen maids working directly for my aunt. She was a bright and cheerful seventeen-year old country girl. With dark, long hair, black eyes, and dressed in a black skirt and white blouse, she looked radiant and fresh. Even after a long day and exhausting journey, I could not conceal my appreciation of her good looks. Every morning, she was up bright and early to bake bread and prepare an early breakfast for my uncle's family. She also took care of the guestrooms. On my previous visits, I spent a fair amount of time chatting with her, flirting, and trying to gather courage to make further advances. She was responding warmly. I had a strong feeling that even though she was older than I, she really liked me.

"Mr. Janusz, since you are sick, I will help you with your luggage."

"Thank you, Anna, and good-bye, Jan," I waved from the porch.

"You are in number two, Mr. Janusz. This is a nice room."

"Thank you, Anna, and how are you?"

The house was dimly illuminated and most of the occupants were sound asleep. In the privacy of the huge entrance hall I touched her arm.

"Not here, Mr. Janusz," she whispered. "Somebody could see us." She looked around.

"Anna, everybody is in bed. Did you miss me?"

She stopped and looked at me seriously. "You are making fun of me. I am not in the mood for joking. We should not be talking like this since we are going nowhere. And now we may even have a war."

I squeezed her hand. "Anna, don't take life so seriously. Did you miss me?"

She smiled, "You are a spoiled young boy, selfish and too young to understand girls like me. But, yes, I missed you." Then she added, "Let me show you to your room."

The morning sun was shining through the venetian blinds. I opened my eyes and checked my watch: nine o'clock, late by Potoczek standards. Breakfast was usually served between eight and nine in the morning, and my aunt didn't take too kindly to people eating late. Normally, maids were cleaning the table after nine and latecomers had to wait until lunch. Since many relatives and guests visited the manor every summer, my aunt ran the daily routine with an iron hand. Food was excellent, and spending a summer in Potoczek was far more attractive than spending it in the best holiday resorts. Potoczek offered tennis, swimming, hunting, and horseback riding as well as long evenings playing bridge in the company of friends and family.

The Przanowski's had one son and three daughters, all grown and married except Halina. She was still at home, a very attractive blonde with a friendly disposition and a long line of suitors. The wealth of Halina's dowry was well known among local gentry. Two older daughters lived in the nearby area. Tola had married an agronomist, and after her father bought her an estate, she was happily settled in Zakrzówek with her new husband and one daughter. Rysia, the oldest sister, had married a professor of forestry. They were also leasing hundreds of acres of dense forest in Lipa, an adjoining village to Potoczek, and owned a large timber export business. They had two children, a boy and a girl, both in their early teens.

My uncle, or the squire—as local peasants called him, was getting old. Michał, his only son and the eldest child, took over management of the land. He was an enterprising businessman and he successfully expanded and further industrialized the estate. In his mid-thirties, he married a young woman from Pomerania and, since that time, he lived with his wife and their son in an adjoining house. It was not as luxurious as the squire's manor, but it was a very comfortable one-story rambler, fully equipped with all kitchen gadgets and appliances available in eastern Europe at that time. A large staff assisted Michał in administering the estate. Jerzy was the chief forester, Stanisław the manager of the distillery, and Paweł in charge of farming and agricultural products. All of the field hands, supervisors, stable boys, mechanics, and gardeners lived in the semidetached houses built on the estate by the Przanowski family thirty years ago. The same families held jobs on the estate from generation to generation. Sometimes treated by the local peasants as second-class citizens, the estate workers maintained dignity and pride in their work. This, combined with their genuine affection for the estate owners, made them indispensable team members responsible for the efficient running of the estate.

The squire was master of their destiny. He established the workers' pay scale, allocated housing and food subsidies, provided nurseries for small children, and welfare assistance for the elderly. He provided opportunities for advancement and was the highest authority in resolving disputes and in decisions about dismissal of unsatisfactory workers. Although the state and national labor laws controlled some aspects of labor and management practices, the individual estate owners were very independent and sometimes capricious masters of their workers' destinies. The squire was also a counselor, informal judge of domestic issues, and peacemaker. Nothing could happen on the estate grounds without his knowledge or approval. The squire's relationship with his workers was almost feudal, a system long ago forgotten by most of the countries of western Europe but still, in some ways, surviving strongly in eastern Poland. I felt strange during my first visit to Potoczek as a child, observing as old men and women kissed my uncle's hand as a sign of respect and formal greeting.

This morning I dressed as fast as I could and rushed downstairs to the dining room. Anna was already passing coffee and serving breakfast to my relatives. I smiled at her gently but she avoided my eyes.

"Good morning, Janusz, and how was your trip?" asked my aunt Antonina. She was Helena's younger sister.

"Good morning, Aunt Antonina, the trip was horrible. The train was overcrowded. People were excited and rude. I hope nothing will happen and we will be able to return to a normal life very soon."

My aunt was not too optimistic. "Janusz, I expect the worst. I talked to Kazik today and he is quite upset. They told him to evacuate his office."

Antonina never married. As the only spinster in the family, she took care of the newborn son of her younger sister, who had died during childbirth. Kazik was the boy's father. After his wife's tragic death, he entrusted Antonina with the care of his infant son. As the deputy governor of Lublin District, Kazik traveled a lot and was unable to provide a proper home environment for his infant son. He also had two other children from his previous marriage, a girl called Emilia and a boy called Paweł, who was about my age. Emilia, nicknamed Emmy, was at a boarding school run by nuns. Paweł lived with his father in Lublin. Both children spent all of their summer vacations with the rest of the family in Potoczek.

I looked around the table. In addition to Antonina feeding the baby jointly with her mother, Grandma Ligowski, and her sister Helena Przanowski, there were several other people whom I had never met before. I understood they were distant relatives from Silesia on their way to eastern Poland. This summer, with an uncertain political situation, which could lead to air raids and food shortages in the cities, there was more than the usual number of relatives visiting the Potoczek estate. Grandma Ligowski, with her daughter Antonina and the baby, arrived from Lublin. Also one of Halina's current suitors, Jan, stopped for a few weeks in Potoczek.

The manor house had ten guestrooms on the second floor, and with spacious formal rooms on the ground-floor level, including large ballroom, there was no concern about overcrowding. Breakfast and lunch were served informally in the dining room at regular times. Dinners were more elaborate, presided over by the chief footman Władysław, and assisted by two maids: Anna and Maria. I loved to watch Anna when sometimes, during Władysław's absence, she served the dinner in his place. I would smile at her warmly and discreetly and she would shyly acknowledge my interest. We both carefully watched my aunts, since flirting with servants was not acceptable in Potoczek.

Władysław, like Jan, was an old fixture in the manor house. His father has served as valet to Squire Przanowski's uncle, and Władysław grew up in this place from his early childhood position as a busboy to his present one of chief footman. Nothing in the kitchen could happen without Władysław's approval. Even the cook had to be diplomatic and played on Władysław's weakness for his favorite dishes. Although his family lived in one of the new houses near the manor, Władysław had his own room in the manor's servant quarters and spent most of his duty and off-duty time away from his family. He liked to drink vodka, but I do not remember seeing this weakness for alcohol affecting his formal functions. In his dinner jacket and white gloves, every evening, he served main dishes around the table and supervised Anna and Maria in providing the most efficient and professional service to the hosts and their guests.

The uncertainty of this summer brought slight changes to the usual routine. The meals were more informal and less traditional. Conversation around the table was somber and serious. The possibility of a German invasion diminished the importance of white gloves and dinner jackets, bridge parties and monthly dances in the ballroom.

The last days of August 1939 were warm and sunny with pleasant light winds blowing occasionally from the west. In spite of the rumors, and concern expressed in radio broadcasts and newspapers, everyday life for farm workers in Potoczek was uneventful, and, for the time being, far removed from the gathering clouds on the political horizon.

The village of Potoczek, adjoining the manor, was small but picturesque. Most of the farmhouses were strung along the road leading from the Zaklików-Modliborzyce highway toward the larger village of Potok Wielki. In the summer, one could hardly see the houses and adjoining barns standing in the shadows of tall, lush, green, and blooming pear and apple trees. Small family holdings did not provide sufficient income to support large peasant families. Most of the village population, in addition to toiling on their own land, worked as temporary hired hands on the Przanowskis' estate. Every morning they gathered in front of the warehouse on the estate backyard to be assigned to special daily chores by Paweł or his two field supervisors. Franciszek, an old man with a mustache, was in charge of horse details, and Tomasz, a skinny and dark—looking fellow, supervised farm hands working in the fields. In spite of this, with the personal pride and self-esteem of a small landowner, the peasants looked down upon regular estate workers who lived in squire houses called "quadruples," and whose livelihood depended entirely on the squire's wishes and prosperity. The estate workers' dwellings were located along the main street leading from the highway to the manor. They were grouped together behind maple trees, close to the farm buildings, and adjoined the village. The dislike was mutual, and occasionally, there were fights in the village inn between estate workers and peasants.

Working the land was a hard and challenging job. The local farmers on their small plots were as much concerned with their crops as my cousin Michał Przanowski with those on his vast estate. The farm work was back-breaking and sweaty. It also required full cooperation from nature. During September, rain was not a welcome event and a dry summer was helpful in getting the crops under roof. This was the middle of harvest season and sunny days were a necessity in taking care of the wheat and corn. The crops were good and plentiful and the warehouses were already full of grain. I watched the field hands working hard and I admired their perseverance in their backbreaking race with nature to bring in all the crops before the rainy season.

As in many rural areas of eastern Poland, there were Jewish families living in Potoczek. Jankiel, who traded with the squire and all local peasants, lived close to the manor. He sold essential housekeeping goods, produced by the Jewish craftsmen in Modliborzyce, to local farmers in exchange for food products, which he in turn retailed to customers in the adjoining towns. Occasionally, he traded horses with Michał or supplied live animals to local peasants. Jankiel had two daughters, Laika and Raisa. Laika, the older sister, lived with her husband in her father's house and was employed at the manor as a seamstress. The younger sister, Raisa, worked for Halina Przanowski in the manor nursery. Raisa had beautiful long blonde hair, blue eyes, and a light complexion. She was very smart, hard working, and always willing to assume additional responsibilities. She was also Halina's lead girl and on many occasions she supervised other girls working on weeding vegetable patches in the nursery. Many village boys had their eyes set on Raisa, but they didn't have enough courage to cross religious and cultural taboos. Village girls were openly jealous of Raisa's good looks, popularity, and friendly disposition and treated her as an unwelcome visitor in the village

The only retail store in the village was owned and operated by another Jewish family. Szymsza and his wife lived behind the store in the middle of the village in a modest house facing the main street. His shop was also well equipped with fancy fabrics and ribbons and local girls were frequent customers purchasing ornamental and shiny trinkets, underwear and stockings. Szymsza's solid business reputation, his honesty and willingness to provide reliable services and reasonable credit to peasants were well known among the local population. While Szymsza traded mainly with peasants, Jankiel's livelihood depended very much on good relationship with the Przanowski family. In the summer of 1939, Jankiel came almost every week to the manor to see Michał in his office. They talked about potential trades, exchanges, and even politics. Anticipating conflict with Germany and rumors of Nazi atrocities against Jews in Germany, Jankiel expressed his worries and concerns about his and his family's uncertain future. Jankiel's humble existence in Potoczek was the subject of many arguments in the manor. Listening to some of the discussions at our family dinner table every evening, I gathered that Wojciech Przanowski, the squire, was not a great admirer of the Polish government's domestic politics.

The squire had been born under the Tsarist regime and was brought up by his uncle among country gentry at the beginning of the twentieth century. Somehow, he developed and retained very strong feelings for social justice and the plight of the underprivileged. I had a hard time reconciling his acceptance of peasants' servitude and ancient demeaning customs with his very liberal views and his concern for the rights of poor and other neglected minorities in new Poland. Squire Przanowski was a strong believer in the education of farm workers and peasants. In the early thirties, he had established a preschool for children of "working hands" on the estate. Once a week, his wife provided counsel to peasants' wives and dispensed free advice regarding some of the social and very personal family problems. Although a very dedicated Polish patriot, the squire often expressed at the dinner table his concerns and his doubts about the government's insensitive treatment of Jews. He challenged anti-Semitic views, so popular with the Polish government, especially after Marshal Józef Piłsudski's death in 1935. He often said: "Remember the Jewish scientists', writers', and poets' contribution to Poland's science, art, literature, and drama. Anybody who talks about Jewish industrialists and Jews taking over our commerce should take a good look at Modliborzyce or Zaklików."

He was right. Every time I traveled through Modliborzyce on my way to Janów, which was the district capital, I went through miles of narrow streets, filled with pale, poor, and undernourished Jewish children playing in front of their small dwellings. The old dilapidated houses with small windows and narrow doors smelled of onions and garlic and displayed many signs of poverty, such as piles of uncollected trash on the streets, and a desperate need for repairs of existing structures. It seemed that the local Jewish population struggled for existence in the impoverished environment.

On the first day after my arrival in Potoczek, I spent most of my time walking around the stables, visiting the distillery and talking to people I knew from my previous visits. I patted the gray mare I rode a few weeks ago and hoped my foot would be better soon. After the recent excitement in Lwów and the chaotic journey to Zaklików, the serenity and the graciousness at the manor house were almost unreal, a welcome change from the fears and speculations in the radio broadcasts and newspapers. Farmers were busy doing their daily chores in spite of the gathering political clouds.

On August 31, after dinner, we all gathered in my uncle's study to listen to the radio. The news was not good. The Polish government had turned down Hitler's request for railroad lines across Pomerania and annexation of the city of Gdańsk. The general mobilization was to be announced any day. The Przanowskis' sons-in-law, who were reserve officers in the Polish cavalry regiments, were mobilized and told to join their units. Tola left her home in Zakrzówek and arrived with her daughter in Potoczek to stay with her parents during her husband's absence. Rysia decided to stay with her children in Lipa. The next morning, on Friday, September 1, during a special broadcast from Warsaw, we learned that the German Army had crossed the Polish border at 4:30 A.M. In a few hours, the Polish government declared general mobilization and appealed to the nation to resist invasion.

To provide a pretext for the invasion, Hitler's SS Guards and Security Police, dressed in Polish uniforms, attacked the radio station in Gleiwitz and broadcast inflammatory statements in Polish encouraging the Polish minority in eastern Germany to fight against Hitler. German impostors left several corpses of concentration camp inmates from Dachau, dressed in the Polish uniforms, at the scene. This was also done to mislead the West.

The mood in the manor house was grim and tense. The following morning, we learned about the heavy bombardment of several cities. Polish radio continuously transmitted coded messages to the front line troops and occasional brief and terse communiqués for civilians. Newspapers were full of horror stories as onslaughts against unarmed, defenseless civilians were cited in the local press. People were uprooted from their homes by the enemy and shot indiscriminately. Within hours after the German forces advance, Jews were being singled out for abuse and massacre by special SS Security units. In some cities and villages, Jews were buried alive in their synagogues. There were no limits to the Germans' brutal anti-Semitic policy of extermination. The Polish soldiers fought bravely, but the might of the German Army and their numerical and technological superiority allowed the enemy to make continuous and steady progress on Polish soil. On September 7, the first German troops reached the river Wisła.

War was getting closer and closer. Recently arrived refugees were tired and tense. Witnesses told about horrors on the highways and destruction of cities. The village of Potoczek and the street leading from the main highway to the manor were filled with hundreds of refugees. Some were on foot and some were on horse-drawn wagons loaded with their earthly possessions. In the distance, one could see frontline troops crossing the fields. The chaos of traffic jams and overcrowded highways were the obvious signs that the front line was slowly inching toward Potoczek.

The civilians were traveling east. In the morning chill, with the sun slowly coming over the horizon, the crowd of refugees gradually but persistently made its way toward Janów. The highway was always crowded and the time of day didn't make any difference to the waves of humanity looking for a refuge from the enemy. The traffic was even more intense in the dark hours of the night, since darkness offered an illusion of safety and the chances of an air attack were less likely with limited visibility under the dark blue sky. Peasants' horse-driven wagons, occasional cars, or even trucks moved down the middle of the highway. The majority of people were on foot, walking slowly and silently on both sides of the vehicular traffic. Loaded with suitcases and personal belongings stacked on bicycles or pushing baby carriages full of family treasures, men, women, and children looked up occasionally toward the cloudless sky in anticipation of enemy planes.

Then we started seeing more soldiers than civilians. Within a few days, long lines of military convoys gradually replaced the civilian traffic and wagons full of refugees. Mounted cavalry units were mixed with infantry, horse-drawn artillery, and Red Cross ambulances with wounded soldiers marching on both sides of the highway. All of them were headed east toward Janów. One of the cavalry units stopped at the manor to requisition food and to exchange tired and worn-out horses. The major apologized to Michał for the inconvenience and offered to pay with Polish currency. Michał would not accept any payment. He told the major, "Take whatever you need. This is the least we can do for our country."

On September 17, panic spread. A radio announcement was made by the Polish government that the Soviet Union, on the basis of their previously secret treaty with Germany, had crossed the eastern Polish border in order to "protect Ukrainian and Belarusian minorities." With Germany moving from the west and the Red Army troops occupying the eastern provinces, Poland's days of independence were coming to an end.

There was great concern in Potoczek regarding the progress of the Soviet army. Nobody knew the extent of the Soviet occupation, so feverish plans for evacuation to Kraków were made by the Przanowski family. The well-known hate and animosity of the Soviet regime toward landlords and intelligentsia spread terror among the local gentry. The choice between two evils, Germany and Soviet Union, was a tough and frightening one.

The sudden invasion by the Red Army came as a great surprise to all citizens, soldiers, and civilians. People close to the Soviet border were in a state of shock. The Red Army now surrounded the main Polish forces east of the Wisła River.

September 18 brought the distant sound of heavy artillery. The next day we could see Polish infantry units with machine guns stationed on the outskirts of the village. The highway was almost deserted except for small groups of soldiers in full combat uniforms rushing around the estate. We could hear an occasional burst of machine—gun fire. The village and the manor were silent. People were scared and hid in cellars. Work in the fields had stopped except for the care of farm animals. The expectation of a bloody battle was on everyone's mind. In the middle of the night all Polish troops left their defensive positions and retreated toward Janów. Potoczek was now in no-man's land.

On September 21, a gray, heavily camouflaged German staff car, with black crosses on both sides, stopped at the entrance to the manor. An officer in a bluish uniform escorted by two well-armed soldiers asked for the owner. One of the soldiers served as a translator.

"I am Captain Beck from the Fourth Panzer Division. I am looking for my staff headquarters. Please, can I look at the house?" Michał spoke German fluently. "Yes, Captain. Please follow me." With Michał and Władysław leading, the Germans inspected the second floor. The captain was pleased. "We will take the entire second floor. Make sure all rooms are available tonight." Since one can not argue with the enemy, we all had to relocate immediately. I ended up sharing a room downstairs with Jan, Halina's friend. Antonina and her mother moved to a spare bedroom adjoining the parlor.

The general and his staff arrived in the evening. Sentries were posted in front of his room. Telephone lines were run to the second floor from the communication truck parked outside of the main entrance. The Przanowskis had become guests in their own house.

Although the general's meals were brought by car from the officers' mess in the village, very soon some of the orderlies ended up in the kitchen working side by side with the cook and her helpers. Security at the manor was very strict as night patrols were watching for intruders and refugees. Armed sentries guarded the general's quarters, staff, and communication trucks twenty-four hours a day.

The general was businesslike but very civil. Talking to Michał on one occasion and seeing his concern about Red Army advances, he reassured him that the Soviets would stop at the river Bug and that this part of Poland would stay under German occupation. Michał was partially relieved and shared the encouraging news with the rest of the family. At least for now, we had to deal only with one enemy. Were Germans better or more civilized than Russians? We had no answer. Recent events of inhumane treatment and the murders of innocent Polish civilians and Jews indicated that we should not expect mercy from our new masters. On the second night, the general and his staff suddenly departed to another location.

The following morning, a small Polish cavalry unit arrived. The officer in charge tried to calm Przanowski's concern. "We are fully aware of the German troops around us and we do not plan to instigate any fights in this area." He continued: "What we need is time to reorganize, store our heavy weapons and carry out our mission behind the enemy lines. If necessary, we may form underground units in the forest." The young lieutenant was outspoken and optimistic: "This phase of the war may be lost, but our fight still goes on." He further explained that Germans surrounded large Polish cavalry formations in the Lipa forest. Some units were ordered by the Polish commanding general to demobilize and go home. This group planned to stay in the forest and carry out partisan warfare.

On September 25, Tola's husband, Stefan, arrived unexpectedly in Potoczek. Since the area was full of German soldiers, he had traveled by night on the backcountry roads. Fully armed and in his Polish officer's uniform, he tried to avoid the enemy in order to reach Potoczek safely. At the reunion everybody was crying tears of both happiness and relief. By the next day, Stefan had discarded his uniform, changed into civilian clothes and departed with his family to their estate in Zakrzówek. Two days later, Rysia sent a messenger from Lipa stating that her husband arrived home, safe from the war. Aunt Helena seemed to be more relaxed, since it appeared that in spite of human suffering everywhere in the country, her family was spared for the time being.

The Wiernicki family was not that lucky. Gradually, through travelers, friends, and private messengers I learned what happened to my parents and my uncles. After the general mobilization, my father had stayed in Lwów to organize the Cavalry Reserve Regiment. Following the short battle with the Soviet Red Army and after the unsuccessful defense of the city, he, along with most of his officers, crossed the border to Romania and through Hungary and Italy traveled west to join the new Polish Army organized in France. My mother, who worked as a volunteer nurse in the military hospital, was forced to remain in the city. She was separated from the rest of the family and was unable to join us in Potoczek. Grandmother Wiernicki, a widow, survived the September invasion by staying with her daughter-in-law Halina. Halina's husband Marcel, who was my father's younger brother, served as a reserve officer with the Fourth Infantry Regiment. He fought under General Kutrzeba at Bzura River. Marcel's unit fought hard for three weeks, suffered heavy losses, and finally surrendered on September 21. He ended up as a prisoner of war and was transported with his fellow officers to the prisoner-of-war camp in Murnau, south of Munich, Germany.

Ryszard, my father's youngest brother, volunteered to join a special-action battalion. He fought near Tomaszów, defending the Wisła crossing as a part of Polish Army "Kraków." Surrounded by Germans and Soviets, his unit, as a part of the Forty-first Infantry Reserve Division, was demobilized on September 24 by its commander, General Biernacki. Soldiers were told to hide weapons and return home. He arrived in Kraków on the last day of September, was denounced by an informer, and had to hide among his friends to avoid arrest by the Gestapo.

September, full of tragic memories, was coming to an end. It seemed that nature cooperated with the enemy. Thirty days of pleasant and dry weather made even the smallest country road accessible to German panzer formations and allowed them to conquer Poland in twenty-eight days. The country was devastated; people were defeated, heartbroken and enslaved by the German tyranny. Artificial demarcation lines and new borders imposed by Germans and Soviets divided Poland into two separate entities. Families were separated and scattered across vast geographical areas.

Thousands of Polish women mourned their fallen husbands, brothers, and fathers. Germans and Soviets took prisoner almost one million troops. Jan Patosz's son Józef was one of the captured soldiers who was interned in Germany. Since the persecution of Jews by the new masters had started on the first day after they crossed the border, Jankiel's and Szymsza's families expected the worst and anxiously awaited their fate under German occupation. The burning of synagogues in the cities occupied by German troops served as a warning about an uncertain future, but Jewish cries for justice were heard nowhere. More suffering and intimidation was planned for the defeated nation in the hands of the Reichsführer-SS Himmler and his associates.

The war had changed our lives forever.

Uneven Struggle

WITH FALL around the corner, the days were getting shorter. Fieldwork and harvesting continued as usual, but it was very difficult to accept the fact that the freedom and independence of a huge country of 35 million people had been lost so unexpectedly and suddenly.

The mood in Potoczek was grim. We shared with the rest of the nation our grief for fallen soldiers, murdered civilians, and destroyed cities. Although somehow isolated in the middle of vast farmland and the adjoining, secluded Lipa forest, we watched for signs of change and expected the worst. How right we were. Soon after the German frontline troops went through this part of the country, SS Police units and civilian administration arrived to govern the conquered land. Janów was declared the capital of the area and a German district chief was appointed. Police units were stationed in Janów, Modliborzyce, and Zaklików. Very shortly thereafter started mass arrests of prominent citizens and the expulsion and extermination of Jews, who were required to wear yellow stars.

On November 5, during a mass execution of local farmers, seven people were murdered by the Gestapo in Potok Wielki. Soon after, all estate owners within the Janów district were directed to report to the German deputy district chief, who was responsible for farm and food production. Each owner was given quotas for delivery of crops, dairy products, and timber. Strict controls imposed by regional representatives of the district manager terrorized the whole area. Of special interest to Germans was the distillery, and within a few days they stationed a small field police unit in Potoczek to protect the plant from saboteurs and partisans. The sergeant and three policemen slept most of the time during the day and patrolled the area around the distillery during the night. They lived together in one of the houses close to the distillery. Since they were nosy and suspicious, their presence forced me to be very careful with my daily activities.

The countryside and the adjoining Lipa forest were still full of armed Polish soldiers who refused to surrender and had organized small independent units. From their hideouts in the forest, they continued to fight with the invaders. At the beginning of the "pacification" campaign, the SS Police units were reluctant to enter Lipa forest. But as they grew in numerical strength and gained the aid of informers, the small isolated villages in the heart of the forest were mercilessly attacked and destroyed. Most of the inhabitants were shot on the spot.

The forest provided a haven for people hiding from the Germans—the vastness of high-density foliage, tall trees, absence of highways, and the isolation of small villages offering partisans protection and relative security against police actions. Fugitives from German persecution and many others with diverse political views were forming armed units and hiding in the forest. Some of the groups were stationed on isolated farms, all the time watching for German intrusion. Others stayed in underground bunkers deep in the least accessible parts of the forest. Although the common enemy was Germany, different units represented different political views, whose configuration varied from radical and conservative right-wing groups to the leftist-oriented People's Guard, which had strong ideological ties with the Soviet Union. Often the partisans quarreled among themselves. Sometimes their differences were settled with angry arguments; at other times, shooting took place between different units. The Polish Home Army, representing a government in exile in London, tried to unite all the groups, disregarding their political views, in order to fight a common enemy, but this was a tough and heartbreaking assignment. In spite of the common danger, the divisions among the partisans were deep. Furthermore, the rapid formation of many illegal gangs of professional criminals, who pretended to represent political parties and ruthlessly terrorized civilians, confused Polish citizens and frightened local population.

There were some changes among the relatives who had been visiting Potoczek. Paweł left for Warsaw to live with his father, but Emmy stayed with us. My first Christmas in Poland under German occupation was sad and somber. My uncle presided over *wigilja*, the family supper and made a short speech trying to lift our spirits. Michał, the oldest son, followed his father's remarks with his own words of encouragement. He appealed to us to be optimistic, maintain our perseverance, and have hope for a better future. Michał felt strongly that the days of Nazi occupation and terror in Poland would soon come to an end and, with the help of the Western allies, an independent Poland would soon take its place among the European nations. In spite of the optimism and encouraging words of the host and his son, a spirit of fear and resignation reigned around the table. The small Christmas tree in the ballroom, with its glittering lights and prewar fancy decorations, was the only cheerful reminder of the holiday season. The customary visit from the farm workers and their families, who usually sang Christmas carols on the portico in front of the manor house, was short and subdued.

Following the traditional custom of breaking wafer with one another, the relatives and household staff exchanged holiday greetings. Then the squire accepted gifts from his employees. I shook hands with Władysław, Anna, Maria, and other friends. The customary joyous New Year celebration was not observed at all this year in the manor.

Silently I participated in the family meals, a strange fear of the unknown future always on my mind. I wished I could share Michał's faith in our Western allies. On the basis of my limited knowledge of European history and military science, I did not think much about the French armed forces and their fighting spirit. Indeed, regardless of our place in the social structure in Potoczek, from the old squire to the youngest help in the kitchen, we all were deeply concerned with the uncertainty of next year and everyday life under German occupation.

During the following two winter months, I spent most of my time reading books from the Przanowskis' library and doing small errands for my uncle the squire. One evening, my aunt talked to Emmy and me together:

"I do not know how long the present condition will last and nobody knows what to expect from the Germans in the future. But I think that both of you should continue with your education. What do you think?"

"Yes, of course," we both agreed. "But how?"

My aunt responded: "I found out that there is a family of refugees from Silesia in the village. The wife is a high school teacher from Wisła and she has agreed to tutor you twice a week."

"Thank you." Emmy and I were very pleased that in a time of national emergency, Aunt Helena still cared about us.

"Then everything is settled. You will start next Monday."

After she left the room, I talked with Emmy. She was two years older than I. For the past four years, she had attended a Catholic convent near Lwów, and most of the summers she spent in Potoczek, where she helped Aunt Antonina care for her stepbrother. Emmy was very smart, the best student in her class, well read, calm, and very mature for her age. With dark hair, brown eyes, and a light complexion, she looked older than her seventeen years. At the very beginning, I treated her almost as an older sister, admiring her composure and common sense. But as we spent more time together, I discovered, under her cover of maturity, a warm and almost romantic feminine touch. She was both pleasant and direct, but somehow when I looked at her slender figure, especially her great pair of legs, my brotherly feeling disappeared. She looked to me like a very attractive female. Since we lived in a very close family circle, although she was not related to me, I tried at the beginning to hide my feelings in order not to complicate our everyday life.

"Emmy, what do you really think?" I asked her after Aunt Helena left the room.

"I think this is a great idea. Since I am more advanced in some subjects, I will try to help you. At least, we will not be wasting our time. Let's try."

I was not completely thrilled or committed, but common sense was telling me that this plan was really in my best interest. "I hope the new teacher will not make us work too hard."

Emmy smiled. "Janusz, do not worry. I will help you."

The school routine, half a day on Tuesday and Thursday, imposed more discipline on my free time. The teacher was a very interesting and serious high school professor from Wisła. She was demanding in her homework assignments, and soon I could see Emmy was doing very well, ahead of me in almost all subjects.

"Janusz," she told me, "do not be discouraged. Remember I was ahead of you in regular school." Days were moving fast and I even began to like my informal classes. The more time I studied with Emmy, the less brotherly I felt. I looked forward to being with her every Tuesday and Thursday. Even Anna appeared to be of less interest. She came every morning to make the bed in my room and we chatted and flirted, but I had no special desire to touch her. Both girls were the same age and I was still torn between Anna's physical attractiveness and her willingness to let me do whatever I wanted and my respect and strong emotions for Emmy. I tried to hide my feelings and acted nonchalant during our private tutoring hours. Emmy was very sweet and pretended that she did not notice my sometimes obnoxious behavior.

One day, in the spring of 1940, Michał asked me to see him in his study. "Janusz," he said, "I know you are busy getting your education and this is great." Then he continued. "At the same time I wanted to ask you if you would consider giving us a hand in the forestry department. The German administration wants to establish a large forestry office that will combine Potoczek, Stojeszyn, and Łysaków under one manager. I am going to hire a highly educated and recommended doctor of forestry to take charge. He will need an assistant who knows the area and would look after the gamekeepers. I think that you are a wonderful candidate."

I was pleasantly surprised: "Sure Michał, I'll be glad to do it."

I was very young and being in charge of gamekeepers appealed to my ego.

"You have to work out the details of your job assignment with Dr. Sowa, but I will make sure that you can continue with your studies."

Dr. Sowa arrived two weeks later. He was formerly in charge of a huge forest estate in Pomerania and since that part of the country was incorporated into territory of the Reich, his family was forcibly relocated east. He was very friendly and informal in dealing with his subordinates. At the first meeting with representatives of the three estates, he established my areas of responsibility, and territorial assignments.

As an assistant forester, I reported to him. My responsibilities included overseeing some of the field activities, such as weekly reports of timber production and inspection for quality of replanting programs. Twice a week I had to visit all gamekeepers, verify fallen timber logs, and look for compliance with fire protection regulations. On sunny days I used my bicycle; this was the most expeditious way to travel in the forest since it never betrayed my presence. The most important advantage was that bicycles were very quiet and at that time the ability to surprise was essential to survive in the wilderness. The Lipa forest was full of partisans with many political views, and one had to be careful not to cross them at any time. The partisans were masters of the forest and fully in control of the lives and destiny of both local inhabitants and all travelers.

Sometimes I stopped in the Lipa village at Stanisław Skrzypek's house. Skrzypek's family was well known in the Lipa district. There were four brothers, Stanisław, Aleksander, Bronek, and Jan. Stanisław and Aleksander lived in Lipa. Bronek and Jan lived in Łysaków, a village adjacent to Potoczek. All of them had served in the Polish Army during September's war and then returned home fully equipped with rifles and a lot of ammunition. When the Polish units were disarmed and demobilized in the Lipa forest, all four brothers saved and buried many weapons in their gardens.

One morning, the German police unexpectedly surrounded the whole village of Łysaków. They arrested many people, among them Bronek Skrzypek. A search for weapons was not successful, but all male residents were locked up in one barn.

Bronek Skrzypek escaped from the barn, but the rest of his friends were shot on the spot in Łysaków. From that day on, the local peasants vowed to avenge their comrades. Since Bronek could not return home for fear of being arrested, he organized a small unit of armed men in Lipa forest and declared his allegiance to the People's Guard, sponsored and supported by the Soviets.

During one of my visits in Potok, I received confidential news from the sergeant of the local Polish police unit that the Germans planned to surround the Lipa forest the next day in search of Bronek and his colleagues. I asked Stanisław to pass this information to his brother.

"Thanks for your help, Mr. Janusz" he said. Stanisław was very grateful. I knew that in his proletarian heart he did not care for local aristocracy and he was not one of Przanowski's admirers. At the same time, we both knew that we needed to work together to defy our common enemy.

The next day, the German's surprise attack in the Lipa forest did not find anybody. Farms were deserted, with no sign of inhabitants or partisans. The SS Police commander was furious. He burned all the houses belonging to Skrzypek's family and searched the adjoining village for an informer. Stanisław joined his brother as a partisan and the rest of the family settled with their cousins in Łysaków.

My early warning earned me gratitude from Polish communists, so from that day on, I was able to maintain friendly contacts with representatives of all political parties hiding in the Lipa forest.

The forestry administration of Dr. Sowa consisted of three separate estates: Potoczek, Łysaków, and Stojeszyn. The family of Jan Karlicz owned Stojeszyn. Karlicz was once a wealthy aristocrat whose ancestors lived above and beyond their means and eventually lost a major portion of their estate to creditors. What was left were a lovely manor house, some farmland, and many acres of forest adjoining Lipa village. The Karlicz family was very sociable and generous, perhaps too generous, well known for wonderful receptions and a flair for the entertainment of their guests. Their servants, always dressed in elegant uniforms, reflected high society's carefree lifestyle, in spite of serious financial problems.

Jan Karlicz and Michał Przanowski were friends and they often visited each other. Karlicz had a son about my age and sometimes I was invited to spend a few days at Stojeszyn manor. They had a wonderful stable and I spent many hours horseback riding and jumping in a paddock specially constructed for equestrian competitions.

The Stojeszyn forestry department was run by Józef Nagórski, who now also reported to Dr. Sowa. Józef was a friendly and energetic young fellow, single, deeply involved in underground operations, and using his job as a cover, in dealing with many partisan units in his area of jurisdiction. The Stojeszyn forest, very deep and secluded, was a center of underground activities for many political parties. My own job was getting more difficult and involved. As a formal German employee, identified by a yellow armband, I was expected to report all suspicious activities to my supervisors. At the same time, as a Polish patriot, I maintained close contact with all underground activities in the area under my supervision. I walked a thin line and sometimes I worried about possible implications and consequences for the Przanowski family. The last thing I wanted to do was to hurt such a decent and supportive family.

Emmy also was concerned about my security. She suspected that I was connected somehow to some of the units and was concerned that eventually an informer would be able to track my connections. Since I was also concerned about my personal safety, I asked Bronek Skrzypek to find me a revolver. I was not comfortable carrying a gun in Potoczek, but at the same time I worried about my safety during inspection trips to the forest. Eventually, I found a special place under the entry to a small barn in Lipa to hide the gun. The gun was my secret joy. Hardly used, it was well preserved, a made-in-Poland "VIS" revolver constructed on the principles of an American Colt, a powerful, semiautomatic weapon that I took great care to maintain in excellent condition. Once, I brought the pistol to Potoczek and showed it to Emmy. Since the possession of weapons was punishable by death, according to German law, Emmy was really upset that I was putting the whole household at risk. She made me promise that I would never do that again.

The first snow and cold weather slowed my activities in the forest. Most of the partisan units had to look for shelter among securely built and isolated farms in secluded areas. To live in underground bunkers was almost impossible. Snow allowed the German police to track movements of the units much better than in the summer and fall and the partisans were constantly on the lookout for Germans.

My studies were coming along well enough. The tutor was excellent, and since Emmy was helping me with the homework, I began to develop a new relationship with her. Torn between my studies, my work, and my secret connections with partisans, I began to rely on her more and more to share my secrets and problems. Emmy was always very supportive and understanding, and I knew that I had found a real friend. Sometimes observing her from a distance, I felt strange sensations going far beyond those of a friendly relationship. I liked her hair and her eyes and many times I felt a strong desire to touch her mouth. I could deal with partisans in the forest but I did not have enough courage to demonstrate my affection for Emmy. Sometimes I had a feeling that she was well aware of my dilemma. She smiled and assured me on many occasions that she had a brother my age and that she knew all about boys.

As soon as the snow disappeared in the forest and early spring brought warmer weather, German police intensified their pacification effort in the Lipa forest. Every day, as I visited villages and gamekeepers' posts, I was told about police action in burning homes, arresting people and deporting them to Germany, frequent executions and outright murders in the nearby villages. Occasionally, I met convoys of SS units passing by in horse-drawn wagons, but my yellow armband and my official documents protected me, at least for the time being.

The police struck the most active political families, and it appeared that they must have had some reliable information in each case. I wondered if there was an informer. One day Anna came to see me. "Mr. Janusz, my sister talked to me and I do not know what to tell her. Please can you help me?"

Her sister, Maria, was married to Adam, one of the gamekeepers who worked and lived in the heart of Lipa forest.

"Anna, what is the problem?" I tried to sound reassuring.

"Mr. Janusz, it is Adam. Maria thinks that he works for the Germans."

Now I understood the deadly success of the German raids. They had a good informer. "Mr. Janusz, Maria is scared for herself and her children. She does not know what to do."

"How does she know that he works for the police?"

"She saw him several times meeting with the police chief from Zaklików and he disappeared the same night there was a raid in the area. They dress him in a police uniform and he pretends that he is a German. He keeps his German uniform and hat at the house."

This was stunning news. To have one of the gamekeepers betraying his own people and exposing all underground activities could result in many arrests, executions, and a certain end to all underground and resistance actions. People's lives were at stake.

"Anna don't cry. However, you must realize that this is very serious. First, ask Maria and her children to move to your parents' house in Potoczek. Use some kind of excuse. Second, I will have to tell the partisans and they will talk to Adam. We really have no choice."

"How can he do it? How can he do it?" Anna tried to control her tears.

I was not certain what to do. Telling the partisans meant death for Adam, not saying anything meant death or execution for some of his neighbors and friends. Adam worked for Jerzy who was chief forester in Potoczek and reported, like me, to Dr. Sowa. I never fully trusted Jerzy and I was concerned about sharing this information with anybody in Potoczek.

I took my bike and went to Stojeszyn to talk to Józef Nagórski, who was really upset.

"One of us is a traitor. I don't like to believe it, but I think this is probably the truth. We must get rid of him. I am sorry for Maria."

I was not happy, since I knew the whole family well. Adam was sometimes a loner, but he knew his job and was, on the surface, reliable and trustworthy.

"What made him do it?" Józef and I wondered.

"Janusz, let me talk to Kowal, one of my gamekeepers. He has good contacts with the partisan unit in my forest. Adam does not know anybody there. Let them talk to Adam. Get Maria and the children out of the house first. Since he does not know me, I may go with them."

"Be careful. There are too many people involved in this," I cautioned Józef.

The next week, Maria moved to Potoczek. Anna was nervous and apprehensive. As I watched her serve in the dining room, I could sense that her thoughts were somewhere else. I thought about sharing this with Emmy. But in the end, I decided not to drag her into it, for none of us knew how this might end. The following week, Dr. Sowa was formally notified by the German District Forestry Office that one of his gamekeepers, Adam, was killed in a shooting with the German police.

I could not figure out what actually happened. The next day Józef came to my small office in Potoczek and told me the whole story. Six members of the People's Guard, Soviet sympathizers, went to Adam's house. It was approximately 8 P.M. and Adam was eating his supper. He was alone. Hearing noises outside his window, Adam took a pistol and went outside to see what was going on. The unit commander jumped him from behind and they dragged him back into the house.

"What is this all about?" Adam screamed as they tied his hands.

"Shut up, you German spy," said one of the partisans. They all started looking through his closets and drawers. "Here it is," one of the intruders shouted, triumphantly exhibiting a German police overcoat and cap.

Adam was white and shivering. "Please, there must be a misunderstanding. One of the gendarmes left this last week. This does not belong to me."

"Quiet, you traitor. We will take good care of you, but not here. Get ready to come along with us to face a military field tribunal."

Adam knew this was just a formality. He knelt and tried to touch the commander's boots. "Please, I have a wife and children. I will work with you. I will do anything."

The commander looked at him coldly and without emotion. "If this was entirely up to me, I would shoot you right now. But we will give you the benefit of the doubt and arrange for you to stand trial. Get ready."

With his hands tied behind his back, Adam marched between two captors on a narrow winding road in the middle of the forest.

"Where are you taking me?" He asked, trembling with fear.

"Never mind, just walk with us. Keep quiet if you want to live." After almost an hour, the road widened and the outline of a village could be seen in the distance. The partisans were silent.

"Who goes—password," suddenly a voice called in Polish a few yards in front of the marchers. All of the partisans stopped, completely surprised. Then, another voice was heard, this time in German. "Hands up, you dirty bandits." A series of automatic pistol shots were coming from both sides of the road.

The partisans threw themselves on the ground. In the commotion, they forgot about Adam, who kept standing and started screaming in German: "Friends, don't shoot! This is your friend, Adam. Help!" He stumbled, running toward the Germans, and one of the bullets went right through his heart.

The fire from the German patrol intensified as more soldiers with machine guns on both sides of the road joined the fight. "Let's run!" screamed the commander. There are too many of them and they did our job for us." He looked at Adam's body. "Serves you right, you traitor!" They all disappeared into the sanctuary of the forest without any loss of life.

The next morning there was a lot of crying in Potoczek. Only a few people knew that Adam was a traitor. A lot of friends participated in his funeral at Potok Wielki. Anna supported her sister at the funeral mass and the priest's remarks were warm and generous. As far as the family knew, Adam's secret went with him to his grave.

The war with the partisans intensified with early spring, bringing more frequent "pacification raids" by the German security units. Families of innocent people were evacuated, some locked up in Janów prison and some, mostly younger people, directly transported to labor camps in Germany. People living in isolated locations suffered the worst fate since the Germans accused them of providing food and shelter to partisan units. During my regular visits in the forest, I saw more and more burned-out houses.

In April, during my routine first inspection I ran across a terrified and exhausted gamekeeper. He stopped me halfway to Lipa, panting heavily. It appeared that he had run a few miles, because his face was sweating and his voice trembling.

"Mr. Janusz, I am coming from Łysa Góra. Germans are killing people and burning houses. They also were holding a group of hostages including Aleksander," he said.

Aleksander was a gamekeeper from Łysa Góra. "Please, can we do anything to help him?" he begged me. I hesitated for a second. Interfering with the German police during a pacification action was a dangerous business.

"Antoni, calm down. I do not know how much good we can do, but let's try. Make sure that you have your official arm band on your left arm."

We verified that our official identification as German foresters was visible from a distance and turned our bikes toward Łysa Góra. "Slowly, not too fast," I warned Antoni. I did not want to surprise the Germans with a sudden and unexpected appearance.

As we were approaching the village, I smelled burning wood and saw smoke above the treetops. On this bright, sunny, spring day, the fire was flickering in the rafters of the first house adjoining the road. Dense white fumes were gently floating above the ground in a northeastern direction. Except for the sound of falling roofs and walls of burned houses, there was complete silence. The combination of flickering fires and blowing smoke made the scene weird and frightening. There was no sign of German police, villagers, their families, animals, or any living creatures.

I looked at Antoni: "Stop, where are the people?" We both looked suspiciously at the dense, silent forest behind the village. Soon we had an answer. As we walked further and passed the first burning house, we saw bodies lying on the ground. Men, women, and children were tangled together in a pile in the open area between two houses. None appeared alive. There was no moaning or crying, just an incredible silence. With closed or opened eyes, sometimes in unique postures, mothers trying with their bodies to protect children from flying bullets, men with hands stretched above their heads, girls in their colorful peasant skirts—all of them were lying silent and motionless on the bright green grass, soaking in patches of red blood. Again, we looked quickly for survivors, but there were none. When I looked closer, I noticed most of the people were lying on their backs. It appeared that the murderers shot them from a short distance. Some of the faces were terribly disfigured and traces of black powder were visible on their clothes. The view of women protecting their small children with outstretched arms and their twisted but silently crying lips for a moment made me numb; then, I trembled uncontrollably.

Antoni was pale. With tears in his eyes, he kept mumbling hysterically. I held his arm: "Antoni, there is nothing we can do for these people. They had to take some hostages and all the animals with them. The only thing we can do is to identify the victims, notify next of kin and make arrangements for a decent funeral."

"Two of us cannot do it alone," I continued. "We need help. Stay here and I will go back to Lipa and send you some help and perhaps some of the relatives will be able to identify the bodies."

Antoni was shivering. "Mr. Janusz, I will not stay alone. I am scared. What if the Germans should come back?"

"You are right, Antoni. Let's both go to Lipa and see if we can get some help. We must also get rid of this fire. It is getting too close to the forest."

I looked around. Houses were burning full force with yellow and red flames, licking the walls and slowly spreading along the burnt-out grass toward the adjoining trees. There was no time to lose. A forest fire would be a disaster for all of us.

"Hurry," I shouted to Antoni as I turned my bike toward Lipa village. It took us two hours to organize volunteers to fight the fire. Relatives from adjoining villages identified bodies, which were subsequently removed and transported to the small chapel. Among screaming and crying relatives, the identities of the victims were again established and verified by the gamekeepers, then their bodies were laid beside a long mass grave in anticipation of the priest's arrival. I was concerned that the Germans might come back. There were too many people gathered in one place. Some of the villagers openly carried rifles and revolvers. Both despair and the desire for revenge grew within the crowd. An unexpected fight with the police would be the worst thing for all of us.

I called my two senior gamekeepers. "Look, I don't know what may happen, but if the police come back, we will not be able to defend ourselves. We do not have enough guns or ammunition. Let's leave a few people to wait for the priest and disperse the rest of the crowd. We do not want more victims."

One of them responded, "Let's hope we won't see the police for a few days. Let us know if you find out in Potoczek what actually did happen in Łysa Góra."

Dr. Sowa waited for me in his office. "Doctor, I just came from Lipa," I said. "I know," he interrupted me. "SS Obersturmführer from Janów called me a few minutes ago and told me about the pacification action. On the basis of the informant's tip, they were looking for guns and ammunition. They did find a few rifles in the barn, so he ordered a mass killing of all the inhabitants and destruction of all houses as a warning to adjoining settlements. Aleksander and other men were taken to jail in Janów."

"Doctor, they killed men, women, and innocent children." I was shaking with emotion.

"I know, Janusz. There is nothing we can do about this. But we must look for another traitor and informant."

After I left Dr. Sowa's office, I could not find a place for myself in Potoczek. I closed my eyes and dead bodies were right in front of me: stiff, white, with glazed eyes and outstretched arms. I went to my room, closed the door and skipped dinner. This was the first time in my life that I had witnessed a mass murder of innocent people. The dead bodies of small children, boys and girls, lying among adults left an incredible mark in my memory and aroused a strong feeling of bitterness and a desire for vengeance. How much must this nation suffer? I had no answer. We all lived under the deadly threats and terror of invaders. For the time being, the Germans were in control. "An eye for an eye" approach did not work, since for one assassinated German there would be hundreds of civilians shot on the spot by the SS and Security units. I did not sleep very well that night, and I heard some noises about midnight, shouting both in German and in Polish. There were also sounds of moving cars and trucks around the manor house.

At 6 A.M., exhausted after a bad night, I walked to the dining room. Anna was crying in the corner.

"What's happened, Anna?" She looked up at me with tears in her eyes.

"They took Mr. Michał last night." I ran to my aunt. Sitting calmly with tears in her eyes and holding her husband's hand my aunt said: "The Gestapo arrested Michał last night."

"Is there anything we can do, Aunt Helena?" I asked.

"I don't know, but I already asked Paweł to go to Janów and find out what all this is about. Paweł knows some people in the Security Police headquarters. Perhaps this was a mistake."

"Of course, Aunt, this could be a mistake." I tried to reassure her. But she did not believe what I was saying.

The following day, Paweł went to Janów to visit those officials he knew. His fluent German opened some doors. Officially, nobody wanted to discuss Michał's case. Unofficially, however, the German district chief, Oskar Rudy, who was a member of the Secret Police and an official of the Gestapo, was willing to inquire about Michał's fate. He visited Potoczek often to inspect the distillery.

"Give me a few days to find out what's going on," he told Paweł.

Rudy's noncommittal response made the whole family feel better. There was a chance, slim, but better than nothing. My uncle and his wife seemed confident that things would work out. I personally did not share any hope for Michał's early return. We learned that on the same day, the Gestapo had arrested many other landowners. All of them were held at the Lublin prison known as the Castle.

Paweł was asked by my uncle to assume Michał's responsibility for the administration of the whole estate. The following day, my uncle asked me to leave my forestry job for the time being and work close by with Paweł to supervise the production of dairy products and, at the same time, to assist him in inspection of work details. Twice a week I had to accompany my uncle in a one-horse carriage to various field locations.

I left my job as a forester with a mixture of regret and relief. I did enjoy working with gamekeepers in isolated and secluded forest locations. Being so close to nature, gamekeepers and foresters developed a sense of comradeship, regardless of rank and position. At the same time, German pacification raids, murders, and the despair and misery of helpless victims generated mistrust and fear. Visits to the forests were risky and unpredictable as the brutal police activities became more and more outrageous. The whole countryside was suddenly full of various German military formations. Something was going on, but we did not know what.

In May 1941, a German horse-driven transport company arrived in Potoczek and was stationed in the village. It consisted of approximate sixty wagons, each driven by two horses, a support unit and one cavalry platoon. The company commander, Lieutenant Von Taub, with his orderly and two sergeants, requisitioned five rooms in the manor house. It was rather strange in an age of advanced technology and abundance of motorized German divisions, to find that a horse—driven unit was still a part of an invading army.

Most of the soldiers were farmhands familiar with animals and highly proficient in taking care of horses. Their horses were heavy, well-fed and well-kept animals. The soldiers showed a lot of interest in Potoczek's animals and often visited the stables and cowsheds. Many of them, talking with our farmhands, expressed their strong preference to stay home and work on their own farms. All of them, of course, tried to flirt with the local girls. The soldiers appeared to be good-natured farmers and farmhands, different from the SS Security units who engaged in the executions and murders of innocent civilians.

Lieutenant Von Taub was a member of the German aristocracy, owner of a large estate near Weimar and very gracious in dealing with Przanowski's family. After talking to my uncle, he even made a few calls to Janów regarding Michał's arrest. Nothing happened, but at least he showed goodwill and sympathy to a distressed family.

One night at the beginning of June, the whole company was put on alert and suddenly departed. Von Taub came to say goodbye to my uncle. He was nervous and distressed. In June 1941 Hitler attacked the Soviet Union. Army units stationed in the Potoczek area were the first-line supply troops, who crossed the river Bug in the early morning of June 22. Now, we all understood the heavy concentration of German armed forces in our district. In spite of visible signs of troop movement and the large number of fully equipped and battle-ready divisions on this side of the river Bug, the Russians did not expect anything until the very last moment before the attack. Stalin dismissed his aides' warnings and his intelligence service reports about Hitler's sneaky intentions. Russian troops were completely unprepared and totally surprised. Front lines were moving quickly east and the Germans were taking thousands of prisoners.

As soon as the German army occupied Lwów, I learned about the untimely death of my mother. She had been killed in a car accident when Polish citizens were forcefully evacuated by the retreating Soviet troops from the city. My relatives in Potoczek, in spite of their own worries about Michał's arrest, were very supportive to me in my grief. Nonetheless, being left alone in occupied Poland, I felt lonely and abandoned.

In July, Rudy informally advised my aunt that Michał might return home sometime before Christmas. There was a very hush-hush rumor that Przanowski paid a huge amount of money, in American dollars and gold, to some of the Secret Police officials in Janów. SS Obersturmführer Rudy was a middleman but the decisions were made in Berlin.

The last day of October at 10 P.M. Michał arrived with Rudy. Pale, undernourished, and thirty pounds lighter than before his arrest, Michał refused to discuss any details of his imprisonment in the German concentration camp in Dachau. One could see that his six months' imprisonment had left visible signs, not only in his physical appearance but in his behavior as well. He appeared to be very tired, exhausted and almost unsure of himself. I could not understand how six months in prison could change him so much.

Since Michał was too weak to assume his responsibilities of managing the estate, my uncle asked Paweł to continue his current duties until Michał had fully recovered. In turn, Paweł asked me to stay on my current job as his assistant.

In spite of my busy work schedule and working with Paweł, I was making progress in my academic studies. The teacher seemed to be satisfied with my effort. Emmy, as expected, was well ahead of me and sometimes helped me with my homework. I did enjoy the long winter evenings when we discussed the next day's assignments and tried to solve some of the math problems. She was very patient as she tried to explain algebraic formulas and the principles of calculus to me. As we studied together, I would watch Emmy sitting across the table from me. Most of the time I dreamed about holding her hand and kissing her on the mouth. I had a feeling that she actually liked me as a person and enjoyed my company. But being a couple of years her junior, I did not expect to be taken seriously by an older girl. With Anna I was assertive, fast, perhaps cynical, but always in control. With Emmy I was shy, romantic, uncertain of my behavior, and unsure of my feelings. Daily routine, short fall days, and long evenings did not allow much time for social life. Potoczek had a well-equipped library and after dinner I would spend many evenings reading Galworthy's and Jack London's books in my room. An occasional visit from some of the neighbors broke the monotony of a rather isolated existence.

However, after a day's work and long hours, I did not have a lot of interest in small talk and socializing with Przanowski's friends. Since my contact with underground units was not as close as when I worked as Dr. Sowa's assistant, I was not aware of recent political developments among the partisan units in the Lipa forest.

I found myself spending more and more of my free time talking to Emmy. After reviewing our homework assignments, we talked about people, family, life in general, and expectations of the future. As I spent more time with her, I became impressed by her personality, intelligence, and strength of character. I also discovered that under her calm exterior there was a passionate heart and strong feelings toward people. We spent more time together talking in the library after dinner. Even my aunt noticed the mutual attraction. There was silent support from the whole family. Occasionally, I tried to analyze my feelings toward Emmy, but somehow I couldn't equate my relationship with her with my relationship with Anna. Surely, I was attracted by her looks, her intelligence, and her positive attitude toward all people and life in general. But aside from my genuine admiration of her goodness and sincerity, there was a strong urge to touch her, to hold her, to kiss her, or even to go beyond innocent flirting. This simplistic and somehow cynical approach bothered me a little as I tried to justify not-so-honorable intentions toward Emmy. After all, she was an attractive girl, and I was running around with my buddies of the same age, looking for emotional and physical outlets for my energy.

I could easily visualize making love to Anna, quick, uncomplicated, very mechanical, and without too much concern about future involvement. With Anna it was mutual convenience satisfying both sides at the very moment without any long-term serious commitments. With Emmy it was different. She was physically attractive, nice, and smart, and a wish for a more permanent, serious, and prolonged involvement was all the time on my mind. When we said good night in the evening, I thought about her most of the night, eager to see her first thing the following morning. There was not only a physical attraction but also a strong feeling of longing and commitment, culminating in a desire to see her and be with her continuously day and night.

This unusual and previously unknown feeling bothered me since it interfered with my regular daily work. "Is this genuine love or am I losing my mind?" I asked myself occasionally. I could not come up with a reasonable explanation. The bloody war, full of surprises, was all the time around us, touching everybody's life in the most dramatic way, yet I was getting seriously involved in a romantic affair that probably was going nowhere. She was a couple of years older, mature, and very responsible. How could she be interested in a sixteen-year-old boy involved deeply with the partisans, playing hero, and flirting with servants?

My previous explorations with Anna were well known among a close circle of manor-house servants. A reputation for amorous skill was very flattering, but it had to be kept away from my relatives, because I knew my aunt's high standards and moral principles. She didn't believe in flirting with servants, not because of the class distinction but because of her deeply religious views and conservative approach to life, sex, and marriage. In her opinion sex had to be enjoyed strictly within the confines of marriage. Simple and uncomplicated lovemaking between husband and wife was intended for the purpose of fathering children and holding families together. Playing around and flirting, according to my aunt, was a distraction leading to sinful acts outside of marriage vows. I didn't expect my aunt to change her views, which were unrealistic and completely out of date, as verified by the continually growing number of unmarried mothers both in the village and among servants. I just tried to stay away from her, never discussed her views, and carried out my explorations with the local girls in a most discreet manner. If Emmy knew about my involvement with servant girls, she never made any comments on this subject. But, as we spent more and more time together, I was losing my interest in Anna and other girls.

One evening, when I tried to kiss Emmy for the first time, she turned her head around and gently avoided my clumsy attempts. "Is this how you practice with Anna?" She asked me half seriously. I was surprised and offended.

"Emmy, don't mix my feelings for you with my advances toward Anna." I sounded disappointed and annoyed.

"Janusz,"—she was serious—"you have to sort out your feelings and make a few serious decisions. I don't feel like competing with the local girls."

I tried to reassure her: "Emmy, please understand that you are not competing with anybody. You are the best thing that ever happened to me. Anna is the past and you are my future. I have already made this decision. Please trust me," I pleaded with her.

"I do"—she said and suddenly kissed me tenderly on my mouth. I was shocked but delighted. At that very moment I felt a strong desire for a long-term commitment, far greater than the simple physical attraction of a first kiss.

That evening marked the beginning of our new relationship. It was exciting but frightening at the same time. As I shaved every morning looking into the mirror, I would ask myself the same old question—"The world is falling apart and you are losing your head. Is this involvement with Emmy really necessary?" As before, there was no answer. I didn't know what the future held for us. I only knew that I was happy and that I looked forward to spending every free minute with Emmy. I wanted this relationship to grow and looked forward to each day with new enthusiasm and optimism, not even knowing what tomorrow would bring. It bothered me that while I was spending all this time with Emmy, my underground activities seemed to become more distant and remote and I was less and less eager to be the dashing hero taking unnecessary risks in fighting Germans. Occasionally, I even had a guilty conscience that my affair with Emmy and my personal feelings toward her were getting out of control. I thought less and less of dying for Poland and more and more of living forever with Emmy.

Christmas came and went uneventfully. News from the outside world was not good. Germans were making steady advances in Russia. The suppression of partisan units was intensified since the underground groups were interfering with vital supply lines to the front troops. Terrorizing and murdering of Jews reached a peak in the resettlement of the Zaklików ghetto and the establishment of Jewish labor camps in Janów and Kraśnik.

In March, Antoni, the gamekeeper who worked with me in the Lipa forest, was unexpectedly arrested. He was my contact with Skrzypek's unit and other underground organizations. Without going into specific details, I discussed Antoni's arrest with my uncle and his wife. They both agreed that because of concern for Michał's safety, I should leave Potoczek immediately.

It was decided that I was going to stay with my Uncle Jan who lived in Matczyn near Lublin. He inherited the estate from his father and, after paying off all his sisters, ended up as the sole owner of approximately three thousand acres of excellent and fertile land with acres of greenhouses. He administered his estate without any help and many times in the past had indicated that he could use my assistance, but I was always reluctant to work in Matczyn because of his dictatorial management style.

This time, I didn't have a choice. My aunt talked to her brother, and he was willing to take me immediately as his administrative assistant with duties and responsibilities similar to my involvement in Potoczek. I left the following day after an emotional farewell to Emmy.

Uncle Jan welcomed me in Matczyn with traditional Polish hospitality. I had visited the manor many times before the war during my summer vacations, but this time, it was different. I was going to work as an administrative assistant and help him manage his estate. Most of it consisted of acres and acres of fertile, black soil, characteristic of this part of the country. Wheat was the main product and Matczyn's high productivity of crops per acre made my uncle a hero among less successful estate owners.

Jan Ligowski and his wife Halina had no children. She was a daughter of Alexander Suryn from Warsaw, a well-known and wealthy family that had lost part of its fortune in Imperial Russia after the Revolution. She also had a sister, Maria, who since the beginning of the war had left Warsaw and moved in to live with Halina. She was an elegant and attractive professional woman who had an excellent job before the war and somehow never married. Matczyn's manor house was a large, two-story structure built around 1840 in a traditional Polish country style. In the center there was an elegant entrance hall adjoining a spacious living room and living quarters. Two wings consisting of a large kitchen and servants' quarters on the right side of the entrance hall and a large ballroom, billiard room, and guestrooms on the left side, reflected a perfectly symmetrical design characteristic of the classic Polish country manor. The house, recently modernized, was spacious, with large windows and high ceilings.

I ended up in one of the guestrooms adjoining the ballroom. Apparently I was not the only person using the guest quarters. In January 1942 the German assistant regional chief for agricultural products in the Lublin district had decided to use Matczyn as both his headquarters and his residence. Hans

Gruchot took over three guestrooms and resided in Matczyn on a permanent basis. He ate in his quarters but was served by my uncle's staff, and all his meals were prepared in the manor's kitchen. I met him the first day after my arrival in Matczyn. Born in German Silesia, he spoke little Polish. His background was in agriculture and he appeared to be friendly and easygoing. Gruchot never wore a uniform and was always dressed in civilian clothes. He drove his own car and carried a lot of weight among German civilians and police. We all suspected he was a Gestapo agent. This was the first time that I met an enemy face to face and had to conceal all my hostile feelings, acting in a civilized and noncommittal way. I was not alone, for Gruchot put a strain on everybody's life in Matczyn.

The day after I arrived, my uncle took me around and showed me his estate. We started with the animals and visited the cow barns, pig pens, then horse stables and warehouses. I met some of his field supervisors. Then we visited the fields. The house was run by the housekeeper, Zosia, who was assisted by Jan, the butler, and two chambermaids: Kasia and Mira. They all served the owner and his guests. Hans Gruchot was, however, their primary customer and required a lot of attention.

The Matczyn estate was approximately six kilometers from Bełżyce, a small town where the German administration established a Jewish camp. Inmates were used for various works in the area and sometimes Gruchot made arrangements to assign Jewish women to work in the fields in Matczyn or other adjoining estates. The laborers were always accompanied by Ukrainian guards who treated them in the most disgraceful and inhumane way.

After a few weeks, I got used to my daily routine. Of course, I missed Emmy and the rest of the people from Potoczek. But since my uncle relied on me to help him supervise various field activities, I enjoyed my work and took it as an opportunity to demonstrate my competence.

Most workdays I rode on horseback from one field to another, watching the farm hands at work. One day, as I was returning home in the late afternoon, I dismounted my horse and walked along the path between two wheat fields.

"Sir, sir . . ." I heard female voice behind me.

I turned around and saw a young woman. She was dressed like a city girl and had tears in her eyes. "Yes . . . What can I do for you?" I stopped and looked at her closely.

"Please, help me. I will do anything but please help me, sir."

"Who are you and what are you doing here?"

"I am Rosa from the Bełżyce camp. We were working all day in the fields in Bychawa, and at the end of the day I decided not to return to the camp.

There was a rumor that they are going to send us to Treblinka. I can't go . . . I am scared."

"Rosa, you know what they will do to you and me if they find us together. First, you must not admit to anybody that you are Jewish and that your name is Rosa. Perhaps I can help you for a few days, but we must be very careful. Let's say that, from this moment on, your name is Maria. You are a Polish Christian girl who lost all her documents during evacuation from Silesia and you are looking for work."

"Anything you say, sir." She listened carefully and stopped crying.

"Look, Maria, walk with me, but please remember do not admit to anybody—and I mean anybody—that you are Jewish."

"Yes, sir," she replied.

I was not quite sure what to do. Hiding Jews was forbidden by German laws and could result in an automatic death sentence for both victims and protectors. I could not have her in Matczyn with Gruchot under the same roof. At the same time, I felt that his presence might be an advantage and partial protection against police searches.

We were approaching the farmstead. "Look, Maria, are you hungry?"

"Yes, but I can wait for food," she assured me.

"I will take you to the greenhouse and you can stay tonight up there. It is clean and warm. I will bring you some food later on. Do not go out and do not walk around. Stay right behind the furnace. I will come to see you later tonight, but first I must talk to the gardener."

Bolek was the chief gardener of Matczyn. He was in charge of five acres of greenhouses where he cultivated flowers and exotic fruits. Most of his products were shipped to the Lublin cooperative. I did not know him very well. I decided that I would have to trust him since I could not think of any other place where she could stay.

I looked at her more closely: "Maria, we both must trust the gardener, but be careful because he may try to take advantage of you. Do you understand?"

"Yes, sir." Her voice trembled a little.

She was perhaps twenty years old with a dark complexion, lovely brown eyes, and long black hair. Her clothes were worn but of excellent quality. Her hands were delicate and well kept. Clearly, she was not a farm girl.

I kept wondering if I was doing the right thing. Hiding her in Matczyn meant exposing Ligowski and his family and taking tremendous risks. At the same time, I could not turn her down and let her stay alone in the field. Local farmers were unpredictable, particularly since she was very attractive in spite of her distress. There were many unpleasant stories circulating regarding treatment by farmers of Jewish escapees.

I knew that I had to come up with a better solution than keeping her in the greenhouse. I just needed more time.

"Wait here," I told Maria as I went to look for Bolek. He was busy watering some of the exotic plants.

"Good evening, Bolek. How are you?"

"Fine, Mr. Janusz. How do you like your new job?"

"I like it very much, Bolek. On my way home, I met a Polish girl from Silesia and she is looking for temporary work. I will try to find her something in the warehouse, but meanwhile, can she stay tonight in the greenhouse behind the furnace?"

"Of course . . . no problem . . . we have to help our fellow citizens." Bolek sounded reassuring.

I brought Maria and introduced her to him. "This is Maria Szpak from Katowice. Maria, Mr. Bolek is the chief gardener, he will help you to find a place to stay tonight and perhaps even some work tomorrow."

Bolek looked at Maria and I saw suspicion in his eyes. Her Polish was excellent, but her city dress and delicate hands could betray her easily.

"Maria, stay with Mr. Bolek. I will see if I can bring you some food." I could ask her to come to the kitchen and eat supper with Jan and Zosia, but I felt that if fewer people knew about her presence, there would be less chance for betrayal.

I was concerned about somebody talking to Gruchot and I tried to prepare a reasonable explanation in case of an unexpected confrontation. The only long-term solution was to find an isolated farm and friendly peasants willing to take a risk and accept her as part of their family. This was not an easy task, since local farmers were frightened and greedy, and I knew far more people in Potoczek than in Matczyn. Transportation to Lipa was, however, too risky.

I brought Maria supper from the kitchen. She was talking to Bolek and trying to answer all his questions. If he was suspicious now, he did not show this in his conversation.

"Mr. Janusz, she will be all right. I can even use her tomorrow for light work in the greenhouse. Do not worry, I will take care of her."

"Thanks, Bolek, and good night." I left the greenhouse with a heavy heart. I was nervous during dinner and could not sleep most of the night.

At 6 A.M. the next day, I went back to the greenhouse. Maria was already working. "I don't know how to thank you," she said. "Do not," I responded abruptly. "We still have many problems." Then I whispered to her. "How is Bolek behaving? Any suspicion?" "He seems to like me. He brought me breakfast this morning and he is very friendly."

I did not like her responses. Bolek's sudden friendliness might signal potential trouble.

"Maria, we must move from here. Do you have any friends in the area?"

"No, I don't. Don't you trust Mr. Bolek?"

I looked at her seriously. "No, I do not. He is a tough and sleazy character. Be careful." I saw tears in her eyes. "Don't cry. We must be tough and practical."

On my way to the stable, I met Bolek. "How are things going?"

"Fine, Mr. Janusz. She is a willing and hard worker. I can use her in the greenhouse."

"Thanks, Bolek. You are a great guy." By now, I knew that I would have to move Maria really fast.

The only person to whom I could confide my dilemma was Jan, the butler. He listened carefully and looked concerned. I tried to explain that I felt bad. Ligowski, my uncle, had offered me a job and a roof over my head and in return, I was putting his whole family at risk.

Jan shook his head. "I understand, Mr. Janusz. I will see if I can find her a shelter with one of the farmers."

That evening I went to see Maria. She was crying. "What's wrong?"

"Mr. Bolek kissed me today. He told me that if I want to stay here I must sleep with him. Mr. Janusz, I can't do it. Please help me. He is getting worse every hour."

The next morning I stopped to see Bolek. "How is Maria?" I began.

He looked at me and smiled.

"Bolek, leave her alone. Otherwise I will talk to my uncle."

He smiled again and looked straight into my eyes. "Mr. Janusz, what are you going to say—that you are hiding a Jewish girl under his roof? Go ahead, talk to him."

"You son of a bitch!"

"Mr. Janusz, if she wants to stay in my greenhouse, it will be on my terms. Otherwise, she will have to go and there is nothing you can do about it."

He was right. I left him in a hurry, feeling helpless and frustrated.

After my day's work and before supper, I stopped in the greenhouse. One of the girls was still there. "Ania, where is Maria?"

She looked around first and then whispered to me: "Mr. Janusz, Maria left this afternoon."

I was shocked. "She left? Where and how? What happened?"

"Mr. Bolek had a terrific argument with her. There was a lot of screaming and pushing. She cried and then he told her to go."

"Go . . . where?" I asked Ania.

"I don't know, sir. All I know is that she was very upset."

I rushed to see Bolek before he left the greenhouse. He looked straight at me: "Your Jewess left this afternoon. I could not take more risks to keep her here and expose my employer and your uncle to danger. How could you bring her here in the first place? And do not try to scare me with Ligowski. He will be very upset when he finds out what his irresponsible nephew is doing." I did not say a word, but turned around and left him.

I never did find out what happened to Rosa-Maria. There were a lot of fugitives from Bełżyce, some of them sheltered and some of them hunted and betrayed by the local farmers. In spite of my searching, none could be identified as Rosa. I now knew that Bolek was my enemy and I would have to watch him closely in the future. After the incident with Bolek, I went back to my routine work, hoping this was an end to our argument. All the time, however, I was concerned that one day he might bring Rosa's story to my uncle's attention.

My regular day started by supervising the early morning milk dispatch to the local dairy cooperative. Then I had a short meeting with the field supervisors about daily field assignments. The work details were usually based on instructions I received from my uncle. Every evening after dinner, we went through plans for the following day. This was a good time to review with my uncle individual people's performance and plans for the next week's accomplishments.

I tried to be reasonably friendly with everybody without getting too close and without being too personal in making daily assignments. Some men, mostly senior supervisors, resented my authority because of my inexperience and age. At the same time, younger employees were friendly and complied with my instructions without challenging my new position. Eventually, I got to know a few people, with whom I had daily contact, a little better than others. They were hardworking peasants willing to toil on the land, deeply religious and committed to the welfare of their families. Mutual trust and friendship developed on both sides.

One of my new friends was Jan, the butler, who had worked for the family for more than twenty years. He knew all the local secrets and gossips and was devoted to both Ligowskis. His wife was an excellent dressmaker and sewed all the clothes for my aunt and her sister. He also served as Gruchot's personal valet and was familiar with his ties to the Gestapo in Lublin. Fully aware about Rosa's case and knowing the sensitivity and potential danger if the story was revealed to the Germans, Jan personally warned Bolek to keep his mouth shut and forget the whole thing. Since he was also familiar with Bolek's black market deals and his illegal sales of vegetables to rich merchants in Bełżyce, Jan was confident that this was the end of Rosa's story. At my request, he also spent some time trying to find out what actually happened to Rosa, but he, too, could not discover any leads.

The political climate was getting worse. The Jewish camp in Bełżyce was gradually liquidated and, except for the most essential workers, all remaining inmates were transferred to an unknown location. There were some stories among local peasants that transports were sent to Treblinka, but this could not be confirmed since nobody ever came back.

The remainder of the prisoners was employed in special workshops, working under German supervisors for the "German war effort." Mostly these were tailors making uniforms for the German army. The strictly enforced death sentences for anybody who helped Jews made it very difficult for escapees to find shelter among local farmers.

One day, my uncle called me to his office: "Janusz, Bolek just talked to me. Is this true?"

I was very upset. "Uncle Jan, Bolek is a liar and a traitor," I said. But my uncle interrupted me sharply.

"Please tell me, is this true?"

I hesitated for a moment: "I do not know what he told you. I just tried to save a human being and find her a home in the village. I did not want her to stay in the manor permanently."

My uncle was distraught: "Janusz, do you realize the consequences of Gruchot finding that we were sheltering a Jew under our roof? How could you do such an irresponsible act in my house?"

"I am sorry, uncle. I did not know what to do. I just wanted to help her because—"

Again, he interrupted me sharply: "Janusz, I have no choice but to ask you to leave Matczyn. I did talk to my sister and they are willing to take you back to Potoczek."

"Are you afraid of Bolek?" I asked my uncle.

"No, I am not, but I worry about my family's safety and I am not willing to take any risks and be at Bolek's mercy."

I felt bad, and said, "I am sorry for all your problems." "Thanks for everything."

My arrival in Potoczek was almost as dramatic as a homecoming from a long exile. I looked forward to seeing my old friends and settling back to my familiar and friendly environment. Above all, I wanted to see Emmy and find out if our friendship had survived several months of separation.

My aunt Helena and her husband were very gracious in taking me back. Michał had recovered fully from his illness and ran the estate as he had before his imprisonment. With Paweł's help, there was no need for another administrator. I realized that Emmy was happy to see me. There was a nice warm feeling of being wanted, in marked contrast to a world of increasingly impersonal disasters.

The situation in Potoczek and the Lipa forest was getting worse every day. Reichsführer-SS Himmler decided to settle a large number of German nationals from the east into the relatively small area of Zamość. After the Jewish population was forcefully deported, all Polish farmers were suddenly expelled from their homes, transferred to labor camps in Germany, or shot on the spot. Whole families and villages were homeless. To protect the local population, the Polish underground designated special partisan units to defend villages and individual farmers. Bloody battles with German military units and police took place, with many killed and wounded soldiers on both sides.

All of this had an impact on units stationed in the Lipa forest since most of the dispersed partisan units looked for shelter near Lipa. Armed men representing many political parties were fighting Germans and each other at the same time.

After a few days of rest, I took my bike and went to see my old friends, the gamekeepers, in the forest to find out how they were surviving. Antoni was back on his job after spending three months in Janów jail. As an unemployed civilian not formally connected any more with the Forestry Administration, I recognized that I faced a certain degree of risk to venture on the isolated country roads leading to the heart of the Lipa forest.

Before I crossed the Zaklików highway, I stopped to pick up my revolver, buried under a large oak tree prior to my departure to Matczyn. It was in excellent condition. With a gun behind my belt, I felt safe as I entered the forest. After a few miles of sandy country road, I was challenged by a group of armed men standing at a small intersection of two fire lines.

I recognized Stanisław Skrzypek. "Hello, Stanisław," I greeted him, pleasantly surprised.

"Mr. Janusz . . . Good to see you. Where are you going? The whole forest is crawling with armed men." And then Stanisław warned me. "Some of them are just plain bandits and robbers. Be careful. They may not like Przanowski's kin."

"Thanks, Stanisław," I responded.

"Do you want my comrades to come with you?"

"No, but thanks anyway. It's easier on my own."

My first stop was Antoni's house. He was glad to see me. "Mr. Janusz, life is going to be more difficult in this forest. We have too many people with guns. Germans are also coming more often in large formations. The whole SS division is fighting with our people near Zamość."

"Antoni, how did you manage to survive your imprisonment in Janów? And how do you cope with this turmoil and why are you still here?"

"I have no place else to go. I am trying to be friendly with everybody who comes here. They usually leave us in peace."

I asked him if he knew anybody who was willing to trade some 9 mm bullets, because I was short of ammunition for my pistol.

"Mr. Janusz, ammunition is a very scarce commodity nowadays. But I do know the commander of the Soviet unit in my area. It is composed of escaped Soviet prisoners of war from German camps and is being led by the senior lieutenant sent by the Red Army. They are very well armed and they use the same caliber bullets. We can try to see if they are willing to exchange bullets for food. Do you want to try?"

I was excited. "Of course, let's go."

"Mr. Janusz," Antoni warned me. "Do not let them know you are the squire's nephew. They do not care for landlords and capitalists."

We walked for about one mile. Obviously Antoni knew his forest. "Halt. Who goes?" A challenge in Russian sounded in front of us.

"Friends," responded Antoni. A well-armed man in a Soviet army uniform came forward to see us.

"Comrade Lieutenant," he was greeted by Antoni. "This is my good friend, Janusz. He is a good worker, the son of proletarians, and he wants to fight Fascists. But he needs ammunition for his pistol. Can you help us? We will trade butter and eggs with you."

"Sure, he is your friend. I will share some of my supplies with you. No trades. I can give you only sixteen bullets."

"This is great." Antoni was sincere. "Thank you. I don't know how we can make it up to you."

"Just kill a few Germans for us." The lieutenant saluted. "Let's have a drink before you go." He pulled a bottle of vodka and a few glasses from his knapsack.

"*Prosit*. Death to enemies."

"Death to enemies." Antoni and I repeated, raising our glasses.

Some of his comrades joined us. I looked with curiosity at the camping ground.

Except for the commander, all partisans were in their early twenties, dressed in a combination of assorted civilian clothes and military uniforms. Most wore hats with a little red star up in front. Weapons were mostly Russian with a few German automatic pistols and plenty of grenades. They looked well fed and in good spirits. The lieutenant talked about the Red Army offensive and the beginning of the battle for Stalingrad. Obviously, they had radio contact with the outside world. In my mind, I tried to compare the Soviets with Polish underground units that I had met before. The Poles were poorly equipped and short of reliable ammunition, since the Polish army recovered most of the weapons from previously buried stocks in 1939 and some of the rifles were not very well preserved. After years in the ground, ammunition deteriorated. I hoped that we would not fight "red" partisans in the near future. They had the might of the Red Army behind their supply lines and we had rare airplane drops from the West and mostly empty verbal promises from our allies.

After we sipped our vodka and chatted about the local situation, I indicated to Antoni that it was time to go.

I thanked the lieutenant again for his generous gift and we left the camp.

"Thanks, Antoni. He did this for you."

"Well, Mr. Janusz, I am glad that I could be of some use to you. I do help them a lot, tracking Germans in the woods. After all, I know this forest like my own house."

"How do they treat local people?" I asked Antoni.

"They are fairly decent to local small farmers and workers, but they hate all landowners and squires."

"Thanks again, Antoni. This was an unexpected treat. I would never dream that I would be getting bullets from the Red Army."

"Be careful on your way home," Antoni warned me again. "There are a lot of nasty people in these woods."

On my way home, I thought about Antoni's comments. He was right. With so many armed people in the forest, some of them genuine partisans and some just plain bandits and robbers, life in the Lipa forest was getting very dangerous. I was fully aware that I knew too many people tracked by the German police. Unexpected arrests and forced confessions of the victims under Gestapo torturers could easily identify members of the underground as well as many innocent relatives. I also recognized that my arrest could compromise the safety and security of the Przanowski family, who had been kind and generous to provide me with shelter for the past few years.

Guilt by association was a well-known policy of the Gestapo. Families and relatives of suspected members of the underground were continually arrested and held as hostages. From one of the informers, I learned that I was on the Gestapo wanted list, and realized I must leave Potoczek soon.

That evening I talked to Emmy. She was aware of my connection with many partisan units and underground organizations. Although, she really wanted me to stay, common sense indicated that in order not to compromise innocent people in Potoczek, I should leave as soon as possible. This was not very easy. I could not return to Matczyn. I did not want to live in any big city, for such places were too dangerous with all the street arrests and continuous rounding up of innocent people for forced-labor camps in Germany.

My options were limited, since I could not join the Polish underground unit in the Lipa forest because too many people in the area knew my face. However, I had some connections with the headquarters of the Polish Home Army in the Lublin district and I wanted to explore the possibility of joining an activated partisan unit in that area.

In an age of suspicion and betrayal it was not easy to cross the line from the "official" and ordinary life into the murky environment of underground activities.

My background and my motives had to be verified by the Lublin District Command and I had to be exposed to a careful check of my credentials. A meeting was set up in Lublin.

Christmas 1942, unlike prewar holidays, was somber and subdued. German propaganda in local papers and on radio glorified sacrifices and successes of the German army in Russia. The Battle of Stalingrad was raging, and photographs of German heroic soldiers were published in daily editions. The winter weather was cold and snowy. Partisans' units in the Lipa forest were less active than during the fall. They were hiding in remote villages, since tough winter weather made it almost impossible to survive in the forest under an open sky. Even German police pacification actions were less frequent as the soldiers stayed inside their warm barracks and were reluctant to venture out in their trucks into a deep snow covering country roads.

Cold weather and drifting snow brought both relief and misery to the few Jewish families from adjoining villages who refused forceful relocation to ghettos. They were hiding from German police in shelters along the Zaklików-Modliborzyce highway. Layers of snow provided additional cover and insulation to their primitive caves dug from frozen soil. The holes were carefully camouflaged with branches of pine trees and provided occupants with the delusion of security and protection from uninvited visitors, but living conditions in cold weather were brutal and food was scarce.

Jankiel and his family had left the village the previous year and hid in a vacant and isolated house close to the mill at the edge of the Lipa forest. Szymsza and his wife were arrested and forcefully evicted from Potoczek and sent to the Zaklików ghetto. Their house and store were taken over by a German settler from East Prussia.

In the manor on Christmas Eve, we all celebrated *wigilja* in accordance with the old Polish customs, sharing the traditional wafer *oplatek* and wishing each other a better future. I kissed Emmy warmly and whispered in her ear my declaration of love and my assurances that she would be my only girl forever. She was very moved and kissed me gently in front of everybody, including my "puritan" aunt. Emmy's eyes were full of tears and emotions. At that time we were both aware that I would be leaving Potoczek soon.

After Christmas, with a heavy heart I said my final goodbye to Emmy. This time we both had tears in our eyes since I was venturing into uncharted territory. It was exciting but dangerous and we both knew it. I left a short letter to my aunt explaining that I was very grateful for her willingness to shelter me for so many years and told her that I was leaving to visit my friends in Lublin. In order to protect my close relatives from arrests by the Gestapo, I obtained from my underground connections in Potok Wielki new identification papers under the name of Janusz Strojnowski. I took with me a minimum of personal belongings and my revolver with Russian ammunition. Using country roads in a small, one-horse-driven sledge, and trying to avoid German patrols with the help of local farmers, I set out on my journey to Lublin for my interview with the district commander of the Polish Home Army.

CHAPTER THREE

Freedom Fighters

THE SOFT-SPOKEN young man sitting behind the desk said "Contact will be established this week." Nobody could suspect that the easygoing employee of the City Resettlement Office was Lieutenant Nerwa, the right hand and confidant of the powerful underground leader Captain Jan, commanding officer of the Lublin District of the Polish Home Army. Here was conspiracy at its best. The office was part of the city government and served as a legitimate cover to hide underground activities of the Polish Home Army. It provided opportunities to establish an active network of secret organizations within an institution that was an extended arm of the German SS Security Services. The Resettlement Office was part of an organization established by the Reichsführer-SS Himmler to control the resettlement of Polish refugees from western Poland, which now was formally incorporated into the German Reich. It was mostly staffed with German civilians but also employed Polish clerks as minor officials.

After waiting for several weeks in a tiny apartment in Lublin for an opportunity to join the partisans' unit operating in the Lublin area, my assignment was now officially approved by the district commander. Lieutenant Nerwa continued: "You will report to Lieutenant Czarnota in Motycz. You may have to stay with him for few days before they will pick you up. Leave all your personal belongings with him."

He told me that Lieutenant Czarnota was a schoolteacher who lived in a small town of Motycz and was using his job as a cover for his underground activities. Together with his wife, he resided in a small country house detached from the rest of the village. During selected nights, active partisans' units visited his home to obtain instructions or new orders and pick up new recruits from the area. The house served as a drop point for "underground" soldiers leaving the unit to enter official existence under German occupation or for people like me who were hunted by the Gestapo and were on their way to join the partisans. Czarnota was able to control this traffic and assist the

47

"right people" in providing false documents and at the same time maintained close contact with partisans.

I knew the area. Motycz was the closest railroad station to Bełżyce, which was located not far from Matczyn, about fourteen kilometers southwest of Lublin. Before the war, the population consisted of local government employees, craftsmen, and many Jewish shopkeepers. It served as an exchange point for agricultural products delivered by local farmers and in turn provided goods and everyday commodities to the local population. The town's commercial character was well known in the area and the Bełżyce market was recognized as the finest place to purchase farm animals. The smallest administrative subdivision, *gmina,* was located in the town. The head of *gmina* and local government officials administered the area. Before the war, a detachment of Polish police was stationed in the town. War, however, had brought unexpected changes to the area. The Jewish population was restricted to a ghetto. Food was scarce and lack of trade resulted in the market closing. The administrative unit was now under the direction of German officials and an SS Security unit replaced the Polish police. The town population was tense in anticipation of an uncertain future. Also, a Jewish labor camp was established in town, the one that Rosa, the Jewish girl, whom I met in Matczyn while I worked for my uncle, had escaped from.

The adjutant to the commanding officer concluded his instructions: "You will be contacted by officer-cadet Zegota, who will accompany you to Motycz. You may also retain your pistol, but be very careful in planning your route. You must avoid German patrols at any cost. Do you have any questions?"

I responded instantly, "No, sir."

"Good luck, Strzemię." He shook my hand as we parted.

Before joining the ranks and participating in the underground activities, every member of the Polish Home Army had to assume a new code name and hide all formal and official personal documents. There was no communication between the partisans and their relatives except in extreme circumstances. German informers watched the suspected families all the time for any contact with the underground world. Usually, "going to the forest," meant cutting off all ties with relatives and friends. Prior to leaving Lublin, I selected *Strzemię* as my code name, which meant "stirrup." This was the coat of arms of the Strojnowski family, my ancestors, and I felt closely attached to it. The "Stirrup" coat of arms had been presented to the family by the Polish king, Jan Sobieski, in 1683 after his victory over the Turks in Vienna. Jan Strojnowski, at his own expense, equipped a unit of volunteers from his home district and as part of the Lisowczyków brigade led a charge of the light cavalry regiment that helped to defeat the Turkish counterattack.

I met Zegota in the house of one of the members of the Lublin Headquarters Command Unit. He was older than I, slim with a small mustache; friendly, and yet businesslike, he appeared to be sincere with a good sense of humor. We talked about our plans for the future without getting too personal. I told him briefly about my background in the Cadet Corps in Lwów and I learned that he had just completed underground training in the Home Army Officers' School and in the future had set his eyes on a career in the air force. The next day, he invited me to meet his parents. They had a small house on Narutowicza Street. We had lunch and I chatted with his parents and his brother Zygmunt. I gathered that the Gestapo was looking for Zegota and he had to leave the city as soon as possible. That evening, as we were making plans to leave for Motycz, I showed Zegota my pistol, which I planned to take with me. In planning our route, we would have to stay away from the Germans. We both knew that possessing a weapon carried the death penalty.

The following early afternoon, we left Lublin on two bicycles. We tried to merge with a group of factory workers who at that time were leaving their work shift in one of the German factories located on the outskirts of the city. The trip was uneventful. German sentries looked mostly for "black marketeers" and did not bother the workers. After a short journey south, at the edge of the city, most of the workers reached their homes, and we were left alone to cycle along the winding country lanes. We looked ahead for German patrols. The early spring sun was bright and pleasantly warm. There were no clouds on the horizon and the countryside appeared peaceful.

Lieutenant Czarnota's welcome was warm and sincere. He showed us a previously prepared space in the barn where we could rest and stay. After a few hours, when it was completely dark, he invited us to his house for dinner. His wife, Krystyna, was also involved in the underground activities. That night, until a late hour, we discussed the diversities and internal struggles among the many Polish political parties. I sensed from our discussion that both Czarnota and his wife were very much aware of political differences, conflicts, and divided loyalties among the civilian population in the Lublin district.

Because of Motycz's proximity to the German concentration camp in Majdanek near Lublin, they were also very well informed about the SS local persecutions of the Jewish population and the German national extermination policy toward Jews. Czarnota, with great concern, described in detail to us Nazi subhuman treatment of Polish political prisoners in the Lublin Castle. He was also well informed about SS atrocities against prisoners in Auschwitz-Birkenau and other camps. It appeared that the Polish underground organization had its own people in each concentration camp, sending secret reports about Nazi murderous activities.

After dinner, we went back to the barn, ready for a few hours of rest before starting the last part of our journey. The house and adjoining farm buildings were isolated from the rest of the village and thus provided some privacy for many visitors. We were told that after midnight a runner from the unit would arrive at the barn to guide us back to the underground camp. I waited anxiously long past midnight, but nobody came to see us.

The next morning, we were awakened by Czarnota, who brought us breakfast and said: "I was unable to contact my courier last night but I expect to see a runner tonight and certainly no later than tomorrow night. Relax, do not worry." Then he added: "I am also anxious for you to leave this house. This is not a very safe place. Recently there has been too much traffic on the highway."

I felt restless. After long preparations and extended efforts by many friends and colleagues, somehow we could not cross that magic line and be true soldiers, full-fledged members of the armed active resistance. That night I cleaned my pistol at least four times, until it was as good as new.

"Relax," Zegota told me. "We will get there eventually. Patience is a virtue of partisan life."

I wondered out loud, "Perhaps they have problems of their own."

On the third day, early in the morning, Czarnota brought us breakfast as usual and announced: "You're leaving tonight."

Again we spent all day in the barn. In the evening, after dinner with Czarnota and his wife, we said good-byes and expressed our appreciation for their hospitality and willingness to help us. As we were leaving the house for our secret hiding place in the barn to wait for the guide, Czarnota said: "This is not good-bye. You will see me many times in the future. There is a lot of work to be done in this area."

Shortly after midnight, Czarnota came again to the barn and said, "Time to get up and be ready in ten minutes." A young man who was standing with a bike in front of the barn said, "Hello, my name is Jelonek and I am your guide. Get your bikes ready."

"My name is Zegota and this is Strzemię," Zegota introduced both of us.

"Any weapons?" Jelonek asked.

"Yes, I have a VIS revolver with me," I responded.

He was pleasantly surprised. "That's good. We are still short of weapons. Follow me."

After two hours of silent cycling, we arrived in a small village. The sky was dark and cloudy. Only the occasional barking of a dog interrupted the silence of the night. Jelonek stopped in front of a large barn. A voice from the darkness called, "Stop. Who goes?"

Jelonek responded with a password, "Night and day." A well-armed guard opened a small side door and let us in with our bikes. Dim light from the old-fashioned oil lamp was flickering on the table and I could see the faces of several people gathered in the middle of the barn.

"Comrades, let me introduce to you our two new colleagues," said Jelonek. "Officer cadet Zegota and cadet Strzemię. They are going to stay with us." We both shook hands with several men. I looked at their faces and their uniforms with curiosity and apprehension. Most of them were in their twenties, dressed in a combination of civilian clothes and Polish Army uniforms. Some held rifles and some had pistols packed behind their belts. Several men were only dressed in shirts and had no shoes. It appeared that they were getting ready to go to sleep. Each man introduced himself. Of course, I could not remember all the names: Mały, Olek, Alex, Gołąb, Rafał, Tom, and many others. I just shook my head and tried to remember faces.

Jelonek continued formal introductions. "This is a mobile group under Commander Jeleń, who reports to Czarnota and who will be with us tomorrow. Our mission is to provide shelter to underground personnel wanted by the Gestapo and to prepare for a general uprising to fight the Germans at the appropriate time. Meanwhile, we are training and trying to recover and preserve weapons buried in this area by the Polish Army in 1939." He turned toward both of us and addressed us directly: "Please feel at home. This is your family. We work, fight, and pray together with one goal in our hearts." Immediately, several voices in the barn responded in unison, "Death to Germans! Death to Germans!" Then, Jelonek concluded: "Guards are posted outside and we can rest here until tomorrow night. Here are your blankets."

I picked up my blanket and looked around for a place to rest. The barn was built on two levels with a large open space in the middle. Some of the men climbed the ladder to the second level, which was full of hay. Zegota and I picked out two spaces along the wall on the lower level. I took off my boots and using my jacket and my pistol as a pillow, lay down on the floor. Zegota spent some time talking to Jelonek. But since I was tired after a long day, I immediately fell fast asleep under the old Polish army blanket.

When I opened my eyes, daylight was already breaking outside. Most of the men were still fast asleep. I gently touched Zegota and using his first real name I asked him quietly: "Polek, what do you think?"

Zegota was very optimistic. "It looks good. I talked to Jelonek last night. This is a training group of almost thirty people under his father's command. We will soon be attached to the regular unit of the Eighth Infantry Regiment. Meanwhile, we must get used to the new way of life and recover some weapons and ammunition from farmers in this area. We are not to attack Germans because of repressions against the civilian population. Until we are ready, we will stay away from the police unless we are attacked first."

We all washed up in the barn and nobody was allowed to go outside. Two friendly, good-looking peasant girls, dressed in the pretty, colorful skirts and blouses typical of the Lublin region, brought us coffee, sausage, and bread for breakfast. I was surprised how nice they looked in their black laced-up shoes and white stockings. Suddenly, I realized that it was Sunday morning and peasants in the village, dressed up in their Sunday best, were on their way to church. I thought, how could I have lost the track of time so easily? But my total commitment to become a soldier in the Polish Home Army overwhelmed me now, diminishing my awareness of time and the life of civilians outside of the forests. The young girls obviously knew all the men. Conversation was friendly and almost sounded like a Sunday morning flirtation before the mass.

I watched my new colleagues with curiosity. Gołąb was a local boy from the village of Wierzchowiska. He apparently had had some problems with the German police and a warrant for his arrest had been issued. Olek was the son of a farmer. He was older than most of the men and talked with a heavy southern dialect. Alex was the son of a Polish officer who was a prisoner of war in Germany. He and his friend, Osa, were involved in a shooting incident with German police in Lublin. The rest were mostly local boys from Bychawa, Podole, and Konopnica.

Jeleń arrived before lunch. He gathered everybody in the middle of the barn and, looking at Zegota and me, made an announcement, "I welcome our two new colleagues. Our group is growing and we must be getting ready to act and fight, if necessary, as an organized military unit. Effective immediately, I am appointing Officer-Cadet Zegota as my deputy. We will intensify our military training but we will avoid fights with the police. We are depending too much on local support from adjoining villages to risk German intimidation of local farmers. Tonight we are leaving for new quarters."

In the afternoon the same two girls brought us a kettle of hot soup and fresh black bread. I noted that there were always two armed guards outside watching for uninvited guests. Inside the atmosphere was informal. Apparently, most of the men knew each other well. The girls were friendly but they behaved more like comrades-in-arms than flirtatious young women looking for a man's company. Later, I found out that both of them acted as couriers for the unit and both had been trained as nurses, in case of an emergency. One of them, Kropka, a tall young woman with long blonde hair, was Jeleń's distant cousin. Deep in my heart, I was disappointed. I had expected to meet a well-disciplined, uniformed, and organized military detachment, but what I saw was a friendly, informal group of people, very patriotic and committed to the cause, but a long way from a highly trained regular army unit.

When it was dark, Jeleń gave the signal for departure. Zegota, in his new capacity as Jeleń's deputy, organized the column. We sent two soldiers up in front walking "point" on both sides of the road. They were our eyes and ears. A hundred feet behind them walked Gołąb, with a light machine gun. Jeleń and Zegota were right behind him. A single line of men followed Zegota. Two soldiers walked a hundred feet behind the unit and protected our rear. The dark blue-black sky was clouded and visibility was poor. We walked rather slowly and silently, watching for any possible signs of ambush.

After a few hours of uninterrupted march, we entered a small village. Typical straw-covered peasants' huts were standing on both sides of the road. The village was isolated in the middle of a valley with a small stream flowing across the main street under a wooden bridge. Except for apple trees behind the houses, the area was open and exposed. There were no trees in the vicinity of the village to provide any kind of cover. I was concerned about our new exposed location and whispered my doubts to Zegota.

He said, "Do not worry. This is Jeleń's home village. We are safe here."

As we approached the first few houses, we heard barking dogs from several farmyards. Jelonek went ahead, called all of the dogs by name and, in no time, quieted them. We all entered a small barn in the middle of the village. Zegota appointed guards and set up other duties. The rest of us looked for a place to rest. An oil lamp hanging in the middle of the barn provided dim light. I found a place between Gołąb and Orzeł. We were all tired after the long march. Some of the men took off their jackets and shoes, and others were getting ready to sleep fully clothed. I took off my shoes and, using my jacket and knapsack as my pillow, closed my eyes and immediately fell asleep.

Friendly laughter and intensified conversation across the barn woke me the next morning. After breakfast, Zegota gathered the group in the middle of the barn and spoke to us: "Starting today, in addition to our duties of collecting weapons hidden in the nearby villages, we will be spending more time on regular training classes and field exercises." Then, he continued: "Day patrols in civilian clothes and with concealed weapons will try to purchase as many rifles as we can from the local farmers. During nights, we will operate as a unit, fully armed and uniformed. However, we will still try to avoid Germans since we must protect the local population from unnecessary reprisals."

"Remember," he added: "Our survival depends on the trust of and good relations with the local farmers. Do not antagonize the local population."

Then Zegota asked Gołąb and me if we wanted to take the first daytime assignments.

We both responded together, "Of course, we will go."

"See me in one hour."

"Yes, sir."

We both were anxious and eager. An hour later, Zegota briefed us about the assignment and explained the background and purpose of our mission. He said: "Our informant, Michał, told us yesterday that in Borów, a machine gun, several rifles, and rather large quantities of ammunition were buried by Kruk's family and Polish soldiers after the September 1939 defeat. See what you can do and how much you can recover. Good luck."

We left our military knapsacks and belts in the barn, and looking like two farm laborers with our pistols hidden under our shirts, started our journey to Borów. It was strange to walk among cornfields in the daytime on our first secret mission. Farmers greeted us in a friendly manner as we passed, but I believed that they were fully aware of our underground connections. We kept our eyes open and looked for German patrols or ambushes along the main road. Since Gołąb was a local boy he knew the area very well.

Finally, we reached our destination. Borów was a small village and we had no problem finding a white house with red shutters. I knocked at the door. A young woman opened the door and looked surprised.

"Good morning." I greeted her. "Please do not worry. We want to talk to Jurek," I said. She seemed to be concerned.

"What do you want from him?" She sounded even more suspicious.

"We have a message from Michał," Gołąb responded.

She turned around and called out loudly: "Jurek, you have visitors."

A young-looking man walked toward us from the farmyard. In his right hand, he was holding a large ax.

"Gentlemen, I am cutting firewood in the yard. What can I do for you?"

I made a sudden decision to bring the whole issue up front. "Jurek, we are from the Home Army, Jeleń's unit. We were told by your cousin, Michał, that you have a machine gun and we would like to buy it from you."

Jurek did not say anything at first. Then slowly he responded: "How do I know that you are who you say you are?" He sounded suspicious.

I was getting impatient. "Jurek, we are with Andrzej Chołaj and we are trying to organize a new partisan unit in this area but we need weapons. Can you help us? We will pay for it."

Jurek asked again: "What's Chołaj's son's name?"

"Bogdan," responded Gołąb.

Jurek seemed to be more relaxed and offered an explanation. "Look, I did not know who you were. There are a lot of informers working for the Germans. One has to be careful."

We shook hands. "This is my sister, Halina. She is a schoolteacher visiting us from Lublin. I am Jurek Kruk, a corporal from the Eighth Infantry Regiment. We do have one light machine gun and ammunition buried in the ground behind our barn." Then he added: "I am not going to sell it. I am going to give it to you. But I can not do it right now. Come back tonight. This will give me enough time to dig it up after dark."

I glanced at my watch. It was almost one o'clock.

"Why don't you stay for lunch?" Jurek suggested. He turned to the girl. "Halina, give us a drink and something to eat." Then he made a gesture and said to us, "Please come in."

We went to the dining room where Halina was setting the table with plates and glasses.

"I am honored to drink with you," said Jurek.

"To Poland's independence," added Gołąb. We all raised our glasses.

I was not used to drinking vodka in the middle of the day, so I picked up a large piece of sausage and a piece of brown bread to modify its effect.

"Excellent bread." I turned to Halina. "Do you bake your own bread?"

She blushed a little and shook her head. "Mother always bakes the bread, I help her when I am home."

Gołąb was talking to Jurek about Chołaj's family.

I looked at Halina again. She was not a typical farmer's daughter. She was dressed like a city girl in a white dress with large blue flowers. Her eyes matched the color of the flowers on her dress and her long blonde hair was tied with a blue ribbon. She looked very attractive and almost out of place in the village of Borów. She must have sensed my curiosity. "I am leaving for Lublin this afternoon to teach my class tomorrow morning."

"Good luck," I said. "How do you manage in Lublin under the German occupation?"

"It is very hard. But I love teaching small children." Then she added: "Do you know that Chołaj's cousin Kropka is my friend? She is my age. I understand that she visits your unit occasionally."

"I am new so I don't know her. But when she comes next time why don't you come along with her?"

She smiled: "Yes, thanks for the invitation. We may see you again soon."

I added: "Ask for long Janusz or for Strzemię if you come to see us. I would like to talk to you more."

Gołąb was shaking hands with Jurek: "Thanks for the food and hospitality. We will be back tonight to pick up the gun."

As we were leaving, I looked back. Halina was waving from the doorway. Gołąb looked at me: "Strzemię, my friend, do not get the wrong idea. You did not join the partisans to play house."

"Of course, I did not. But she is a good-looking girl," I protested.

This time he was serious: "Take my advice. Don't start anything you will not be able to finish. We have too many problems already."

I reassured him: "I know. Do not worry but please don't say anything to the boys in the unit."

Zegota was pleased. One additional machine gun, hopefully in good condition and loaded with ammunition, was an asset to the organization and considerably increased our firepower. I was slowly getting used to our daily and nightly routines. Partisan lifestyle at that time was fairly primitive and unpredictable. We never stayed longer than two nights in one village, and we were always eating, sleeping, and relaxing in a state of readiness to face the enemy or to escape from a closing trap. At the beginning, I slept fully dressed. But gradually, I developed enough confidence to undress at night and sometimes I even wore my colorful pajamas, which I had brought with me from Potoczek. This was the subject of many humorous comments from my friends, since nobody shared my preference for comfortable and informal night attire. Every evening, as I was getting ready to retire, Gołąb would make a comment: "I would like to see you in the middle of the night running from Germans in your pajamas. You may even scare them."

Our contacts and good relations with the local farmers were essential to our survival, not only because they provided us with food and shelter but also with vital intelligence. In each village, we had an organized group, mostly of young women, who informed us about the movements and activities of German police and the German army.

Night marches were always dangerous, exciting, and very tiring. We had to continuously watch out for Germans as well as for other underground units. The area around Lublin was crawling with many different underground groups representing many political factions. Peasant Battalions, supported mostly by poor local farmers and not affiliated with the Home Army, were strongly represented in the Bełżyce District. In addition to Polish and Jewish formations, there were also Soviet units consisting mostly of escaped prisoners of war under the command of Red Army officers who had parachuted behind the German front lines. Both German Ukrainian police and Soviet partisans spoke Russian. To find out who was confronting you in the middle of a dark night, cursing or shouting in many different languages required tact, diplomacy, and steady nerves. Most of the time, we shot first and then asked questions. Other people, of course, did the same thing. This led to many disturbing confrontations.

At the beginning of April, our night route from Moszna to Jastków required crossing the Lublin-Warsaw highway. As we approached a ditch on the west side of the highway, we received sudden and unexpected heavy machine gun fire. Our lead patrol responded with a rapid burst of fire from machine pistols. Very soon the ditches on both sides of the highway were blazing with flying bullets in all directions. Then, we heard voices across the highway screaming to each other in Polish, "We need more ammunition." Zegota passed the word to cease-fire. We called back in the best Polish we could master under the strange circumstances, "Stop shooting. Who are you?"

A voice responded, "This is the First Battalion of the Polish Peasant Army. Who are you?"

"This is special unit of the Polish Home Army. Do not shoot."

A person with a white handkerchief on his rifle stepped up on the highway. "Brothers, we all fight against the same enemy. Save your ammunition for Germans."

Both groups met in the middle of the highway, talking. No one even remembered that a few minutes before we were ready to kill each other.

We spent most of our days sleeping, training, recovering weapons from local farmers, and cleaning and preserving our equipment. My revolver worked like new and most of my colleagues looked with envy at my prize possession as I cleaned the gun each day. Every night, I put all of my equipment under my jacket and used this as a pillow. Having my revolver close to me all the time gave me a feeling of security.

One morning, as I opened my eyes and checked for my prized possession, I found that my revolver was missing, though everything else was there. I was devastated and could not understand what had happened. Usually, we slept in barns and each man had a rifle and revolver by his side. Personal belongings and ammunition were kept in our military knapsacks. Other items were mostly stacked close to our sleeping bags or army blankets.

I looked around and searched for the revolver, but could not find it. I went to see Zegota.

"Polek, my revolver is missing." He was also surprised. "Are you sure? Did you look around?"

"Yes, I am sure."

After breakfast, Zegota called the whole group together. Everybody was present except Orzeł. We all looked for him. Nobody remembered seeing him since last night. This was strange. Orzeł and my revolver were both missing. This could be serious for all of us. Apart from my personal loss, desertion from a partisan unit was punishable by death. None of us knew Orzeł very well. Was he an informer, traitor, adventurer, or thief? Zegota talked to Jeleń, who knew the area and all underground units regardless of their political or military associations.

Jeleń was very reassuring: "It may take a little while but we will find him."

All that week we carried out our regular routine: training, weapon recovery, day patrols and the never-ending change of quarters every second night. The loss of the revolver was always on my mind. Then one day Jeleń came to see us and called me. "We found Orzeł." I was really excited.

"He is staying with the Red Army Unit in Kawka near Kozłowiecka Forest. My courier tells me that the commander is willing to talk to us. I will set an appointment for tomorrow. You may want to take Olek with you since he speaks good Russian."

Late afternoon the next day, Olek and I were waiting patiently for a contact at the entrance to Kawka cemetery. Suddenly, I heard a voice from behind the stone wall, "Comrades, greetings from the Red Army."

We passed the entrance gate to meet a middle-aged civilian who told us in fairly good Polish: "Follow me." We both walked behind him, left the cemetery, and entered the forest. About half a mile from the edge of the forest we met the first outpost: "Stop—who goes!" He challenged us. "Friends," responded our guide. Then we entered the compound. Beside a small fire in the middle of an open area there was a wooden table with several benches. A group of armed and uniformed Red Army soldiers were standing around the table. I could not see Orzeł.

An officer with an insignia of senior lieutenant stepped forward: "I am Senior Lieutenant Kabushkin. What can I do for you? I understand Polish."

I talked slowly and looked straight into his eyes, "Comrade Lieutenant, I am Cadet Strzemię and this is Corporal Olek. As an officer, you must understand that this is a serious matter. We believe that one of our soldiers who deserted with stolen weapons is in your unit. We came to bring him and our weapons back to our camp."

The lieutenant responded in fairly good Polish, "Comrades, a few days ago we welcomed a soldier, who of his own free will, joined our forces to fight Fascists. We respect his decision and he will stay with us."

I asked the lieutenant, "Can we talk to him?"

He shook his head, "He does not want to see you."

I recognized that we would not reach any understanding with the Soviets and that Orzeł was under their protection. I tried to salvage my revolver. "Comrade, I am requesting that you return my pistol which was stolen by the deserter."

The lieutenant turned around to one of his soldiers behind him. The soldier disappeared for a few minutes and came back with my revolver and my old leather holster. He handed me the weapon with a brief comment, "Comrade, since we are fighting the same enemy, I am returning the revolver as a sign of good will. Now you must leave the camp." There was no purpose in arguing our case. I took my revolver, turned around, and walked with Olek toward the cemetery. There was complete silence among the Russian soldiers. Not hate, but I could feel a cold indifference. The same guide accompanied us back to the main gate.

After our return from Kawka, I discussed Orzeł's desertion with Zegota.

Our options were limited. We could not fight the Soviets. They were well armed and undoubtedly we would incur some losses. We decided to screen more carefully all newcomers to our unit, in order to avoid similar problems in the future. I never saw Orzeł again. Recovery of my revolver brought me peace of mind and I could again concentrate on my military training and field exercises.

At the end of April, there were minor changes in our unit. A few local boys left. Some went back home to help with the farm work and some were assigned to other duties. Except for occasional visits, Jeleń, practically speaking, left the group and Zegota was in charge. Zegota told me in secret that there were going to be further changes in the organization. Our small unit was scheduled to join Lieutenant Spartanin's group, which was officially identified as the fourth platoon of the Eighth Infantry Regiment. The name of this formation was "Spartanie" and they operated in the Bychawa region. He did not know the exact date for consolidation of both units but it was expected to happen fairly soon, sometime in July. Meanwhile, we were to carry out our business as usual and cultivate a friendship with the peasants and local population.

As we moved from village to village, we learned from the underground press, dispatched to us by Czarnota, about the Warsaw Ghetto Uprising. This was a tough struggle. Isolated and forgotten by the rest of the world, Jews were fighting with dignity and honor for their survival. Knowing well from our own experience what it meant to be outnumbered and outgunned by the German police, we found their fight an encouragement for us to concentrate on our own mission to survive, improve our military skills, and cultivate our friendship with local peasants. Those were essential elements for operation "Tempest," a national uprising scheduled for the following year, prior to the entry of Soviet troops into Poland.

The local people had some fear of German retribution, but they were willing to take a risk in supporting the fight for independence. In tough war times, among misery and fear imposed by the Germans, an oppressed and hunted population looked desperately for any meaningful signs of resistance and unity of purpose. Although suffering was enormous, down-to-earth, stubborn peasant spirit was far from being broken. Celebrations with partisans bonded the local villages with the fighters.

On the third of May, we took a day of rest to celebrate the national holiday, an anniversary of the first Polish Constitution of 1791, with the local population of Majdan. On this warm, lazy, and pleasant afternoon in the middle of spring, we were also celebrating the success of our unit. Our small group of freedom fighters had survived several months and, over the past eight weeks, we had recovered a considerable amount of weapons and ammunition. In the heart of the struggle for independence, success was measured by the quality of weapons and the quantity of ammunition. At that time we had plenty of both.

After a long, all-night forced march, we crossed the Ciemięga River, and arrived in Majdan. Wiktor, the *sołtys* as the head of this small village buried deep in the Kozłowiecka forest near Lubartów, greeted us warmly: "Welcome to our homes and our hearts." As a respected official, he was the formal host to Zegota's partisans' being entertained by local folks. Good news traveled fast and our presence was unwisely magnified from village to village. By the time we met Wiktor, local farmers were already treating us with reverence, as if we were real heroes. Nothing was too good for freedom fighters. "Let's take a real day of rest," concluded Zegota. "Strzemię, set posts around the village and have one guard on the main road."

"Yes, sir." I saluted smartly and designated sentries around the village. A day of rest in a partisan's life usually meant relaxation, sharing food with hosts, cooking with women, drinking with men, and flirting with girls.

As soon as news spread that we were staying in the village, the large barn, which was used as a command post, gradually began to fill with visitors. Since this was Sunday afternoon, local peasants, dressed in their Sunday best, stopped to wish us well and gossiped with the soldiers. Men wore white starched shirts and long black boots; married women, somber dresses with white scarves covering their heads; and young girls, colorful skirts, silk blouses, white socks, long, laced-up, high-heeled shoes, and fancy jewelry. The joyful combination of colorful dresses and the glittering of jewelry brightened the spartan furnishings of the barn and enhanced the informality and festive spirit of the gathering.

Some people brought food, some brought drinks, and soon favorite local dishes appeared on the table. Suddenly, we heard the sound of accordions.

"Toast to our defenders," called the villagers.

"Toast to our hosts," responded the partisans. "Let's dance!" called one of the soldiers. In no time at all, to the rhythmic clapping of hands and the happy sound of accordions, several dancing pairs appeared in the barn's open area. The sight of dancing couples was unreal under the circumstances. Only rifles and machine guns piled in the corner reminded us of somber realities.

Zegota called me, "Somebody is here to see you." I turned around, and in the corner of the barn, behind the large table, I noticed a tall blonde girl talking to my comrades. She was dressed differently than most of the village women. Her city clothes, tight black skirt, white silky blouse, and high-heeled shoes made her look even taller. Slender with long blonde hair tied with a red ribbon and enormous blue eyes, she looked like a Greek goddess from my history textbook. It took me awhile to recognize Halina.

"Halina, I am glad to see you." She smiled: "This is a great surprise. I have never seen real partisans." I sounded conceited: "Well, here we are. You can even touch one." I took her hand and put it on my shoulder and walked with her away from the crowd.

"Not so fast," she smiled again. "I hardly know you."

"Yes, I am aware of our unique circumstances. But time is a luxury for people like me. We don't have a chance for long and formal introductions. We live for today since we may be dead tomorrow."

"Are you scared?" She asked more seriously.

"Of course I am, but by now I am used to living and playing with fear. Can we go outside? This place is too noisy and our conversation is too serious."

The spring day was slowly coming to an end. Shadows from tall pine trees appeared to be longer and the warm sun was gradually disappearing behind the houses. In the serenity of the peaceful village, memories of yesterday's battle were remote and almost forgotten.

Halina looked up and then suddenly I kissed her slowly. Not sensing any resistance, I put my hand gently under her silky blouse. It felt wonderful. After days of isolation and hiding in the forest, it was strange and exciting to be so close to a warm and beautiful human being.

"Not so fast." She held my hand back. "Not yet." She added, "Do not rush, please. There are so many things I would like to talk with you about."

"Halina, I never felt like this before . . . so unexpected. I am really confused and you have to help me."

"Janusz, slow down. We just met." She held my hand and said: "I am sure we will meet again."

I felt disappointed and partially betrayed. "In my line of business, we must take advantage of every minute because we can't plan for tomorrow."

She obviously felt offended. "Do you think that, as part of my patriotic duties, I should go to bed with you right now?"

"Halina, I didn't mean it that way. But our life is so dangerous and full of surprises. I believe every moment offers opportunity to start something between us that will go even beyond today. Apparently you don't feel like this."

"I do. I really like you, but you know," she looked at her watch, "I've known you for exactly twenty-seven minutes. How can we be even half serious about the future after this unexpected and very short meeting?"

"Halina, I can't make any promises or plans for future dates. But I do believe that this is the start of something special between us and we will both be winners after all."

This time she kissed me slowly and gently. "Janusz, I have a feeling I will see you a lot in my life. Let's go back inside. I feel like having a cold drink."

I held her hand gently. A feeling of genuine tenderness mixed with feelings of shame and betrayal brought me back to my senses. Suddenly, the thought of Emmy made me unsure of my true intentions.

As the guests and visitors were leaving, I hugged Halina and apologized for my behavior. She smiled, "Do not worry. I did enjoy this visit and I plan to see you again."

After our celebrations in Majdan, we returned across the Warsaw-Lublin highway back to Miłocin. Following the pattern of the past few months, we moved from village to village in the Nałęczów-Lublin-Niedrzwica triangle. Because of the recent departure of local volunteers, the unit was smaller. However, our spirits were high and we were anxious to try our recently acquired military skills in a real confrontation with German Security Police. Zegota, however, was cooling our enthusiasm, "Don't take unnecessary risks and expose the local population to German retributions." And then he added, "Unless you are in danger."

As we rested in Moszna at the end of May, Jeleń's brother Chołaj arrived in the village. Full of excitement, he came straight to see us in the barn. "Germans are on their way to this village to select people for slave labor in Germany!" he said.

"How many?" asked Gołąb.

"Just one car with an agent from the Gestapo and two policemen from SS headquarters in Lublin."

"Where are they now?" asked Rafał.

"They should be here any minute," responded a nervous Chołaj.

There was not enough time to move the whole group during the day to an adjoining village. This could be too risky and too visible. Since there were only three officials, we had a good chance of ambushing them somewhere away from the village.

Zegota made the decision: "Gołąb, Strzemię, Rafał, and Janek see if you can intercept them between Moszna and Sieprawice. Hurry up!" We picked up our rifles and ammunition in a hurry and in no time we were running toward the Warsaw-Lublin highway, bypassing our village as much as possible. I carried my rifle, and my revolver was stuck behind my belt. In the distance we could see dust generated by a fast-moving vehicle across the field.

"Here . . . here they are!" cried Gołąb triumphantly. We ran as fast as we could to reach some cover from a few isolated willows standing on both sides of the winding country road. My heart was beating fast. I hardly had time to reload my rifle and take aim at the oncoming vehicle. The car was almost on top of us when all four of us started shooting.

"Hands up!" We all screamed at the same time.

The sound of rapid fire, the screaming of the passengers and the tinkling noise of the cracked windshield broke the silence and turned a pleasant spring day into a nightmare. The car slowed down, abruptly turned towards the ditch on the left side of the road and came to a stop. The left front tire was damaged and flat. A person in a blue uniform whose face was white as a sheet opened the door and while holding one hand to his left eye, whispered in Polish: "Why . . . Why do you want to kill your own people?" The driver who was still sitting behind the steering wheel was wounded. He held his stomach with both hands.

Rafał looked into the car and asked the driver, "Who are you?" The driver, shivering with fear and pain, responded, "This is the Polish Commandant of the Fire Department in Lublin, Galant and I am his driver. Why did you shoot at us? Why?"

"Why did you drive across the field like the Germans do?" Rafał asked angrily. The Commandant, still holding his left eye responded, "I wanted to save time on our way to Sadurki. We both need a doctor."

"Yes, we know. We will see what we can do for you," said Gołąb nervously.

Rafał, who used to be a mechanic, looked at the car and immediately started to fix the flat tire. We were all terribly upset, but there was no time to analyze the blame or to justify the terrible mistake.

"We are all going to see the doctor," Gołąb suddenly announced. He opened the door of the car and ordered everybody to climb in except for Janek. He turned to a startled Janek and said, "Take our rifles and return to the camp."

In no time, Rafał was sitting behind the steering wheel with me in the front seat and the wounded driver in the middle. Gołąb and the commandant were in the back. "Let's see the doctor in Nałęczów," decided Gołąb. Rafał squeezed the gas pedal with his foot and shifted gears with both hands on the wheel. Soon he was driving as fast as the sharp, winding turns in the small country road would allow.

In the beginning, the doctor would not talk to us. He told Gołąb in an arbitrary tone of voice that it was against the law to assist the wounded. He absolutely refused to look at either of the wounded men. But Gołąb would not accept the doctor's refusal. Instead, he pulled his revolver from its holster and put it right to the doctor's head. The doctor was sweating.

"Please, do not do anything silly," he mumbled, "I will see what I can do." His hands were shaking when he undressed the wounded driver. He looked at the stomach wound and hesitated. "There is nothing I can do for him. If you want to save his life, you must take him immediately to the hospital. He is bleeding a lot."

There was silence in the room. I looked at Gołąb and Rafał and said: "Let's talk outside." Then I turned to the doctor, "Stop his bleeding as much as you can and take care of the commandant's eye."

We went to the adjoining room and let the doctor work on both of the wounded men.

I said, "Look, nobody knows me in Lublin. I am willing to take them to the hospital if Rafał is willing to drive." Rafał did not hesitate and said quickly, "I will go."

Gołąb thought for a short time, "I agree. Two of you must drive to Szarytek Hospital in Lublin. I will stay here and keep an eye on the doctor." Then he added, "Contact Olek Łukasik. He is one of us and he will take care of the wounded. Be careful and good luck."

In a few minutes, we were driving toward the city. The commandant with his bleeding eye sat next to Rafał. I was supporting the wounded driver in the back seat. On the outskirts of the city and in front of the previous army barracks of the Eighth Infantry Regiment, there was an armed German sentry. He was pointing a rifle in our direction. He raised his hand and motioned for the car to stop. Rafał slowed down without a complete stop and the wounded commandant was loudly repeating in German, "German firefighters attacked by Polish bandits. Emergency call! We need medical help. Please let us pass, there is no time to spare . . . Emergency call!" The sentry hesitated, then seeing the bloody faces of the wounded firemen, he opened the barrier and waved us through. As soon as we passed the checkpoint, I looked around and saw him talking on the field telephone in the guardhouse.

"This is not the end," I warned Rafał. Fortunately, Rafał was driving very fast. He knew Lublin well. Without any hesitation, he passed Aleja Racławicka, turned right into Krakowskie, slowed down on Staszyca Street and stopped in front of the emergency entrance to the hospital. A medical orderly and a nurse ran to the car and, without any questions, removed both wounded firemen immediately. The engine was running. There was no need for any explanations.

I felt better that both men were finally getting proper medical attention, but I still worried about the sentry at the checkpoint. "Let's go!" I told Rafał. He turned the car around and both of us at the same time spotted a big German police car turning the corner in our direction. A police sergeant with three gendarmes in steel helmets with machine pistols at the ready was in the car. The tall sergeant was waving at us and screaming in German to stop, "Halt, halt!" He stood in the open field car next to the driver.

"Let's go, Rafał—faster, faster!" I called again and pulled my pistol from under my shirt. The car jerked suddenly and we were driving at high speed through the city streets.

The German police car did not lose any time. They were right behind us, driving with a blasting siren. The sergeant standing next to the driver held on to the top of the windshield with his left hand. With his right hand, he was aiming and shooting at us with his revolver. I turned around on the back seat. The streets were uneven and the ride was bumpy, so it was almost impossible to aim with the pistol. Nevertheless, I opened the side window, took my revolver in both hands and emptied the magazine at the standing policeman. They were getting closer and closer. I could see the sergeant's angry red face under the steel helmet. Now, since they were closer, I was more selective in my shooting. I aimed at the driver and his standing passenger. I could hear whistling bullets on both sides of our car and then I realized that their windshield was cracked and shattered glass obstructed their view.

"Hold tight!" screamed Rafał and suddenly turned left into narrow Lipowa Street. The impact of the unexpected change threw me to the floor. I held to the door, still trying to aim at the Germans. The German police car overshot Lipowa Street and went straight towards Aleje.

We lost them and in a few minutes we were passing the cemetery. We took a different route to reach the city limits. Away from the downtown area, there was hardly any traffic. Rafał slowed down, pretending that we were just one of many officials leaving town for formal inspection. We looked at each other and smiled. We both felt good. Our sense of shame for a tragic misunderstanding was somewhat reduced, knowing that both men would receive proper medical attention. Slowly we left the city behind us and, after a few minutes, we were in the open country driving south.

"What are we going to do with this car?" Rafał asked me. It would be a pity to give it back to the Germans and it would be a waste to destroy a perfectly working automobile. Perhaps, we could save it for future use.

"Let's hide it," I told Rafał. Half way to Konopnica was an isolated barn standing in the middle of a vast field, away from traffic and villages. At one time, it had been used for storage of agricultural equipment but now it was abandoned and long forgotten by the owner and neighbors. The road was empty, and there was nobody in sight. The narrow, unused country road led us straight to the forgotten barn. We parked the car inside, covered it with straw and completely closed the gates. Rafał patted the steering wheel and, with considerable emotion, said: "Good-bye! You served us well." We walked the rest of the way to one of our "safe houses." The farmer and his family were part of Czarnota's organization and we spent the night in their barn. The next day, we got up very early and caught up with the rest of our group.

Gołąb had already told everybody the whole story. We were not proud of the whole adventure and, although I cherished my exchange of shots with the

German police in the middle of a large city, we did not brag about this incident. I found out later on that both firemen recovered completely. That news made us feel better and we were more careful in selecting our future targets.

After our risky delivery of the wounded Polish firemen to the Szarytek Hospital in Lublin, German Security Police increased their activities in the southwestern part of Lublin County. Continuous pacification actions and increased police patrols along the Warsaw-Lublin railroad forced us to move further south.

In June, the unit crossed the Bystrzyca River and looked for temporary quarters in the Niedrzwica, Bychawa and Prawiedniki triangle. We changed our location almost every night and we worried continuously about informers. Local farmers were still friendly and supportive, but one could feel a sense of resignation and fear among the villagers. Czarnota told us to maintain a low profile and not to instigate further fights with German police or Ukrainian Guards who patrolled the area. Most of the time we spent on military training and learning basic army regulations. We tried to avoid any pattern in moving from village to village in order to make it difficult or impossible for the Germans to anticipate our future moves. Cool and fresh spring weather gave way to hot and sunny summer days. We stored most of our heavy clothes and many blankets with the farmers who belonged to the Home Army. This allowed us to travel relatively lightly with only essential camping equipment, weapons, and ammunition.

At the beginning of July, we arrived in the small village of Tuszówek where we planned to spend a few days. The village was located to the west and, not too far from the Biłograj-Lublin highway. Farm buildings were spread out on a gentle hill, which allowed us to have an extended and unobstructed view of the terrain. A small, wooded area adjoined the northern part of the village. To the west of the village was a large open cornfield. Parallel to the western edge of the cornfield was another, smaller road leading to Lublin from Bychawa. On the other side of the road, to the west, was the beginning of a small pine forest, which spread toward the banks of the Bystrzyca River. Farmers in Tuszówek and their families were friendly but not really thrilled with our presence. I understood their feelings and their fears. German police units from Lublin had a well-known reputation of punishing civilians, burning their homes and often whole villages. They would arrest the entire family of anyone who was accused of providing shelter to partisans.

On the first day, we all rested peacefully in a big barn in the center of the village. Sentinels were posted outside. We talked about the possible unifying action of all Home Army units in the Lublin District. Zegota also mentioned the possibility of leave passes to visit families and relatives in the near future. The following day, we started working early on our regular morning chores, since in July, the sun was usually up at six o'clock. When I opened my eyes and looked around, a few soldiers were already getting water from the nearby well. Some were slowly putting their sleeping gear together. In one corner of the barn, hot water was boiling over a small fire. The smell of coffee was pleasant and inviting. While we were busy with our morning chores, the door to the barn opened suddenly and one of the sentinels, Pantera, screamed at the top of his voice, "Germans . . . a whole company is coming from the east side."

I jumped up and pulled all my personal belongings together; trying to tie my belt and holding my rifle I looked through the open door. No further than two hundred meters away, I saw a long line of German Security Police moving slowly toward the village. Behind the line of men, I could see field cars with machine guns mounted on the top.

Zegota stepped outside and in a moment was back, directing everybody to leave the barn through a small door at the north wall. "Let's move to the woods," he shouted. We all started running for cover toward the adjoining woods. Except for some of us calling each other and Zegota's impatient encouragement to run faster, there was complete silence outside and no shooting. All of us left the barn. Half way to the woods, we received sudden, heavy machine gun fire from the wooded area to the north. Apparently, another unit of German police was waiting ahead of us. We all started shooting at the same time, but we were no match for their firepower. Bullets were flying in both directions, and all of us were confused. Germans were coming from behind us and we faced a steady front line of another police unit ahead of us. The only possible way out of the ambush was to turn west and run to our left toward the sanctuary of tall pine trees across the road. Zegota gave a signal and we all turned west amidst confusion and flying bullets.

Together with Zegota and Gołąb, I ran away from the Germans toward the safety of tall pines, growing in small bunches and forming an edge to the pine forest behind the Bychawa-Lublin road. The rest of the group spread to the left of us in a long line, and crossed the cornfield in the same direction. Occasionally we stopped, knelt, and began shooting in the direction of the oncoming Germans who also turned left and followed us across the field. There was hardly any time to aim and shoot properly as we had been trained to do. I could hear hundreds of bullets whistling around me but, at that time, I was not aware of anybody being hit.

The road still appeared to be a long way away. The pursuing line of gendarmes was moving closer and closer.

"They are closing in on us," I shouted to Zegota. He shook his head, turned around and started shooting with rapid bursts of fire from his machine pistol. Staggering with exhaustion, Zegota, Gołąb, and I reached the ditch on the east side of the road. Using the steep banks as a cover, we all started shooting at the same time in a more organized and disciplined way. Tom, who carried a light machine gun on his back, was breathing heavily, completely exhausted and drenched in his own sweat. However, as soon as he reached the ditch, he turned around and opened fire from his machine gun. This stopped the Germans. They were now lying in the middle of the corn-field exchanging individual shots with us, but unwilling to move forward.

Out of the corner of my eye, I could see other staggering partisans join-ing us in the ditch. Very soon we had almost the whole unit, protected by a low stone wall, shooting continuously at the police. I saw some of the parti-sans throwing hand grenades to discourage the gendarmes from further pur-suit. The noise of the explosions was terrifying.

Zegota called to Tom, "Stay here with Gołąb and Rafał and cover us." Then he added, "We will wait for you in the forest." Tom nodded and waved to show that he understood the message.

Slowly, one by one, we started crawling across the road. After running a few hundred yards into the forest, we all dropped on the ground, panting with fatigue, trying to catch our breath and to recover from our shock and confusion.

"Who is missing?" Zegota asked. We all started to look around. Six peo-ple were missing. We rested in silence and waited for Tom, Gołąb and Rafał.

Tom appeared first, tired but happy, followed by Gołąb and Rafał. Three people were still missing.

"Germans are not coming across the road for sure," Tom declared. "I think I hit two gendarmes."

"They will never enter the forest," Gołąb and Rafał confirmed.

After resting for a few more minutes, I reloaded my rifle and counted my ammunition, I still had plenty of bullets.

"Let's move!" Zegota gave the order.

We formed our small marching procession: two partisans far ahead of the unit and two soldiers closing our rear about a hundred meters behind the main group.

We all silently wondered what had actually happened. Were we be-trayed? Was there an informer or was it just pure coincidence? The ambush was too well organized to be coincidental. The German police were well pre-pared and they knew the terrain. It looked more and more like betrayal. Now we worried about our missing comrades. Where were they? Nobody knew. We marched in silence with heavy hearts.

We walked through the forest for about two hours, and finally we came across a few isolated dwellings. Zegota ordered us to stop. He went inside the first farmhouse and talked to the owner. The farmer and his family were frightened. In spite of the distance, they seemed to be fully aware of the fight. We calmed the farmer down and decided to stay in the barn for the rest of the day. With two sentries posted outside, we all lay motionless in the barn trying to recover before our evening departure. I piled all my equipment by my side. My heart was still racing, my shirt was wet and soiled from crawling across the road, and my spirit was shaken.

"That was a close call. A few more minutes in Tuszówek and there would have been an end to Zegota's partisans." Tom was trying to add some humor, but nobody was laughing.

The farmer's wife brought us hot tea and fresh brown bread. Two younger sons brought containers with soup. Zegota paid for the food, which we ate in silence. By evening, we were ready to continue our march. Before our departure, Zegota disappeared for few hours to meet a messenger from the regional headquarters. He was back before midnight.

"We are joining Spartanin's group tonight," he announced. "I also found the rest of our unit and they are coming with us tonight. We lost Olek. He was killed by the police at the Tuszówek cornfield." There was silence in the barn. This was our first casualty. Zegota told us that the Germans shot Olek as he ran from the village toward the road. They found him shot several times in the middle of the field. Police took his rifle and ammunition. The local villagers buried him in a simple pine coffin. His grave, with a wooden cross, was very close to the Bychawa-Lublin road. His old French helmet that he carried with him was put on the top of the cross. There was no sign on the grave since nobody knew his real name. We all reflected in silence about our lost comrade and the fate of a partisan's life and death.

With excitement, anger, and sorrow in our hearts, we tried to act again as professional soldiers and maintain a positive and stoical attitude about the unpredictable events of underground warfare.

"Get clean and check your uniforms and equipment. We want to look like real soldiers, not a bunch of civilians!" Zegota announced before departure.

Tom and Rafał walked point, a hundred meters ahead of the main unit. Pantera and I were guarding the rear. After two hours of marching, we reached the village of Prawiedniki.

"Halt, who goes there?" called a voice in Polish in front of us.

Tom responded "Zegota" and the voice concluded: "Proceed and welcome to Spartanie platoon."

In spite of the bright moon, I could not see very much in the small cleared area among the tall pine trees. Gradually, I was able to identify several horsemen, three horse-driven wagons, and a group of armed men standing in a formation. One of the riders came in front of the group. He stopped his horse and said, "I am Lieutenant Spartanin, commanding officer of the fourth platoon of the Eighth Infantry Regiment, called Spartanie. We welcome you to our group. I heard about your fight with the Germans in Tuszówek. Any losses?"

Zegota came closer and saluted. "Officer Cadet Zegota with a special mobile platoon reporting. We lost one soldier."

"Thank you." Lieutenant Spartanin turned to the rest of us and said, "We are happy to have you here. We must leave this area right now, but I'd like to talk with you as soon as we arrive in our new quarters." Then he signaled his troops. "Proceed . . . let's go." The wagons started to roll.

As we marched toward our new quarters, I had a chance to get a closer look at our new fellow partisans. All of them were dressed in old Polish uniforms and they looked smart and crisp. They also were well armed. Each partisan, in addition to his rifle, carried two hand grenades behind his belt. On one of the wagons, I noticed three barrels of heavy machine guns. Later on, I learned that before 1939, the machine guns belonged to the Polish Air Force. During the war, they were mounted on a light bomber that crash-landed in the Lublin District. After the crash, the guns were dismantled by the crew and given to the Polish Home Army.

Lieutenant Spartanin, in the full field uniform of a Polish army second lieutenant, rode an elegant, light brown horse. He had a fully equipped saddle, as in a prewar Polish cavalry regiment. His VIS pistol and light brown leather holster were new and shining.

I was impressed with the appearance, weapons, and spirit of the new platoon. It looked as if this unit faithfully carried out military traditions of the Polish army from before 1939. There were at least four riders and forty foot soldiers. Three horse-driven wagons carried a lot of equipment and supplies. Two riders rode in front of the column headed by Lieutenant Spartanin, followed by the wagons and the rest of the foot soldiers. Our group walked together behind the last wagon. As soon as we arrived in the village, all wagons were hidden in different barns and we all were divided in several groups and directed to different houses. Zegota, Tom, Gołąb, and I all stayed together in a small farmhouse in the middle of the village.

Lieutenant Spartanin came to see us. "Again, I welcome you to our platoon and look forward to working with you to build the best partisan unit in the Lublin District. I would like you to embrace the spirit of our small organization and be proud that from now on you are part of the Spartanie."

After serving my first few days with the Spartanie, I found that this was a friendly group of dedicated young men, mostly local boys from the Bychawa area, well organized along principles of military discipline. The second in command was Lieutenant Janota, previously a reserve army officer. He was also friendly but kept his own company most of the time.

Corporal Konny was the leader of the small horse—reconnaissance patrol. After our arrival, he asked for volunteers to join his unit, which at that time consisted of three riders. Rafał and I volunteered the same night, and on the following day we picked up two horses held for us on a nearby estate. My horse, Zawisza, was a veteran from the Twenty-fourth Polish Lancers Regiment, which, before the war, was stationed in Kraśnik, not too far from Bychawa. The estate owner kept the horses that were abandoned in 1939 by the defeated Polish army. After three years, he returned both animals with full equipment and saddles to the "Spartanie" platoon.

Being part of the cavalry unit meant more work and less free time. In addition to other duties, I had to worry about maintaining, feeding, and cleaning my horse. We helped each other all the time, and our small cavalry unit developed a well-deserved reputation as an "elite" within the Spartanie organization.

Slowly I was getting to know other soldiers, and I was impressed by their willingness to help each other under any circumstances. The trust among fellow freedom fighters was an essential element for survival in an underground organization. During our long marches, the mission of the horse squad was to provide protection to our horse-driven wagons, to scout new territory, and to act as the eyes and ears for the group. Occasionally, Lieutenant Spartanin ordered us to assume other duties, such as delivering urgent messages to other units, patrolling unsecured areas, or helping requisition food and supplies essential for the operations and survival of our group.

I was quite happy with my assignment since I enjoyed my duties in the horse reconnaissance squad. Every night, I looked forward to riding point in front of the unit, even if this was a dangerous venture. In case of ambush, both horse and rider were primary targets of the enemy. While I was getting along quite well with my new colleagues from Spartanie group, I noticed that Zegota was not too happy. He had no official function in the new organization. All of us from the old Jeleń's group looked up to him for direction and guidance. At the same time "old Spartanie" soldiers treated him without special recognition, just as one of them. I could easily understand that Zegota, who was used to taking charge in Jeleń's organization, was not too pleased with the current command structure. He felt underutilized and unappreciated.

One evening, when we stayed in the same village a second night, Zegota came to talk to me. We went out for a short walk outside the barn. In the distance, I could see guards posted on the outskirts of the village. Inside, soldiers cleaned their weapons and talked with the host and his wife who brought us hot soup. More enterprising partisans flirted with local girls in the shadows of farmyard buildings. In great secrecy, Zegota told me that he seriously was considering returning to the Motycz area. He wanted to know if I would come with him. I was surprised, since I was aware of some rumors and dissatisfaction among our old fighters from Jeleń's group regarding Lieutenant Spartanin's leadership, but after all, we were a military organization. One can hardly expect to vote on the popularity of the commanding officer. At the same time, I had already spent several months with Zegota and other friends from Jeleń's unit and I felt a strong sense of loyalty to the group. It did not take me very long to make up my mind.

"Polek," I told Zegota, "if you leave the Spartanie, I am coming with you."

Zegota was happy: "That's great. You will not have any regrets," he said and then he added: "We may be doing something very interesting. Czarnota has been asked by the Regional Home Army Headquarters to organize a special 'air drop' unit. He is considering using our old Jeleń's group for this purpose. Allied airplanes from Bari in Italy will fly and drop containers with weapons at secret drop sites in the Lublin District. Our mission will be to protect the supplies and dispose of all containers."

This was interesting and exciting. I asked Zegota, "How about Lieutenant Spartanin?"

He explained, "Czarnota will talk to him shortly. He is also considering granting some of you a few days of leave to visit your relatives or your families before we are fully reorganized."

This was good news. After a few months of sleeping in barns most of the time fully clothed, eating on the go, shaving with cold water, and surviving in the most primitive hygienic environment, I was ready for a short break. I looked forward to regular meals, hot baths, and decent and regular changes of underwear. A partisan's life may have appeared glamorous but the reality was quite the opposite. It was a hard, tough, and dangerous way of living.

I wanted to see Emmy, but I knew that I could not go to Potoczek. I had not seen my grandmother for several years, and since she was completely unaware of my underground activities, this was a good opportunity for a short visit. After the war ended in September 1939 and Marcel was held as a prisoner of war, she decided to stay in Kielce with her daughter in-law, Halina, and help her to take care of her two teenage boys.

I asked Zegota, "Can I get my old papers from Czarnota and perhaps additional false documents to allow me to visit my relatives?"

"I do not see why not," said Zegota. "But let me talk with Czarnota first. In order to avoid bad feeling with Lieutenant Spartanin and his boys, I must very carefully review this transfer with regional headquarters."

The following week Zegota disappeared for two days. I knew that he went to see Czarnota who was still commanding officer of the First Region in the Lublin District of the Home Army. Zegota joined us on the third day in our temporary quarters in Babin. After a long meeting with Lieutenant Spartanin, he came to see me, "Strzemię, you have a five-day pass to visit your family. All your papers will be ready next Friday. I have talked to Czarnota and Spartanin and you have all the necessary approvals."

I was excited. Coming back to the real world, after several months of underground experience, was quite a thrill and a pleasant surprise. On Thursday, I reported to Lieutenant Spartanin and said good-bye to my old comrades from Jeleń's unit and my new friends from Spartanin's organization. Zegota and Gołąb were my closest friends. I said an emotional good-bye to both of them and asked Zegota to keep my VIS revolver until my return. We had a few drinks for the sake of old times and adventures. On Friday, I went to see Czarnota. He gave me back my original papers, *Kennkarte,* under the name of Janusz Strojnowski and a counterfeit exemption from the service in *Baudienst,* a compulsory labor service for selected Polish males born between 1921 and 1925. Since the Strojnowski name was still related to the Wiernicki family, I was to use these documents only when I was visiting my genuine relatives. For traveling on the train he gave me a set of false documents with a different name and different birth certificate exempting me from *Baudienst.* I was to use the above documents in transit only. The purpose of two sets of documents was to make it difficult for German police to trace my family roots and my connection with the Polish Home Army. I also received 650 *złotych* as part of my earned pay while serving with the partisans. I changed back to my civilian clothes in Motycz, and after saying good-bye to Lieutenant Czarnota and his wife, I boarded the train for a journey to Kielce.

At the beginning of my journey, I experienced strange feelings. Unarmed, I felt as if I was naked and vulnerable. In a regular passenger train with endless crowds of passengers, mostly "black marketeers," I sat in the corner of the compartment and observed with curiosity the world that I had left a few months ago. Trains were overcrowded. Separated from the Germans, who used special carriages, a cross section of the population could be seen using this popular method of public transportation, the only one available. The majority of the passengers were women of different ages, carrying a multitude of suitcases and parcels. Food was scarce in the cities, and part of the population earned a living by buying food cheap from the peasants and selling the same items on the "black market" in the city at inflated prices. Officially, this was an illegal activity, and many people were arrested or imprisoned during frequent inspections of city-bound trains.

This time the travel from Lublin through Radom to Kielce was uneventful. The train, puffing and whistling, slowly entered the main terminal at the

Kielce railroad station. Of course, there were new German signs everywhere. A large crowd of German soldiers traveling from the East front to visit their families in the Fatherland was waiting for the next train west. Well-armed German Security Police, Military Police, and Railroad Police patrols guarded all sensitive areas, such as the communication tower, the train master's office, and the traffic control center. All civilian passengers were checked at numerous points for the proper documents. After a wave of "black marketeers" left the train in a large group, I walked silently along the platform and stopped at the exit to have my documents checked. The German Security Police inspected my *Kennkarte* and let me pass. From the station, I walked along Sienkiewicza Street toward Bazar Square. Then, I turned right on Zagórska Street and started looking for Marcel's villa. A few years before the war, Marcel and his wife had built a lovely house for their young family. It was on the outskirts of the city, on the opposite side of town from the railroad station. The walk was long, but the weather was very pleasant and many of my old memories were coming back. Every step was a reminder of my previous visits. As I crossed the Main Street in the heart of the city, I looked curiously for changes.

The cobblestone city streets and concrete sidewalks looked the same. Most of the existing buildings were seriously dilapidated. Lack of proper maintenance could be seen everywhere. The local population, all civilians, was shabbily dressed. Most of the pedestrians, carrying large parcels and brown bags, were continuously on the lookout for black-market opportunities. Food was scarce and expensive. A large number of uniformed Germans paraded in the middle of the sidewalks, looking down on the local inhabitants with the ego of a master race who was racially superior.

Jews were already restricted to the ghetto, and occasionally one could see special labor details crossing the street under German police supervision. Ukrainian armed sentries were guarding the working details. Jewish properties, shops, and businesses were confiscated by the SS and given to Germans and Gestapo informers. The synagogues were closed and cemeteries abandoned. Once a vibrant part of a small provincial capital, the Jewish community was ruthlessly starved and exterminated. A small number of survivors were left in the isolated ghetto area to do "essential work" in Wehrmacht factories. They were waiting for their turn to be taken to the unknown destination.

Many shops were closed. Commercial transactions among the local population were performed on side streets, on Bazar Square, or in the dark passages between apartment houses. In spite of the sunny summer day, the city and its inhabitants looked run-down and depressed, a very different city than the one I had known.

I rang the bell at Marcel's villa. My younger cousin, Jurek, opened the door. "Yes, sir, what do you need?" he asked me, and then turned around and called, "Grandma, somebody is at the door."

My grandmother had changed a lot. Her hair was white and her face was tired and full of wrinkles. She looked at me for a second and then cried, "Janusz, my grandson!" We both had tears in our eyes. My aunt Halina, Marcel's wife, and her two sons came to the entrance hall, "Janusz! Janusz is here!"

Everybody was screaming. It took awhile to calm my relatives and explain my unexpected arrival. Then, in tears, they brought me up to date on what was happening to the rest of the family. Ryszard had married last year and he lived in a house across the street. Marcel was in an officers' prisoner-of-war camp in Murnau, Germany. Karol, my father, was in the Polish army in England and occasionally sent his mother a brief postcard through the Swiss Red Cross. Everybody was under the impression that I had come from Potoczek, and I did not say anything to the contrary.

In the afternoon, I went to see Ryszard and met his new wife, Nina. Both of them welcomed me warmly into their home. The decision was made that I should stay with them and visit my grandmother daily to spend some time with my two younger cousins, Jurek and Janek.

Apart from my close relatives, there was nobody I knew in the city. I felt depressed and isolated. I also realized that the painful impact of the German occupation was more noticeable in the city than in rural areas. In the city, German police, security agents, German army, and civilian bureaucrats were more visible and more arrogant every day. The restaurants with signs "only for Germans" were crowded with eating and drinking German soldiers. The possibility of sudden street closings and arrests hung in the air and made the local population nervous. After four days, I was ready to return to my unit. Life with the partisans looked more promising than city existence accompanied by constant fear.

I said good-bye to everybody on Tuesday morning, packed my personal belongings in my small suitcase, and left the house for the long walk to the railroad station. The terminal was unusually overcrowded with Germans and Poles. People were waiting for trains to Kraków and Radom that were late. My train to Lublin was delayed one hour. I sat patiently in a corner of the public waiting room and read my book.

Suddenly, there was a commotion at the entrance. German Security Police appeared at every door in the waiting room. Two uniformed members of the Gestapo, and one civilian in a leather jacket and green hat were making rounds in the waiting room and checking passengers' documents. My heart started to beat a little faster. I did not move, pretending that I was totally absorbed in my book. "Your documents please," said an SS Oberscharführer in front of me. I stood up and gave him the documents that I used when visiting my relatives, under the name of Janusz Strojnowski. He looked at my registration card and exemption document from *Baudienst*. Then he asked me to join a small group of four people, already standing in the corner. They were all young men about my age. After they went around the waiting room checking papers, two more young people joined the group. The civilian waved all of us to enter one of the rooms adjoining the public waiting space. We waited there under the Security Police guard while the civilian and two SS men interviewed us individually in the next room, behind closed door. I was concerned because nobody was coming back. As soon as I entered the adjoining room, I was told to open my suitcase and undress to my underwear. The civilian spoke Polish. They carefully looked through my personal belongings, my jacket and trousers.

"Are you Jewish?" One of the SS men asked me in a highly suspicious voice.

"No, sir," I replied nervously.

The SS man ordered me to lower my underwear to see if I was circumcised. After brief inspection, he barked. "Put your clothes on fast, you idiot."

I was ready to get dressed when SS Oberscharführer asked me to give him my boots for inspection. He looked carefully and slowly and then he spotted a narrow opening on the top of my left boot inside the lining. With a pair of scissors he slowly pulled out my hidden set of other documents. His face turned red and he shouted in German, "What is this, you Polish bandit? How come that you have two *Kennkarten*?" Not waiting for my response, he hit me in the face with an open palm. I lost my balance. The SS Unterscharführer standing nearby kicked me with his heavy boots as I was lying on the floor.

"You damned Polish bandit" he cursed at the top of his voice.

I tried to stand up. But then both of them started kicking me again. As I was trying to protect my swollen face and eyes, I wondered silently: "Are they going to kill me here—at the railroad station?" I had a vision of Czarnota, Zegota, and Gołąb in front of me. I knew that under no circumstances could I talk. Would I be able to take the punishment and not betray any secrets? After a few minutes, they stopped kicking me. My lips were cut and blood was seeping on the floor.

"Get dressed . . . Fast!" growled the SS Oberscharführer. The Security Policeman put handcuffs on my wrists and dragged me out through a different exit to a large covered military truck.

CHAPTER FOUR

Devil's Empire

SIX OF US were sitting close to one another on the floor of the enclosed military truck. Two armed SS guards stood by the exit tailgate holding machine pistols in their hands. After a short ride from the station, including some slow driving along a steep and winding street, the truck suddenly stopped. The SS guards jumped out first and opened the tailgate. "All out," they shouted. As I climbed down from the truck, I took a quick look around the area. I recognized the place immediately. We were at Zamkowa Street in front of what used to be the City Municipal Prison. Built before the First World War, the complex of offices, interrogation rooms, and cells served between the two wars as a city prison for criminals and serious offenders. The jail was now under the direct administration of SD, Sicherheitsdienst Polizei, the security police that was part of the Gestapo.

"Fast, fast!" urged the SS guards. We all walked through the guarded gate and then turned left, passed another gate with a sentry and entered a large office. There were several uniformed Gestapo men, with the insignia *SD* on their left sleeves, sitting behind desks. A long counter separated a small waiting space from the office. "Wait here," we were ordered by the guards. Soon it was my turn to see one of the clerks. I entered the office accompanied by the SS guard.

As I stood in front of the large desk, I looked with curiosity and fear at the seated SS man's face. I recognized that he was only an admission official, but I did not know what to expect. He shuffled some papers around on his desk and picked up one file. Then he looked up from his typewriter. "What is your true name?" he asked in German. I knew that from this moment I must stick with the same story and be consistent during interrogations. We went through all the names and dates as listed in my original *Kennkarte*. He typed all of this without making a comment.

The SS guard, who stood behind me, checked all my pockets, removed all my personal belongings and piled them on the desk. "Cell 10," said the admission clerk, and then he added, looking at me, "Leave your belt before you go." The SS guard removed my belt and pushed me with contempt through the door. We walked through a long corridor, down a stairway, passed an iron gate and stopped in front of cell no. 10.

The unarmed Polish jailer opened the door and the SS guard shoved me brutally inside. The cell was a dark room, without any furniture and with one small barred window high above the floor, just under the ceiling. The room was crowded with at least ten people. They all looked at me with curiosity, but nobody said a word. Most of the men sat along the wall. They seemed tired, defeated, and scared. There were three men lying side by side on the concrete floor. Their faces were white and swollen. One of them, whose eyes were closed, mumbled a few words occasionally and held both hands close to his chest.

I found an empty space near the wall and feverishly pondered my situation. I knew they would call me soon for interrogations. I must have a good, realistic story to put as much distance as possible between myself and the underground. I must isolate myself from my underground activities and service with the partisans. The names of Czarnota, Zegota, and Gołąb must be forgotten forever. The future and the survival of the Lublin District Home Army Organization rested on my shoulders. It was a heavy responsibility.

I wondered if the Gestapo regarded me as a fugitive from *Baudienst* or as a potential underground conspirator. The possibility of connecting my arrest with the Lublin Home Army activities made me shiver. This was not only because of my certain death sentence but also because of the tragic involvement of other brave people and the possible end of the organization. With a firm resolution not to involve anybody else, under any circumstances, I was getting ready to face my oppressors.

Then I heard footsteps and noises in the corridor. I could smell the aroma of cooked food. The tinkling of kitchen utensils drew closer and closer. Doors opened. An inmate with a kettle of soup in front of him gave everybody in the cell a small bowl of soup, each prisoner using his own spoon. I had none, so I looked for a way to eat or drink my portion.

A young man in his late twenties approached me. "When I finish, you can use my spoon."

"Thanks," I responded.

After lunch, he sat beside me and we talked a little. Each one of us was very careful about sharing personal observations. We did not know each other, and we were scared of informers. "Don't trust anybody." It was an old underground motto engraved in my mind by Czarnota when I was with the partisans in Motycz. It was very real and appropriate in Kielce prison.

Then the door opened again and a name was called. A young fellow, well dressed in city clothes, stood up, crossed himself several times and, with clenched fists, left the cell. The men sitting close to him looked sad. Nobody felt like talking. Nearly two hours passed before the door opened again. Two Polish jailers, with an SS man behind them, carried the fellow who had left a few hours ago. His face was bruised, swollen, and covered with blood. His fingers on his right hand were smashed and twisted. They protruded from his palm in many different directions, like a set of broken pencils. His eyes were half closed.

The jailers dropped him by the wall without a word and closed the door. Some of the men gathered around him. The minute he opened his eyes, they whispered "How do you feel?"

"They smashed my fingers in the door jamb. It hurts a lot. I need water, please."

We looked all around. There was not even a drop of water in the cell. The man was only half-conscious, holding his injured palm with his good hand. I felt terrified. Would I be able to hold to my resolution? I had no answer.

The evening meal was served, the same soup with a small piece of bread. My new friend again shared his spoon with me. "I am Jurek from Busko near Kielce. I have been here since June and my best friend Antoni is in the cell across the corridor. Don't worry, you may be lucky. Maybe they will let you go home." "Thanks," I whispered, but I knew that this would never happen.

After dinner, the lights were dimmed as a signal for getting ready for the night. Everybody picked out a space on the concrete floor and, without blankets, using our own jackets as pillows, we settled down for the night. I could not sleep. When I did close my eyes, images of my relatives, friends, and fellow partisans swirled in my head. I tried desperately to forget all those people and let them disappear into obscurity. But they kept coming back in spite of my wishes. Sometimes I had the strange feeling that they were all sitting around me in cell no. 10. The cell was very quiet, except for the occasional groans from the interrogation victim and the snores of some others. I was very much aware that some of my cellmates lay on their backs with open eyes, unable to fall asleep, uncertain of their future, if any.

When I opened my eyes in the morning, I could see the first rays of sun coming through the small window. Some of the inmates were still asleep. Others sat quietly, waiting for breakfast. Our door was opened. We were allowed to wash for a few minutes and, under armed guard, return to the cell. Breakfast was served, a black liquid—so-called coffee—and a piece of bread. I was hungry and ate my portion immediately. After breakfast, I waited nervously to be called for interrogation. Suddenly, screams were heard coming from the floor above. The sound of a male voice, pleading and begging in Polish and German, mingled with the hysterical crying of other victims and the shouting of guards. The sounds traveled fast and clear along the old stone walls and connecting concrete corridors and stairways.

We all sat, still and silent, listening.

Jurek turned to me and said: "It's started." "What?" I asked. He looked at me with the experience and superiority of an old prisoner: "Beatings. They are interrogating and torturing prisoners from the upper floors." Then the screaming stopped abruptly. We all listened for any further signs of activity upstairs. There were none. Jurek whispered, "They probably killed him . . . the bastards!"

Late that afternoon, my name was called. Jurek wished me good luck and shook my hand. As I was leaving the cell, a tall SS Unterscharführer prodded me with a rubber truncheon to move faster on my way upstairs. I was scared but calm. He took me to the floor above and instead of turning right toward the exit told me to turn left. This was a dead-end corridor without doors or windows, about thirty feet long. In the middle, facing the stairway was a huge desk with three men seated behind it and one empty chair in front. Various shapes and sizes of filing cabinets stood along the wall. A bright light was hanging above the desk.

My guard clicked his heels and as he stretched his right arm out in a Nazi salute, he reported to the civilian seated in the middle behind the desk: "Heil Hitler, Herr Inspector." An SS Oberscharführer in uniform sat on either side of the inspector. The man on the left side was big and heavy, with large hands casually holding a long rubber truncheon. The other man was skinny. He looked at me with contempt and, with a sarcastic smile, played with a similar rubber truncheon, which rested on his knees. His eyes were ice-cold and cruel. The inspector gestured with his hand to indicate that I should take a seat in front of the desk. Then he said slowly in reasonably good Polish with a heavy Silesian accent:

"If you cooperate with us, then you have nothing to worry about. Tell me why do you have false papers? If you do not answer my questions honestly and truthfully, then I can not guarantee anything. Do you understand?"

"Yes, Herr Inspector," I responded.

Since my future and perhaps my life depended on this man's decisions, I studied him with curiosity and fear. He was perhaps in his mid-forties, blond, with watery blue eyes. He was dressed in a greenish civilian suit, brown party shirt, and black tie. On his left lapel was a swastika pin. His appearance projected an image of bureaucratic indifference and German efficiency: cold, inhumane, and orderly. I already had concluded that I must be consistent in my responses and under no circumstances must I mention my Lublin connections. It was essential that I also stick to the same story, regardless of the number and nature of my interrogations.

I looked at the inspector and responded in the most natural voice I could master, "I obtained false papers to exempt me from the service with *Baudienst*. The registration was sold to me on the street in Warsaw. The seller would not give me his name or address."

The inspector looked at me and smiled sarcastically: "Do not play games with us. I want the name of the person who sold or gave you the documents. You have one minute to think about this."

I pleaded with him, "I honestly did not know this man. This was purely a business transaction."

The inspector sounded annoyed and irritated: "I am not going to waste my time on you. You give me no choice but to ask my colleagues if they can persuade you to be more cooperative. Their language is much more effective than mine."

"Herr Inspector, please, let me explain." I sounded intentionally apologetic and scared.

He looked at both SS men and nodded his head. They both jumped from behind the desk. The big man yelled to me in German: "Kneel down and put your head under the chair." He leaned on me and forced me down. The skinny SS man pulled my arms around the chair's rear legs and put handcuffs on my wrists. This was not a very dignified position with my head under the chair and my back and buttocks up in the air.

Then both of them hit me with rubber truncheons on my back and buttocks. I screamed. The pain was sudden, excruciating and terrifying. The guard who brought me for interrogation joined in beating me with his own leather whip. All three screamed at me, "You dirty Polish swine." I struggled under the chair. By now I was getting hysterical, the pain increasing with every blow. "Please, please, stop!" I pleaded in Polish and in German. The skin on my back and buttocks was giving in and I felt blood seeping into my underwear. Sharp pain generated in my back and traveled across my body. One of the SS men pounced on me and held my head further down under the chair. I closed my eyes. Every new blow produced penetrating flashes in my head. The big man shouted louder with each blow. I could sense that he was getting personal satisfaction from my punishment. As I knelt with my head under the chair and my buttocks up in the air, I began to feel dizzy and as if I was slowly losing touch with reality.

Out of the corner of my eye, I watched the inspector calmly writing his report. Occasionally, unemotionally, he would look at my oppressors and me. His eyes were full of contempt and indifference to pain. My back and my buttocks were a bloody pulp, cut into strips of flesh like ribbons. Blood was now seeping through my underwear and pants onto the concrete floor. I choked and could not breathe any more. When I closed my eyes again, I thought about my childhood, my friends in Lwów, my relatives in Potoczek, and my comrades in Lublin. My mind searched desperately for an answer, "Is this the unexpected end of my short career in the Polish underground? Why, why?" I tried to look up for an answer from heaven, but the only thing I could see was an ugly Gestapo face above me, red with rage and contempt and fury. The world crumbled around me and I collapsed unconscious.

When I opened my eyes, the first thing I saw was the high window just below the ceiling in the cell and a patch of blue sky. I lay on my back on the concrete floor and everything that my body touched felt like fire. My back and buttocks were puffy, bruised and cut into long, narrow open wounds. My shirt, underwear, and my pants were almost red with dried blood spots. Fresh blood was oozing slowly from my wounds.

"What happened!" I whispered. Jurek, who sat next to me, responded quietly: "They brought you back last night. You were bleeding a lot and you were unconscious."

I felt hot and exhausted. "Water," I whispered.

Two of the inmates tried to help me turn on my stomach. This was a far better position. The burning sensation was less obvious. "Water, please," I whispered again.

One of the inmates responded: "I'll see what I can do." He banged on the door, calling for the Polish jailer. The door opened and the jailer stuck his head in: "What do you want?"

"Look, this fellow is almost dying. Bring us some water. You are a Pole, after all."

The jailer took a careful look down both sides of the corridor. In a few minutes he was back with a small canister of water which he put next to me. Then he said: "You know that I am risking my job and my life." Then he quickly left the cell.

I drank most of the water. Then I took off my bloody shirt, dipped it in water, and tried to clean my back. One of my cellmates helped me and held my hand steady. This was not an unusual situation for the inmates. At least half of them had already gone through a similar experience. The rest of them looked at me silently in anticipation of the same treatment. The water helped a lot, making the fire in my body more bearable. I managed a weak smile at Jurek, "Looks like I have survived the first Gestapo treatment."

The inspector let me remain in the cell undisturbed for the next few days. My wounds and cuts were slowly healing. My body, especially my back, was still very sore and painful. I did get a new shirt from the jailer. Most of the time I lay on my stomach except when I had to get up for my meals or take short walks to the bathroom. While all parts of my body hurt badly and I could hardly walk, my face was not affected, not even scratched. I wondered if this was Gestapo policy.

One week after my interrogation, my name was called again. The same tall SS man was at the cell door. "Did you learn your lesson?" He barked at me. Slowly, I climbed the stairway. I was really concerned that I could not survive another beating. If they beat me again in the same places, the fresh wounds would open and I would bleed to death. During the past few days, I had figured out a slightly different approach. Now I wondered if it would work. The inspector sat behind his desk with two SS men on either side. He looked at me with a sarcastic smile. "Sit down," he ordered.

"Thank you, sir, but I would rather stand." I tried to be as polite as possible.

His face reddened and he screamed, "You fool, when I tell you to sit, you sit." The SS Unterscharführer who had walked with me from my cell brutally pushed me down. My back and buttocks were again on fire. As I sat on the chair, I clenched my teeth and trembled inside.

The inspector looked at me again, "No more games this time. This is your only chance to tell us what you know."

I knew he was dead serious, which is why I had planned a slightly different approach. I hesitated at first and then I responded, "Herr Inspector, the first time I was so scared that I did not remember everything. Today my head is clear and I remember who gave me the false papers. His name is Stanisław Kowalski. He lives near Zaklików in the Janów District. I paid him two thousand złotych to obtain an exemption from *Baudienst*."

The inspector looked at me closely: "I hope for your sake, that you are not lying. If this is not the real truth, you are going to be very sorry. I do not have time to chase rainbows. You better be right this time." After he made a few notes, he had a short and private discussion with both SS men who sat beside him. "Out . . . take him away," he told the SS Unterscharführer and waved his hand. I could not believe my ears. The guard yanked me from the chair and pushed me down the stairway.

I thought about my "confession." The name and address of Stanisław Kowalski, whose estate was adjoining Zaklików, were true and real. At one time, he was suspected of cooperating with the Germans, though it was never proven. Just before my departure from Potoczek, he had been executed by the partisans. I hoped I would be able to talk my way out of this. If they did come back with accusations that I had given them a false lead, I would have to stick with my story and claim I never knew about his death.

I was concerned with the simplicity of my plot. However, this was the only possible explanation that did not tie me to the Lublin connections. I also hoped that, with so many people being arrested by the Gestapo all the time, the inspector would not have time to verify the details and specifics of my story. I returned to the cell with a heavy heart. Nobody asked me anything and I did not volunteer any explanations.

My wounds still bothered me. My short stay on the chair during the second interrogation made things worse. Most of the time, I lay on my stomach in a corner of the cell, trying to recover as fast as possible. Out of the original inmates in the cell when I first arrived, two were removed the following night and never came back. There was a rumor in the jail that they were interrogated by the inspector, judged by the Special Police Court, and shot immediately in the courtyard. The rumor was also going around that the Gestapo would soon arrest large numbers of Polish citizens. Subsequently, the present inmate population would soon be removed, transferred from Kielce prison, to provide room for the new victims. Nobody had any idea what the Gestapo planned to do with us.

It had been almost three weeks since my arrest. I was wondering if my relatives in Kielce were affected by my imprisonment and if the local police had questioned Ryszard, the only male in the family. I hoped that since my last name was different from everybody else's in Kielce, it would provide a buffer and some protection for my innocent relatives.

I was losing track of time. To help us keep count of days during imprisonment, every morning one of my cellmates marked the day on the wall and announced the date to all the others. I still remember when he said: "Today is September 13, 1943. I hope it is our lucky day." I did not know at that time the significance of that date. After breakfast and our trip to the washroom under guard, we heard a lot of traffic on the upper floors. Footsteps, closing doors, and occasional shouts by the guards were heard all morning. Then, the SS Unterscharführer who escorted me to my interrogations stood in the door. He slowly read the names of the prisoners. I listened carefully. My name was last on the list of six.

"Everybody out," he shouted.

All six of us were told to wait in line along the corridor, facing the wall. Transport or execution, we wondered.

I felt a tight chill around my throat. My heart was wildly pounding and I was sweating as I stared at the blank wall in front of me, expecting the worst. There was a fair amount of activity in the other cells. People were pushed out into the corridor and told to wait, like us, facing the wall. Pretty soon, the whole length of the corridor was full of standing men. I looked at both sides and, seeing so many people, felt a sense of relief: "They can't shoot all of us." I tried to calm Jurek, who stood next to me.

Then I saw armed SS guards forming a line in the middle of the corridor. "Turn around," yelled the guard commander. "Put your hands in front of you."

I turned around, stretched out my hands and the nearest guard tied my wrists with a piece of wire.

"Left turn, march," called the commander.

We all walked slowly in a single line, downstairs to the courtyard, this time with guards on each side. There were approximately two hundred people in the courtyard. We formed columns of five. I saw at least forty women included in the marching formation. The SS Obersturmführer gave the signal. The column of prisoners with armed guards on both sides passed through the prison gates, turned left on Zamkowa street and then left on Sienkiewicza Street. I knew then that we were marching to the railroad station. On this early September morning, we marched in the middle of the street. The pedestrians looked at us with sympathy and compassion.

I was wondering silently: "Is this my last look at Kielce?" As we marched onto the railroad platform, a special area detached from the regular passenger terminal was assigned to us. A company of SS guards with pistols at the ready watched us carefully and isolated us from the general public. The train was late. We stood in the middle of the platform, surrounded by SS guards, wondering about our future. Muted conversation and speculation were ongoing among the prisoners. Everybody had a different idea about our destination.

"Silence!" called the impatient guards. After an hour of waiting, a train consisting of two locomotives, several passenger cars, and a long line of box cars, used to transport cattle, pulled slowly into the station. I could see that some of the cattle cars were already full of people. SS men responsible for guarding the prisoners occupied the passenger cars. As the train stopped, railroad officials opened the cattle cars. The prisoners' column was divided into three groups. All the women went together to a separate carriage while all the men climbed into two designated cars. SS men standing by the entrance cut the wire and freed my hands. Each of us received a small portion of brown bread. There were approximately eighty men standing close to each other when the railroad car doors were finally closed. Two small windows in each cattle car were covered with barbed wire. A pail stood in a corner for personal use.

The train was detained for at least one hour. Then we heard voices of railroad officials. Somebody shouted "Attention!" A few short blasts of the train whistle and we were on our way. By watching railroad signs and the names of stations as we passed by, we were able to determine that we were traveling south on the Warsaw-Kraków-Vienna main railroad line. Almost all the prisoners ate their meager portions of bread immediately and now were thirsty. None of us knew how long we would have to travel before we reached our unknown destination. There was not enough room in the car that we could sit on the floor, so we were squashed close together, speculating out loud about our future.

In the early afternoon, as the train was passing stretches of isolated and uninhabited areas, there was a heated discussion about the possibility of a mass escape. The prisoners' views differed, and arguments on both sides were very emotional, but equally convincing. One group argued that the only possible avenue of escape was through the windows, but they were very high from the floor, difficult to reach, and secured by barbed wire. An armed guard with a machine gun was posted in a small tower constructed above the roof of each car, making an escape nearly impossible. The risk of jumping from the fast moving train was great. Possible repercussions against persons left behind must also be taken into account. After a long discussion and many arguments, supporters of the escape plan gave in. A majority decided to stay with the transport and see what would happen.

A few hours into the journey, punctuated by the occasional whistle of the train and by the staccato clicking of the wheels, we were all sleepy. Discussions and speculations became more sporadic until, totally exhausted, we stopped talking completely. Deep into our very personal thoughts, we wondered about the future and remembered the past. I recalled my childhood, my happy years in Lwów, and in Potoczek. Images from my carefree prewar life were now returning so persistently that I had a hard time comprehending how my life could be changed so drastically in such a short time.

Three weeks ago, I was a soldier in the Polish Home Army fighting for my country's freedom. My beloved pistol, VIS, was my pride and a priceless possession. My horse, Zawisza, was my faithful companion. The danger and excitement of active and armed resistance in a country suffering under German occupation had offered challenges to the undefeated spirit. I was a free and proud soldier. Today I was traveling with a lot of strangers in a guarded cattle car toward an unknown destiny. I had lost my freedom, my pistol, and my horse. Tortured by the Gestapo, with my body still aching, at eighteen years old, I felt tired, lonely, and abandoned. As I looked carefully at all the faces so close to me, my feeling of loneliness intensified. I thought about the people I had left behind: Emmy, Czarnota, Zegota, Gołąb, and others, my relatives and friends, and I could not control the tears in my eyes. They came from nowhere and were slowly drying on my cheeks. I wiped my eyes discreetly.

One has to be tough. I whispered, "tough, tough, tough," to myself. "Tough, tough, tough" responded the monotonous clattering of the train wheels. Suddenly the wheels changed their tune. The rhythmic sound lost its urgency and the train slowed down. The limited view through the barbed-wire windows showed mostly a dark blue September sky. After switching through several railroad lines, puffing its way among railroad junctions, and whistling occasionally, the train reduced its speed even more and moved slowly toward an endless string of glowing lights.

CHAPTER FIVE

Auschwitz-Birkenau

THE LONG LINE of railroad freight cars was moving slowly through switches, the monotonous sound of wheels interrupted by the jerking of cars signaling changes of tracks. The slow puffing of the locomotive indicated that the train was entering the central railroad junction. Suddenly there was a whistle. The train stopped. The stop was unexpected and most of the men standing tight against one another lost their balance. Only the extreme density of the crowd squeezed shoulder to shoulder in the railroad freight car prevented everybody from falling down. People close to the door were screaming. The car was in total darkness. The train started moving very slowly and then stopped again. Crying and moaning in the car was reduced to a whisper or a quiet sob in expectation of the unknown. In silence we listened to the outside voices and the sound of unlocking doors. "Everybody out!" Doors were suddenly opened wide.

My first impression was of the dark sky above with many sparkling stars. Below one could see a yellow glare from endless lines of perimeter lights. Our destination looked like a network of rectangular streets in a large city with brightly lit avenues enclosing dark shadows of wooden barracks. On the horizon, a bright yellow flame was flickering from a huge chimney on the top of a large structure. The contrast with the blackout in the railroad cars was both surprising and frightening. The SS guards on both sides of the door started shouting: "Out, you dreadful bandits." The guards were joined by a group of people dressed in striped white and blue suits that looked like pajamas. With sticks in their hands, they were screaming at the top of their voices. Some were wearing yellow bands on their left arms with black letters saying "Capo." They looked unreal and terrifying.

The first wave of men close to the door jumped from the railroad car. "Form lines of five," shouted one of the Capos. An SS guard with a big Alsatian dog entered the railroad car and started kicking the prisoners unmercifully. Panic swept through the car. Some people were slow; some were trampled by others who were terrified of the dog. In the midst of the pushing,

screaming, and beating, a column of five was formed on the railroad platform. In front of our car two bodies lay on the ground. The workers in the
blue and white uniforms threw them out of the railroad car. An SS guard was
shouting and counting people. The dead bodies, lying in a pile in front of the
railroad car, were also included in the count.

"All accounted! Forward march!" He barked an order to the Capo, who
replied: "*Jawohl,* Herr Rottenführer . . ." The column of prisoners started
to move slowly.

Suddenly, the SS guard leading the column screamed: "Run! Run, you
dirty dogs!" Half conscious, tired after the long journey in cattle cars, the
prisoners, completely confused and disoriented, slowly started to run.
Guards on both sides of the column encouraged their dogs to scare the people.

"One, two, three," screamed the SS guard at the rear.

"One, two, three," echoed the Capos running on both sides.

After the initial shock and brief confusion, the column of prisoners was
moving fast. People were already exhausted by the long journey with little
food and no water. Some elderly men could hardly keep their balance. I saw
three people fall to the ground, one in front of me and two on my right side.
"Move!" screamed the guard and a huge dog jumped on top of the prisoner.
The man on the ground covered his face and sobbed hysterically. "Stop!"
called the guard in front of the column. Unaware of the new command, people at the back of the column were bumping into each other. The screaming
of the guards, shouting of the Capos and barking of the dogs generated
sounds of fear and terror. We passed through the entrance into a building
with a tower in the middle, turned left, passed another gate and stopped in
front of a one story long brick building. It was one of a few structures located
within a barbed wire enclosure and separated from the rest of the camp-
ground, which was also enclosed by barbed wire strung on concrete posts.

As we entered the first building, I looked around the area. We were all
crowded into a large room with a concrete floor. A long line of small, square
windows could barely be seen below the ceiling. We were led into this room
through the vestibule doors of the main entrance. A number of exit doors on
the opposite wall were tightly closed. The room was lit with a series of single
lamps hanging high above the floor. Except for a long line of tables set up
against the wall, there was no furniture. The whole scene suggested a large,
impersonal waiting room. Waiting for what?

After the all-day journey in crowded boxcars, people were completely
dazed, confused, and very thirsty. I tried to stay very close to the men with
whom I shared my prison cell, but in the confusion of many conflicting orders issued by the Capos, I lost my place in the crowd and found myself surrounded by complete strangers. Looking around the room, I realized that the

women prisoners from the train transport were not with us anymore. Some of the men were desperately clinging to their comrades, begging for support and assistance. Others whispered, "Help, water." "Where are we?" Nobody knew for sure. I looked at the windows high above the floor, hoping to find an answer or at least an indication of our location.

"Be quiet and do not move," said one of the Capos. After a few hours of waiting in silence the early morning light appeared on the coated window panes and dark shadows were slowly disappearing. A small door opened. "Form a single line," called one of the Capos. An SS man standing by with a long, large stick in his hand was forcing all prisoners to form a long line. As we formed the line each of us was given a paper bag. In a corner, there were people dressed in blue-striped pajamas sitting at tables or standing behind them. At the opposite end of the room, there was another group of inmates. They were all waiting for us. "Undress and put all your personal belongings in the paper bags. Return the bags to the table, report your names and move ahead fast, fast, fast!" These were the instructions called out to us by Capos dressed in well-fitted blue-striped uniforms. The order was given continuously and repeated in German and Polish.

A Capo with a yellow band on his left arm stood on a table and, with a large wooden stick, controlled the traffic. "Faster, faster!" he screamed occasionally. His associates were circulating freely in the crowd, encouraging men to undress without hesitation.

After we undressed and left our personal belongings in paper bags, naked, we were forced to enter an adjoining brick building where we were pushed to form several columns in front of a group of barbers. They were also dressed in prisoner's garb and had an assortment of brushes and clippers. Above them, a sign painted on the wall *Eine Laus dein Tod* proclaimed "One lice is your death." In no time, my head was shaved. I also lost all my body hair. Another prisoner applied disinfecting fluid to all my shaven areas. I had hardly any time to look around and see myself among a hundred naked, shaved, and confused men. It seemed somehow that suddenly, stripped of our personal belongings and human dignity, we all looked alike and acted like a flock of frightened sheep.

We were all shivering when they forced us to move to another room. This was a bathhouse, as indicated by projected showers. As soon as the room was filled with people, a freezing stream of water made us scream at the top of our lungs. Then, within a minute, there was a boiling stream of water running down our necks. We screamed again, louder and louder. "Silence," the Capo said waving his stick. Then the water was freezing again. In spite of the warning signs not to drink this water, some men tried to lick the cold drops. I could not swallow even one drop. The water was terrible, smelly and yellowish. Then the water stopped. The Capo screamed again "Everybody out!"

We entered another room. A bundle of clothes was thrown at me. I picked up underwear, a jacket and a pair of pants. I also grabbed a pair of shoes with wooden soles. A Capo stood on top of the table and screamed: "Get dressed. Fast, fast!" My jacket fit well but the pants were too short. I looked around and found a short, middle-aged fat man holding an extra-long pair of "pajama" pants. "Can we exchange?" I asked him. "Sure!" He was anxious to complete our trade.

The shoes were terribly uncomfortable. I could hardly walk. Shivering, half-wet, and dressed in an almost comical combination of civilian dress and prisoner's garb, we all stood confused and bewildered in the middle of the large room. Again, as in the undressing room, there was a line of tables with prisoners sitting at them. Our names were called in alphabetical order and we had to form a single line as directed by one of the Capos. The clerk behind the table asked me the usual questions: name, place of birth, address of closest relative, as he filled out a registration form. I hesitated over the "address of closest relative." I was arrested by the Gestapo and they knew my grandmother's address. I felt that I should be consistent and use the same information. Considering my grandmother's age and the fact that she was an elderly widow, I hoped that the Gestapo would leave her alone, regardless of my circumstances. I desperately wanted to exclude even a small possibility of connecting me with Potoczek and my underground activities.

After that process, I received a small piece of paper with a number. At the next table, I was asked to lift my left arm. In no time, with a very sharp needle, one of the inmates skillfully tattooed my new number. It hurt at the beginning and my skin was slightly swollen and reddish. I could, however, read clearly as I looked with apprehension at my bleeding arm . . ."150302." A prisoner of KL Auschwitz was born. From that moment on, it was my new name, my new identity, and my new official identification number, which would stay with me for the rest of my life. I felt that something personal was taken away from me and replaced by an obscure six-digit number. "Move on, *Schutzhäftling* 150302." A powerful kick from the Capo brought me back to reality. Later I learned in the camp that the *Schutzhäftling* term meant "Protective Custody" and was given by the Gestapo to all prisoners incarcerated for an undefined period of time.

As the people behind me were registered by the Schreibers and tattooed by the artists, a small commotion was heard at the entrance to the hall. An SS Hauptscharführer, slim with reddish hair, accompanied by several SS men, walked slowly toward the middle of the room. One of the SS men shouted: "Silence! Anybody speak German?" Several people raised their hands. The

SS Hauptscharführer called for the closest volunteer. "Where did you learn German?" The man stood at attention: "Corporal Hanz Plicha, 314 Infantry Regiment, Kaiser's Army, First World War, Herr Hauptscharführer." The SS Hauptscharführer seemed pleased: "Very well, translate my words." In a high pitched voice, with a leather whip in his hand, he started talking in German. Except for a whisper of people still being registered, there was complete silence in the room. The translator repeated each word in Polish. "This is a Concentration Camp in Auschwitz and you are here because of your unwillingness to support the German nation in our deadly struggle with communists and the decadent West. This is not a recreational area. You are here to work, work hard, and demonstrate your allegiance to Germany. If you do not obey orders and comply with regulations, you will be punished. If you commit acts of sabotage, you will be shot. For unwilling and stubborn creatures, there is only one way out from this place." Then he pointed his whip to heaven and said: "The fastest way to leave this camp is through one of the chimneys. Meanwhile, you must work since work makes you free men." He turned to the Capo and said: "Continue with the disinfection process."

I closed my eyes. Now I knew. This place, as suspected by some of the people on the train, was Oświęcim, or Auschwitz, as it was called by the Germans. Of course I knew about it. I had learned about Nazi concentration camps when Michał was arrested and sent to Dachau. I also remembered from my short stay with Czarnota and his wife in Motycz that the Home Army had a reliable and specific knowledge of what was going on in the concentration camps. I recalled that underground leaders were familiar with the history of this camp and plans for liberation of Auschwitz were made a long time ago by the local partisans.

Auschwitz had the worst reputation of all Nazi concentration camps. This camp was initially established on Himmler's order by SS Sturmbannführer Höss for Polish nationals, and later on for Russian prisoners of war. It became operational in summer 1940 and the first Polish transport arrived in June. In September 1941 the SS performed the first experimental gassing of Russian prisoners of war and sick inmates. Later that same year, in accordance with Himmler's new directives, Auschwitz became an extermination camp for European Jews. In the winter of 1942, the existing crematorium in the old camp in Auschwitz was used for the gassing of selected Jewish transports. After the so-called Wannsee Conference, in order to maintain full secrecy, from early spring of 1942, the gassing of Jews took place in one, and later on, in two houses in a wooded area in Birkenau. After the deportation of local farmers, the houses were modified to serve as temporary gas chambers. Corpses were burned on pyres under an open sky and ashes were dumped in adjoining ponds. The systematic gassing of Jews using both houses, referred to by the SS as "bunkers," began in the summer of 1942. In the spring of 1943, four crematoria in Birkenau were hastily completed, tested, and put in operation to expedite the extermination process of hundreds of Jewish transports from all the areas conquered and occupied by the Nazi. Because of the rapidly growing camp population, the existing buildings were expanded, and new facilities and additional camps were continuously added. Yet, the whole complex retained the old name of Auschwitz Concentration Camp. Actually, the camp consisted of three independent and separate compounds: Auschwitz, which was the original old camp organized by Höss and renovated from the Polish army prewar artillery barracks; Birkenau, the extermination camp, constructed in 1942, which included four crematoria with a complex of several camps for men and women; and a chain of several small camps that provided slave labor to the German war industry, such as Buna, Jawiszów, and Monowice, all located in the general vicinity of Auschwitz. All individual camp leaders, who were SS lieutenants or captains, were known as SS Lagerführers, and reported to the SS Kommandant of Auschwitz. Each SS Lagerführer was assisted in the supervision of the camp by SS Rapportführer, usually a roll-call SS sergeant, who supervised several SS Blockführers, mostly SS corporals in charge of individual blocks. SS Kommandoführers, who were SS men of various ranks, supervised and led all work details inside and outside of camps areas.

I was devastated. How would I survive in this factory of death? There was a silence among the prisoners. People were desperately trying to cope with the news. I looked for Jurek for encouragement and reassurance, but could not find him in the crowd. On the opposite side of the room, a group of tailors was busy sewing new numbers on the newcomers' jackets. A newly assigned number, as tattooed on the left arm, was stitched on each prisoner's jacket. My tailor, a man in his late forties, had a four-digit number on his jacket with a letter "P" on the red triangle. "How long have you been here? And what place is this?" I asked him. Without stopping his work, he responded, after carefully looking right and left: "You are lucky that we were told to help you out. Usually you have to sew it on your jacket yourself and pay dearly for it with your daily ration of bread. This is Birkenau. I have been here for almost two years."

"Who is this fellow?" With my eyes I indicated the Capo on the table.

"That is Capo of the bathhouse. He is Jewish. He yells a lot but he is not a murderer."

"How about the sergeant?" I asked again.

"I never saw him before but I believe he is SS Hauptscharführer Palitzsch and this is an unusual visit. He is the worst. This SS bastard can shoot you in cold blood." Seeing surprise in my eyes, he continued: "He was SS Rapportführer in the old camp in Auschwitz and an executioner on Block 11. Now I understand that after a transfer to Birkenau he works in the Gypsy compound. There is also a very strange rumor that as a result of recent SS investigation of the Political Department, he is leaving Auschwitz shortly to take charge of one of the camps in Czechoslovakia. Watch yourself and good luck to you."

After he attached my red triangle with the letter "P" and my new number, he concluded, "It looks good. Now you are a real inmate and a millionaire." Then he added: "Watch out for Franek and Mietek at the Quarantine Camp. They are real killers." I did not understand his comments. Why "millionaire?" Who are Franek and Mietek? Only later, I learned from my comrades that my red triangle indicated that I was designated by the Gestapo as a political detainee in protective custody. At the time of the assumption of power in Germany, Nazis established a rigid classification system for all concentration camps inmates. A red triangle designated political prisoners, a green triangle was assigned to criminals, a violet triangle was given to Jehovah Witnesses, a black triangle marked prostitutes, a pink triangle was used for homosexuals, and brown for Gypsies. The capital letter within the triangle designated inmates' nationality. Jews were forced to wear the Star of David with their numbers.

My number was very high and because of this I was referred to as a "millionaire" in the camp jargon. Numbers were assigned in a consecutive order to all newcomers, unlike the methods in all the other concentration camps, and never reused, even in case of death or deportation. Subsequently, in Auschwitz the respect of the camp's population toward the "low" numbers was based on their length of imprisonment and ability to survive early persecutions.

New "high" numbers or "millionaires" had to go through the same selection process. Like low numbers, they had to demonstrate their ability to survive adverse conditions in order to gradually and slowly climb up from the bottom of the social ladder to a safe administrative position or assignment to a good *Kommando*. If they could not make this progression within the first six months, then unsuccessful "millionaires" would become destitute Mussulmans—tired, decaying, living skeletons heading toward the certainty of selection for the crematorium. Mussulmans were on the very bottom of the camp social structure. With broken spirits and at the very end of their physical limits, with glossy eyes and weak undernourished bodies, resented by their healthy comrades, the forgotten prisoners were forced to join the worst possible work details with the most inhumane Capos. Their survival rate was very low.

The acceptance and registration process had been completed and we waited in front of the bathhouse for further orders. Complexities of ranks and responsibilities of functional prisoners confused me. After talking briefly to a few low-number prisoners working in the bathhouse, I began to understand the internal camp structure imposed by the SS.

The head of each camp was Lagerältester or Camp Senior Prisoner selected by the SS Lagerführer. The Lagerältester, in turn, with SS approval appointed Blockältesters or Block Senior Prisoners. Each block had a deputy called Schreiber or clerk/writer responsible for prisoners' personal records. Housekeeping functions and food distributions were performed by Stubendiensts or room orderlies.

Similar structure among prisoners applied to work details. The Obercapo, usually a low-number prisoner, was in charge of large groups of working inmates. Capos supervised individual *Kommandos*. The Undercapo was in charge of small group of workers within each *Kommando*.

"Form the column," called the Capo. Five men abreast, a long column was formed in the open field in front of the admission barrack. "Fast! Fast!" screamed the Capo, running between uneven lines of prisoners and kicking and pushing the half-dazed inmates. We all stood in our new uniforms with our new numbers displayed on our jackets and in our wooden shoes. The Capo was counting us endlessly and the Schreiber was making notes. "Everything checks out," he reported to the SS Unterscharführer. The transition was completed. The September sun was slowly rising over the horizon.

About three hundred inmates from SD Polizei Radom/Kielce transport stood silently in front of the bathhouse. Shaved, wearing ill-fitted uniforms, we hardly fit the description of the Third Reich's mortal enemies. The Capo ordered: "Turn right—Forward march—left, right—left, left, and left!" The column moved, passed the barbed wire gate and turned right. At that point armed SS guards with machine pistols surrounded us. Some of them were holding big Alsatian wolves on short leashes.

This was my first opportunity to see Auschwitz in the daytime. As we moved quickly toward a long brick building with a tower and semicircle arch in the middle, I noted several canals and deep ditches being excavated by a group of prisoners. Beyond the working group, I could see endless lines of wooden barracks in neat straight rows, divided by miles of L-shaped concrete pylons strung with barbed wire. Wooden watchtowers were located every two hundred meters outside the wire fence. As far as one could see, wooden barracks stretched for miles in all directions. The wide, straight streets built between the wooden structures projected an illusion of order and rigidity, and the miles of stretched barbed wire made me feel that I was trapped in an enormous cage. On the horizon, behind the lines of barracks, I could see four massive structures with tall brick chimneys. A gentle wind moved some of the light clouds in our direction. The sweet smell of burnt meat was in the air.

This was a beautiful dry and sunny September day. I remembered, as I walked with my comrades toward an unknown destiny, that it was the fourth anniversary of the beginning of World War II. The happy times in Potoczek, my underground connection, and life with the partisans flashed through my mind. These memories were so vivid and yet so distant that I began to feel sorry for myself. But not for long. My feet were killing me and I could hardly walk and keep pace with the column. The wooden shoes were too small and hard. Every step was a torture, and I could not slow down because the huge dog walking with a guard on my right side kept barking at me. As we passed the archway, the column turned left. On one side, behind barbed wire and along a large ditch, I could see wooden barracks with people standing in large groups behind each building. After walking for a few minutes, we turned left again and the column stopped in front of a closed gate. An SS man appeared from the SS Blockführerstube, a single-story military barrack located by the entrance gate to each camp. Two prisoners in smart and well-fitted uniforms accompanied him. One of the prisoners with a black armband and white letters, Lagerältester, talked briefly to our Capo.

The gate was opened. An SS man, with his stick in hand, counted us as we passed him in our formation. We marched five abreast. "All accounted for," called the Lagerältester. The gate of the Quarantine Camp closed behind us. As we passed the entrance gate, a single line of wooden barracks was on our right. A fence of electrified wires separated the Quarantine Camp from the adjoining campgrounds. On the other side, a long line of electrified barbed wire fence strung on concrete pylons enclosed the whole camp and separated an open area on the left of the barracks from the main access highway. Wooden watchtowers accessible to the SS guards from the main road overlooked the campgrounds. We stopped almost in front of every barrack as the Capo called out newly assigned numbers. I could hardly remember mine when it was called. With a group of about twenty inmates, I was told to wait in front of one of the wooden barrack.

A young man in a striped but custom-tailored uniform with a red armband saying Blockältester took us into an open area between two barracks. "I am Mietek, your new Block Senior. All of you have been assigned to spend quarantine on my block so you can learn about the camp's regulations and to prepare you for the productive life in the Men's Camp. As long as you do what I tell you, you have nothing to worry about." He waved his hand and continued: "Remember, this is not a resort and you are not on vacation."

Then he turned abruptly to one of the functionaries standing by, "Take over!" A group of prisoners watched us from the sidelines with curiosity. It appeared that most of them knew each other very well and that they had some kind of administrative positions on Mietek's block. They all were reasonably well dressed and I noticed that all of them had normal shoes or boots. Later on I found out that all of them were Mietek's Stubendiensts or room-orderlies responsible for housekeeping functions in the block.

My feet were swollen and I looked with envy at their leather footwear. On the basis of my discussions in the bathhouse with the tailor, I now understood that they were low numbers, the first prisoners in Auschwitz who survived the trying times at the beginning of the camp. It was well known that during the camp's construction in Birkenau in 1941, hundreds of people were murdered every day. I was gradually beginning to understand the new prisoners' traditional respect for low numbers.

The Schreiber, or the writer, second in command at each block, asked the newcomers to gather around him. I looked for my friends from prison, in Kielce, but I could not find anybody. My friends had disappeared mysteriously and apparently had been assigned to different blocks. The frightened faces of strangers surrounded me. I felt forgotten and humiliated. Within the last few days, I had lost my name and my identity. I also lost my clothes, my dignity, and my willingness to take risks, which had served me so well in my partisan's life. I looked with despair at my fellow prisoners dressed in ill-fitting, striped uniforms and I could imagine that I, too, looked dreadful.

The Schreiber sounded friendly: "I will give you a few minutes to go to the latrine and then I want everybody back on the open area between the blocks. You will learn the camp's customs and regulations."

"What customs?" somebody asked.

"You will see," the Schreiber responded. "Don't drink any water from the bathroom regardless of how thirsty you are," he added.

In half an hour all newcomers were lined up on the open area. The Schreiber talked slowly in Polish: "The Quarantine Camp, or BIIa was opened in August 1943. You are the fifth transport. Today you will learn how to greet SS Blockführers. There are two most important commands which you must learn by heart in German: '*Heftlinge—Mutzen ab and Mutzen auf.*' It means 'Prisoners—hats off and hats on.' Always remember to take off your hat before you address SS guards. Like this." And he demonstrated the movement. "Now, all together—hats off!" We all tried to do the same thing. It sounded so easy. In an energetic movement, one had to pull the hat off and clasp it firmly against the right side of your pants. But it did not work very well. Some people did not understand the German command and some were late and clumsy. The Schreiber was annoyed but patient. "You better try harder. The SS Blockführer will not have much patience with you. Let's try once again"—and so we tried again and again. After half an hour, my arm hurt a lot, but group performance finally became better and the Schreiber dismissed us. The group broke ranks. We all looked for friends or even casual acquaintances to share our emotions. In particular I looked for red triangles with the letter "P," but I could not find anybody. We were surrounded by previous transports representing many nationalities. A young man in a striped uniform approached me, "Do you speak Polish?" he asked.

"Of course," I responded.

"I am Moniek from Zawiercie. I've been here for the past three weeks. Where are you from?"

"I am Janusz from the Radom transport and this is my first day in Birkenau," I answered and looked at his number. On his striped jacket, he had attached the Star of David consisting of the overlapped yellow and red triangles, and a six digit number." How are you surviving this madness?" I asked him quietly.

"I don't know yet. Three weeks is not enough time to reach any conclusion. I was here in the Quarantine Camp with one of the first transports. But we both have bad luck because we ended up in Mietek's block. He is a killer."

I did not understand and Moniek explained to me: "Tonight look for a space on a top bunk. Since there are only three of us at my place, if you like, you can stay with us." Then he added:

"Don't ever sleep in a lower bunk in Mietek's block. Almost every night he gets drunk and after all lights are out, he pulls people from the lower bunks and kills them in cold blood."

Seeing my expression of disbelief, Moniek continued:

"Mietek, his buddy Franek, and SS Rapportführer Kurpanik usually drink every night in Mietek's room. After lights are out, they drag innocent people from the bunks for their own amusement. After abusing their terrified victims for hours, they usually kill them in front of everybody. The whole block is watching when Mietek takes a shovel, places it on the victim's throat and jumps with his two feet on one side at a time. It takes a minute to kill the man."

"How can he do it?" I was stunned. "Did you actually see this?"

"Yes, with my own eyes, two nights ago. He can do anything he wants as long as Kurpanik covers for him. This is a living hell and we are part of it," he continued quietly.

Moniek was a few years older than I. He told me that before the war his family lived in Zawiercie. He was ready to graduate from a Polish high school and enter the university to study medicine. I gathered that, although the family retained their Jewish identity and were very religious, they tried to blend with the Polish society and be good citizens of the new country. His Polish was excellent and his knowledge of Polish history was impressive.

Soon after the defeat of Poland, the SS moved Moniek and his whole family to a ghetto, where they all worked in the German clothing factory. Life in the ghetto was hard and Moniek's father died of a heart attack. During the liquidation of the ghetto, Moniek, his mother, and his sister were transported to Auschwitz with a large group of workers from the factory. At the selection process on the railroad ramp he lost touch with his mother and sister. Some of his coworkers went to a different camp. Only a few ended up on quarantine and, since his arrival, he was assigned to Mietek's block. He was resigned but calm as he was telling me his story.

"I wish I could find out where my mother and sister are."

I tried to reassure him: "Moniek, we will leave this Quarantine Camp soon and then you can look for your family on the women's side."

He looked at me with his sad eyes, "Janusz, you don't understand. I am a Jew and for my people there is only one way from this inferno." He turned around and showed me the flaming chimneys on the horizon. Then he added, "My father was a pious Jew, but I have some doubts. How can I believe in the God of Abraham after seeing this?"

"Don't get discouraged," I pleaded. "They can't burn all the Jews."

He looked at me again: "Yes, they can. Who is going to stop them?" His voice was cracking. Then he abruptly changed the subject and said, "Before we make any plans for the future, let's worry about today and see if we can find a good spot before roll call starts."

At the end of the day, roll call was held at the same time in all camps in Birkenau. As the *Kommandos* reporting from work details gathered slowly on the *Appellplatz* located between the wooden barracks at each camp, Blockältesters at the Quarantine Camp lined up their prisoners for the same purpose. We stood almost an hour between two barracks in a rectangular formation, ten people deep. Five hundred bewildered and frightened human beings waited patiently for the SS Blockführer to arrive and complete the roll call.

Mietek was in front of the formation standing half way on the main street and waiting for the SS man's arrival. Suddenly, he turned toward us and barked in German: "*Heftlinge—Mutzen ab.*" An SS man on a bicycle stopped in front of the block. Mietek completed his report and the soldier walked briskly in front of the formation, counting the rows of prisoners. On the left side of the unit, dead bodies were lying on the ground. They were part of the roll call. Another command: "Heftlinge—Mutzen auf." In a reasonably coordinated movement, we covered our heads. Moniek, standing beside me, whispered: "This is SS Rottenführer Baretzki. He is a mean beast." I shook my head. We stood for another hour. "Dismiss!" cried the Blockältester. We broke ranks. A sense of relief could be felt among the inmates. . . . Supper time!

Since our arrival in Birkenau yesterday, I had not had anything to eat. I was hungry and thirsty, but the dramatic events around me and the strange environment made me forget even the most essential needs. Now they were coming back. We all lined up in front of the blocks. As we entered the compound through the large wooden gate, each person was given a small piece of brown bread, a small square of margarine and a thin slice of sausage. A sip of ersatz "coffee" known as *Avo* was also provided in one bowl for two prisoners. With a small piece of bread in one hand and a bowl of *Avo* in the other hand, Moniek and I found empty spaces on the heating duct, that ran in the middle of the blocks' floor. Moniek warned me: "Leave some bread for tomorrow morning. Make sure that it is well protected. There are a lot of thieves in the blocks."

I carefully looked around my new "home." The middle of the block looked like a large stable, forty meters long and ten meters wide with large doors at each end. Near the front entrance on either side of the corridor, two small enclosed rooms provided quarters for the Blockältester on one side and storage for food supplies on the other side. A small enclosure near the rear entrance served as temporary and portable sanitary facilities for the prisoners' use during night hours only. The inmates were not allowed to leave the blocks after lights-out. In the middle of the open area there was a horizontal heating duct running from the front to the rear of the block, which was connected to two brick chimneys at each end. There were two open passages on both sides of the duct adjoining rows of three-level bunks, providing sleeping quarters. Paper mattresses filled with straw and occasionally an old blanket were provided at each level. There were no windows except for the small, glazed openings along both sides of the central portion of the elevated roof.

Moniek explained to me that our blocks were originally designed by the manufacturer as prefabricated stables for horses. To expedite construction process, the SS administration decided to use this type of block for rapid expansion of the Men's Camp in Birkenau. The stables intended to accommodate fifty horses each now provided housing for about five hundred prisoners in each block.

After we all finished our meal, Moniek asked me to follow him to his bunk, which was in the middle of the block. There were already two prisoners lying on the straw mattresses. An elderly man, about fifty years old, greeted us in a friendly voice, "Moniek, who is your friend?"

"Major, this is Janusz from yesterday's transport. I hope you don't mind. I asked him to stay with us."

The older man's voice sounded irritated and annoyed. "Moniek, for the last time, don't call me Major." He turned to me, "Janusz, it's nice to have you here if that is possible to say in this place. Where are you from?"

"Lwów, but I was arrested in Kielce," I responded.

The other prisoner, a man about twenty, turned around and shook my hand, "I am Tomasz. Welcome to our private hotel." He tried to smile.

Major spoke to all of us, "I suggest that we should get ready for the night before they turn down the lights."

I ended up on the edge of the bunk with a good view across the barracks, which was now full of people eating, talking, arguing, and desperately trying to preserve human decency and normality in this abnormal environment.

The "free time" in the evening was running out fast. After a few sounds of gongs from outside on the main street, the camp was slowly getting ready for the night. A last dash to the latrine. I hid my bread under my jacket that served as my pillow. I took off my wooden shoes. My feet were swollen. This was a bad sign and I knew that I would have to do something to find a new pair of shoes.

The lights were dimmed. I lay with my eyes open on the edge of my bunk and watched the misery and suffering of my fellow prisoners down below. Then I picked up the sound of singing coming from Mietek's room. The sentimental words of "Rosamunde" were floating through the corridors of the block. The sound grew stronger and stronger and, by now, the whole population in the block was fully aware of the festivities in Mietek's quarters. There were several men's voices singing German words.

The bright lights in the block went on. Completely drunk and unsteady on his feet, Mietek, dressed in a white shirt and striped pants was slowly walking on the surface of the heating duct. He yelled at the top of his voice: "I need a good singer to help us in our recital. Any volunteers?" There was complete silence on the bunks. People on the lower level covered their heads with blankets and pretended that they were fast asleep. Mietek was getting impatient: "If I don't find a volunteer, I am going to teach you a lesson that all of you will remember for the rest of your lives."

The whole block was silent. He jumped down from the duct and ran along the passage. Then he stopped in front of a lower bunk. In a dramatic gesture, he pulled the blanket from the prisoner. The man was still pretending that he was fast asleep. Mietek was getting mad: "I'll show you who runs this block." He hit the man hard with his fist. "Get up, you miserable creature." The frightened prisoner was struggling to his feet. "Can you sing?"

"No, sir, I can't," mumbled the frightened inmate.

"Then I will teach you. Sing, you bastard!"

"I honestly don't know how."

Mietek was furious. "Wait here. I will refresh your skills." He turned around, ran to his room and came back with a shovel in his hands.

"This is your last chance. . . . Sing!"

The man knelt in front of Mietek and begged: "Sir, please let me go."

Mietek hit him full force with the shovel. As the man lay on the concrete floor, Mietek placed the handle of the shovel on his throat and jumped with both feet on the opposite end of the handle.

"Music!" he screamed toward his room. Standing on top of the inmate and, as if he were playing on the see-saw, he swung the handle of the shovel with his feet up and down in rhythm with the "Rosamunde" melody. He was slowly choking and suffocating his victim. In a few minutes, the victim was dead.

Mietek looked around: "This man needs company. He is lonely. Any volunteers?"

All of the inmates covered their heads with blankets, pretending to be fast asleep. Except for the music coming from Mietek's room, there was silence.

"Since there are no volunteers, then I will make my own selection. . . . How about you? Where are you from?"

An old man in his sixties mumbled: "Warsaw."

"I love that city," Mietek screamed. "Sing for me Tango Milonga."

The prisoner gasped for air and started singing this well-known, prewar Polish popular ballad. His voice sounded terrible. Fear of death was in his eyes. Mietek listened for a minute and then in a drunken voice whispered: "Your singing is pretty bad. You don't deserve to live."

He hit the singer with the blade of the shovel and split his head into two halves. Blood gushed on the floor. The man, half-dead, lay still. Mietek jumped on his chest and with a single movement cut his throat with the sharp blade of the shovel. The shovel and his white shirt were covered with blood.

"You dirty dog! Are you still fighting back?" Mietek screamed at the top of his voice. He threw the shovel away and staggered toward his room. "I need a new shirt," he called to his drinking companions. Then he turned around to the Stubendienst and night watchman on duty.

"What are you waiting for? Clean this mess up before I teach you a lesson."

I shivered uncontrollably under my blanket as I watched both murders from the edge of my top bunk. I tried to reason with myself that perhaps the harsh conditions brought unexpected changes in human behavior. I still couldn't understand how good-natured people, ordinary normal human beings, came to be so cruel, vicious, and indifferent to the sufferings of others.

The power of functionaries, which they exercised over the lives of their fellow inmates, corrupted the most responsible and decent individuals. I wondered silently if Mietek and Franek were actually mature, decent, and responsible citizens in their precamp existence. I had no idea about their lives and their backgrounds. Right now, both of them were cruel, mean, and brutal oppressors, tormenting and killing their fellow prisoners. Perhaps, the instinct of self-preservation in subhuman conditions was stronger than anything else? I realized by now, that I had entered a strange and different world that was deprived of any moral constraints and genuine human decency and was completely removed from the normal standards of human behavior. The heart of the SS evil empire in Birkenau had one aim: to destroy the mind and the body of prisoners. It took me a long time to fall asleep.

The first thing I did when I opened my eyes in the morning was to look at the spot where Mietek killed two prisoners last night. I could not locate the place. The concrete floor was clean everywhere and there was no sign of bloodstains. I could not believe my own eyes. Was I dreaming last night?

In the center of the block, morning preparations before roll call were at their peak. People were dressing, eating, talking to one another, and running around doing a million errands to make life more bearable. With so many people squeezed in a highly congested area, it was very difficult not to bump your neighbors regardless of what you were trying to accomplish. I climbed down from my top bunk and tried to reach the adjoining bathhouse and latrine. As I was leaving the block, I noted two naked bodies lying by the exit door. I recognized the inmate with the split head. Blood covered his upper torso. Glazed eyes, wide open, looked at passersby almost with contempt and accusations: "Where were you when I was murdered?" they seemed to ask. I turned my head away and, full of guilt, joined the crowd and quickly ran to the bathhouse.

Lines in the bathhouse were enormous and I did not have any time to wash my face. I returned quickly to the block to collect my belongings from the bunk and then stood in another long line for ersatz coffee. I barely had time to eat my piece of bread before the Stubendiensts were screaming and throwing us from the block to attend morning roll call.

Again, we stood for one hour before Baretzki arrived on his bicycle. Mietek smiled and joked with him and with the Stubendienst. I looked at Mietek's face for signs of remorse, but looking in his eyes from a short distance as he marched behind Baretzki in front of the formation, I found nothing. The brutal instinct of a killer was ticking inside his heart like a hidden bomb, ready for the next explosion.

I began to understand that the purpose of quarantine was to terrorize the prisoners, force them to unconditional obedience, and expose them to the natural selection and elimination process. The weak and sick with no stamina to resist brutal and inhumane treatment were usually the first to die. Stronger and tougher individuals who managed to survive were, after a few weeks, transferred to the Men's Camp. Then, they were either forced to work in the German armament factories or assigned to special working squads responsible for improvement and expansion of the camp's facilities.

Following the morning roll call, we were usually divided into groups of about a hundred men. Under Capos, or in some cases SS Blockführer's direct supervision, inmates with knowledge of trades or special skills worked on the improvements of internal Quarantine Camp's facilities. Since I had no trade or skills, I was usually assigned to a special squad and performed various all day camp "sports" for the amusement of SS men and Capos. These included a number of forceful and strenuous physical exercises, accompanied by cursing and beating from Capos. For no reason except to provide our oppressor an opportunity to hit us, we were forced to carry hundreds of bricks from one place to another. We had to maintain a fast pace all the time. Prisoners unable to keep up with the group were unmercifully punished. This took the form of cruel beatings by the Capos and other functionaries.

By lunchtime, we were exhausted, both physically and morally drained. Then a Lagercapo appeared from nowhere. He was an expert in providing additional entertainment for visiting SS men during the official lunch break. Usually, he selected a group of resting prisoners and made us squat in a knee-bent position for the duration of the break. After a few minutes our legs were stiff and numb. We could hardly maintain our balance. With a sarcastic and a sadistic smile, in his elegant uniform, he towered above us with a large cane in his hand and he barked his orders: "Hands up! Knees bent! Jump, jump, jump!" Inmates who couldn't move or jump high in this ridiculous position received a powerful kick on their buttocks. In no time, this strenuous "sport" made us hot and sweaty and ready to return to our less challenging tasks of carrying the bricks around the camp. By the end of the day, dead bodies of brutally beaten and murdered inmates were neatly stacked against the blocks' rear walls. They also had to be accounted for during the evening roll call. After a week of the exhausting "sports," I was slowly losing my strength. Painful hunger and thirst was increasing with each day. There was never enough food to satisfy my empty stomach and there was never enough time to search for precious drinking water.

One night I woke up as heavy rain started pounding on the roof above my bunk. I lay quietly with open eyes, listening to the melancholic music of falling raindrops and pondering about my chances to survive the terrors of Quarantine Camp. I could not sleep for the rest of the night. At 4 A.M. all lights went on and several orderlies ran along the horizontal duct in the middle of the block shouting at us to get up and form a line for morning ersatz coffee. Half asleep and tired after a restless night, I climbed down from my bunk and decided not to go to the washroom. A heavy rain and misty fog made going outside very discouraging. I knew that eventually we all would be forced to stand for hours at the morning roll call and I wanted to prolong the comfort of the dry enclosure as long as possible.

During a long and confusing roll call, one inmate was missing and all prisoners were ordered to wait until a search was completed. We were told by SS Rottenführer Baretzki to stay outside in full formation under the wet sky. In one hour we were soaked and cold. Steady rain drenched our cotton uniforms and penetrated our underwear. We stood shivering, isolated and forgotten, hoping for the rain to stop soon. Meanwhile, our Blockältester, in his room, entertained Baretzki with food and drinks.

The rain kept pounding. That day I did not feel very well. My stomach was giving me a lot of problems. I prayed that this was not the beginning of dysentery, which was common among all inmates. After looking carefully around, I decided to take a chance and ran to the nearest latrine. I left my place in the last row and hiding behind my comrades' backs, I covered my head with both hands against rain and ran as quickly as I could. I carefully tried to avoid potholes full of mud and dirty water. Then, unexpectedly, I heard a high-pitched scream in front of me. "Stop!" I raised my head and saw Baretzki in a heavy motorcycle raincoat, with a cane in his hand, standing in front of me. I was confused, since he was the last person I would expect in the middle of camp on a rainy September morning.

I pulled off my cap, waiting anxiously for his next move. He screamed at me. "Who gave you permission to leave your formation. Do you understand?" He was all red in the face and very excited. His eyes were mean. I answered him promptly in my best German. "*Jawohl*, Herr Rottenführer." I stood straight holding my cap in my right hand. He suddenly raised his cane and hit me on the left side of my head. I screamed hysterically, flashes appeared in my eyes, and as I tried to protect my head from the oncoming blows, I lost my balance and fell down. As I lay on the ground he kicked me unmercifully with his enormously heavy army boots. My head was split and I could feel warm blood seeping behind my ear, down my neck, and under my shirt. I also felt a sharp pain around my kidney. I made an attempt to stand up when he hit me a second time with his cane across my back. I lost my balance again. Black circles vibrated in front of my eyes and I was on the verge of losing consciousness. Baretzki looked at me lying on the ground at his feet and then he screamed again. "This will teach you a lesson. Do you understand?" "*Jawohl*, Herr Rottenführer," I whispered, looking up from the ground at my oppressor when he put his right boot on my chest. He looked at me again, kicked me hard once more with his boot, turned around, and disappeared into the mist of the foggy Birkenau morning.

My head was still bleeding. I looked around to see if there was anybody nearby to help me. The camp seemed deserted since all inmates were still standing between blocks in roll-call formations. Raindrops mixed with blood from my fresh wound washed my face and stained my jacket with red spots. I struggled in the middle of the wet and muddy street to get up on my feet and find my way to the nearest washroom.

I begged the washroom chief, "Please let me clean my face." He looked around to see if the SS troopers were close by and then let me inside his "kingdom." Clean water was a blessing and a relief, and I slowly regained my balance. The washroom chief was very sympathetic. "This looks pretty bad. You better see a nursing orderly. Perhaps I can help you." He found an old paper bandage and dressed my head wound. Then he told me, "You must return to your block's formation until they release all roll-call units." By lunchtime the roll call was over. The missing inmate was found dead behind the kitchen and all prisoners were allowed to enter their blocks. Slowly, I found my way to my bunk and lay down trying to recover from my unexpected meeting with Baretzki.

"Is this the beginning of the end?" I wondered every night.

Although we slept on the same bunk, all four of us were assigned to different work details in the Quarantine Camp. Major, with the help of his friends, found work in the kitchen, peeling potatoes. This was a choice assignment since the work was under a roof and kitchen employees received an extra portion of soup every day. Sometimes in the evening, he brought a few boiled potatoes back with him and shared them with us. I admired his courage and willingness to take a risk since the punishment for stealing potatoes from the kitchen was beating and reassignment to the Penal Company.

Like many other Jewish prisoners, Moniek was assigned to the worst and the toughest drainage Kommando. He spent all day digging dirt and widening existing ditches within the Quarantine Camp's perimeters. Prisoners in intolerable conditions carried out this work. It required standing continuously, up to the knees, in mud or dirty standing water. Tomasz, the third comrade from our bunk, who used to build houses before the war, volunteered as a carpenter and was assigned to a small Kommando of Dachdeckers. His group maintained the roofs on all Quarantine blocks.

At the end of each day, we all met on the top of our bunk, and completely exhausted, shared the day's experiences. After one week of "sports," I started saving bread to exchange for better shoes. Every evening I ate half of my ration and saved the other half for my new pair of shoes. I was hungry each night. It took a strong will not to eat the whole portion. But my feet were worse every day and I knew I had no real choice.

One evening Moniek told me: "Janusz, one of the Stubendiensts has an extra pair of size 12 shoes. He wants two bread portions. Are you interested?" I was thrilled. The next evening, we went to see the shoes. They were in good condition and the right size. "One and a half." I tried to barter. The Stubendienst looked at me with a sarcastic smile: "Two or nothing. Your choice." Reluctantly, I gave him half the loaf. I may have been hungry for two days, but the shoes felt great. I could walk and run again like a normal human being. Even the difficult and demanding "sports" were more bearable than before. My head wounds improved sufficiently that I did not have to wear the paper bandage.

Every night the whole block waited with apprehension for Mietek's further outbursts, but for five days nothing happened. There was less and less tension among the prisoners. Then, on Saturday after all lights were out, well before midnight, we unexpectedly heard drunken voices and the sound of loud music coming from Mietek's room. The whole block was paralyzed. We pulled our blankets over our heads, kept quiet, and listened carefully to the sounds of a wild party. Mietek and Franek, who was Block Senior of the adjoining block, both completely drunk and unsteady on their feet, came out of Mietek's room and stopped in the middle of the block.

"I want two good fighters . . . right now!" Mietek screamed at the top of his voice.

Nobody moved. He pulled the blanket from one of the men on the lower bunk. "Can you box?"

"No, sir."

"Then you will learn today." Mietek waved his hand and then stepped in front of another bunk: "First man . . . out! Are you a boxer?"

"No, sir. Please let me go." The man almost cried.

Mietek was getting mad. He pushed both men on the top of a heating duct. "Fight!" he insisted. "Otherwise you have to face me."

Both men assumed boxing positions pretending that they were trying to hit each other with closed fists.

"Hold it!" Mietek shouted. "I need a referee." He pulled an elderly prisoner from the middle bunk. The man was trembling. "Go up and act as a referee," he ordered the frightened, shaking victim. The man reluctantly climbed on top of the duct.

The two victims pretended they were fighting each other. The referee acted clumsily. All three moved slowly in an unnatural, grotesque way. Mietek was mad. He held his shovel and then, in a sudden, swift move, hit the referee below both knees. The man lost his balance, fell down on the concrete floor and began screaming.

Mietek put his shovel handle against his throat and jumped with both feet on both ends of the shovel. He broke the man's neck.

The two men left on top of the duct were hysterical. They tried to run toward the exit door, but Franek stood in the middle of the corridor. He also had a shovel.

The men turned around toward Mietek. He used his shovel only twice and in no time both prisoners were lying on the concrete floor. Blood was everywhere. Then, he finished both of them in his customary way. He quickly put the shovel across their necks and then jumped with both feet. They groaned for a second and then everything stopped.

There were three bodies lying still on the floor.

Mietek shook hands with Franek and screamed: "Stubendienst, clean this mess." Completely drunk, both men staggered back to Mietek's room and, in no time, the sound of music blasted louder and louder. The noise coming from Mietek's room was unbearable. In the rest of the block, there was a complete silence.

The next morning we carried out our daily routine. There were nine bodies beside the exit door. In addition to Mietek's three victims, six people died during the night. Devastating demands for athletic performances and inhumane treatment were slowly taking their toll. I asked Moniek how long we had to stay in quarantine. He did not know but Major volunteered his view, "Two to four weeks." I looked forward to the moment of transfer, though I did not know what to expect at the Men's Camp. I was fully prepared for the worst, expecting more hardship, more hunger, and more inhumane treatment. All of that sounded less dangerous than staying one more night in Mietek's block.

That evening Moniek was subdued. I asked him: "What's wrong?" Moniek told me that after roll call, the Schreiber told him to report at the main gate tomorrow morning.

That meant a transfer. But where? Moniek tried to cover his nervousness, "I know that they are only calling Jews and I don't like it," he whispered.

I tried to reassure him, "You are young and healthy and they want you to work. Do not worry."

In the morning, we all shook hands with Moniek. He was calm but pale and trembling, "Good luck. I hope to see you all after the war." Then he smiled: "We Jews are tougher than Hitler thinks and we will be here a long time after he is gone." Then he turned to Major: "Can I ask you for a favor? I know that sometimes you visit the Women's Camp to bring new potatoes to our kitchen. Could you please, next time, ask there about my mother and sister?" He scribbled their names on a piece of paper: "I don't know their numbers, but they were from the Zawiercie transport in August. Tell them I am doing fine."

Major took the paper, "Moniek, I will try to do this on Monday. If you can, let us know where they are taking you. Good luck!" he added. We watched him in silence when, right after morning roll call, he went with the Schreiber to the main gate. That night only three of us were left on the top bunk.

After almost two weeks of confinement in Birkenau, I was extremely depressed. The transition from the "outside world" to the concentration camp had been terrifying. This strange world of dehumanizing experiences, blunt terror, murder, and complete disregard for human life was far beyond what many ordinary people sent to Birkenau were able to accept.

Every morning and evening roll call was a confrontation with fear. The SS Blockführer walked slowly counting the inmates and dead bodies lying by the side of the block. Occasionally, he stopped and without any provocation or even one word spoken, he hit the prisoner standing in the front row at full attention. If the man tried to protect his face he was kicked unmercifully and beaten with a large cane that most of the SS men carried with them.

Sometimes during roll call, the SS man would call for specific numbers. After verification of numbers by the Schreiber, the victims had to fall out from the formation and the functionaries forcefully dragged them toward the main gate. It was a well-known fact that this was the Political Department recall of inmates who were previously sentenced to death by the Gestapo and who were kept temporarily in the Quarantine Camp to await their final verdict. As Gestapo formally closed their cases, they were summoned to be transferred to Block 11 in the old camp in Auschwitz for execution. We never saw them again.

Sudden changes of circumstances, loss of freedom, and exposure to inhuman quarantine practices, generated a feeling of resigned despair among inmates. Suicide was one of the free choices left to completely confused and heartbroken inmates, who could not face the reality of persecutions in Quarantine Camp.

The number of suicides in quarantine was growing day by day. The simple way to take your own life was to touch the electrified wires or cross the post lines. SS guards on duty were ordered to shoot every prisoner who crossed the security perimeter ditches. In each case, after shooting the prisoner, the SS guard was awarded a few days of leave.

After Moniek's departure, I felt lonelier than ever. I had not known him very well or for a long time. But under the unique camp conditions, a friendly and sympathetic soul goes a long way to make up for the horror of other people's behavior. I thought about the tragic circumstances that brought people of many diverse cultures, backgrounds, and nationalities together in Birkenau. Moniek was born in an independent Poland and his family wanted very much to be part of the new country. They had a hard time being fully accepted as they faced prejudice and ignorance among their neighbors. Yet, in spite of the many disadvantages that Moniek encountered, he considered himself a Polish patriot. His ambition was to become a doctor. I had grown up in the same country taking my freedom and independence for granted and enjoyed full benefits and privileges of the free society without restrictions or prejudice. If it were not for the German occupation of Poland in September 1939, we would probably have never met.

Idealistically, I wanted to think that in Birkenau, the common danger and a strong will to survive would bridge all the differences among the inmates. After my short stay in the Quarantine Camp, I knew that I was wrong. As the living conditions here were getting worse and worse and brutal SS men and functionaries terrorized their victims, greed, intolerance, prejudice, and indifference among the fellow inmates grew stronger and stronger.

Sitting on the top of my bunk, I tried to sort out my situation and find a way to survive. I was aware that as long as I was still breathing, I was in a far better position than the Jewish prisoners. They were systematically killed just because they were Jews. Providing that I could stay healthy, I would still have a slim chance of survival. By now, I was fully aware that in the early days, internal camp administration was in the hands of German criminals who were willing to serve the SS bureaucracy without hesitation and who demonstrated their allegiance to the Nazis by inhuman treatment of their fellow prisoners. I was told by Major that at the very beginning of the camp's existence, in 1940, Höss asked Palitzsch to bring from the concentration camp in Sachsenhausen thirty professional German criminals. They were appointed to the highest administrative inmate positions in Auschwitz and were the core of an unscrupulous and cruel functionary's clique. Later on, the first Polish prisoners who were detained in the camp and assigned low numbers, and who were thus able to outlive gas selection, brutal treatment, hunger, typhus, and other camp disasters, became camp functionaries. But some of them conspired, and struggled to attain power and authority, which would help them to survive the system. They maintained and defended their positions of privilege above the ordinary human masses, with the vested rights of life and death over less fortunate inmates, and were not much better than the German criminals. Mietek and Franek, although both Polish nationals, were typical examples of men with twisted minds and raw animal instincts.

Since 1941, the camp's underground circles tried hard to replace mean and unscrupulous officials and put in the responsible positions their own trustees, who would be willing to help and assist their fellow inmates. Many functionaries, mostly red triangles, appointed to their jobs after 1942, were decent human beings. They used their positions to assist and to help less fortunate inmates. In spite of many temptations, this group never lost their decency and concern for the suffering masses. With the extensive arrests of

Poles and their massive transports from the Gestapo prisons to Auschwitz, the German criminals were slowly losing their power in the internal struggle for leadership in many camps. Yet, in spite of this general trend, in the fall of 1943, all of the most senior prisoners' camp positions at the Quarantine were in the hands of German criminals. A few selected Poles and Jews shared the remaining functions of Blockältesters and Capos with Germans. Although, there were some exceptions of compassionate functionaries, the majority of Block Seniors at the Quarantine Camp were indifferent to human suffering and pain. They looked up to Mietek and Franek to set an example of inhumane, cruel, harsh, and often deadly treatment for newly arrived transports.

Life at the Quarantine Camp was tough and cruel. The victory of political prisoners in the struggle for internal control of camp administration was uncertain. In addition to my personal exposure to the SS terror of SS Rottenführer Baretzki, my brief experience at the Quarantine was a brutal awakening and harsh lesson about the intensity of social and political power struggles among prisoners at all levels. We all hated Germans, but we also resented other national and racial groups and were suspicious of one another. The Quarantine Camp population, at the very beginning of camp existence, consisted of many nationalities. We all lived together behind barbed wire, under one roof. We shared the same crowded bunks, but we were separated from one another by our racial and national prejudices. There was a feeling of distrust among Poles, Russians, and Jews as we all struggled to survive and perhaps outlive one another. Although ugly, strong feelings of anti-Semitism occasionally surfaced among Polish chauvinists; on our bunk, however, we had treated Moniek as one of our own. I missed him a lot. Yet, in spite of the crowded blocks and the constant milling of people around me, there was a strange and recurring feeling of loneliness. Every time my personal circumstances changed in Birkenau, I experienced deep depression, feeling lost and forgotten by everybody.

During the day I had to be careful and hold onto all of my personal possessions all of the time. When I washed or used the toilet, I had to carry and hold dearly to my personal belongings and never lose sight of my jacket, my shoes, my spoon, or my metal bowl. If I left those items unprotected for a minute, in no time, my fellow inmates would steal them. When I slept, I put all my "valuable" belongings under my head and used them as a pillow. Half asleep, I had to watch for scavengers crawling across the bunks in the darkness of the night looking for a chance to steal anything. Even with the few trusted friends on my bunk, the continuous awareness that I must fight, argue, and scream for a place in line, for food rations, or for a decent space in the washroom made me confused and exhausted well before the beginning of the "official" day's work.

We all knew that our days in the Quarantine Camp were coming to an end and very soon we would be transferred to the Men's Camp. Some evenings, after roll call, and during our so-called free time, I stopped for a few minutes behind my block to watch life across the barbed wire in the adjoining Theresienstadt family camp. Moniek told me that the first prisoners from Theresienstadt included men, women, and children who were brought to Birkenau in special rail transports only one week before my arrival.

The camp was formally designated as BIIb-family compound, although I saw men and women with children housed separately in different blocks. They were allowed to mix during the day only. Most of the prisoners retained their personal belongings, and some men wore white-and-blue-striped uniforms. Their hair was not shorn and it appeared from the distance that their food was better than ours. Since the camp was not completely finished, most of the young men like us were forced to work on the completion of the blocks and adjoining grounds. Hundreds of them worked every morning under strict SS supervision in digging large stones that were used to pave the main street in the camp and in hauling them from the nearby depot. Their morning and evening roll calls were held at the same time as ours. There was a strange feeling, almost an illusion of "normal life," when I saw for the first time men, women, and children living together in what appeared to be more relaxed and less stringent conditions. Close observation indicated, however, that this was an erroneous assumption. The prisoners of BIIb camp, regardless of gender and age were as much harassed and persecuted by the SS Blockführers and the functional elite as the rest of us. The mortality rate was very high and every evening I saw corpses piled against the blocks' walls waiting to be transferred to the camp mortuary. The "family life" was a cruel hoax and political gimmick to serve the SS propaganda machine, which was eager to mislead the whole world.

After evening roll call on Monday, Schreiber called out many numbers including mine. I knew that meant transfer, but where? Major and Tomasz were not on the list. The following morning a group of about two hundred people gathered in front of the main gate. Schreibers from many different blocks carefully checked our numbers. "Everything checks out," Kurpanik reported to the SS Lagerführer.

"Turn right . . . Forward march." As we were passing the main gate, SS Rapportführer again carefully counted the column. The Capo heading the group turned left. We passed the Theresienstadt and Hungarian camps, turned left again, and stopped in front of the SS guard barrack leading to the Men's Camp, or BIId. Another check at the gate and then we marched inside.

This camp was twice as big as the Quarantine Camp. Wooden blocks were identical and located symmetrically on both sides of the main street. I was assigned to Block 28, which stood at the very end of the camp near the washrooms and latrine barracks. It was located across from the electrified wires, facing an open area and FKL or the Women's Concentration Camp across the wide access street. As I looked at the Women's Camp in front of me, on my right side I saw the Gypsy Family Camp and on my left side a special camp for Hungarian Jews. All camps, although adjoining one another, were separated by electrified wire fences. The crematoria, with their continuously flaming stacks, seemed to be closer than ever.

CHAPTER SIX

Men's Camp BIId

EXCEPT FOR functional officials and small crews of prisoners working in the kitchen or on the maintenance of buildings and campgrounds, the Men's Camp was deserted. The blocks and streets were also empty. Approximately fifteen thousand men housed in the camp worked all day in various *Kommandos,* or prisoners' working parties, employed outside of the camp area. Ten hours daily they were sweating, struggling, building up and expanding the might of the German armament industry. The camp dignitaries and SS officials mercilessly hunted people who decided early in the morning to hide in the blocks in order to avoid work. If found, they were punished in the worst possible way. In addition to regular beatings, they were required to perform exhausting "sports" or assigned to an extra heavy work detail.

The Schreiber from Block 28 grouped us together and led us to his barrack. "Since everybody is working," he said, "I will assign available empty bunks to you and you can stay here until evening roll call." This was a pleasant surprise. I also noted that the Stubendiensts were friendly and accommodating. There was no shouting or beatings.

Again I ended up on the top bunk. This was a good location, except when the roof leaked. In that case, if it rained, all straw mattresses and blankets, if any were available, became wet. Unfortunately, there was no way to change places. Five of us were assigned to the new bunk, two Poles from Warsaw, two French Jews from Paris, and myself.

Antoni, one of the Stubendiensts, or Toni as his friends called him, was born in Lwów. As soon as he found out that we came from the same town, he tried to make my first day in the Men's Camp more bearable. I came to see him in his bunk, which was next to the Blockältester's room. The mattresses were much better than ours and he had plenty of blankets and pillows. A built-in shelf added to the everyday convenience. I saw several personal belongings placed in the corner. He had an extra pair of shoes and an overcoat, which was neatly folded on the bed. This was luxurious living by Birkenau standards and I was very much impressed with Toni's housekeeping.

He asked me to climb up to his bunk and, in reasonable privacy, we talked about our experiences. As a prisoner from one of the first transports, after working in the construction *Kommando,* he had a job as a nurse in the old camp in Auschwitz. Then, in 1942, he was transferred to Birkenau as a Stubendienst. He was a low number and old prisoner by camp criteria, but a young man in his late twenties by the standards of the normal outside world. He sounded like a responsible, warm, and compassionate human being.

"Janusz," he told me, "this is a terrible place, but we must help each other if we expect to survive." Then he added, "you are lucky that you were assigned to this block. The Blockältester Stanek is German. He came to Auschwitz in 1941. His Schreiber, Kazik, is Polish. He is good to people in the block and most of the Stubendiensts were handpicked by him personally. We try to be fair to everybody regardless of where they came from.

"How did you manage to survive?" I asked him.

He shook his head. "At the beginning it was tough. As we were working on the expansion of the old camp in Auschwitz, we lost thousands of people. Brutal extermination of all prisoners and daily killings of inmates during working hours were part of a normal routine. There are not that many comrades left from my transport. Later on, with the shortage of labor force, and changing fortunes of war, the SS administration changed its priorities from unnecessary killings to forceful exploitation of slave labor. Inmates were coerced to work until they dropped dead from sheer exhaustion. Eventually, some of us were able to find better jobs. Being a Stubendienst is a good assignment. We used to go to work with our *Kommandos* but now some Blockältesters allow us to stay and clean the blocks during the day. Perhaps the most important responsibility is the distribution of food rations to all inmates in the block."

"There is a lot of abuse," he continued, "In some blocks, they are stealing food rations and some inmates are fed with meager leftovers. Kazik, or Kaz as we call him, is an honest man and he does not allow the Stubendiensts to 'organize' food and distribute reduced portions to the inmates."

"The first priority for now is to find you the right *Kommando.* Some of them are really deadly and people are dropping like flies," he continued. "The Capos are inhuman and work is very hard and demanding. I know one Undercapo. His *Kommando* works in our old camp, which is currently assigned to women prisoners. This is known as BIb or the FKL area, and as soon as they finish work on the bathhouses and latrines, they will move to Mexico."

I did not understand. The name "Mexico" sounded exotic and hardly fit into the deadly camp surroundings. Seeing my puzzled face, he explained, "Mexico, or Section C, is the proposed new camp across the street from

Men's Camp. There is nothing up there now except for a few unfinished wooden barracks." He continued, "The BIb, our old camp, is very close, a short walking distance. Many of the Block Seniors are Slovak women who are friendly and compassionate. You may even get an extra bowl of soup up there."

I went back to my bunk. There was not much conversation among my comrades. We had a hard time talking pidgin German with the two Frenchmen. They were depressed and worried about their families, which had been separated from them at the railroad ramp in Auschwitz. "Get ready for a roll call," called one of the Stubendiensts to all the newcomers. All newly assigned inmates formed a small group between the blocks.

We stood silently and watched thousands of men make their way toward the camp. I saw a number of stretchers behind each column. Exhausted inmates carried their sick and dead fellow prisoners. In the distance, I saw *Kommandos* coming through the Main Gate. They all marched to the loud and rhythmic sounds of German marches played by the camp orchestra. The music sounded strange in this place where misery and death were everyday occurrences. All *Kommandos* in columns of five deep marched with their Capos toward their blocks and then waited with the rest of the camp for the beginning of the roll call. The camp SS administration made an attempt to group specific *Kommandos* in the same blocks, but since some of them required specialists or last minute replacements, often prisoners from the same *Kommando* lived in many different blocks.

Getting ready for a roll call required a lot of patience and understanding. Some of the workers, half dead after the day's work, could hardly stand on their feet and wait for the roll call to start. A few, sick and desperate, ran to the latrine despite the ranting and pushing by Stubendiensts who tried to maintain order and count the number of prisoners in each block before the official counting. As the *Kommandos* were arriving through the main gate, thousands of tired and miserable people gradually began to fill the previously deserted camp. They walked like robots, dragging their exhausted bodies to the rhythms of the music and looking for a not too exposed place in their block formation. Nobody wanted to be in the first row and directly face the SS Blockführers. Gradually the *Appellplatz* between blocks was getting crowded with people. I noticed that on our block most of the inmates were Greek Jews from Saloniki. They all looked exhausted. Thousands of the weak and sick had died a long time ago. Birkenau's cold weather and damp, rainy autumn, with muddy, clay soil, did not help the Jews from Saloniki, who were used to a gentle Mediterranean climate. Most of them didn't speak German or even Yiddish. As a group, they also had a problem communicating with others and because of this, they experienced a sense of isolation in the camp. In no time, the majority of them reached the status of Mussulmans and were dying in large numbers. The survivors developed a strong sense of unity among themselves and were respected by their fellow prisoners. The devastating camp experience had made them wise and ferocious. Those who survived developed a determination to live at any price. The majority of them succeeded eventually in obtaining better jobs and gradually secured for themselves a respectable place in the camp's social structure. However, new transports from Greece had to go through the same natural selection process. The passive, sick, and even the most decent prisoners usually ended up joining the ever growing ranks of Mussulmans. They all stood together, talking to one another and arguing with their hands and raised voices.

"Don't pay any attention," Toni told me. "They always talk like this. But watch out after roll call. They are clever thieves and great organizers."

The music stopped playing. The Blockältester turned around: "*Heftlinge—Mutzen ab!*" We stood straight in columns of ten with caps in our hands.

The SS Blockführer, on a motorcycle, stopped in front of the block. He walked slowly and counted the columns of prisoners. Then he looked down at his chart.

"Everything checks out" he told Stanek as he mounted his motorcycle. "*Heftlinge—Mutzen auf.*" We stood in formation; there was complete silence among the prisoners since talking was forbidden. Then we heard: "Dismiss." The roll call was over and we all ran to receive our meager portions of food. As usual, I tried to save half my bread for the next morning, but the temptation was enormous. I was very hungry and I knew that I was losing weight.

After "dinner" I took my trip to the latrine and washroom. Slowly we were all getting ready for the night. My new Polish comrades were not too eager to talk. The French Jews kept to themselves. Silently, from my top bunk, I watched my fellow prisoners in the block.

Toni stopped at my bunk: "It is all set. You will work with the *Planierungskommando*. The group forms in front of Block 8 after morning roll call. Talk to Undercapo Witek. He is expecting you. Good luck!"

"Thank you, Toni. I am really grateful." I shook his hand more than once.

As I vividly remembered my frightening nights in Mietek's Quarantine block, I could not go to sleep. I kept expecting something monstrous to happen. The lights went off. The night watchman was sitting half asleep by the exit door. At least that night nothing happened.

After the usual morning activities and roll call, I gulped my ersatz coffee and looked for my new *Kommando*. About a hundred men strong, the group was ready to march. I found Witek easily since he had the yellow armband of an Undercapo. "I am Janusz. Toni sent me," I whispered to him.

He looked at me. "I know. I've been expecting you. Stay in the first row and hold this place for me."

Four of us were standing at the head of the *Kommando*. The group always marched in rows of five prisoners abreast. The fifth spot in the front row was reserved for Witek. The Capo, a middle-aged German with a low number and green triangle was circulating around the column and watching that nobody would leave the group for other *Kommandos*. Up in front, we heard the sound of music. "Forward march!" "Left, right, left!" Endless lines of formations, gathered in different parts of the camp, were slowly finding their way to the main gate.

We passed the orchestra and the gate where official SS personnel on duty and functional prisoners from the Labor Office were checking and counting the columns marching by. At the gate, we picked up our SS Kommand-offührer and SS guards. They marched at each side of the column with machine pistols ready to shoot. We turned right on the main street and then, after a few hundred yards, we turned right again. On my right side I recognized the entrance to the Men's Quarantine Camp. Once more we turned right, passed under the control tower and turned left toward the Women's Camp. We passed the men's *Sauna* or bathhouse where I had spent my first night in Birkenau and turned right to the Women's Camp BIb. Then we stopped in front of a wooden shack and Witek started to distribute shovels and other tools.

"Take this one," he said, handing me a shovel. Witek told me that Russian prisoners of war and other inmates built the first camp in Birkenau. Thousands of men perished during the intensive construction from October 1941 until March 1942. In the spring of 1942, some of the old prisoners from Auschwitz and the surviving Russians were transferred to the new Birkenau Men's Camp, BIb. After completion of the new section BII in July 1943, the men were again transferred to a newly completed camp BIId, and old camp BIb was designated as an extension of the women's compound.

As I looked around, except for the designated fenced area for the acceptance of new male transports, I saw that the rest of the camp was crowded with women. I understood from Witek that our job was to repair existing blocks and grade the ground for an extension of the new bathhouses and latrines, which were located at the east side of the camp, adjoining the perimeter fence. The sanitary facilities consisted of several one-story buildings. Washrooms had a series of faucets mounted above long metal sinks that looked like a large gutter for collection and discharge of running water. The latrine barracks had a long single ditch in the middle and a raised concrete cover above it with circular openings for individual prisoners.

Although there were several wooden barracks similar to those in the

Men's Camp, the majority of blocks for women were one-story brick units. The buildings were approximately twelve meters wide and forty meters long with a single entrance and a long corridor in the middle. Inside there were two small rooms adjoining the single entrance. The first room was used by the Blockältester as her sleeping quarters. The second served as the bread storage area for the whole population in the block. On both sides of the corridor, there were sixty internal, built-in partitions. Two small iron stoves were installed at each end of the block, but there was no running water. One block could accommodate approximately seven hundred prisoners sleeping on three levels.

All female inmates assigned to working *Kommandos* inside and outside of the women's compound were forced to live in a harsh, unsanitary, and overcrowded environment. Thousands of women, of all ages and from many different European countries, struggled for survival after the day's work in these unheated blocks. Fighting with rats, covered with lice, always hungry and thirsty, in filthy "quarters," they were completely unprepared to face the realities of camp existence. With limited access to latrines and washrooms, where even cold water was scarce and dirty, the stench of their blocks was terrible. Some of the women, already sick and helpless, lay quietly on their bunks, unable to make any effort to reach for their primary needs: food and water. They looked at us silently as we walked through their blocks trying to repair their wooden bunks, fix the deteriorating brick walls, and patch the holes to prevent the rainwater from coming inside.

Mice, rats, and lice were everywhere. Big, well-fed and brazen mice ran openly during the day among the women's blocks. Pushy, curious, and not intimidated or scared by the women inmates' screams, they searched relentlessly for hidden bread portions in the blocks and crawled among the women's bunks. Witek told me that in the darkness of the night, huge rats would leave their burrows, crawling among the sleeping prisoners, in search of food, often scavenging corpses piled outside of each block. The Women's Camp was also full of mud. Dark, brown, rich, and moist Auschwitz clay was everywhere. It stuck to our wooden shoes and made every step an effort. Fragile and hungry women fought bravely, with every step, trying to cross the main street in search of water and food. As I tried to concentrate on my work, I watched how they struggled and felt helpless and frustrated.

The area close to our workstation was isolated from the rest of the Women's Camp and designated as a temporary quarantine for recently arrived Jewish women.

This part of the camp was internally run and administered by Jewish women who came to Auschwitz from Slovakia in March 1942. They were all held together in the old camp in Auschwitz but subsequently had been moved to the newly constructed blocks in Birkenau. The new location, known as BIa, was opposite the Men's Camp, which they eventually inherited in 1943.

Like everybody else, the Jewish women from Slovakia went through harsh and inhumane treatment during the construction of the women's concentration camp in Birkenau. Thousands died and perished in the early years working on the demolition of the existing houses. But the survivors ended up with better jobs and functional responsibilities in the newly established Women's Camp. They were not required to shave their heads. While the German Blockältesters were mean and cruel, Slovak functionaries were tough and assertive, but somehow never lost their feminine touch and compassion for their less fortunate sisters. They desperately tried to help newly arrived inmates, but their means and resources were very limited and were strictly controlled by the SS.

Working in the Women's Quarantine area, I observed with sadness that hundreds of starving newly arrived young Jewish women wandered around their blocks in their skimpy dresses, half naked with bare feet. With colorful scarves covering their shaved heads, from a distance they looked like exotic tropical birds. But as I looked at them more closely, I saw frightened young women, hungry, confused, milling around the blocks and wondering what would happen to them. They watched us working, asked us about their relatives, cried, and made attempts to beg for food, soap, and clean drinking water. They were willing to trade everything they had and they did not have very much. With dehydrated bodies covered with sores and ill-fitting summer dresses without underwear, with shaved heads and frightened eyes, they were sadly unappealing. Although by now I was getting used to the primitive living conditions that I had experienced at Men's Camp, still I was appalled by the plight of the starving and persecuted women inmates and their subhuman existence in the Women's Quarantine.

Our *Kommando* was divided into five squads, each one supervised by a Vorarbeiter or foreman. In Witek's group there were several Poles recently transferred from Buchenwald. There were also a few Greeks and French Jews. Most of them did not speak German and they had a hard time communicating with the rest of us. I tried to stay close to Witek, who supervised two squads. Every time the SS Kommandoführer was close to us, Witek screamed at us and waved his stick. Nobody took him too seriously. We all knew he was a "good guy" and would never hit us or harm us. However, he pretended to be tough and harsh in front of SS personnel.

We had a half-hour break for lunch. The food was brought from the kitchen on trucks and set aside while we all waited for the official Capo's whistle to stop working. The Capo personally distributed the soup. One could feel the sense of power and satisfaction radiating from his smiling face as he carefully used his ladle to serve floating potatoes to his friends and favorites. The Greeks were at the end of the line waiting impatiently for a bowl of watery and tasteless fluid. After the first go-around, all functionaries were entitled to a second helping and Witek shared his portion with me. It was smelly and tasteless, but it did have a few meager potatoes and I was grateful for the favor.

At six o'clock in the evening, the Capo called the *Kommando* together and, with the SS Kommandoführer leading the group and our SS guards on both sides of the column, we started marching toward the Men's Camp. "Left, Right, . . .One, two, three," we marched again in rhythm with a military march played by the camp's orchestra at the Main Gate.

The camp authorities had organized the prisoners' orchestra, and every SS Lagerführer took pride in selecting the best and most talented European musicians to play in the band. At the very beginning of the camp's existence, except for the Kapellmeister and a few music scribers, its members worked during the day on field *Kommandos,* like all other prisoners. The orchestra members were last to leave the camp in the morning and usually returned to camp an hour sooner in the evening, in order to play the music for the outgoing and incoming *Kommandos.* Each major camp had its own orchestra. At the old camp in Auschwitz, musicians worked in the kitchen and played every day standing by the well-known entrance gate with the sign, *Arbeit Macht Frei,* (Work makes you free).

In Birkenau, the men's orchestra played by the entrance gate to the Men's Camp BIId on a specially designated spot. As the marching *Kommandos* approached the gate, the Capo called: "Hats off," then "Eyes right." Passing in front of the SS guard house, he shouted: *"Kommando's* number," "Number of persons" and "Confirmation of number." Then, as he passed the post, he called: "Hats on." Prisoners, with their eyes turned right and holding their hats, marched to the military cadence, holding their breath and praying that they would not miss steps in front of the watchful SS guards. Inmates from the Women's Camp marched to and from work to the music played by the women's orchestra.

"The great music lover," Marie Mandel, the cruel SS Head Supervisor of the Women's Camp, had organized this band. It was formed from the best women musicians and soloists from the whole of Europe. Beginning in the summer of 1942, on Sundays the orchestras played at public concerts organized by camp authorities and attended by privileged prisoners. Some of the orchestras, divided into small teams, also played for smaller, private gatherings of Capos and other camp functionaries. This was an attractive arrangement since the musicians were compensated with extra bread rations, sausage, or margarine. Occasionally, even the SS Lagerführer requested that the prisoner-musicians entertain SS troops and their families. Being in the orchestra was a choice assignment. Members of the orchestra eventually had been assigned lighter camp duties. They spent most of their time practicing music or teaching others how to play. The music lessons were usually given to camp functionaries for a small compensation, such as an extra piece of bread or perhaps an additional bowl of soup.

At the gate, the SS men counted incoming *Kommandos*. Occasionally, they stopped the column and selected individual prisoners for personal search. They looked everywhere for everything: food, messages, additional and illegal clothing. If anything was found, they pulled the prisoner from the column. His punishment was harsh and he could expect beatings, "sports," and imprisonment in the Auschwitz bunker at the famous Block 11.

Sunny and pleasant days were coming to an end, but the fall weather was still very mild. Early October was warm and only in the evening could one feel the light westerly winds that carried the ubiquitous smell of sweet, burnt flesh. I occasionally looked west at the crematoria smokestacks. The yellow and red flames could be seen most of the time above all four crematoria buildings.

As we struggled every day for survival in Birkenau, trains full of Jews, squeezed together in packed cattle cars, were pulling in at the distant railway platform in Auschwitz. Hundreds of innocent and frightened people were unloaded, sorted, selected, gassed, and then disappeared without a trace. Only mountains of luggage were left behind each transport. "Canada" men were working feverishly to load the suitcases as quickly as possible and move them to the adjoining barracks before the arrival of the next transport. "Canada" was a term in prisoners' camp jargon, describing the abundance of goods looted by Nazis from Jewish transports, sorted out, and stored in Birkenau barracks. The "Canada" *Kommando*, formally known as *Aufräumungskommandos* or housekeeping work details were groups of men or women prisoners assigned to collect and sort personal effects and luggage left on the railroad platform by the incoming Jewish transports. At the beginning of 1942, all property requisitioned from Jewish transports was stored in a few barracks. Since 1943, with the considerable increase of incoming transports, additional barracks had been constructed in the area adjoining the men's hospital and located between Crematoria III and IV.

Women prisoners, who as a part of *Aufräumungskommando* sorted and disinfected requisitioned property, enjoyed better working conditions than most of their fellow prisoners. They had opportunities to pick up better clothes and on many occasions smuggled some of the valuable items from barracks to the Women's Camp and exchanged them for food and other personal services. The SS Kommandoführer of the women's "Canada" section took personal pride in selecting the most attractive women, providing good warm clothing for "his girls," accessories to create a uniform physical appearance and supplementary soup during lunch time. As they marched from the Women's Camp to the clothes storage area every morning, they could be easily identified by colorful and attractive headscarves of the same color and design. If it were not for the tragic circumstances of the camp's existence, one could almost enjoy watching columns of several hundred young and healthy women walking through the camp's streets and bringing patches of bright colors to the dreary landscape of Birkenau.

Although trading in gold was punishable by death, some of the gold coins and jewelry stolen by "Canada" men did find its way to the Men's Camp and were exchanged or "organized" on the black market for other items. The irony of some people dying from hunger and other people trading gold for French wine, fine food, or sex, yet all living under the same roof, was beyond comprehension to people unfamiliar with the Birkenau "culture." Sometimes I had the impression that I was living in two separate worlds.

By mid October, train traffic was intensified. Jewish transport from Theresienstadt, with many children and their caretakers, was sent directly to the gas chambers. From other transports only a few lucky survivors from the railroad ramp selections, mostly young and healthy men and women, eventually joined us in our blocks and were assigned camp numbers. I tried to track the origins of new arrivals by checking their numbers. Meanwhile, our population in the blocks increased dramatically. We were forced to accommodate eight people in each bunk. Several French Jews arrived from Drancy and I met quite a few Polish Jews from Zawiercie. One evening I asked Toni, "How many more people can we take?" He scratched his head, "We are already overcrowded but there's nothing we can do. You can't argue with Rudolph Höss and Schwarzhuber."

Several Jews were assigned to our block. The new person in our bunk was Icek, a young Polish Jew from Sosnowiec. He came to Birkenau about the same time as Moniek but they did not know each other. Icek was born and raised in Lwów before moving with his parents to Silesia. Since I used to live in Lwów, the first evening we spent talking and reminiscing about old times. He had been separated from his parents and a sister at the railroad ramp and was very much concerned about their well-being. Icek asked us that evening, "Can I save one space for my father on this bunk?"

We all said, "Yes, of course." None of us had enough courage to tell him the truth.

Since he did some carpentry work in the Sosnowiec ghetto, Icek looked for his friends and tried to join the carpenters' *Kommando*, where one of his relatives was already assigned. I wished him luck in the morning and after the familiar call, "Form your *Kommandos*," went to look for Witek and his group. We marched through the main gate as usual, met our SS Kommand-ofűhrer and our SS guards, and in no time were in Section BIb.

The work at the Women's Camp was very popular among men prisoners since it offered many opportunities for "organization" or trading of various commodities among men and women. Food and cosmetic items were highly sought after by women's camp functionaries. These women controlled food distribution for their less fortunate sisters and occasionally exploited their privileges.

The luxuries of the outside world were easily available from "Canada." Electricians, carpenters, and other men's working parties at the Women's Camp provided messengers and delivery services. Some of the women functionaries traded in other commodities. As strange as it sounds against the background of chimney fumes, there were many genuine romances among the prisoners. Some of them reflected true and honest feelings among re-signed people prepared to face death together. Some were cold and calcu-lated exchanges of goods available on the market. Sex was not excluded, nor were homosexual or lesbian relationships among prisoners uncommon.

Many Blockältesters from the Men's Camp, after obtaining their jobs and positions of authority, looked for understanding, compassion, friend-ship, or even love from female functionaries in the Women's Camp. The BIa and BIb areas provided excellent opportunities for various exchanges among prisoners, civilian workers, and SS guards. The latter were fully aware of for-bidden relationships among prisoners, but generous bribes from the inmates helped them look the other way. The jewelry, money, gold, and other per-sonal items stolen from Jewish transports offered an irresistible temptation to simple-minded, uneducated, and not very wealthy guards. When the women Blockältesters were entertaining men prisoners in their quarters, all Stuben-diensts provided discreet lookout services for them. Officially, contact be-tween men and women, in all camps, was a punishable offense. We were forbidden to talk to any women when we worked around their blocks. One had to be careful since bribes did not always work with all SS guards. Some of the soldiers were still dedicated Nazi fanatics, and no amount of gold could change their blind faith in the party system and the supremacy of their race.

One day, as I worked with my shovel grading the soil, a well-dressed woman prisoner with a Star of David on her jacket stopped by. She looked around and then asked me in heavily accented Polish, "How long have you been in Birkenau?"

I looked at her and recognized her immediately. She was the Schreiber from the block where we had done some repair work the day before. She was very attractive, perhaps twenty years old, with short blond hair and sad blue eyes. She smiled in a friendly way. I looked quickly left and right. Except for a few Greeks, there was nobody in sight. "Four weeks," I responded.

"Where are you from?" she asked me.

"I am from Lwów in Poland."

"How are you surviving in this place?"

"Not too good." My answer was truthful.

She looked around this time, "Come and see me in my block during lunchtime."

"I will." I looked around. The Greeks stared at us with surprise but since they did not understand a word, they carried out their grueling work.

She turned and went away. This was the first time I had actually talked to a female since my arrest. I closed my eyes for a second. The danger in this situation was obvious. Here I was fighting for my survival, not knowing in the morning if I would last until evening, desperately trying not to join the ranks of the Mussulmans. And here, this lovely creature had invited me for lunch!

Since this brief conversation was so unexpected and almost surreal, I looked for some proof that I was not dreaming, that this was still Birkenau. I turned around and looked north. Crematoria II and III were blasting full speed. Red and yellow flames roared from both chimneys. Now I did not have any doubts. This was still the Birkenau extermination camp. I was curious and excited as I went to see my new friend during lunchtime.

"My name is Vera and I am from Propad," she said. "I came here last year with one of the first transports. If you can stay for a few minutes, I will get you a bowl of soup."

I was impressed and embarrassed. "Thank you. My name is Janusz."

She brought me a bowl of soup. It was not regular camp soup, watery and tasteless. This was fat, tasty, solid potato soup with pieces of meat. I looked at her with surprise.

"Oh, we cook our own soup with the Blockältester on this block. Don't worry, we are not stealing from anybody. She has friends in "Canada" and they send her food from the transports." Then she added: "Relax and eat your soup. My friends are on the lookout."

I was puzzled. I was almost certain that with my worn-out jacket, striped blue-and-white pants, shaven head, and tired and exhausted looks, I was not the most attractive male among my *Kommando* friends. There were a number of electricians parading all the time around the women's blocks. Most of them were low numbers, well dressed in custom-tailored, striped jackets, and had excellent connections with SS guards. They were trading and organizing all the time, smuggling items from "Canada" and offering women functionaries various gifts and promises.

Vera was young and attractive and I had nothing to offer. After lunch, I asked her, "Why me? I can't do much for you. I just arrived and I am a millionaire."

She smiled: "Remember that I have been here for a long time. The camp makes you a good judge of character. You look honest and decent and you are too new here to be cynical and calculating." Then she smiled, "I like tall men. I would like you to be my friend."

I was flattered. "Sure, I am really pleased that I met you. I hope we can continue this friendship after we leave this camp."

Her smile was melancholic. "Perhaps we will. I have been here too long not to be aware of what is going on." She pointed toward the crematoria chimneys on the horizon. Yellow and red fire was blasting from both smokestacks.

"Vera, you never know what is going to happen in the future and you can't give up under any circumstances." I tried to be reassuring.

"Jonas"—as she called me—"I am too tired after almost two years in Birkenau to talk about this. One day this camp may disappear and nobody will miss us."

I saw that she was really serious. "Vera, don't talk nonsense. I will visit you in Propad after the war."

She smiled this time. "My mother won't like it." Then she added calmly, "If she is still alive. She always wanted me to marry a Jewish doctor in Propad."

The end of the lunch period was officially announced by the Capo's whistle as he chased the Greeks back to their workstations.

"Thanks for the soup." I waved to Vera: "I will see you tomorrow." I was puzzled and pleasantly surprised by my encounter with Vera. For the first time since my arrest, I started looking forward to tomorrow. I was not worried about being cheated, exploited, or taken advantage of. I wondered as I kept digging, "Is this being homesick? Does she remind me of Emmy?" I had no answer.

"Faster, Faster," said the Capo as he ran after a few of the workers with his stick. Some of the Greeks were still finishing their lunch. They licked their bowls and always looked for an opportunity to organize or trade for more food.

The SS Kommandoführer looked on indifferently from a distance. His sarcastic smile indicated clearly that he was disgusted with the animal-like behavior of the inferior race. He was both amused and angered by the Capo's performance and he barked in his Bavarian German, "Capo, get your house in order before I take care of you." We all started grading the soil for the new barracks.

Like everybody else, I was so absorbed in the act of survival every day from 4 A.M. until "lights out" at 9 P.M. that I hardly noticed the changing seasons. Days were gradually getting shorter. A westerly wind was bringing fresh but cold air. One could feel the changing weather especially in the grayness of the daybreak, when we were getting ready for the long and painful workday. We gulped our morning "coffee" and ran after the roll call to look for our *Kommando*. I silently wondered during morning roll call: "What is going to happen to us when it starts snowing?" The idea of facing a cold winter here was depressing and scary. We were neither dressed nor equipped to face a rainy November and snowy December, let alone January, with snow storms and freezing temperature. Even now in October, there were a lot of prisoners walking without shoes. Work under a roof was a priceless commodity, sought by everybody through friends, connections, bribes, and intrigues.

I decided to talk to Toni and see if there was a chance to change my *Kommando*. However, I was not absolutely certain that I wanted to do this, since my visits with Vera meant a lot to me and every day I anticipated talking with her during lunch time. At the same time, I recognized that the instinct of survival was stronger than an innocent romantic involvement. There was neither resolution nor any future in our friendship. This was just the loneliness of one person looking for sympathy and understanding from another human being. I tried to analyze my feelings, but the continuous fear and the will to survive dwarfed any other commitments or sympathies. This was the wrong time for both of us to be involved in a hopeless experiment in human compassion.

The next day I tried to explain my feelings to Vera. She was sad but very understanding. "Jonas, I have learned to live day by day. I have no idea or any control over my future. The view of the crematoria and my people being murdered without any mercy kill all my initiative and faith in the human race. We don't even like to talk about tomorrow because it may never come. We all live for today." Then she added: "I know that it looks silly to put curtains in our rooms in the blocks when people are dying all around us. But we have been dying for the last two years and we look for reassurances that we are still alive. Since we don't know how long we have to go, we like to enjoy every minute, to exploit every opportunity to pretend life is normal. And if curtains in the windows make us feel better, so what. We are not harming anybody. Perhaps this concern with the betterment of our life in these dreadful circumstances keeps us sane in a world of madness."

She had tears in her eyes. I did not know how to respond, so I kept quiet, thinking, "She is very mature and responsible for her age. Perhaps, after two years in Birkenau, we are all going to be young-old people with the maturity of our grandparents and expectations of small children."

My contacts with Vera had reflected my need for diversion from everyday problems and disasters. These meetings were, if not the highlight of my day, certainly the most pleasant and memorable experience. Of course, I had to be careful, since getting close to women was a capital offense for men prisoners. Usually some of the girls in her block maintained watch while I ate. In spite of restrictions and very strict regulations, contacts between working men and some of the women were an everyday event. The search for understanding, sympathy, or even love was stronger in Birkenau than fear of punishment, "sports," or detention in the Auschwitz bunker. At one point, I wanted to kiss and hug Vera, or cry with her, if this would only help us. I could not do anything. There were hundreds of people around us. Her friends the Stubendiensts looked at me and my high number with suspicion and cold indifference. My Greeks, with no understanding of our conversation, looked at Vera as an opportunity to get extra food.

That evening I marched with a heavy heart to the Men's Camp. The Capo screamed: "Left, right . . . one, two, three." I had a hard time concentrating on marching in step with the music. Witek whispered to me, "Pay attention or you will get all of us in trouble." As we passed the gate, I noticed a large number of SS personnel near entrance to the SS duty barracks. The Lagerführer was standing among his staff. That evening roll call was unusually long. We stood and stood in formation between the barracks and waited for the SS Blockführer to arrive. Weak and sick prisoners, after a day's hard work, looked around for a chance to rest or sit down. This was not permitted and we supported each other, standing and waiting to be counted. Then, from a distance, I saw a group of SS men walking along the main street toward our block. The SS Rapportführer, accompanied by four SS Blockführers, was making his way in our direction. They slowly bypassed other Blockältesters and were getting closer and closer to us.

Stanek, as usual, stood on the main street waiting for the SS Blockführer to appear for a roll call. As the dignitaries came close to our block, he turned around and faced us: "*Heftlinge—Mutzen ab* " he called. The SS Rapportführer stopped in front of Stanek and talked to him briefly. Stanek turned around toward our formation and called a number. From the first row of the group a middle-aged man took one step forward. I was standing in the last row. From the distance, together with the rest of the inmates, we watched carefully what was happening.

The SS Rapportführer stopped in front of the inmate and, without saying a word, hit him with an open fist. The victim, surprised by this vicious and unexpected attack, tried to protect his head. After a heavy blow in the groin he fell on the ground still trying to protect his head from future attacks. As he lay on the ground, the other SS Blockführers continued to kick him rapidly in the groin and hit him with heavy sticks. All of this was happening in front of the whole formation standing at attention. The Schreiber, second in command, was visibly shaken, white and trembling. Two SS Blockführers pulled the inmate to his feet. "You traitor, we will teach you a lesson." SS Rapportführer yelled at him and hit him again on his left cheek. This was so unexpected that the poor man did not know what was going on. He still held his hand up to protect his face. One of the SS Blockführers twisted his arms behind him and placed him in a pair of irons. Then, having placed him between the two SS Blockführers, they started dragging him to the main gate.

Inmates standing still in the block formation were silent. The Blockältester took one step forward and turned around: *"Heftlinge—Mutzen auf."* The prisoners covered their heads in a submissive and resigned movement. We knew that this was the last time we would see our comrade.

It took an extra hour to complete evening roll call. As we were going back to barracks, I asked Toni what had happened. He explained to me that a few days ago several prisoners were taken to the bunker at Block 11 in Auschwitz. The majority of arrested prisoners were regular Polish army officers who had organized a secret military group in Birkenau. The victim was a close confidant and friend of Tadeusz Lisowski, whose real name was Palone. Tadeusz was a professional soldier, a captain in the Polish Army. He arrived in Auschwitz from Tarnów jail in June 1940. His number was 391 and in Auschwitz he used to be Capo of the vegetable store. In the camp, he was detained under a false name. He was a real patriot and used his position in the camp to assist less fortunate fellow prisoners. The victim was Tadeusz Palone's contact in Birkenau. Both prisoners used their positions in the camp to carry out underground activities and to organize Polish military resistance movement among Birkenau prisoners. After mass arrests that evening, we suspected that there was an informer on our block. From then on, I was very careful when I talked to strangers. Later, I learned from Toni that most of the leaders of the Polish Union of Military Organizations, twenty-eight men altogether, including Tadeusz Palone, were executed at Block 11 in the old camp in Auschwitz.

I was slowly getting used to the hardships of camp existence, if this was possible. Occasional soup from Witek and a fairly regular lunch at Vera's place helped to control my hunger. I tried hard to maintain both mental and physical discipline and, except for closer friends like Witek, Toni, and Vera, I minded my own business. My colleagues from the bunk lived in their own world and there was a time that we hardly talked to one another.

I looked forward to my secret meetings with Vera, although I was somehow embarrassed about accepting her generous offer of an extra meal. Our backgrounds and upbringing were very different but we managed to find many topics of mutual interest. She was very familiar with German and Polish literature and had a good understanding of life in prewar Poland. Her aunt used to live in Warsaw. Sometimes in the middle of the night, when the snoring of my companions kept me awake, I thought about her and compared her with Emmy or perhaps Anna. I tried to convince myself that if I could think about the opposite sex in my present circumstances, that meant that I was not ready to be depressed, give up, and become a Mussulman.

Toni once told me that in this camp everybody who had enough food and sleep was thinking about women all of the time. From my own observations during work hours, I noted that a longing for companionship, sympathy, or even genuine love played a strong part in relationships between men and women prisoners. It could be true feelings or just an outlet of energy well preserved among camp functionaries. They even had a bordello set up in Auschwitz for the camp aristocracy. Good conduct, hard work, and the approval of camp officials were needed to obtain the necessary passes to visit this establishment.

Just after my arrival at the Men's Camp, I learned from Toni that twice a month, non-Jewish prisoners were allowed to write letters home. This helped to establish an illusion of contact with the outside world. It boosted prisoners' morale and, in many cases, strengthened inmates' will and determination to survive. I decided that the only person I would contact was my grandmother. Her official address was in my Gestapo file. She was an old, harmless widow and I could not see how the Political Department, which was part of the Gestapo organization in Auschwitz, could punish her for my "criminal" and "revolutionary" acts. With Toni's help, I composed my first letter with the mandatory sentence at the beginning in German: "I am well and happy." Later on I mentioned that food parcels are allowed and that I remembered and loved the whole family.

Anxious and full of expectations, I turned over my letter for censorship and approval by camp SS administration. The first parcel arrived four weeks later. After an evening roll call, the Schreiber called me to his room. In a brown cardboard box, opened previously by the censors, I found bread, fat, sausage, and a small cake. I could not believe my eyes. This was not only a necessity, but also almost a luxury, a treat and a ticket to survival. Apart from the illnesses, physical exhaustion, and beatings, hunger was the worst enemy. Tortured and hungry people were dying every day. Food from home was a ray of hope, a sign of independence, and a wonderful change from watery, tasteless camp soup. Furthermore, it offered an opportunity to "organize" and exchange valuable food for the necessities of life in the camp. One could buy everything from underwear to gold watches for a small portion of homemade bread.

After I tried everything and shared my sausages with Toni, I gave the Schreiber my package for safekeeping in the block food store. This was the only safe place for keeping food parcels. Since starving prisoners were willing to do anything to steal food, food storage in the block was well guarded all day by Stubendiensts and the Schreiber.

My situation changed considerably for the better. Having decent food, I could use my camp portions to organize many essential items to improve my comfort and appearance. Using my daily portion of bread as the established and acceptable camp currency, I bought a better jacket, a new pair of pants, and new underwear. Most of the items were available on the black market from "Canada" men who collected and sorted all luggage left by Jewish transports at the railroad ramp.

I looked better and felt better. The next day I carried some of the food to Vera. There was a risk of a search at the gate but I hid small items on my body and we were not searched that time. Vera was pleasantly surprised yet almost disappointed that my dependency on her generosity was coming to an end. I left with her one container of animal fat for cooking her soup and I shared with her my homemade cake. Since I did not bother to collect my official portion of soup from the Capo, I asked Witek to give my portion to one of the older Greeks who worked next to me most of the time. In no time, he came to see me. "Thank you, thank you very much," he repeated in French and looked gratefully at both of us.

After we had a real feast behind Vera's block, guarded by her Stubendiensts, I returned to my *Kommando*. I felt good and looked forward to my "private" dinners, courtesy of my grandmother. There were days when I was amazed how well I adjusted to my life in the unique accommodations of Birkenau's horrors. Rather than plotting ambitious plans for a happy return to normal life after the war, I established for myself short-term goals to be able to survive one day at a time from morning to evening roll calls. I did this because I was too scared and confused to speculate about the future. The flaming chimneys from four crematoria dominated Birkenau's landscape. We could not help wondering when and if our time would come.

I could see that our work in the Women's Camp was coming to an end. Plumbers and electricians were staying behind to complete the job. I asked Witek about our next assignment and even he did not know where we would be going or how soon. I was not really happy with the change since I had looked forward to my lunches with Vera and secret discussions with other women prisoners from the Warsaw transport that I met during my assignment at the Women's Camp. One of them was Maria, who had been in Auschwitz since October 1942. Sometimes, I carried letters or messages back to the Men's Camp. There was a risk involved in case of a search at the gate, but I usually hid the letters in the lining of my hat and I never had any problems. During a search, I kept my hat in my right hand in accordance with camp regulations.

After a few weeks, I knew our routine by heart. Every morning we passed several men's *Kommandos* working along outside the perimeter road. They were digging drainage ditches. The Birkenau camp was located between two rivers, the Wisła and Soła. The water level in the area was high. In order to maintain healthy and sanitary working conditions, urgent improvements to an inefficient drainage system were a top priority. The work was demanding and all the men worked up to their knees in water. The SS guards stood above the ditches on the edge and watched for marauders and slow workers. Capos ran along the ditches yelling all the time. "Faster . . . Faster!" while waving long, wooden sticks.

One day, on our way to work, as we turned right under the formal entry tower to Birkenau, I noted the men's *Kommando* extending railroad tracks toward Crematoria II and III. The new unloading ramp was to be built along fences enclosing all Men's Camps in section BII and across from the women's compound. Witek made a crude comment, "Look, how good are our SS masters, they try to save the Jews from having a long walk."

I was not happy with Witek's comment but remained silent and wondered, "Are we going to be next after they are through with the Jews?"

I was also not surprised by Witek's comment. When we were all imprisoned behind barbed wires together, facing a mortal enemy and fighting for our lives, Jews, because of Nazi racial policies, were the most obvious victims of SS persecution. They were rounded up in ghettos, transported to camps, selected, and gassed without mercy and without exception. Although officially in April 1943 the policy for gassing of terminally ill non-Jews was discontinued, the gassing and shooting of "political" Poles was still going on in Auschwitz and Birkenau. It was done now in a more selective way, on the basis of real or false accusations of underground activities or hostage situations.

Every month the SS *Polizeistandgericht,* known as Police Summary Court, under the command of SS Obersturmbannführer Mildner, from Katowice, was held in Block 11 in the Auschwitz compound. Hundreds of people accused of working with the Polish underground were brought to the camp from Gestapo prisons in Silesia, sentenced by the SS Court and either executed by the SS Rapportführers or gassed in the crematoria. In addition to the formal court hearings in the presence of the visiting Gestapo officials, the Auschwitz Political Department, jointly with the SS Lagerführers, routinely inspected files of prisoners detained in the bunker of Block 11 for various illegal activities in the camp. Death by shooting against the wall between

Blocks 10 and 11 was a normal outcome of each review. Yet, in spite of a common peril, there were incidents of antagonism, political and national animosities, and anti-Semitism among prisoners.

Since Auschwitz began in 1940 as a concentration camp for Poles, low numbers from the first Polish transports eventually succeeded in achieving important positions. Many of the functionaries like Kaz were compassionate human beings trying to help everyone regardless of race or national origin. But there were also incidents of anti-Semitism among non-Jewish functionaries and strong preferences in helping less fortunate inmates strictly according to national, political, and religious affiliations. Facing extermination and certain death, Jews, who suffered enough under the brutal Nazi regime, looked helplessly and sometimes unsuccessfully to their Aryan brothers for help. Feelings of selfishness, distress, and suspicion were common among the prisoners, and the cruel instinct of survival at any cost showed its ugly face on many occasions.

We passed the workers grading the soil for the future railroad connections, and as we did every morning, turned left and marched through the gate leading to the Women's Camp. On the left side was the old women's section, BIa. On the right side were the new women's quarters, BIb. Straight ahead was a Birkenau bread store currently serviced by forty Russian prisoners of war who were the survivors of the first Russian transport to Auschwitz. On the misty fall mornings, watchtowers that hovered above buildings and people took on a ghostlike appearance.

In late October, all prisoners in all camps celebrated SS Oberscharführer Schillinger's sudden and unexpected death in Crematorium II. A Jewish woman had killed him. However, we had to pay a price for her courageous act. The following evening, in retaliation, SS guards shot several people in Birkenau at random from their watchtowers. The story was going around in blocks that they had killed twelve people and wounded forty.

As the SS Kommandoführer of the men's kitchen in Birkenau, Schillinger had been a mean and tough supervisor. Later on, he was in charge of leading Jewish transports from the railroad ramp to the crematoria. The woman who shot Schillinger also wounded SS Unterscharführer Emmerich, who eventually recovered but was left with a crippled leg for the rest of his life. I could not help but admire this desperate and courageous act of defiance by a brave woman.

There were many rumors circulating among inmates about Schillinger's death. The next day, Toni came to see me and told me in detail what he heard from his friend who had good and reliable connections with the *Sonderkommando*. On the evening of October 23, a large convoy of trucks arrived at the courtyard of Crematorium II. The Lagerführer of Birkenau men's camp, SS

Obersturmführer Schwarzhuber, the SS Lagerarzt, Dr. Thilo, and other SS officials in charge of the crematoria met the convoy. After unloading people
from the trucks, Schwarzhuber made a polite speech welcoming the new arrivals and informed them that they would have to go through the disinfection
process before departing for Switzerland. This was a special transport of
Jews from Bergen-Belsen who had paid the Gestapo a large sum of money for
visas to South America. People in this transport were convinced that, in accordance with the Nazis promises, they were already on their way from Germany to the neutral Switzerland. They considered the disinfection process a
part of normal immigration procedures.

From the courtyard the special transport was led to the underground facility. In the changing room downstairs, they were gently encouraged by the
SS men to get ready for disinfection and showers. Some of the people undressed and left for the adjoining room which was equipped with shower-
heads; the remaining crowd hesitated, stopped undressing, showed signs of
alarm, and tried to delay the process. The SS men were slowly losing their patience. Very soon, equipped with sticks, the SS men pushed stragglers, in an
unusually brutal way, to undress quickly and move swiftly to the next room.
The people, fearful for their future, still ignored the threats. The SS men
shouted obscenities and struck at the crowd with sticks. Quickly, a few heads
had been injured so blood was flowing, and the victims were completely terrorized with a powerful kicking and beating by the agitated SS guards. Reluctantly, they began to undress. The SS men stopped the beating and
leeringly watched the undressing women. Their attention was drawn to a
strikingly beautiful young woman with black hair, elegantly dressed, who
was gracefully removing her clothes. When she removed her blouse, half-
naked, she suddenly struck SS Oberscharführer Quakernack with her shoe
and quickly grabbed his pistol from the already opened holster. She looked
around and shot the nearest SS man, Oberscharführer Schillinger, who fell to
the concrete floor.

Pandemonium broke out in the changing room. A crowd waved and
pushed against the wall. The remaining SS men grabbed Schillinger and
pulled him to the door. Another shot was fired. One of the helpers, SS Unterscharführer Emmerich, was shot in his leg. The door was bolted and lights
went off. There was a commotion among SS troops in the crematorium
courtyard. Very soon SS Kommandant Höss arrived at the crematorium and
instantly ordered the shooting of all Jews left in the undressing room. The
part of the transport previously undressed and gathered in the gas chamber
was treated with the usual portion of Zyklon B that was dropped through
the specially constructed vents in the crematorium roof. All of the Jews died
instantly. The *Sonderkommando* men watched in silent grief the tragedy and

the heroism of their own people. Toni's story was shocking and inspiring. Would we ever have enough courage to rebel against our SS masters in BIId?

One day, on a chilly and misty November morning, as we were trying to form our *Kommando* after roll call, Witek greeted me with bad news, "We are not going to FKL any more," he said. "Today we will start working in Mexico." I was deeply upset.

For the past several weeks, I had managed to organize my life around my most essential needs. Parcels from home helped me to survive hunger. Work with Witek was hard but bearable. Seeing Vera every day added a human touch to the brutal and inhuman camp environment. I felt that if things wouldn't change, I might have a good chance of surviving. The war was not going well for the Germans, and we secretly counted days and months waiting and hoping for an early and miraculous liberation.

After learning from Witek about our new job location I realized that I would not be able to see Vera any more. I would miss her company and her "homemade" tasty soups. Secretly, I was ashamed to admit that, although company and conversations were of great importance to maintain sanity, the food and secret lunches were added attractions to our brief and sincere acquaintance. I was so used to seeing her every day that the unexpected and sudden change in my routine made me sad and frustrated. I did not even have a chance to say good-bye to her and make plans for possible meetings in the future.

By now, I understood that this was a normal course of events and that stability had no place in Birkenau. The camp's administrative principles were based on uncertainty, terror, drastic changes and surprises, including sudden transfers to other camps, and far from least, the brutality of SS masters.

The low numbers and functionaries, powerful and influential in Auschwitz and Birkenau, were reduced to nothing when transferred to other camps and had to start their careers from the very beginning. It was a well-known fact among Birkenau camp inmates that Buchenwald's "red" functionaries, mostly German communists, could not stand functional prisoners from other concentration camps and tried to make life for Birkenau transfers as miserable as they possibly could.

Staszek, who worked with me in Witek's *Kommando* and who spent almost two years in Buchenwald, confirmed the fact and shared with us horrible stories of cruel treatment of the Polish prewar intelligentsia at the hands of "red" Capos that he witnessed as a prisoner in Buchenwald.

As I was learning more about the camp's way of life and death, common sense encouraged me to accept the changes and carry out my fight to survive regardless of circumstances. There were days that I felt deeply sorry for myself.

I could not understand the cold-blooded and systematic SS practice of gassing innocent people by the thousands every day. As I occasionally watched the Jewish transports entering the crematoria, I had a strong feeling of guilt about my comrades' indifference to other people's suffering.

Now the sudden change in my work assignment made me fully aware of my unimportance and insignificance in the deadly game played by the SS masters.

I walked slowly behind Witek, deep in my own thoughts, occasionally missing a step. Witek turned around and impatiently touched my shoulder. "Shape up, Janusz! Every time you have a personal problem, you mess up our marching formation. You may get all of us in trouble with the SS Kommandoführer."

I nodded. He was right and I picked up the rhythmic beat of the camp orchestra as we were marching through the gate. I tried to march briskly, watch my steps and look calm and composed.

"One, two, three . . . *Mutzen ab*" screamed the Capo.

As we entered "Mexico," I looked around. This was the site of a future Section C of the camp to be constructed as a mirror image of the recently completed Section B. At this time, it was a deserted area partially enclosed with a temporary fence and a few uncompleted blocks at the far end of the compound. Section C was to be located across the street from Section B, with the SS headquarters and SS barracks at the east end of the street and Crematoria IV and V at the opposite side. We were told by the inmates employed in the SS Central Construction Office that the camp would be ready by early spring 1944 to receive Jewish transports from Hungary and other Western European countries. It looked like a lot of effort and sweat would be required to meet that deadline. The rainy autumn weather and anticipation of a harsh winter after snow in December and January would make the schedule almost impossible.

Every morning after our arrival, Witek distributed tools to all workers and, in squads of ten, we prepared ground for foundations and footings of the future barracks. A number of other *Kommandos* worked feverishly with us on the "Mexico" site. After surveyors completed the measurements and layout for the main roads, the Highway *Kommando* was busy constructing connecting streets. Another *Kommando* was excavating around the camp perimeter to provide a proper drainage system and reduce the level of underground water. As expected, "Mexico" 's site, being close to the confluence of the Wisła and Soła rivers, represented an engineering challenge to provide decent sanitary, working, and living conditions for thousands of future prisoners.

All day long, including lunchtime, we were exposed to dismal weather conditions, and I noted that the Greeks could not handle the long working hours, the wind and cold, and the accelerated tempo of work. Every evening our *Kommando* carried at least twenty sick prisoners on stretchers. Colds, pneumonia, high fever, not to mention occasional typhus cases, slowly decimated our ranks. Witek was constantly looking for replacements. I, in turn, was desperately looking for another *Kommando*. The all-day exposure to rough weather and the accelerated tempo of work required unusual physical strength and an almost superhuman resistance to the toughest working conditions. I practically lived on the food received weekly from my grandmother and considered myself extremely lucky. Jews and Russians, however, were not allowed to get any help from the outside. The number of Mussulmans was growing every day within our working group, and fear of contagious diseases was constantly on my mind.

With the food I received in my parcels, my "organizational" abilities allowed me to exchange official daily bread rations for the most essential and otherwise unavailable items that helped me to maintain my personal hygiene and acceptable sanitary conditions. In order to protect myself from catching typhus or any kind of contagious disease, I tried to change my underwear once a month, watched carefully for lice and, in spite of cold weather, tried to wash every day. This was easier said than done, since both lavatories and latrine barracks were always overcrowded. The little free time we had in the evening was not sufficient to spend hours waiting in line to use the sanitary facilities. Occasionally, a small bribe to the Scheissmeister, or washroom supervisor, allowed one to beat the crowd.

Dirt and subhuman sanitary conditions were an inseparable part of our daily existence. Sicknesses from typhus to dysentery, from simple colds to incurable pneumonia, took a daily toll on many prisoners, regardless of their position in the camp hierarchy. Mussulmans and newly arrived transports were more susceptible to the infectious diseases devastating the ranks of all prisoners.

Better jobs and better living conditions offered some protection to camp functionaries, but the deadly spread of typhus found its victims among senior prisoners and touched even SS personnel and their families. There was gossip circulating around the camp that last year SS Rapportführer Palitzsch's wife died of typhus. Toni told me this with a sarcastic smile and said, "It couldn't happen to a nicer guy."

But when death among functionaries and SS ranks was almost an exception, the ordinary prisoners were dying in hundreds. Our ranks were reduced daily by the range of diseases and by the brutal selection of the SS doctors who tried to prevent the spread of the infection by sending all sick Jews to the crematoria. The situation was even worse at the Women's Camp. The SS doctors continuously selected hundreds of sick and fragile Jewish women for gassing. After each final selection, the unlucky victims were locked naked in Block 25 at the Women's Camp BIa and transported during the night in the SS trucks to the crematoria.

The SS Lagerführer declared typhus enemy number one. Every Sunday afternoon was designated for delousing and personal inspection of prisoners' clothes. All this had very little impact on the improvement of sanitary conditions. Lice were part of our lives. Even disinfection in the *Sauna* was unable to kill the insects, which remained alive and active in the disinfected clothes returned to us.

Shortage of drinking water contributed to the spread of infectious diseases. Dysentery, affecting hundreds of inmates, was a result of unsanitary water supplies that came from the primitive and contaminated well. The uncontrollable thirst of exhausted Mussulmans, returning from work every night, was by far stronger than pleas from experienced inmates to stay away from the poisonous water.

The typhus epidemic was a constant companion and deadly threat to all prisoners all the time, regardless of their positions in the camp hierarchy or their functional responsibilities. The prospect of sudden illness leading to a trip to the crematorium hung above our heads all the time. Now, with the sudden change in my *Kommando* assignment and more demanding working conditions, my resistance to infectious disease and my stability were increasingly challenged.

One evening, Toni stopped at my bunk to bring me up to date with what was going on. Apparently the story was circulated among prisoners that Höss, the first Kommandant and organizer of Auschwitz, had left for a new job in Berlin and been replaced by SS Oberstumbannführer Liebehenschel, who had the reputation of being less brutal.

Prisoners in the bunker at Block 11 in Auschwitz were suddenly released back to their camps. An expectation of better working conditions was floating among the inmates. The new Kommandant divided the camp into three independent jurisdictions. Under the new organization, Auschwitz I, organized in 1940 by Höss, remained the Main Camp. Birkenau was renamed Auschwitz II, and SS Sturmbannführer Hartjenstein was appointed as the new Lagerführer of all camps in Birkenau. All the remaining smaller subcamps such as Buna, Jawiszów, and others, were combined as Auschwitz III, with headquarters in Monowice, under command of the SS Hauptsturmführer Schwarz.

All of this, however, did not mean much to me. I saw Höss several times from a distance in his chauffeur-driven car or walking with his dog and surrounded by his staff when he visited the Men's Camp. His was a strange, unfamiliar face to most of us. I was much more concerned about avoiding Kurpanik, Baretzki and others. Confrontation with one of them usually ended with a brutal beating or the fatal shooting of a prisoner. There were also some changes at the lower administrative level among our oppressors. Palitzsch, a cold-blooded murderer, after being investigated by the Political Department for corruption, left Auschwitz for another camp in Czechoslovakia. Baretzki was transferred from Quarantine to the Men's Camp as the SS Blockführer. With the abundance of wealth brought to the camp by the Jewish transports, most of the guards, corrupted by greed, were indifferent to our living conditions. Secretly, they looked for opportunities for personal enrichment by trading gold and diamonds with "Canada" prisoners, though publicly, they were full of contempt for their "subhuman" victims and trading partners.

At the beginning of December, in spite of the continued heavy rain mixed with light snow, we were forced to work long hours each day. Half of the Greeks were sick with pneumonia. In the evening they walked like skeletons, holding one another, thin, exhausted, with swollen legs and sore feet. Every step back to the camp was a painful effort. Too weak to argue among themselves, with sad eyes they begged silently for mercy and for relief.

The *Kommando* was slowly changing from what it used to be, a reasonably efficient working unit, into a gathering of ghostly figures. Witek tried to help me, but he was also under pressure to exploit prisoners. As the word about inhumane treatment and bad working conditions was spreading among prisoners in the Men's Camp, it was more and more difficult for Witek to gather the necessary number of inmates every day to staff the full *Kommando*. Every morning, Witek asked me to guard the new prisoners forcibly selected and assigned to our *Kommando*. I owed him a lot and he was my good friend. Nevertheless, I could not see myself walking with a stick and screaming at terrified and frightened Greeks. I refused the assignment and this strained our friendship. Now, I knew that I had to look for a different *Kommando* as soon as possible.

Christmas was coming, but none of us had any time or interest in celebrations. Only a letter from my grandmother and a more generous than usual food parcel reminded me of the coming holiday season. Continuous light snow in December made our work difficult and dangerous. The ground was hard and covered with patches of wet snow. My warm underwear, which I obtained from "Canada" boys for my grandmother's butter, and my warm sweater, which I hid under my shirt, did not prevent me from catching a bad cold. I could not get rid of a persistent cough, which was getting worse every day. My appetite was poor and I thought I had a fever. A few days before Christmas, as I was digging frozen ground, I felt really bad. I stopped work and looked around. Suddenly the whole camp whirled around me. I closed my eyes. My heart was pounding and as I looked around for help suddenly I fainted.

When I opened my eyes, I was lying on the ground behind the tool shed, shivering. My old Greek friend who used to eat my official soup in the Women's Camp was kneeling by my side. "*Monsieur*—very sick" he was telling me. I touched my head. It was hot and perspiring. At the same time, I was trembling with cold and my hands were freezing. If this was the beginning of typhus, it was the beginning of my end in Birkenau. If it was pneumonia, then I might have a chance to recover. I looked for red spots on my body, but could find none. Perhaps I had just a very bad cold? With my friend's help, I managed to march with the *Kommando* back to the camp.

I went to see Toni, who took me to see the nurse. They checked my temperature. It was very high, and I was still shaking. Toni had a conference with the Schreiber: "Tomorrow, after morning roll call we will try to move you to the hospital. But we need the certificate from one of the prisoner doctors. I will see what can be done to avoid SS exterminators." He left the block, but was back in a few minutes. "We have to bribe one of the inmate doctors. It will cost you one pound of your grandmother's bacon." I nodded in agreement. I felt that my fever was rising rapidly. Shivering all night on my bunk, I waited hopefully for my transfer to the hospital. At the end of the morning roll call, the Schreiber called a few numbers, including mine. After checking and verifying our names and numbers, he led a small group of sick, shivering prisoners wrapped in thin blankets toward the main gate. Since I did not plan to return to my block, I carried with me my brown parcel full of food. At the gate SS Rapportführer was checking our numbers. "Move" he barked to the Schreiber. After we collected our SS escort, we marched slowly, still wrapped in our blankets, towards BIIf, Birkenau Men's Hospital. I walked right behind two nurses who carried a sick prisoner on a stretcher. Occasionally, I touched the stretcher to keep my balance. Although the hospital was very close, right behind the Gypsy Camp, I had the feeling that we were walking for hours. The food parcel was heavy and inconvenient to carry, but I held on to it for dear life, knowing very well that this could be my ticket to recovery. After a short but strenuous march, I was totally exhausted when we stopped in front of the hospital entrance gate.

First day as a cadet at the military academy in Lwów, 1938. Courtesy of the author.

Manor house in Matczyn, 1942. Courtesy of the author.

Working in Potoczek, 1942. Courtesy of the author.

Lieutenant Czarnota-Szaruga and his staff,
1944. Courtesy of Dr. Jerzy Krzyżanowski.

Lieutenant Czarnota-Szaruga and his partisans, 1944. Courtesy of Dr. Jerzy
Krzyżanowski.

Central watchtower and main entrance to Birkenau, 1945. Courtesy of Auschwitz-
Birkenau State Museum (Państwowe Muzeum).

Central bathhouse in Birkenau, 1945. Courtesy of Auschwitz-Birkenau State Museum (Państwowe Muzeum).

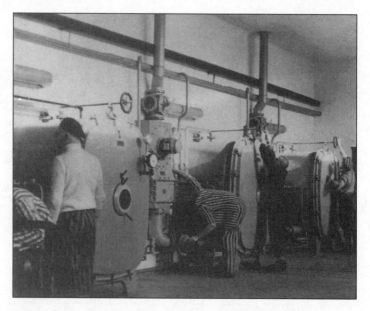

Steam room in the bathhouse in Birkenau, 1944. Courtesy of Auschwitz-Birkenau State Museum (Państwowe Muzeum).

Prämienauszahlung für den Abschnitt B II/d   den 27.Juli 1944.

Blockpersonal:
Blockälteste.Blockschreiber,Blockfrisöre
Blockstubendienste.

Lagerältester........................5.-
Rapportschreiber.....................5.-
Arbeitsdienst 1......................5.-
Arbeitseinsatz.......................5.-
Aufsicht.............................5.-
Arbeitsdienst 2......................4.-
Prämienverwaltung....................4.-
O.Capo Kontrolle.....................4.-
Lagercapo............................4.-
R.Sch.Frank..........................3.=
                                    44.-
...erwehrcapo........................4.-
Feuerwehr............................25.-
Häftl.Schreibstube...................30.-
Postpaketstelle......................24.-
Lagertischler........................28.-
Kapellmeister........................3.-
Lagerkapelle.........................33.-
Capo Rollwagen.......................3.-
Capo Wäscherei.......................3.-
Wäscherei............................10.-
Capo Holzhof.........................2.-
Wasserpumpen.........................14.-
Lagerarzt BII/d......................3.-
Pflegerpersonal......................13.-
Zahnärzte............................6.-
Lagerältester FL.....................3.-
O.Capo Desinfekt.....................3.-
Entwesungszug........................14.-
Kalfaktoren..........................10.-
Reiniger Block 2.....................2.=
                                   230.-

Block 3.............................6.-
Block 4.............................6.-
Block 5.............................6.-
Block 6.............................6.-
Block 7.............................6.-
Block 8.............................6.-
Block10.............................6.-
Block 12............................6.-
Block 13............................6.-
Block 14............................6.-
Block 16............................6.-
Block 18............................6.-
Block 20............................6.-
Block 22............................6.-
Block 24............................6.-
Block 25............................6.-
Block 26............................6.-
Block 27............................6.-
Block 28............................6.-
Block 29............................6.-
Block 30............................6.-
Block 31............................6.-
Block 32............................6.-
                                 138.-RM.
Lagermaler..........................6.-

Für die Richtigkeit der Prämienauszahlung
in Werthöhe von 418.-RM,

Der 1. Rapportführer des Kl.Au.II

SS.- Oberscharführer.

List of functional prisoners who received bonuses in Birkenau, 1944. Courtesy of
Auschwitz-Birkenau State Museum (Państwowe Muzeum).

Preparation for selection of Jewish transport in Birkenau, 1944. Courtesy of Auschwitz-Birkenau State Museum (Państwowe Muzeum). The man on the far right has been identified by prisoners of Birkenau as SS Rottenführer Stefan Baretzki.

Dr. Heinz Thilo selecting Jews at the railroad platform in Birkenau, 1944. Courtesy of Auschwitz-Birkenau State Museum (Państwowe Muzeum).

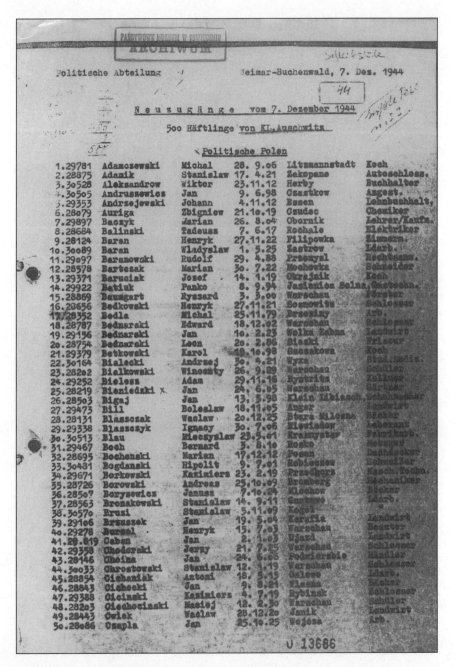

Prisoner transfer list to Buchenwald, page 1, 1944. Courtesy of Auschwitz-Birkenau State Museum (Państwowe Muzeum).

351.28861	Blotwinski	Klemens	23.11.24	Częstochowa	Buchbinder
352.30087	Smacki	Michal	28. 8.12	Nagowice	Ldarb.
353.29658	Smagacz	Marian	26. 8.12	Lwow	Beamter
354.30103	Sobala	Stanislaw	28. 1.16	Jedrzejow	Friseur
355.28075	Sobczak	Jozef	19. 3.09	Ludwikowo	Ldarb.
356.30075	Socha	Henryk	15. 7.15	Kielce	Friseur
357.28161	Sosnowski	Jozef	13.11.16	Brzeszcze	Schlosser
358.28927	Sosnowski	Vaclaw	19. 6.00	Szelkow	Beamter
359.28247	Sowa	Boguslaw	23. 8.14	Strelitz	Mechaniker
360.28062	Spiewak	Marjan	14. 2.28	Wolfsdorf	Kutscher
361.29282	Sulich	Stanislaw	8. 5.12	Warschau	Kraftf.
362.29258	Surowiak	Julian	1. 2.14	Bazanowka	Ldarb.
363.30608	Swiergala	Franz	24. 8.85	Wilkowice	Weber/Kutsche
364.28911	Swiergula	Tadeusz	18. 2.03	Laskowa	Landwirt
365.28904	Sywak	Bronislaw	27. 6.19	Wieniawka	Tischler
366.28109	Szablowski	Zygmunt	13.10.19	Wasewo Kol.	Gärtner
367.30525	Szafranski	Stefan	14. 8.26	Warschau	Ldarb.
368.30202	Szaran	Witold	10. 7.17	Blgw	Milobmmbjn
369.29609	Szawlowski	Zbigniew	2. 5.17	Warschau	Arzt
370.29982	Szczepanski	Zygmunt	21. 4.21	Bartodzieje	Koch
371.28107	Szlacheta	Wladyslaw	27.10.81	Lasy	Arb.
372.30008	Sztark	Marek	3. 6.15	Torahek	Beamter
373.30262	Sswaja	Jan	23.11.22	Pilica	Schmied
374.28668	Szybinski	Stefan	25. 7.21	Warschau	Schäler
375.29297	Szyc	Piotr	14. 7.95	Warschau	Glaser
376.28122	Szydlowski	Wladyslaw	3. 1.11	Wiszniew	Kraftf.
377.30072	Szymorek	Feliks	10. 9.21	Zelow	Autoschloss.
378.29285	Schary	August	23.11.98	Poremba	Heizer
379.29494	Schikora	Jozef	14. 3.07	Orzegow	Koch
380.29093	Schindler	Wiktor	11. 1.89	Podwoloczyska	Beamter
381.28833	Schmidt	Emilian	23. 7.02	Zdunska Wola	Weber
382.28375	Schulz	Franciszek	17.9.99	Frankenau	Buchhalter
383.29751	Stachowiak	Andrzej	24.11.18	Wrzesnczow	Fleischer
384.28809	Stan	Stefan	3. 7.96	Warschau	Schlosser
385.28214	Staszkiewicz	Jozef	14. 9.11	Bolmin	Schuster
386.28184	Stefanowicz	Jan	29. 1.09	Warschau	Buchhalter
387.30191	Stolarski	Gustaw	2. 4.19	Janow	Schlosser
388.30492	Stolarski	Stanislaw	20.11.93	Wlaznow	Schneider
389.29272	Strojnowski	Janusz	28. 7.25	Sarny	Student
390.28890	Stryj	Franz	5. 1.12	Ruda	Kaufm.Angest.
391.30338	Strynkowski	Jozef	20. 2.05	Warschau	Drucker
392.28328	Tabor	Edward	8. 6.00	Warschau	Buchbinder
393.30047	Tarchalski	Bogdan	11. 3.99	Furmanow	Maschinist
394.30410	Tarkowski	Roman	30. 9.12	Tomaszow Maz.	Elektriker
395.28974	Teklowicz	Marian	4.12.10	Posen	Zimmermaler
396.30088	Tomaszewski	Czeslaw	16. 5.16	Baltimore/USA.	Bäcker
397.30488	Tomaszewski	Jozef	13. 3.05	Gorki	Landwirt
398.29147	Topszewski	Zygmunt	11. 3.14	Warschau	Fabrikarb.
399.28892	Trzeciakowski	Czeslaw	29. 4.01	Posen	Kaufmann
400.28886	Trzeciakowski	Janusz	30. 4.25	Schroda	Schüler
401.28148	Turek	Stanislaw	7. 9.23	Wodzislaw	Gärtner
402.29502	Tyszka	Kazimierz	25. 8.25	Andrzejki	Schneider
403.30031	Tytyk	Eugen	13.12.20	Forombka	Angest.
404.28350	Uchman	Stanislaw	1. 3.15	Aleksandrow	Mechaniker
405.29151	Urbaniak	Stanislaw	5. 5.10	Zbara	Landwirt
406.30408	Wadiak	Wasyl	27. 4.91	Szklary	Beamter
407.30196	Walas	Franciszek	17.4.09	Janina	Landwirt
408.29960	Walentynowicz	Felix	23. 5.08	Krakau	Pfleger
409.30195	Walutek	Marian	26.12.21	Oseladz	Angest.
410.28863	Wapinski	Wieslaw	8.11.26	Warschau	Kraftf.Mechan.

ᴜ 13692

Prisoner transfer list to Buchenwald, page 7, 1944. Courtesy of Auschwitz-Birkenau State Museum (Państwowe Muzeum).

Ovens in Buchenwald crematorium, postwar photograph.
Courtesy of the author.

Entrance to tunnels at Jonastal Valley near
Ohrdruf, postwar photograph. Courtesy of
the author.

General Eisenhower accompanied by Generals Bradley and
Patton examine the corpses of prisoners executed by the SS
in Ohrdruf, 1945. Courtesy of National Archives and U.S.
Holocaust Memorial Museum.

American troops inspecting SS atrocities in Ohrdruf, 1945. Courtesy
of National Archives and U.S. Holocaust Memorial Museum.

CHAPTER SEVEN

Dr. Thilo's Hospital

I CROSSED the hospital main gate with a heavy heart. The Men's Hospital in Birkenau had a reputation as both a killing ground and a waiting room for the crematoria. The services and facilities were very primitive. Without medications and drugs and hardly any medical equipment, the hospital staff—doctors, nurses, and orderlies—had very limited means of providing proper medical care to sick prisoners. They tried, but people were dying all the time, either from lack of medications or because of the advanced stages of their illnesses. Selections of sick and terminal Jewish patients were held continuously under the stern supervision of SS doctors. There were also many rumors about experimental facilities and medical research performed by SS physicians on prisoners in different parts of Auschwitz and Birkenau at specially designated blocks. The frequent killings of sick prisoners by phenol injections in Block 20, in the old camp in Auschwitz, was a well-known "secret" among the inmates in all Birkenau camps. Injections were administered to the victims' hearts by the SS orderlies, who were aided in those deadly tasks by the group of degenerated prisoners working in the hospital as nurses. In the Women's Camp BIa in Birkenau, a special Block 30 was designated as the experimental laboratory for sterilization of Jewish women. Based on stories circulating among prisoners, hospital facilities in Auschwitz and Birkenau did not offer much encouragement or hope of recovery to sick prisoners.

Passing through the hospital gate, I looked for familiar faces among the nursing orderlies but could not find anybody. As sick as I was, I was wondering silently if I had made the right decision to enter the prisoners' hospital in Birkenau. At this point, there was no way back.

We passed the guard post and a number of small but sturdy buildings and entered a large washroom. Our group was ordered to undress and after a quick shower, all of us were given paper shirts and told to wait for the SS doctor. I asked one of the orderlies what we were waiting for. He told me that the SS Lagerarzt, who was in charge of the hospital, was concerned that too many healthy inmates were admitted for treatment. Because of this, he personally wanted to know what kinds of admission standards prisoner-doctors were practicing.

In the cold winter weather, I shivered in my flimsy paper attire. Tired and confused, I was also anxious to quickly pass the admission process and looked forward to rest in a regular bed. One of the prisoner-doctors examined me and prepared a written diagnosis. The SS Obersturmführer entered the room and, after a brief conference with the Lagerältester, senior prisoner-doctor, ordered each of us to take off his shirt and walk in front of him. Then he looked at each inmate and the chart submitted by the prisoner-doctor before directing the inmate to the left or to the right. I tried to walk briskly, straight and firm, showing signs of vigor and energy. He looked at me, then at my chart, and sent me to the smaller group on the right. The senior prisoner-doctor took my chart, noted my number, and after deciding that I had pneumonia, assigned me to an observation block.

I noted that the majority of Jewish prisoners were sent to the left side and assigned to Block 12. At that time I was not aware if that decision had any significance. Later, I learned that Block 12 was designated for terminally ill Jews. Most of them suffered from incurable dysentery, and were dying every day in large numbers. This was a favorite barrack for frequent and unexpected selections by the SS Lagerarzt. Condemned men lived without proper medication for a short time in terrible conditions, without mattresses or blankets, and usually died in a few days. Every morning corpses of dead prisoners were piled high in front of each block. Block 12, constructed like the prefabricated barracks in the Men's Camp, had a special extension that served as a mortuary, with part of it designated as a primitive and hardly used dissection room. The washroom, officially designated as Block 16, located between Blocks 8 and 10, was also used for holding selected prisoners overnight prior to sending them naked by truck to the crematoria.

Accompanied by the orderly, I entered a large hospital room, full of wooden bunk beds standing close together in order to provide limited circulation space. The orderly told me to climb up to the top level of one of the beds. I reached the top and, surprisingly, found that a tall and thin Greek inmate was resting peacefully on a thin straw mattress. I turned to the orderly: "This bed is already taken." He shrugged his shoulders. "Yes, I know, this is your new partner."

I could not believe that I had to share my bed with another person. The Greek was thin but tall, and his large frame filled most of the bed. I hesitated for a moment. Seeing my indecision, the orderly smiled sarcastically: "If you don't like it, we may send you back to the Men's Camp."

Reluctantly, I climbed into the bed. We lay with our heads at opposite ends. His feet were in front of my face. I noted that my new partner was completely dehydrated. He had hardly any stomach, his skin was wrinkled, and his half-closed eyes were burning with fever. I tried to stay on one side of the bed without touching his body. He opened his eyes, looked at me and made an effort to smile: "Me, Saloniki . . . I am dying," he whispered and closed his eyes again.

In the afternoon, I felt that my fever had returned. My lips were dry and I was thirsty and weak. I tried to attract the nurse's attention. All of the nurses were low numbers, secure in their privileged positions. Some were seeking protection in the hospital from hard labor in field *Kommandos* at the Men's Camp and some were dedicated and compassionate souls trying hard to make life easier for their sick comrades. The job of a nurse was particularly demanding in such primitive conditions, the lack of the most essential medications making the work frustrating and unrewarding. No amount of human attention could overcome the deficiencies of such inadequate medical facilities.

After one week as a new patient with regular supplies of food parcels from home, I received some attention. Nurses were more accommodating, and other patients looked at my food parcels, which I used as a pillow, with envy. When I felt better during the day I exchanged my homemade cookies for bowls of dietetic soup. The food for all the sick prisoners was prepared at the Men's Camp kitchen and brought everyday by a special *Kesselkommando* to the hospital. Władysław Klocek was the Capo. He was friendly and sympathetic to his crew and other inmates. Occasionally, he was able to "organize" a barrel of soup for distribution among the terminally sick patients. There was also a small hospital kitchen in Block 13 preparing dietetic food for German nationals and selected functionaries like doctors and nurses. By exchanging some of the food sent to me by my grandmother, I was able to obtain a bowl of dietetic soup every day from one of the orderlies.

Every afternoon, I was given two aspirins. My fever was slightly reduced, and after two rough weeks in the hospital, I felt better, but my bed partner ate hardly anything. The nurse warned me: "Don't try to be good and feed him. He can't eat and your rich food from home may kill him." Nonetheless, I shared some of my drinking water with the Greek. He whispered occasionally: "*Merci, merci*" and smiled at me. His eyes were always half-closed and glazed; he had an unhealthy pink rash on his cheeks.

"How is he doing?" I asked the nurse. He shrugged.

"He won't make it and it looks like he does not care. All Jews from Greece are dying like flies."

Nights were especially bad. I could not find a decent or comfortable position without touching my Greek bed partner. As he lay motionless and moaning, his skin was burning hot and he could hardly make it to the bathroom. He was so weak that nurses had to carry him from the bed to the nearby latrine. I could see that his condition worsened every day and the sickness was taking over his body. Early in the morning, he waved his arm to me but even this was an effort. Surprisingly, after two weeks we did get used to each other and I was able to maneuver in my bed and find a reasonably comfortable position.

Every bed in the room had two patients. Some of them, sick and exhausted, lay without a sound. Others argued all the time. Being in the prisoners' hospital, we were very much aware that contagious diseases, especially typhus and tuberculosis, had claimed many victims in Birkenau camps since the great epidemic of 1942. I was told that in the Men's Camp a monthly exchange of underwear was now carried out on weekly cycle. Every Sunday, there was a distribution of new shirts and underpants. However, the disinfection process was not very reliable and most of the newly exchanged underwear was full of lice, which survived the chemical treatments.

In January there was a rumor among the orderlies and nurses that the SS Doctor Mengele, Lagerarzt of the Gypsy Camp, was sick with typhus. Panic spread among SS personnel. In our hospital, a special committee was organized headed by the SS Blockführer and several prisoner doctors including the Lagerältester, the Lagercapo, and the Leitenderarzt from the Men's Camp, to monitor the delousing of patients in all barracks.

All sick prisoners, regardless of their condition, were forced to walk naked to the washroom in Block 16. After brief showers and disinfection of our private parts with the special fluid, we were each given a pair of wooden shoes and told to wait in front of our block for the completion of the disinfection. The Desinfektionskommando treated our barrack with Zyklon B canisters, similar to the gas used in the crematoria. Since it takes several hours for the gas to evaporate, we stood silent and naked in the chilly winter morning waiting for permission to enter our ward. I shivered as I held the Greek's arm. He was half-conscious, delirious, and hardly able to stand on his own. Our blankets and shirts were transferred to the recently opened bathhouse at the end of Section BII for disinfection. I looked around and saw many prisoners desperately holding each other and also noted a large number of bodies lying on the ground among our ranks.

It was not even much of a satisfaction that all functionary prisoners, such as doctors, nurses, and orderlies were treated the same way and shivered with us waiting for their clothes. Then some of the more compassionate nurses moved between our lines and tried to encourage us: "Wait . . . Hold on . . . It won't be long." In the afternoon our clothes were returned. New paper shirts were thrown from the truck onto the ground and we had to se-lect whatever was available.

In the late afternoon, our barrack was inspected and declared "clean" by one of the SS Blockführers and we were allowed to go inside. Four of us had to carry the Greek to our bed. I did not feel too well and I was concerned that my fever might return after today's ordeal. Without medication, decent food, or proper medical attention and completely exhausted after disinfection, my Greek companion was slowly sinking into a deep coma. One night I could not sleep. I lay on my bed thinking about happy times in Potoczek. Then, I touched the Greek's foot to move it away from my face. It was cold, so I reached for his arm. It was also cold and lifeless. I tried to shake his hand. His fingers were stiff and frozen. In the middle of the night, I screamed hysteri-cally: *"Fleger* . . . Nurse, nurse, nurse!" The night guard and nurse on duty came, half-asleep, to see me. "What's wrong with you?" he asked me angrily. I pointed to the dead man lying peacefully in my bed and I whispered to the nurse: "Please, take him away. He just died."

The nurse looked at me: "So what? People are dying here every day. You must wait until morning. I can't carry him by myself."

I was perspiring as I climbed out of my bed. "I can't stay with him. Please help me out."

Covered with the blanket that we used to share, I stood and shivered on the concrete floor. "Please let me stay here until you take him away," I begged the nurse.

He nodded his head: "It's okay with me. Use the temporary stretcher standing in the corner until morning roll call. Be quiet and do not disturb anybody else."

"I will, I will, thank you!" I was both sad and grateful that I did not have to share my bed for the rest of the night with my deceased comrade. After his body was removed in the morning, I stretched out on the bed for the first time. It was strange not to see him any more and, in a way, I missed his com-panionship. I did not even know his full name. Occasionally patients from the adjoining room had come to visit him and talked among themselves in their native language. The only part I understood was that his first name was Maurice.

It was an early morning in February when one of the orderlies stuck his head into our ward and screamed: *"Blocksperre!"* I had no idea what he was talking about, but noted that his announcement had a terrific impact on all patients. Only the seriously sick prisoners, half-conscious and almost dying, failed to respond to this call. The majority of recovering patients were really excited. They climbed out of their beds and walked in circles and between beds briskly and energetically. Others were doing vigorous physical exercises. It looked as if they were trying desperately to convince somebody that they were well. I was puzzled and asked one of the nurses: "What's going on?" He looked at me as if I was from a different planet: "Don't you know? This is selection."

Two prisoner-doctors with charts assembled everybody at one end of the room. People who could not walk were told to sit without shirts on their beds. The Lagerältester, Dr. Schuster, walked in accompanied by the Lager-capo. We all now waited for the Lagerarzt SS Obersturmführer, Dr. Heinz Thilo. As he entered the room, accompanied by two SS Sharführers, I recognized him from my admission examination on the first day in the hospital. He was tall, smartly dressed in the SS bluish uniform with the silver insignia on his shoulders. After a brief report from Dr. Schuster, he looked over some charts. All Jews were ordered to form a special line. They went first in front of Dr. Thilo. Then one of the SS men told the rest of us to take off our paper shirts and walk in a single line in front of the doctor. He looked at each person briefly and moved his finger left or right.

The room was silent. One could feel a shadow of death standing behind the doctor who, in a businesslike and impersonal manner, sorted out first the Jewish prisoners into two separate groups. Every time his finger turned left, a shivering chill of death could be seen in the eyes of a victim, the group of which was growing rapidly.

Most of the patients walked looking down with tense fear in their eyes. I was also scared and confused, but my spirit of adventure and my curiosity made me glance at the doctor's face. I expected to see hate and arrogance, rage and contempt for the inferior race. I saw none. As he selected Jewish patients, he was calm, impersonal, and businesslike, moving his finger from left to right. His movements were mechanical and determined. I saw no contempt nor any signs of superiority, just indifference. I walked holding my head up, very brisk and energetic. He sent me to the non-Jewish group on the right.

At the end, he walked in front of the beds to look at the patients seated there. Dr. Schuster was right behind him taking notes. In a few minutes, Dr. Thilo and his staff left the room. Orderlies pushed selected Jewish bedridden patients down to the floor. They could hardly hold their balance. Prisoner doctors called the numbers of prisoners selected by Dr. Thilo to move to Block 12. All of them were Jews. Some of the victims cried, some of them moaned hysterically, but a majority, perhaps too sick to be aware of what was going on, walked silently, resigned to their fate, too weak to express their fear. In a few minutes, the room was half-empty. As I returned to my bed, I noticed many vacant beds around me.

The next day, a new group of patients arrived. I convinced one of the orderlies to let me stay alone in my bed. It took half a pound of butter from my food parcel to accomplish my goal, but it was worth it. My new bed was next to the window.

It took almost ten weeks since my arrival in the hospital before I started to feel better. I had no temperature, my appetite improved and the regular supply of nutritious food in my parcels from home nursed me slowly back to health. Being alone in my bed was a luxury. When I started walking around the room, one of the doctors asked me to help nurses and orderlies take care of other patients. My tasks were simple. Most of the time I assisted orderlies in the distribution and serving of food to very sick patients, and twice a day I helped bedridden prisoners visit washrooms and latrines.

From my window, I could feel the cold March wind penetrating the uninsulated barracks walls. I watched with apprehension as light snow accumulated on the ground. Looking at the floating snowflakes outside my window, I dreaded the time of discharge from the hospital and my inevitable return to the Men's Camp.

I did not know any doctor well enough to ask him directly for a job and an opportunity to stay permanently in the hospital. This decision would require approval from the Lagerältester, who was the senior prisoner-doctor in the men's hospital. In March, Dr. Zenkteller replaced Dr. Schuster and was appointed Lagerältester. One of the orderlies told me that Dr. Zenkteller had been arrested by the Gestapo in Poznań and in September 1941 was transferred to Auschwitz. I tried to avoid him as much as possible. His reputation was questionable and there were many rumors among prisoners about his rough treatment of patients. I was told by many inmates that he was fair, stern and tough, well organized and very authoritarian. I understood from nursing orderlies that he was also a very demanding supervisor and treated some of the younger Jewish doctors with a dose of military discipline. Every time he entered the ward I tried to stay out of his way.

However, I knew Wiktor Sawik well enough, a low number, 2861, who was a professional barber from Warsaw. In 1940, the Gestapo arrested him for his involvement with Polish underground organizations. He was jailed in Pawiak Prison and, in August 1940, transported to Auschwitz. In 1942, Wiktor was transferred from Auschwitz to Birkenau, where he became sick. After recovering from his illness, he was allowed to stay in the hospital and work as a member of *Entwesungskommando*—the delousing squad. In the evening he cut hair and shaved very sick patients. Wiktor and I became good friends. As a low number, he knew quite a few functionaries and he was on very friendly terms with the hospital's Lagercapo. Wiktor also worked as a messenger to coordinate disinfecting activities in Birkenau. This function allowed him to visit all the camps with his SS escort and maintain secret contacts with the camp underground organizations and *Sonderkommando*, which at that time was housed at Block 13 in the Men's Camp.

Sonderkommando was a group of healthy and young Jewish prisoners selected by the SS men and forced to work in the crematoria. They were handling all of the jobs required for extermination and disposal of the condemned victims. This included acceptance of incoming transports, assistance in the undressing of unsuspecting victims in bathrooms adjoining gas chambers, and transport of corpses to the ovens. Prior to cremation, they had to remove hair and inspect all dead bodies for gold, jewelry, and other valuable items hidden by the victims. After the removal of all gold teeth and the cremation of corpses in specially designed furnaces, ashes were disposed of in selected spots or buried within the crematoria compound.

At the beginning, the newly selected Jewish prisoners did not know what kind of work they would be assigned to. By the time they discovered that they had to bury their own brothers and sisters, it was too late to dream about escape. They were well guarded and isolated from the rest of the prisoners. In order to maintain full confidentiality and secrecy of this inhumane operation, every few months the whole *Sonderkommando*, except for a few Capos and specialists such as bricklayers and stokers, was liquidated and gassed in other camps.

From the very beginning of the Men's Camp BIId in Birkenau, *Sonder* men were assigned to Block 13, adjoining the Penal Company, which was housed in Block 11. High masonry walls separated those two blocks from the rest of the camp and, at the same time, provided an enclosed courtyard. The *Sonder* men and the prisoners in the Penal Company shared the same washroom facilities, divided in the middle by a solid wall. Contact between the *Sonder* and the rest of the prisoners was limited but not impossible, and with the help of messengers like Wiktor, news from *Sonder* men was passed to the outside world. Wiktor was usually up-to-date about what was happening on the eastern front and he was well informed of the camp's activities and any changes in the SS administration. Occasionally I shared my homemade food with him, trying to learn from him his practical wisdom about survival in Auschwitz.

As I was getting better every day, I knew that eventually I had to be discharged from the hospital and sent back to the Men's Camp. Looking for other solutions, one evening I shared my concerns with Wiktor. He listened carefully to my explanations and before he left he told me: "Janusz, perhaps I can help you, but I must talk to Tato first before we can consider any option for you to stay longer in the hospital. Dr. Thilo is obsessed with the idea that prisoner-doctors are sheltering healthy patients in the hospital and we must be very careful before any arrangements can be made."

I knew that Dr. Thilo had a reputation of being very strict and very impersonal in the treatment of all patients. He spread terror and fear among terminally sick prisoners. His daily inspections of the hospital were limited to superficial visits to a few barracks. He spent most of his time on the selection of terminally sick Jews for gassing, review of medical charts of non-Jewish prisoners, and attendance at medical briefings presented by the prisoner-doctors. It seemed to most of us that his goal was to release as many so-called cured inmates as possible from the hospital to the working *Kommandos* in the Men's Camp.

With great anticipation I looked forward to Wiktor's next visit. His willingness to help me was very encouraging. Tato was a well-known hospital Lagercapo and carried a lot of weight in the administration of the hospital's work assignments. His real name was Józef Bernacik and he was from Poznań. As political prisoner number 15517, he had arrived in Auschwitz in May 1941 from Dachau. Tato always carried a stick with him and was very vocal, always screaming at prisoners when SS men were close by. In reality, he was very compassionate, helpful, and friendly with all inmates. Because of his positive attitude and willingness to assist prisoners in distress, he was called Tato, which meant "Daddy" in Polish. He and Wiktor were old friends from 1941, when they had both lived and worked in the camp clinic for men in Auschwitz. Wiktor came to see me the following evening: "All set. You will report to *Strassenreinigungskommando* next week and you will be transferred to Block 18."

I could not believe my luck. Block 18 was designated as a transit block for convalescents, but several of the hospital's working *Kommandos* were also housed there in specially designated areas. It was staffed with a dedicated group of Polish, Jewish, and Russian doctors and orderlies, who spared no effort to help the sick inmates. In close cooperation with the underground organizations, the prisoner-doctors used this facility as a temporary shelter for invalids and the chronically sick who would have hard time surviving in the Men's Camp. They also provided refuge for prisoners engaged in the political underground activities.

The following week, with an anxious heart, I reported to my new job. There were two bunks dedicated exclusively to the *Strassenreinigungskommando* or street-cleaning crew. Six people, led by a foreman, were assigned to clean the streets of the hospital and maintain clean grounds around the barracks. I shared my bunk with Hans Bankier, a German Jew, and Johann Mikas, a Polish political prisoner. There were also two Frenchmen and one

Greek working with us. Hans Bankier was born in Silesia and spoke German. He was a gardener by profession and, perhaps for this reason, he was assigned the job of cleaning streets and landscaping the hospital's grounds. He was the foreman of the group and, from the beginning, he tried to help me settle down in my new job. Mikas was a small farmer from Odrowąż, very quiet and sincere, minding his own business and worrying all the time about his family.

Bankier explained to me that our work required maintenance of clean streets and all grounds in the hospital area. I was given a bucket and a stick with a nail at the end in order to be able to pick up loose papers and other trash lying on the ground. The Hospital Camp was divided into five sections and each of us was responsible for a designated area. Bankier, as a foreman, supervised all work. My area included the washroom; Blocks 10, 11, and 17; the sport field grounds adjoining the Gypsy Camp up to the corner of the new railroad ramp and Crematorium III.

Occasionally, we were called to help the small *Leichenkommando,* whose job was to load bodies of recently deceased prisoners on trucks heading for the crematoria. With a two-wheeled wagon, we walked around the camp collecting bodies of prisoners who had died of illness within the last twenty-four hours. The bodies were piled outside of each block, and our job was to bring them back to Block 12, the hospital's main dispatch center for corpses. Collecting and loading naked corpses, stiff and frozen and looking like skeletons, was a grim task. We worked with gloves and tried not to get too close to the bodies because of the high potential for transmission of contagious diseases. We also watched for rats that crawled among the corpses.

In time, we improved our way of handling the gruesome duties. Since some of the corpses were tangled together, we had invented new methods, and with wooden hooks we tried to separate the bodies before loading. Then, holding their arms and legs, two of us in a swift movement threw the bodies one at a time on a large pile in the wagon. I looked at men's faces, open and glazed eyes, bloated bellies, and long limbs with bones so thin that we worried about breaking them. Wrinkled skin full of sores was stretched on visible ribs and collapsed chests. A large number was written in pencil on each body. I had an uneasy feeling that the corpses were looking at us with their glazed eyes and tried to remind us silently about the inevitable end of passage for all prisoners in Birkenau. I looked at their twisted lips and wondered about their last words. Perhaps they were a farewell to families, perhaps a cry for mercy, or perhaps a promise of revenge. After all, they had mothers and fathers, perhaps wives, sisters, daughters, and sons.

In spite of the conspiracy of lies and silence imposed by the SS masters, the dramatic news of heartless murders would eventually reach the outside world. Perhaps there would be somebody waiting and hoping for a happy re-union that would never happen. Perhaps there was nobody left at home to receive a tearful message. The morbid duties were draining my spirit and what was left of my natural instinct for survival. I felt sick. After the job was finished, I washed my hands endlessly and lay quietly on the top of my bunk, looking forward to my regular street-cleaning assignment.

After a few months of staying in bed and sharing my bunk with Maurice, I appreciated the work as a street cleaner. The bright spring days with cloud-less skies were a welcome change after cold and windy winter weather. Every morning I carried my bucket, and with my stick in front of me, I walked around the blocks, picking up papers and discarded bandages and dressings. I cleaned the grounds around the blocks, and then I walked along the fence of the adjoining sanitary waterworks plant and Crematorium III. At the inter-section of the almost completed railroad ramp and the crematorium grounds, I turned left and walked inside the fence, along the railroad tracks, which were nearly finished. Then, I turned left again. Walking along the fence by the Gypsy Camp, I crossed the sports field diagonally and returned to the barracks. Except on Mondays, the day after sporting events, the field was pretty clean and deserted.

The Gypsy Camp was separated from the hospital grounds by a ditch and barbed-wire fence, which was not electrified during the day. The camp was full of families, men, women, and children who lived together in wooden barracks similar to ours in deplorable hygienic conditions. They all suffered from hunger and malnutrition. The abuse and exploitation of Gypsy women by SS guards and functional prisoners were well known across all camps in Birkenau. The black market and "organization" or exchange of gold and jewelry for food and sex was part of the daily routine. Gypsies, treated by Germans like "happy-go-lucky children," tried hard to survive their incar-ceration like the rest of us.

The hospital's Special Block, at the back of the Gypsy Camp, was uti-lized by Dr. Mengele for his anthropological experiments and provided un-limited opportunities for abuse of principles of humanity and practice of medical science. His study was in the *Sauna* building behind Block 32. I had to be very careful with my observation of the activities going on at the ramp, since Dr. Mengele's schedule was unpredictable and he spent many hours in his study.

As I stood in the middle of the soccer field pretending that I was collect-ing trash and enjoying the "peaceful" atmosphere, I carefully watched the brutal and inhumane activities happening continuously around me. Except for occasional gunshots from the crematorium, the camp was quiet and de-serted during the day. All the time I kept my eyes open in order not to be surprised by an unexpected SS Blockführer or other camp functionary out for a daily walk on the sport field.

Crematorium III was hidden by an approximately six-foot-high wicker screen, behind electrified fences. There were gaps in the enclosures and I could observe long lines of Jews walking through the main entrance gate. The entrance to the underground chambers was on the opposite end of the building and could not be seen from the hospital grounds. Knowing about the gassing process from Wiktor's explanations, I watched with apprehension. All of those people, completely unaware and innocent, were walking in columns of five from the railroad ramp in Auschwitz to the crematorium. Women and children walked slowly, holding hands and looking concerned and frightened. Men in separate columns walked faster, looking around with suspicion and frustration. After a few weeks, I began to recognize the origin of individual transports. Civilians transported from the ghettos of Western Europe were well dressed. They were forced to leave their furs, hats, and expensive handbags on the railroad ramp. Transports from other camps were more subdued, with pale and tired faces. The clothes were modest and they carried no hand luggage. Groups from other concentration camps were dehydrated, dressed in rags and wooden shoes. They looked hungry, with fear and resignation painted on their faces.

I felt like screaming and waving across the barbed wire. I wanted to warn the marching columns about their destiny. But I recognized that this would be a useless gesture and would most likely get me into a lot of trouble. With so many people from large transports arriving at the same time to the crematorium courtyard, smaller groups were sometimes held back near the hospital fence, waiting for their turn to enter the building. I could hear the *Sonder* men talking to new transports at the crematoria and assuring them about their future: "You are going to be washed and disinfected. Don't worry. Look at us; we are still alive." The reassuring words had a calming effect on the newcomers. They seemed less nervous as they walked down the steps to the underground gas chambers.

At first I was angry with the *Sonder* men for deceiving their own people. Then I began to understand. False reassurances prevented last-minute panic, shouting, and screaming, creating, perhaps, a sense of dignity and peace for the already condemned victims. I thought that perhaps it was better for them to find out the bitter and cruel truth about their tragic destiny at the last minute rather than carry the burden of facing death during the long and exhausting walk from the railroad platform to the crematoria.

Since I was highly visible from the hospital grounds, I had to be careful not to stay too close to the fence while watching the transports. Observation of the "special handling" by prisoners was forbidden under penalty of death.

I looked discreetly around and pretended every few minutes to be diligently picking up trash and discarded paper bandages.

The only person who occasionally came across the field was Tato, who was responsible for recent street improvements and also supervised the work for the grading of the soccer field, which was used occasionally on Sundays by the prisoner hospital staff to play football. This job was Tato's favorite project and he was very proud of it. Tato would wave to me with his stick and talk briefly about the soccer field construction progress. He was not only very humane and people-oriented but, at the same time, he was smart to be able to get along with other Capos and with hospital personnel.

On this particular day Tato joined me on the field. We both looked silently at the marching crowds. Neither of us said anything. People were continuously walking in long columns in the direction of the crematoria. The April day was hot, sunny, and cloudless. This time the women's dresses suited the warm weather; they were bright and colorful. Some of the men removed their coats and jackets, marching in their white shirts. Children, holding their mothers' hands, looked curiously around and small boys, being boys, kicked the occasional small stones lying on the ground.

This was a large transport, and the long line of people was making its way toward the solid masonry buildings. From a distance, they looked like a well-disciplined crowd walking slowly to participate in a holiday event. However, a closer look revealed tired and apprehensive men, women, and children walking along, completely unaware of their destiny. Tato hesitated and then he turned his head to me: "Take care, Janusz, and say hello to Wiktor when you see him." "Yes, Tato" I responded, keeping my eyes on the walking column.

May brought longer days and warmer weather. The railroad ramp on the outside of the hospital's fence was almost completed and ready. The ramp was located in the wide and open area dividing the hospital grounds from the Women's Camp. The railroad line was extended from the Auschwitz station. It ran under the arch entry of the Birkenau main watchtower toward Crematoria II and III. Two additional side rails were constructed almost across from the main entrance to the Women's Camp adjoining the long, concrete platform. The drama of unloading and selecting Jewish transports for gassing in the crematoria moved from the obscure stop in Auschwitz to the newly constructed facility in Birkenau.

One evening before "lights out," with a somewhat guilty conscience, I went behind our barrack to look from the distance at the railroad platform. Like everyone else, I was so engrossed in my own affairs and the continuous struggle to survive each day that sometimes I forgot the background of our dreadful existence.

The first train transports started arriving at the recently completed platform on an accelerated schedule. Every few hours I could see or hear a new train with a huffing and puffing locomotive pulling a long line of boxcars to the platform. The routine, which by now most of us knew by heart, was always the same. Unlock cars, unload frightened passengers, collect luggage, form columns, select, and depart. The "Canada" *Kommando* always stayed behind to sort out the luggage and clean the ramp to make it ready for the next transport.

In the evening under electric lights, one could see only masses of people being grouped together and occasional human shadows being pushed, screamed at, and threatened by supervising SS personnel. One could also hear the hum of thousands of innocent victims being led by their SS masters through the selection process. Occasional shots claimed some newcomers' lives before they could face the selecting officials. Even from a distance, the howling of dogs, screams from sentries, shots, and the puffing of a departing locomotive generated an atmosphere of fear.

I stood silently as I watched the unfolding human tragedy and wondered: "Are we so callous and so engrossed in our own fight to survive that we are unmoved by the mass murder of innocent people going on all the time around us? How can we forget so quickly the flaming smokestacks on the horizon and so easily accept this mass murder as a natural part of the Birkenau landscape?" Then I tried to reason with myself. "What can we do?" Every day terror and strict camp discipline did not allow us to take any action unless we were willing to end up in one of the crematoria ovens ourselves. Uprising on a large scale was impossible and not realistic. The instinct of self-preservation was strong enough to control and constrain emotional outbursts. We watched silently as victims of the Nazi extermination policy walked daily from the railroad platform to the crematoria. We wondered when it would be our own turn.

In addition to the ramp activities, the SS doctors, in all camps, selected for gassing all terminally ill Jews. Every day, trucks full of naked prisoners brought the victims to the crematoria and dumped them like sacks of potatoes from the mechanically operated vehicles. Hydraulic lifts, at the front of each truck, automatically raised the confused, screaming, and tangled bodies of selected naked victims and tumbled them rapidly to the ground. They lay there howling and moaning.

Most non-Jewish prisoners detained in camp had a slight hope for survival, which helped them to overcome the exploitation and abuses of the SS guards. If they did not die from hunger or infectious disease, they gradually became stronger in anticipation of an allied victory and freedom. For the

Jews selected in the Birkenau camps or at the railroad ramp there was no such ray of hope, no promise for the future.

With the completion of the new ramp and the relocation of the unloading operations to Birkenau, just outside of the hospital security fence, I could observe the whole process of arrivals, selection, and disposition of new transports at a reasonably close distance. May was a busy month. Trains bringing Hungarian and French Jews were arriving every day. The "Canada" men worked in shifts for twenty-four hours without interruption, sorting and collecting luggage left by new transports on the railroad ramp. I could see most of the action from my camouflaged position in the hospital as I pretended to diligently pick up trash along the hospital's fence.

Nobody paid any attention to a simple *Schutzhäftling* trying to do a good job. However, from a distance, I could not recognize the individuals working on the platform. In particular, I wanted to see the faces of the people participating in this unreal drama. I was very much interested in seeing the expressions of courage and determination on the faces of the innocent victims. I wanted to be able to look closely at the faces of SS selection officials and their helpers as they were sending thousands of innocent people to their death. I wanted to remember their faces, names, and ranks, hoping that when freedom came, the murderers would be caught and made accountable for their deeds.

One evening, I approached Bankier: "Herr Bankier, you know so many people in the camp. Do you think you could help me?"

"Janusz, what do you want?" Bankier sounded suspicious.

"Could you find me a pair of binoculars?" I asked him with a straight face.

He jumped and started waving his hands: "You must be crazy or stupid! If they find you with binoculars, you are dead."

I was calm: "I know Herr Bankier, it is risky, but nobody will find anything. I will be very careful." Then I added: "I am sure that there are plenty of binoculars in 'Canada's' barracks hidden in the luggage of Hungarian or French Jews."

Bankier shook his head: "I do not want anything to do with this." I looked at him again: "Herr Bankier, you have many friends in the 'Canada' *Kommando*. I will give you three apples and two onions." My proposal had a positive impact. Bankier thought for a second: "I will see what I can do. Give me four apples and three onions but don't you admit to anybody that I had anything to do with this."

I smiled: "It is a deal, Herr Bankier. Thanks."

The camp was flooded with stolen Hungarian and French jewelry, gold, money, and canned food. But there was still a shortage on the black market of fresh fruit and vegetables so they carried a high price. Food was more valuable than gold. On the third evening, Bankier brought small opera binoculars and, in great secrecy, gave them to me hidden in a blanket. We traded our goods. I was then the proud owner of a very beautiful pair of opera glasses made in Paris.

The next day, I started my work early and, in the middle of a bright and sunny May morning, I arrived close to the fence line separating the hospital from the ramp. This was a good location for watching the unfolding human drama across the barbed-wire fence. However, I had to be very careful to look out for any activity on the hospital grounds. I did not want to be caught unexpectedly by the wandering SS man who could cross the sport field. There was no sign of the typical morning mist. The sun was bright and visibility was good. After a careful check to make sure that I was alone, I unwrapped my binoculars from the tissue paper used by orderlies for hospital dressing and looked at the railroad platform.

The "Canada" *Kommando,* gathered in small groups, already stood in the middle of the platform waiting for the train. SS armed guards were stationed along the full length of the ramp. A military vehicle arrived and an officer stepped out. I immediately recognized SS Obersturmführer Dr. Heinz Thilo from my previous hospital selections where, as the Lagerarzt of the Birkenau hospital, he selected sick prisoners for gassing.

Two large army trucks entered the platform and were parked near the exit. Dr. Thilo, accompanied by another officer, paced the platform and occasionally looked at his watch. A large number of SS personnel stood in small groups, talking in loud voices and laughing at the same time. All sergeants and corporals carried large wooden sticks. Then I also recognized my old adversary Stefan Baretzki, who was now one of the SS Blockführers at the Men's Camp. He was cruel and well remembered by all prisoners from the Quarantine Camp for his punishment methods and excessive "sports."

As I looked at all the people gathered on the platform, I realized that the carefully planned and improved extermination process in Birkenau had reached the highest level of perfection and was ready for the final test. Hungarian transports were generally prosperous, well equipped with gourmet food and valuable personal belongings such as jewelry and gold. The impact of this wealth was already felt on the camp's black market.

"Canada" men, responsible for sorting luggage, were the main source for distribution of stolen property from the sorting barracks. Some of the perishable food taken from the transports was occasionally given to the prison's main kitchen to upgrade the watery taste of the typical Birkenau meal. The "death angel" of newcomers and the "greed angel" of old-timers worked hand in hand. The unwritten rules of the camp allowed prisoners working on the ramp during unloading operations to collect discovered fresh and perishable food for their own use. Gold, jewelry, and all valuable items were property of the Reichsbank. SS officers specially appointed for duties on the platform carefully watched all prisoners sorting and collecting luggage. All gold was collected from each transport and transferred to the SS Main Administrative Offices in Berlin to finance Hitler's war. Jewelry and expensive gold watches were sold in Switzerland, and cheap watches were distributed among SS troops fighting on the eastern front. There were some exceptions to this rule, and occasionally, greedy SS guards were tempted to steal valuable items discovered on the platform for their own personal use. If caught by their superiors, they were court marshaled, shot, or sentenced for a long stay as prisoners in one of the concentration camps. Some of the more courageous prisoners also tried to "organize" or to steal gold from the luggage collected on the railroad ramp. This was, however, a risky business, punishable by death.

Suddenly I noted excitement among the people gathered on the platform. The incoming black locomotive pulling a long line of cattle cars whistled from the distance and then slowly puffed its way along the railroad ramp. Then it stopped and unexpectedly released clouds of white steam from one of its side cylinders. For a second, the whole ramp, train, SS guards and prisoners were lost in the clouds of white and foggy mist. All of the people standing on the platform looked from a distance like dark and menacing shadows waiting anxiously for their victims as in Dante's *Inferno*. When trains were unloaded from the track adjoining the Men's Camp and the hospital area, the view was completely obstructed by the long line of boxcars. We couldn't see what was going on. But when the incoming Jewish transports were unloaded from the middle track, closer to the Women's Camp, the dramatic ramp selections were clearly visible from the hospital grounds. Only then did I have a chance to use my binoculars and watch the drama unfolding before my eyes. This time, the train arrived at the middle track.

Soon a gentle westerly wind carried off the clouds. The train stopped. In the small windows of the cattle cars appeared human faces. Women with begging, sad eyes, unshaven men with fear and frustration pained on their faces, gazed with suspicion at the reception group on the platform. They all looked exhausted after their long journey. Thirsty, they pleaded in strained voices: "*Wasser . . .* Water!" The SS man walked slowly along the train, banging at each door with a wooden stick: "All quiet and all out. Leave your luggage behind . . . Keep moving!" He screamed in a loud voice. "Canada" men opened the door of each cattle car. The people inside each car, tired, thirsty, and squeezed very tight for many days and nights, pushed toward an opening. There were no excuses and no customary politeness. Men pushed harder and they were the first on the ground. Women and children made the second wave. The sick and old were left behind lying helplessly on the dirty floors of the cattle cars among piles of luggage, blankets, and human excrement. They all begged for help and assistance.

I looked closer at the railroad cars. The signs were in Hungarian. This was a Budapest transport. The "Canada" men jumped into the cattle cars and tried to assist the invalids and the sick. With a mixture of compassion and indifference, they gently guided disabled persons to descend from the high steps of the cattle cars to the railroad ramp.

The newcomers tried desperately to find answers from the "Canada" men: "Where are we? Where are we going?" They pleaded and begged the old inmates for a response. The prisoners pretended to be busy as they unloaded the luggage, avoided eye contact, and stayed silent. Some of them pretended not to understand Hungarian. Once unloaded, SS guards with huge dogs inspected the empty cattle cars. They went from car to car. Whenever the guard found a person left behind, he let the dog attack the victim who, frightened by the ferocious animal, gathered all his or her strength and desperately jumped screaming from the cattle car.

People were helplessly lying on the ground, crying for mercy or help from members of their families or close friends. It appeared for a moment that panic was spreading among the Hungarian Jews. One of the SS Obersharführers called out in a reasonably friendly voice: "Please be calm, ladies and gentlemen. Form a column of five—men on the right side, women and children on the left." The friendly tone of his voice had a calming effect on the crowd.

Diligently, they formed two long columns along the full length of the railroad platform. I noted also a small group of men with Red Cross armbands standing on one side. They were the Jewish doctors who arrived with the transport and who waited their turn for selection. All groups were facing Dr. Thilo. As soon as men were formed in an orderly column five abreast, each person was told to move forward, one at a time and face the SS doctor. After a brief assessment of each individual, the SS doctor started to move his finger. As he turned his face toward me, I really appreciated my new binoculars. Although, the platform was quite a distance away from the hospital fence, with my new equipment I could see him very well.

However, I was disappointed when I looked at his face and his eyes. I expected to see a spark of humanity, anguish, contempt, perhaps even anger or hate. What I actually saw was a calm bureaucratic indifference. His face was expressionless and impersonal. His eyes were cold. He just stood there, in the middle of the platform, with his left arm behind his back holding his leather gloves and with his right arm outstretched in front, flicking his finger from left to right. Young, robust, and healthy men moved to the right while the older men were forming a new column behind the army truck on the left. "Canada" men helped sick and disabled men to climb on the truck. Within a half-hour, the job was finished.

The SS man heading the column made a sign to the driver of the truck. The long line of old men moved and walked silently behind the truck carrying the sick and disabled people. They crossed the rail lines as they walked toward the entrance to the Women's Camp. In front of the SS guard post, they turned right and walked along the railroad tracks toward the entrances to Crematoria II and III. The short column of young men followed the first group and walked in the same direction. After a few hundred yards the truck and the column of old men turned right and entered the courtyard of Crematorium III. The column of healthy young men bypassed the entrance to the crematoria and marched farther down the winding road to the bathhouse.

The women left behind on the platform were confused and scared. Families had been torn apart. Children cried and, in voices full of emotion, called: "Daddy, Daddy!" Nobody knew what was going on. The women and children waved to the departing men: "Good-bye, Daddy! Good-bye, Uncle! Good-bye, my love!" The men's eyes reflected both resignation and fear. Wailing and screaming was heard everywhere. The SS man on the platform tried to reassure the women: "Do not worry. You will see them again soon. Stay in columns of five." The SS men on the platform were too busy and too absorbed in their deadly assignments to pay any attention to what was going on outside the platform perimeter. I was so close that I could hear SS men barking orders and some of their loud remarks.

Dr. Thilo was already selecting women left behind on the platform. Young and healthy girls stayed on the right. Older women, grandmothers, and granddaughters below the age of fourteen were left together on the left. Sometimes the doctor stopped the selection process and talked to the people. I was sure that he asked the same old question: "How old are you?" Then he made his decision.

A young, beautiful, tall woman, well dressed, slender, with dark, long hair, who had been sent to the right side, pleaded in a highly emotional and loud voice with the doctor for permission to join her mother and grandmother sent to the left side. Dr. Thilo seemed to be accommodating in this case. He smiled, moved his head in an affirmative way, and let her join her family. Unknowingly, she had selected death.

"Canada" men helped old women and invalids and small children to climb on the second truck. From a distance, I could see through my binoculars that people sitting in the truck were relieved and less nervous. They sat watching the end of the women's column passing in front of Dr. Thilo.

"Where are we going?" This unanswered question hung above everyone's head and nobody was willing to offer any explanation. The doctor reached the end of the women's column and sent mostly young and healthy girls to the right. Immediately upon completion of selection, the column of young women from the right side was led by SS Unterscharführer across the railroad tracks directly to the Women's Camp. The long line of mothers, grandmothers, and children followed the second truck heading toward Crematorium III. A Red Cross ambulance passed the marchers. Inside, canisters with Zyklon B were delivered by SS men to the crematoria, to make sure that there was a sufficient supply of poisonous gas to take care of the Hungarian transport.

"Canada" men were left behind on the platform to collect and sort out all luggage. Thrown in large piles in front of each cattle car, the mountains of suitcases offered tempting opportunities for theft. Large and small, expensive and cheap, made of leather or plywood, the tossed luggage was sorted out by "Canada" men under the watchful and suspicious eyes of the SS guards. Damaged and half-opened suitcases full of clothes, food, jars of fat, bread, sausages, and bottles of wine lay on the platform in the middle of cleaning activities, tempting both prisoners and the SS guards. As the "Canada" men discretely eyed valuable personal possessions, they also looked around carefully to see if SS guards were still watching.

The train stood empty on the platform. Dr. Thilo left with his driver, the people had gone, and only small groups of "Canada" men worked diligently to make room for the next transport. There was a whistle on the platform signaling the beginning of train-cleaning activities. A special squad of "Canada" men went to each car to clean the floor and wash the walls. The cleaning crew threw out of the cars trash, human excrement, soiled underwear, and corpses left abandoned and covered by pillows and blankets. Stiff bodies of infants, hidden by terrified mothers before their departure, were collected in a separate pile for transport to the crematoria.

The "special handling" of the Budapest transport was coming to an end. Then I heard the whistle. The train moved backward. Wheels turned slowly as the steaming locomotive pushed the long line of cattle cars toward the main watchtower. SS guards holding automatic weapons still guarded the remaining suitcases, coats, briefcases, parcels, and the damaged, half-open trunks. Occasionally, a Capo with a yellow armband crossed the platform, screaming at the few remaining "Canada" men to work faster.

I watched the arrival of this transport for almost two hours. There were approximately twenty cattle cars with eighty persons in each car. One thousand six hundred people: men and women, old and young, adults and children, and infants were "processed" by efficient and businesslike camp administrators. A majority of the new arrivals ended the journey in Crematorium III. In spite of the fact that I watched the whole process, I could not believe that it actually happened. Walking silently back to my block, I wondered: "Will anybody believe me that this actually took place?" I had serious doubts.

Block 18 looked peaceful and almost friendly. Herr Bankier greeted me at the door. "What's wrong, Janusz?"

I could not answer. I shrugged my shoulders and told him: "I just watched the Hungarian transport going to the crematoria. It makes me sick. I still can not get used to this." Bankier was philosophical: "Janusz, you can get used to anything." Then he added: "Just wait. My concern is that we may be next."

We both sat silently on the top of our bunks without saying a word. Somebody called: "Lunch, get ready." We collected our bowls and both of us waited patiently in the line in front of the block for our soup. As usual, it was tasteless and watery, with a few pieces of floating turnips. After a few sips, I could not eat any more. I returned to my bunk for a short rest. I closed my eyes and the tall girl with beautiful, dark, long hair was still in front of me arguing with Dr. Thilo. I picked up my stick and bucket and went out to clean the grounds around the hospital barracks. I did not even dare to look back toward the railroad ramp.

CHAPTER EIGHT

Desinfektionskommando

SPRING OF 1944 brought the beginning of very special activities among SS ranks in all camps in Auschwitz I, II, and III. The first indication of something unusual was the return of the previous Kommandant, SS Obersturmbannführer Höss. His arrival at the beginning of May made most of the inmates nervous and suspicious. Crematoria compounds were screened from the rest of us with additional evergreen plants and solid wood fences. The *Sonderkommando* was enlarged and almost nine hundred men were assigned to gruesome duties in the gas chambers. Open ditches and large pits were dug behind Crematorium V.

While these preparations were going on, the railroad traffic at the Birkenau unloading platform steadily increased. At least two trains arrived every day and additional transports were unloaded every night. The brightly lit railroad ramp served as the focal point for selections among Jewish transports. With the powerful searchlights located on both ends of the platform, one could read a book in the middle of the night. Thousands of confused and tired Jews—men, women, and children—arrived every day and night at the railroad platform, and within a few hours these same people walked silently beside the hospital's fence on the paved road that led to all four crematoria. Only a few preselected young and healthy men and women were transferred from the platform to one of the camps. Some were registered, tattooed, and included in the camp records. Others were later employed in Buna or other war plants around Birkenau, and some of the new arrivals were held in a transit camp, such as "Mexico," without registration, before they were shipped to work in Germany.

The stench of burnt flesh was everywhere. We ate, slept, and worked in the middle of these murderous activities. The overworked smoke stacks of four crematoria discharged red and yellow flames every day and night. They generated an abundance of grayish clouds that hung heavily all day over Birkenau's misty landscape. We watched this drama unfolding in front of our eyes and with heavy hearts wondered about our own destiny.

According to underground gossip among the inmates, the eastern front was moving rapidly west and some people claimed that the Red Army had already crossed the old Polish-Russian borders. The future existence of the camp was threatened. Deportation and transfer of inmates to other concentration camps located in the heart of Germany increased rapidly. Some of the trains that brought Jews left Auschwitz with transports of prisoners for Buchenwald and Mauthausen. None of us knew what to expect the following day. The unloading on the railroad ramp behind the hospital's fence was now guarded by SS armed sentries with dogs and I could not go close to the fence any more. The electrified fence around Crematorium III was further screened with closely planted pines to prevent us from seeing anything inside the courtyard. I wondered if I should attempt to ask for a transfer from the hospital to the Men's Camp. The proximity of the crematoria, the stench in the air, and the flames overhead reminded us constantly of our uncertain future.

One evening Wiktor stopped to see me and to tell me what was going on in Auschwitz. His information, gathered from many different sources, had been very reliable in the past. He confirmed that Höss was back and was acting as SS Camp Kommandant. SS Sturmbannführer Baer replaced SS Obersturmbannführer Liebehenschel and assumed command of Auschwitz I. SS Hauptsturmführer Kramer, who replaced SS Sturmbannführer Hartjenstein, was put in charge of Birkenau. SS Hauptsturmführer Schwarz was reappointed Lagerführer of Auschwitz III, including all subcamps, with headquarters in Monowice. Kramer was Höss's adjutant in 1940. His sadistic persecution of women inmates was remembered very well. Since his new appointment, he and his chauffeur continued their old practice of terrorizing every woman prisoner they met during Kramer's inspection tours. He was a big man. He walked slowly, with his chauffeur right behind him. On many occasions, the chauffeur carried a drawn revolver in his hand. His reputation and his sadistic behavior spread a wave of terror through the entire Women's Camp in Birkenau.

Wiktor also learned from his secret sources that in view of the rapid advances of Russian troops on the eastern front, a decision had been made in Berlin to expedite the extermination of Jews from Europe. Himmler had given the task of destroying Hungarian Jews to Höss. Höss brought with him a "result-oriented" team of experts to expedite the handling and gassing of new Jewish transports. Under the direction of SS Sturmbannführer Eichmann, who was responsible for the transportation of Jews from existing ghettos in Europe, thousands of innocent people were to be transferred to Birkenau for selection or death in the gas chambers. Trains full of new deportees were already arriving every day. SS Hauptscharführer Moll was appointed new director of all crematoria.

Wiktor also confirmed that the total Auschwitz complex was to be gradually liquidated. Existing records were to be removed or destroyed. Every day hundreds of worn-out inmates were transferred to other camps in Germany. However, in spite of the accelerated evacuation of inmates, the camp's population, especially in the women's compounds, was steadily growing. Although a majority of new arrivals were immediately sent to the gas chambers, young healthy women and robust men were retained at transit camps. All camps in Birkenau, except for the Men's Hospital, were overcrowded. Because of this, SS doctors were concerned with the possibility of another epidemic of infectious diseases. An effort was made to accelerate and expand existing delousing procedures. As a part of this program, new and expensive disinfection equipment was installed at the Women's Camp.

Wiktor was a disinfection specialist, who worked in the *Entwo sungskommando,* or delousing squad, when they were using Zyklon B for disinfection of prisoners' clothing. This method was discontinued in Birkenau when a hot air system was introduced in women's and men's bathhouses. Now Tato asked Wiktor to provide necessary training to the newly formed Women's *Desinfektionskommando* in Camp BIb. SS Doctor Thilo, as the Lagerarzt of the Men's Hospital, approved this assignment. Wiktor continued his story of how Tato explained to him that most of the work would be done by women. However, a few men were needed as mechanics to service the equipment and to operate the electrical controls of the disinfection trailer. The work hours were based on the already established schedule for delousing of all women's blocks in Camp BIa and BIb. It was also stipulated that some of the disinfection processes might be carried out at night. That meant that Wiktor and his crew would have to work night shifts and rest in the Men's Camp during the day. The job required standing in one place for many hours, but the work was not very heavy, since most of the packing and unpacking of special sacks of clothing were done by women.

Wiktor was not absolutely sure what was expected of him and his operators. He looked at this new job as an opportunity to maintain contacts with the Women's Camp and to move away from the hospital where both sick and healthy prisoners, as well as the staff, faced an uncertain future. He also indicated that he had accepted his new assignment with the full approval and support of the Camp's Underground Central Committee. I was not aware of the extent of his involvement with such a secret organization since he was not very specific and I did not ask for details.

Wiktor continued, "Janusz—I am looking for people I can trust and who do not ask too many questions. This could be a very interesting job." Then he asked me directly, "Would you be interested in working with me in the *Desinfektionskommando?*"

I was really surprised by this offer, "Wiktor, this sounds like a very inter-esting assignment, but can I take a day to think about it?"

Wiktor promptly agreed. "Remember, I am not pressing you and you do not have to take this job, but I think this may be a good time to leave the hos-pital and SS doctors like Thilo and Mengele." Then he added: "I will stop by again tomorrow evening."

That evening I could not sleep. Wiktor was right. This was an opportu-nity to leave the hospital and, to a limited extent, control my own destiny. However, it was a major personal decision with many unknown factors. In spite of my previous fear of the Men's Camp, I had already thought about leaving the hospital. With the establishment of another clinic at the Quaran-tine Camp, the flow of new patients to the hospital was considerably re-duced. Most of the recently admitted newcomers were terribly sick Jews who, after a short stay in the hospital, were selected by Dr. Thilo for the gas chambers. The gradual reduction in the number of incoming patients and frequent selections among the terminally ill Jews slowly reduced the hospi-tal's population. There were fewer patients and less trash to pick up. We even had fewer corpses in the mortuary since every day, most of the Jewish pa-tients arrived alive and naked in huge trucks and were transferred directly from their barracks to crematoria for gassing. There was even talk about transferring *Strassenreinigungskommando* to Mauthausen. This was the last place I wanted to go. My future in the hospital did not look very good. Also, of course, there was Vera. Going back to work in the Women's Camp, I would perhaps see her again if she were still in Birkenau.

The next day I talked with Bankier and asked his advice. He felt that the sooner we left the hospital, or even Birkenau, we would be better off. "Janusz, I would like to get away from the hospital and Auschwitz as fast as I can. I would even take a chance on another camp as long as I am away from the smoking crematoria."

Perhaps he was right. Being next door to the crematoria and witnessing the destruction of human lives made me severely depressed. I recognized that the Men's Camp was not that much further removed from the crematoria than the hospital. The smoking chimneys could still be seen everywhere, as they overshadowed the rest of the camp's facilities. But even a short distance removed from these "death factories" would make me feel better since the air further away was less foul and I could not hear the screams of the con-demned people. All of this helped me to make up my mind.

The next evening I told Wiktor that I would like to work with him. He was pleased that I had decided to go with him to the Men's Camp and as-sured me that he thought I had made a good decision. "I may ask you to do something special occasionally, but we will talk about this later on." Then he added, "Yesterday I found an old and trusted friend of mine on Block 28. He is Tadeusz or Tadek Deperaszyński and he is coming to work with us."

Wiktor explained to me that Tadek was a native of Radom, a Polish political prisoner who had been arrested by the Gestapo in 1942 with his wife. They spent several months being interrogated in Radom jail before his transfer in May 1943 to Birkenau. His wife arrived in the same transport and was sent to the Women's Camp. Both were accused of printing and distributing underground newspapers. They left two teenage children at home who were currently living with relatives. Wiktor knew Tadek from the time when they both worked at the clinic in the Men's Camp before Tadek was admitted to the hospital. Tadek wanted desperately to establish contact with his wife and looked for every opportunity to work in the Women's Camp. He was eager to go and had already left the hospital last week, waiting for us to join him in the Men's Camp. After our conversation, Wiktor went to the Hospital Labor Office and talked to the senior prisoner in charge of work assignments to make appropriate arrangements for our transfer.

The next morning both of us were included in the transfer group of convalescents returning to the Men's Camp. In a column of five abreast, twenty of us marched together with an escort from the hospital to the Men's Camp. The column stopped in front of the SS guardhouse: "*Mutzen ab,*" called the senior prisoner. He reported our arrival to the SS guard on duty and then, with the Men's Camp Lagercapo, they checked and verified the roster and numbers. After a six-month absence, I was back in the Men's Camp. "*Mutzen auf,*" screamed the Lagercapo as we passed the gate. Wiktor was assigned to a block that was set aside for functionaries and low-number prisoners. I went to Block 28 to meet Tadek. There were changes in my old barrack. The Blockältester Stanek and the Stubendienst Toni both left in transports to other camps in Germany. The new Blockältester was Piotr Lisowski. Kaz was still the Schreiber. They both welcomed us warmly and we were assigned one of the better sleeping bunks, adjoining the food storeroom.

The newly reorganized *Desinfektionskommando* consisted of two separate groups. Wiktor, Tadek, and I, as a part of the first group, were assigned to service the new disinfection trailer. Women inmates supported us in our work.

The second group, consisting of about eight Russian prisoners of war and a German Capo, was responsible for disinfecting the women's blocks, including all furniture and mattresses. This was accomplished by the use of Zyklon B containers similar to those used in the crematoria gas chambers. The SS Sanitätsdienstgrade or SDGs, specially trained SS sanitary personnel in gas masks, installed and opened gas canisters at the designated block. After waiting several hours, to make sure that all the vermin were exterminated, the group of prisoners in gas masks entered the building and opened all possible windows and doors for ventilation until the toxic gas evaporated. Meanwhile, deloused women prisoners usually waited naked for their clothing, which was processed in the disinfection trailer by Wiktor, Tadek, and me. Upon inspection and approval by the SS SDG personnel, inmates, after recovering their disinfected clothing, were allowed to enter the building.

Tadek was about forty years old. He looked reasonably well, if one considered his long stay in the Radom jail. He was of medium height, slim, and he projected an image of fairness and confidence. We both talked about our prewar lives, imprisonment, camp experiences, and our hopes for the future. His main concern was to find his wife, and he was anxiously awaiting our first day of work in the Women's Camp.

The following morning, which was bright and sunny, Tadek and I met Wiktor at the Men's Camp main gate. We had to wait for all large outside *Kommandos* to leave the camp first and take our turn with smaller groups reporting our formal departure at the SS guard post. We went through the usual routine: *"Mutzen ab"* and *"Mutzen auf"* and marched in front of the SS Rapportführer on duty. Outside the gate, a SS Unterscharführer in a crisp, new uniform was already waiting for us. He was slim, in his late twenties, with short, blond hair and blue eyes.

The previous night Wiktor had told us that the SS Kommandoführer Omlauf was in charge of the disinfection program for women. He was a demanding supervisor, a stickler for rules who believed in discipline. Wiktor used to work for him at the old camp in Auschwitz. Now, in his new capacity as the SS Sanitätsdienstgrad (SDG), Omlauf was part of the SS Desinfektion unit reporting to SS Obersturmbannführer, Dr. Wirths. As the SS Standortarzt or Chief Doctor of the Auschwitz garrison, Dr. Wirths supervised all SS and prisoner doctors in Auschwitz and was responsible for medical and sanitary conditions of all SS troops and prisoners. Dr. Wirths reported directly to the SS Kommandant of the Auschwitz Concentration Camp and also submitted reports about camp's health problems to his SS medical superiors in Berlin.

The specially established SS disinfecting unit, staffed by highly trained SS Sanitätsdienstgrade, or SS male sanitary orderlies, was responsible for control and containment of infectious diseases among the SS troops and prisoners. They oversaw disinfection of inmates in all *Saunas* and supervised the disinfection processes of clothing carried out by the prisoners from the *Entwesungskommando* in the specially designated disinfection chambers. The SS Sanitätsdienstgrade also played a major part in the extermination activities in all of the crematoria, during massive gassing of Jewish transports. They opened Zyklon B canisters and discharged the poisonous gas through special openings in roofs or walls of the gas chambers.

As we walked around the Quarantine Camp, I recognized a familiar route following the same path we had taken the previous year in Witek's *Kommando*. The street between camps BIIc and BIId, leading directly to the Women's Camp across from the unloading railroad platform, was closed in anticipation of the arrival of a new transport. This time I noted far more prisoners behind the Quarantine Camp's barbed wire. Traffic on the main street seemed also more active than before. SS trucks full of prisoners standing close together were traveling in many different directions. "Mexico" Camp was still full of new deportees dressed in their normal "civilian" clothes, waiting for transfer to other camps.

We turned right, walked down a passageway under the main watchtower and then turned left toward the Women's Camp. As we entered the bathhouse compound, I remembered quite well my first night in Birkenau. Nothing had really changed from the previous year except that now the barbed-wire fences around these buildings were removed and the main structure was designated exclusively as the women's bathhouse.

A huge, dark green trailer stood between the bathhouse and the adjoining blocks. The trailer looked almost like a small house with a flat roof on huge rubber wheels. It was at least three meters wide and fifteen meters long. Wiktor stopped in front of the trailer and, as we walked around the equipment, explained to us the basic operation. At the back of the trailer facing us, I could see wide doors and a canopy forming an overhead roof. Below, there was a glazed panel full of electrical switches and control valves. Along both sides there were two rectangular openings located opposite each other with a small, inside conveyor belt connecting them across the width of the trailer. During the delousing process, women's articles of clothing, including blouses, skirts, and underwear, were packed in sacks and loaded through one of the openings onto a conveyor belt. Because metal objects were not allowed to enter the machine, women helpers cut out all metal buttons and zippers and removed hidden metal spoons and forks. As the clothes moved on the conveyor belt across the trailer from the "dirty" side to the "clean" side, they were exposed to an extremely high temperature. The high temperature killed all insects and lice. Disinfected and warm sacks were unloaded on the "clean" side by a specially trained operator.

All of the packing and unpacking was done by women. Tadek and I were designated as the operators processing the sacks through the trailer. Tadek was assigned to the "dirty" side and I was given the task of unloading on the "clean" side. The *Desinfektionskommando* of approximately twenty women was divided into two teams, "clean" and "dirty." The "dirty" team was responsible for gathering, sorting, and packing all articles of clothing into small sacks that would be delivered to Tadek for processing on the conveyor belt. On the "clean" side, disinfected sacks would be received by me and given to the woman handler for delivery and unpacking at the central site for distribution to already bathed, shaved, and disinfected women.

After listening to Wiktor's instructions, we walked around the trailer in order to become more familiar with its operations. We were also told that controls would be operated by the SS man who must always be present when this equipment was in use. I was impressed with the advanced technology of the new machine and, at the same time, surprised that this costly and complex equipment was being used to benefit "enemies of the Reich." According to Wiktor, this trailer was previously used by troops at the eastern front and now was on temporary loan from the German Army to the SS Camp Administration.

SS Unterscharführer Omlauf, who disappeared into the bathhouse after our arrival at the Women's Camp, came out accompanied by three SS troopers. Omlauf stopped in front of Wiktor, turned around to his fellow soldiers and said, "This is Wiktor who used to work for me in the old camp in Auschwitz and these are his two helpers." Then he looked at Tadek and me, "Do you understand German?"

In unison, we replied, "Yes, *sir.*"

"That's good. At least we can communicate. In a few minutes we will start this operation and I want you to listen very carefully to SS Sturmmann Pherbinde's orders."

The youngest looking of the three soldiers, Pherbinde was not more than eighteen years old. With a very serious expression on his face, he inspected both of us. Apparently, he was an electrician in charge of controls. Then Pherbinde took his place behind the glass panel. The remaining two SS Rottenführers were to assist Omlauf during the operations. One was in charge of the "dirty" side and the other was to stay with me on the "clean" side.

"Where are the women?" Omlauf asked one of the SS Rottenführers. He said he would check and disappeared into the bathhouse. In a few minutes, he returned leading a procession of the Women's *Desinfektionskommando.* All of them were young, dressed in marked-up civilian clothes of decent quality, with shaven heads covered with colorful scarves. The Capo was a petite young woman with dark eyes and a light complexion. Her head was not shaved, and her hair covered her eyes in a boyish haircut. She talked to her group in Hungarian as they formed a circle around the trailer.

Two SS women supervisors came from the bathhouse and joined the SS men standing in front of the trailer. The Women's Camp had an SS administrative structure similar to that in the Men's Camp. However, functions of SS Blockführers were held by SS Aufseherinnen or wardresses, young German women, mostly from the working background and not highly educated.

Some even had a dubious past, including criminal records. They were crude and cruel in their treatment of women prisoners, and one could feel their arrogance and contempt as they screamed at the confused and frightened inmates. The SS Aufseherinnen wore uniforms similar to those of the men and carried canes in their hands and pistols at their belts. They wore capes and knee-high boots and were referred to as "angels of death" by women prisoners. They were ruthless, with no compassion whatsoever for their victims.

All inmates in the *Desinfektionskommando* were Jewish women from Budapest. They were handpicked by Omlauf to work with him. As all of them were new arrivals, they still looked healthy and fairly attractive in spite of their shaven heads, which they covered with scarves. The Capo, although small and almost fragile looking, was an energetic and assertive leader of the group. In spite of the gloomy environment, she was able to maintain both compassion and a sense of humor.

She came to the three of us standing by the trailer and said in perfect German, "I am Pepi and this is my *Kommando*. We are very happy that we can work with you." Then she turned to her group and announced, "Silence! I want you to listen to Herr Unterscharführer carefully."

Omlauf first looked around at his colleagues, two SS women, the three of us, and the group of women inmates. Then in a pompous voice, he explained the work, stressing the need for high sanitary and safety standards and discipline. I was really surprised. Up until now it sounded almost too good to be true. In my Birkenau experience, this was the first time that an SS man did not bark his order and threaten us with heavy penalties.

After his short speech, we went to the designated work station and waited for our "customers" to arrive from their blocks at the bathhouse compound. Five women assigned to the "clean" side stayed with me on the same side of the trailer. A young, tall girl with a colorful scarf covering her head came to see me as I was standing by the opening in the trailer. In broken German, she said: "My name is Olga and I am your helper. With my four friends, we will unpack and sort all the disinfected clothing."

She looked at my number and the red triangle on my jacket, "Are you Polish?" she asked. "Yes," I responded. Then she said: "I am from Budapest. My whole family came to Auschwitz in May with the Jewish transport, but I can't find anybody. My older brother was sent to the Men's Camp. Do you have many Hungarian Jews in your camp?"

"Yes, we do." I responded. Then I added: "Do not worry. It is almost impossible to find anybody here now. My friend, Tadek, has been looking for his wife for several months. That is why he is here today. It takes time and patience."

I looked at her again. She had tears in her dark eyes. "Take good care of yourself and you will find everybody. This war cannot go on forever."

My German was getting better but I stopped our conversation abruptly as one of the SS Rottenführers was coming closer to the "clean" side. We both pretended to be busy getting ready for work. He walked around us without saying a word. He was of medium height and slim in his SS uniform, carrying a cane in his hand. He looked around and then turned back and walked away whistling melodies of German folksongs. Later on, I found out that his name was Charwin and he was Volksdeutsch, born in Lithuania. After graduation from the School of Music in Kowno, he was called in 1941 to serve with SS troops. First he was assigned to the concentration camp in Majdanek and then transferred to Birkenau.

Suddenly, I could hear the sound of hundreds of miserable women being pushed into the bathhouse and told to undress by the Blockältester and her Stubendiensts. Their clothing was to be packed by Pepi's *Kommando* and delivered to Tadek for processing.

SS Sturmmann Pherbinde called out to both of us, "Get ready!" and switched on the electrical controls. The machine was on. I watched the conveyor belt coming toward me and I felt the heat generated by the equipment. The sacks were hot and heavy. I collected them from the conveyor belt and passed them to Olga. She in turn took them to the table where her four friends were unpacking sacks and sorting articles of clothing. Then they dumped them on a big pile in front of the bathhouse.

This was an exceptionally bright and sunny morning. Birkenau's mist had disappeared and a warm, pleasant wind was blowing from the west, carrying the stench of burned flesh from the crematoria sites. The first group of bathed and shaven women emerged from the bathhouse and were told to wait naked in front of the trailer for their clothes. In columns of five, they were ordered to stand still and wait patiently until the first batch of disinfected sacks was ready for distribution. They represented all ages and all nationalities. All of them had clean-shaven heads as well as bodies shorn of body hair. Pushed by Capos, screamed at by their supervisors, confused and disoriented, they stood in columns of five and watched us working around the trailer. Women's life in the camp was a hell. They had to face lice, dirt, rats, mud, terror, incredibly unsanitary conditions, heavy physical work, hunger, and fear of the unknown. After a short stay in the camp, the most assertive and courageous women became ghostlike shadows. In spite of the sunny, warm day, some of the women were shivering. With their eyes wide open, they all stood naked, half-dry and half-wet, since towels were not available in the bathhouse.

Seeing SS troopers and inmates working around the trailer, the first group, especially the younger women, tried to cover their breasts with folded arms. Several healthy, young, and well-built girls—probably newcomers, or *Zugangs* in camp jargon—could be easily identified from the rest of the crowd by their bashful behavior. Others, older, tired, and humiliated women who had spent years in concentration camps and were familiar with the impersonal and cruel disinfection practices, were not bothered by their nakedness. They seemed to be resigned to their undignified circumstances. They stood patiently in formation waiting for their clothing. The older, sick and fragile women looked like walking skeletons, with drooping breasts, swollen legs, scabs, and tired eyes. They were supported on both sides by their younger companions.

I hardly had any time to observe them since the sacks were coming fast on the conveyor and I had to concentrate my attention on my work in order not to miss a delivery. I almost threw the sacks to Olga and she would run the short distance to the table where her friends were unpacking the disinfected sacks. Seeing so many naked women at the same time was a demeaning experience. I felt humiliated by the way they were treated by their supervisors and SS troopers, who pointed their canes to different parts of the women's bodies looking for hidden personal items. Nothing was allowed to be carried from the "dirty" to the "clean" side. Consequently every delousing meant the loss of valuable personal treasures and souvenirs. The only visible links with home and family, such as letters and photographs, were brutally torn from prisoners by their supervisors and the SS troopers.

After the first batch of disinfected sacks was delivered, inspected, and sorted out, the Blockältester gave a signal to the waiting crowd to start picking up their clothes. They all ran fast toward the pile, trying to pick up the best articles of clothing. Some women looked for their own dresses marked with their numbers, and others looked for the best available clothes regardless of to whom they used to belong. There were serious arguments, screams, and even fights. The Blockältester and her Stubendiensts with sticks and canes ran around among the fighting women and tried to restore peace. The fully dressed first group, with some women looking almost grotesque in their ill-fitting dresses, was led by one of the Stubendiensts to the already disinfected barrack. At noon, Omlauf announced a lunch break. The machine stopped. The SS troopers and both SS women disappeared for lunch. The water in the bathhouse was turned off and the barbers and disinfectors also left to eat lunch. Meanwhile, the second group of naked women left the bathhouse and stood in front of the trailer waiting for their clothing.

The bathhouse was serviced by a special women's *Entwesungskommando*. It was organized to accept new prisoners but also was used to provide delousing services to inmates. The *Kommando* consisted of low numbers, German and Slovak girls with a German woman Capo in charge. A very small *Kommando* of men coming to work every day from the Men's Camp supported this group. They were specialists, plumbers, and electricians who looked after bathhouse operations, water supply, and mechanical and electrical systems. Both groups had worked together for some time and I could sense very intimate relationships among some of their members. They treated Pepi's *Kommando* and us as outsiders or temporary help. However, since Omlauf was the highest SS authority in the bathhouse and we were part of his crew, they did not have much of a choice but to accept us as "equals."

Four women from Pepi's *Kommando* brought two cauldrons of soup. One was given to the women waiting for their clothing in front of the bathhouse. The second belonged to Pepi's group. From my work station, I watched the crowd of naked women standing in line under the pleasant summer sun as they silently and patiently waited for their rations. The Blockältester, assisted by her Stubendiensts, carefully served the soup into metal bowls, which were stacked behind her on the ground. This was a moment of glory and absolute power for her and she enjoyed every minute, lording it over her subordinates. All eyes looked at her ladle as she slowly picked up floating pieces of vegetables from the bottom of the cauldron for her friends and favorites. Each woman in complete silence, naked, with outstretched hands accepted a red metal bowl half-filled with tasteless and watery vegetable soup. From the distance, it looked almost like an ancient religious ritual. Block functionaries looked in their bowls for small pieces of floating vegetables graciously given them by their chief. The women quickly drank their meal from the metal bowls. There was no need to use spoons, since there were no solids to be lifted. As soon as they finished, all of the naked women formed a circle around the Blockältester and her cauldron, waiting anxiously for a second helping. The Blockältester scraped the bottom of the kettle and showed an empty cauldron to the inmates surrounding her. Nothing was left. There were no seconds. All of the women standing close, disappointed and still hungry, moved forward one step, looking for a chance to lick the empty cauldron. The Blockältester looked around and, after selecting a group of younger and healthier women, gave them the empty cauldron: "Clean this, but don't fight," she ordered.

Pepi acted more dignified and friendly as she dispersed her cauldron of soup among her workers. I picked up my bowl of soup from her and went behind the trailer with Olga. Sitting on a pile of sacks in the shadow of the trailer, between sips of watery soup, I tried to make a conversation in my best high-school German. Olga told me about her background. I learned that before the war, she had lived with her parents, one brother, and two sisters in Budapest, where her father had a business. Then, in 1942, they were evacuated to the country and in May of 1944 they were transported to Auschwitz. She had studied to be a music teacher and was already an accomplished pianist.

Olga acted very mature, calm, and composed, in light of the sudden changes in her life, especially the separation from her family and the daily fears and cruelties at the Women's Camp. She seemed to have an unusual ability to get along with people and to survive under the most difficult circumstances. During her first day in Birkenau, she somehow persuaded the barbers not to shave her head completely. Still showing beautiful short dark hair under her headscarf, with delicate features and dark eyes, she looked very feminine and attractive even in the ill-fitted dress. I noted that some of the plumbers had already looked her over in the bathhouse. She was a friend of Pepi, the Capo, whom she greatly admired. Right after their arrival in Birkenau, when most of the women were hysterical and cried day and night, Pepi was asked by the Blockältester to organize a group of women for the cleaning of washroom facilities. She selected the best workers, calmed them down, worked with them for a few weeks, and inspired them with confidence and hope. When asked again to volunteer for the sanitary work, she took her old group and organized the *Desinfektionskommando*, accepting the position of a Capo.

During our first morning, I watched her from a distance and noted that in spite of her youth (she was perhaps twenty-two or twenty-four years old), she acted with firmness and authority. At the same time, she treated all her workers with compassion and understanding. They in turn were willing to work hard and stay together as a newly formed and closely bonded family. They helped each other and looked after their mutual interests. Pepi was prepared to argue with anybody, including SS Blockführers, to defend "her girls." After listening to Olga, I told her, "Try to stay with this group as long as you can. This is a good *Kommando* and it will be easier for you to face hard times with a group of friends."

Omlauf and his staff, including two SS women supervisors, arrived back from lunch. Tadek stopped at my workstation to let me know that one of the women from the bathhouse would look for his wife. He sounded optimistic. Pherbinde gave the signal to start. The conveyor jerked and moved slowly. The afternoon was hot and humid, and the additional heat generated by the equipment made me sweat. I had to take my jacket off, and I worked in my undershirt. Olga was running from the trailer to the pile with many sacks. She looked tired but she still smiled when she picked up my sacks. By the time we finished the job of delousing six hundred women, we were all exhausted. The last group of women gathered their clothing and left the compound. The bathhouse was quiet. The only reminder of the pain and abuse suffered by hundreds of women were some articles of clothing left lying on the ground in the middle of the bathhouse yard. Sitting in the shadow of the trailer and trying to gather my strength after a long day's work, I watched Pepi's *Kommando* cleaning the yard and collecting assorted articles of clothing left behind. Tadek left his post and went to the bathhouse to search for news about his wife.

I sat behind the trailer and talked to Olga. We both knew that any contact, including conversation between men and women, was strictly forbidden. Both of us watched carefully for SS personnel wandering around the bathhouse and the trailer. I told her about my life in Poland prior to my arrest, omitting all reference to my underground activities. The fate of her family was on her mind all the time. She was generally aware of the gas chambers and the German extermination policy, but in her heart she hoped that her family was still held in one of the transit camps in Birkenau. Her mother was still a young woman, her brother was a healthy youngster, and both her sisters were teenagers. I did not have the heart or courage to tell her what SS Dr. Mengele did to thousands of deportees from Theresienstadt who were held in BIIb Camp. Last March they were transferred to the Quarantine Camp BIIa and then most of them were sent straight to Crematoria II and III.

Wiktor came and told me to be ready to leave as soon as Tadek came back from his quest for information about his wife. In a few minutes, I saw Tadek walking slowly across the courtyard. By looking at his tired and pale face, I sensed that the news was not good. He told me with tears in his eyes, "Janusz, they sent her to Ravensbruck last month."

I tried to reassure him: "Tadek, at least you know that she is alive. It may not be such a bad idea to leave this place. There is too much destruction going on and we are too close to the crematoria."

He looked at me and shook his head without a word. I did not think that he heard what I was saying. Then suddenly he turned to me and said, "I hope you are right."

I could see that he took the sad news about his wife's departure very hard when he quietly said to himself, "What am I going to tell my children if I ever see them again?" For the rest of the afternoon, as we waited for our escort, Tadek said nothing.

Wiktor came along with SS Rottenführer Charwin and said we should go back to the Men's Camp. This time we walked together, all three of us abreast. The SS man walked right behind us whistling one of his arias. We arrived early at the main gate. The camp orchestra was just setting up their instruments at the SS guardhouse, getting ready to play military marches for incoming field *Kommandos*. Charwin talked to the SS guard on duty and he waved us in.

"*Mutzen ab,*" called Wiktor as we marched through the main gate, making sure that we didn't miss a step.

The Men's Camp was almost empty since all healthy and able to work prisoners were still working on "outside" *Kommandos.* They were not due back from work for another hour. We rested on top of our bunk getting ready for roll call and the evening distribution of our daily ration of bread and margarine. Tadek was very quiet all evening and I respected his privacy. I could see that he had to have time to accept the fact that his wife was deported from Birkenau into an uncertain future somewhere in Germany.

The next morning Charwin waited for us outside the main gate. I remembered him well from our first day of work because most of the time he had spent talking and flirting with one of the SS supervisors. She was tall and slim, with blonde hair and blue eyes; a typical German woman glorified in the Nazi propaganda posters. She was very strict with her subordinates, including Pepi, and the Hungarian women stayed away from her if they could.

We walked our usual route and by the time we arrived at the bathhouse, Pepi's *Kommando* was already there. As we waited for the women designated for today's delousing, I went inside the bathhouse to see if some of the men from last year were still working. Capo was not there and all the men were strangers. The old crew was now working in the new men's bathhouse completed last December in section BII and located between "Canada's" barracks and Crematorium IV. Back at my post, I was ready to start working. Pherbinde stood behind the control panel. We all waited for his signal. Olga looked good that morning when she came to see me. I presented her with an apple from my food parcel. At first, she would not take it, but as I explained my situation and the fact that every week I received fresh food from my grandmother, she was very grateful for the gift.

The block scheduled for delousing was late and Omlauf was impatient. He turned to me unexpectedly and said, "*Langer*"—as Omlauf used to call me—"see what's holding them up."

"*Jawohl,* Herr Unterscharführer," I responded, pretending that I was honored by my new name and this assignment. I went to the bathhouse; the first group of women scheduled for delousing this morning were already there in an undressing room, a large hall with benches along the walls and metal hooks above. Most of the women were already undressed, holding their underwear and clothes in their hands and waiting. Like yesterday, younger women, recent arrivals with better-looking bodies and healthier skin, tried to cover their nakedness and hide behind others in the naked crowd. Older women, indifferent to what was going on around them, did not care about anything. Without paying attention to the SS men who were walking around or to male prisoners, they all waited silently, resigned to their fate. They all knew from their long camp experience that the delousing process was an unpleasant and humiliating task.

I asked the Bathhouse Capo, "Why don't we start? Omlauf is losing his patience." The Capo, a German woman with a green triangle looked at me, shrugged her shoulders and said, "We ran out of rope to tie their underwear and dresses together before they are packed in your sacks." Then she added that she would be getting more string in a few minutes.

I was not terribly keen to explain to Omlauf the reason for the delay. I thought about the old story of "shooting the messenger who brings bad news," and I decided to wait for a few minutes until new supplies of rope were delivered. The women "barbers" waited for their customers by their stools. The shower room was empty and a group of disinfectors stood patiently holding canisters of calcium chloride ready to spray the shaved areas of all women after their showers. The Capo called to me from across the hall: "We have the rope and we are ready to start." Relieved, I went outside and reported to Omlauf: "Herr Unterscharführer, they are ready to start." "It is about time," Omlauf muttered to himself. SS Sturmmann Pherbinde pushed the control button: "Go!" The conveyer started to move toward me as Tadek loaded sacks at his end.

The day passed so quickly that we hardly had time for lunch. I figured that we processed eight hundred sacks. By late afternoon, I was exhausted. Olga looked tired and in the warm spring air, her face was sweating as she ran with hundreds of sacks from the trailer to the distribution pile. I wanted to take some time to look for the old block where Vera used to be, but I had no time to wander around the camp. Men were not allowed to walk unescorted to the women's blocks. By SS standards, this was considered a serious breach of discipline, and if one was caught, assignment to the Penal Company was almost guaranteed. On the way back to the Men's Camp, Tadek tried to convince himself that perhaps his wife's transfer to Ravensbruck was for the best.

Life in Birkenau grew more hectic every day. Hungarian transports were coming around the clock. Thousands of young women were still held without registration in the old "Mexico" camp. As we walked every morning to work, we watched hundreds of desperate and dehydrated women, whose ranks were increasing continuously. The washrooms, latrines, and open spaces between barracks were full of undernourished and confused shadows holding dearly to life but aware they were moving slowly and persistently toward death. Some women, tired of their miserable existence, deliberately "walked to the wire" toward the forbidden zone of electrified fences to be shot by SS guards stationed at the watchtowers.

In the Men's Camp, roll calls were longer and more troublesome. Newcomers not familiar with the camp's layout and forgetting the number of their blocks were missing their roll call places. SS Blockführers assisted by Blockältesters ran through the blocks tracking missing inmates. Some of the missing prisoners were too sick to be bothered with roll calls. Others were half-conscious, and many of them were dead. All of them, however, had to be accountable to the Blockältester at roll-call time.

For the first two weeks in June, we had to work long hours. At least one full block of approximately eight hundred women was scheduled for delousing each day. Although the work was very demanding, the assignment at the Women's Camp was still considered to be one of the better *Kommandos* and many of our friends envied our luck. By the end of June, the tempo of all activities on the ramp, as well as in the camp, was even more accelerated.

Quite often the bathhouse was visited by the senior SS officials. Marie Mandel, SS supervisor of the Women's Camp, along with her staff, stopped occasionally and watched the long lines of naked women standing in front of the bathhouse and waiting their turn to enter the shower room. They also observed operations at the disinfection trailer. The SS Unterscharführer Omlauf explained the working process and the basic elements of the equipment. I noted that SS wardresses were more vicious in treatment of women inmates during those visits. The functionaries, Blockältesters, and Capos screamed louder and used their canes more often in front of their bosses. The smallest disobedience or wrong move by one of the inmates was punished in front of Mandel with a ferocity and vengeance unknown to civilized people. As the crowd of women stood in front of the bathhouse before undressing, the Blockältester looked for the most trivial offenses and punished the offenders without mercy. If a woman fainted in a waiting formation, a brutal kick in the behind was the forceful encouragement to get up and hold her place in line before entering the shower.

Behind the bathhouse and across the barbed wire, next to an adjoining street leading to the crematoria, trains from Hungary were coming day and night. The railroad platform was always full of people waiting in long lines for selection, and the sweetish stench of burning flesh was getting worse. The "Mexico" camp had reached its full capacity, and some of the transports were on temporary hold at the old Theresienstadt camp prior to deportation to other camps in Germany. *Sonderkommando* was moved from Block 13 in the Men's Camp, split into smaller groups, and relocated to each crematorium, using lofts as living quarters.

One morning I mentioned to Wiktor that I wanted to take a short walk during lunch time and look for Vera. He was noncommittal and warned me, "Be careful, and I don't want to know anything about your escapade." I skipped the soup during lunchtime, looked carefully around as I entered the main street at the Women's Camp, and walked toward Vera's old block. There was hardly anybody inside, so I knocked on the door to Blockältester's room.

A young woman with a green triangle opened the door. This was not Vera's old friend. "What do you want?" she asked in German.

Calmly, I tried to explain: "I am looking for Vera who used to be Schreiber here last year."

"Oh, Vera! She and all the Jewish whores left for Ravensbruck last March. Anything else?" She looked hostile and her response was like a sudden bolt of lightning.

I noted her Blockältester red armband, "No, thank you." I turned around, disappointed and disillusioned.

As I walked slowly toward the bathhouse, I did not pay too much attention to what was going on around me. I tried to argue silently with myself that I should not be surprised that Vera had left Birkenau. With so many changes and so many deaths, one should not get used to or attached to anybody. Losing friends was part of Birkenau's tradition. "Stop!" I heard a sharp command in front of me. I raised my head and saw an SS officer with the silver insignia standing by the bicycle in front of me. I looked closer, pulled off my cap and recognized SS Hauptsturmführer Mengele, Lagerarzt of the Gypsy's Camp. Mengele had quite a reputation among the prisoners in Auschwitz. I remembered seeing him before on the men's hospital grounds when he visited the Jewish block, accompanied by other SS doctors. Also I had heard about him from prisoner doctors, nurses, and patients in the hospital. His name and his presence terrified everyone. I also remembered that he frequently participated in the selections at the ramp and in the hospital. He was deeply committed to the Nazi ideology and obsessed with medical research on children, especially twins. I remembered his office in the Gypsy Camp, which I could see clearly during my routine work hours as street cleaner in the men's hospital.

He was tall and slim, well-dressed and almost elegant in his bluish uniform. Holding onto his bicycle, he looked at me and asked in a slightly irritated voice, "What are you doing here?"

I responded in my best German, "I am working for the *Desinfektionskommando* in the women's bathhouse, Herr Hauptsturmführer." He looked at me closely. "You know that you are not allowed to wander alone in the Women's Camp?"

Although I was trembling inside, I stood straight at full attention, "Yes, Herr Hauptsturmführer."

He waved his arm in the direction of the bathhouse: "Go back to work now. If I ever see you wandering again, you will be punished. Do you understand?"

"Yes, Herr Hauptsturmführer." I watched for him to signal my dismissal. My heart pounded heavily. I knew that if he asked for my number, I would face an even more uncertain future in Birkenau. Detention in the Penal Company, deportation, and other forms of punishment flashed through my mind. Mengele waved his arm and said, "Go back to your work and stay there."

"Yes, Herr Hauptsturmführer," I responded in a shaky voice as he mounted his bicycle. He did not ask me for my number.

I walked fast to the bathhouse wondering if I should say anything to Wiktor. I decided not to mention this incident in order to avoid lectures and complaints. Tadek was waiting for me by the trailer, "What's wrong? You look terrible."

I tried to sound calm, "Oh, nothing. I could not find Vera. She left camp a few months ago. I don't even know where she is now."

This time Tadek was sympathetic and said, "Don't worry. Look, you hardly knew her. This is not the right place to get attached to anybody." With the image of Mengele in front of me, I responded calmly, "You are absolutely right. Let's not talk about it any more." I closed my eyes. Mengele somehow disappeared, and I could see Vera talking to me for the last time.

I looked around at the people mingling in the bathhouse enclosure. I had just lost a friend and I was certain I would never see her again; just like Icek, Witek, Toni, Maurice, and many others. Sitting on a pile of disinfected clothes, I wondered, "How can one be surrounded day and night by thousands of people and be so terribly lonely at the same time?" SS Sturmmann Pherbinde arrived back from his lunch, ready to start the afternoon shift. He called to one of the SS women supervisors. She waved her cane to the Bathhouse Capo and the conveyor started to run.

Walking back at the end of the day, all three of us were silent. Tadek thought about his wife, I was wondering about Vera, and Wiktor seemed to keep his thoughts to himself. I noted that during the day Wiktor occasionally disappeared from the bathhouse. Nobody seemed to pay any attention to his prolonged absences. I knew that he was meeting somebody in one of the women barracks, but I was not sure if he was socializing or carrying out underground work and acting as a messenger for the secret military organization. Remembering what he told me a few months ago in the hospital, I never asked him any questions.

After the first few weeks of intensive work at the women's bathhouse, we were getting more familiar with the disinfection procedure and the new environment. The work was demanding and the pace was very fast. We were processing several hundreds sacks a day, more than ever. Sacks were well packed and heavy. We all felt that we were being pushed very hard by the SS Kommandoführer and his staff. At the same time, I recognized that in spite of the physical hardship this was a good assignment. We were sheltered from backbreaking work like digging ditches or carrying heavy loads of building material in all kinds of weather. We were also free from capricious abuses of Capos and other camp officials. Once a week we were allowed to take a shower and have our clothes disinfected.

However, I was bothered by the cruel treatment of the women prisoners. The SS men and women were very callous and indifferent to the pain and suffering of hundreds of the deloused victims, humiliated and struggling every day through the disinfection process. All day SS men walked with their canes among naked women and looked for the smallest breach of discipline. Beatings and kicking of the innocent prisoners happened all the time, and the screams of persecuted women were heard coming from the bathhouse day and night.

As we watched every day the inhumane treatment of women prisoners, we felt angry and helpless. I could see that both Wiktor and Tadek were very upset. I recognized that there was very little that we could do, except observe and remember some of the most painful incidents and hope that one day we would be able altogether to even our scores with the oppressors.

On a slow day, when the arrival of women inmates was delayed for many different reasons, I had a chance to talk to Olga and listen to her hopes, fears, and expectations. My own problems were slowly gathering on the horizon. Until now, the weekly delivery of food parcels from my grandmother had been very regular. All the time I recognized how much effort and sacrifice she had to make in order to keep sending costly food products to Birkenau. The cost of a single food package was high so I knew that the total cost of weekly packages over the year must have been enormous and it was a real financial hardship for my family. I deeply appreciated those sacrifices since my grandmother's food parcels were the lifeline that kept me alive in the camp. With the front line getting closer and closer, I dreaded the time when I would not be able to receive my weekly food supplies.

One day during our short lunch break, when Tadek and I were resting in the shadow of the disinfection trailer, Wiktor came to see me and said.

"Janusz, SS Unterscharführer Omlauf wants one of us to go with him to the old camp in Auschwitz. Can you go?"

With some apprehension, I said I would. This was my first opportunity to leave Birkenau and visit the old camp in Auschwitz, and I was both concerned and curious.

"This task should not take you more than a couple of hours," Wiktor explained to me and then added, "During your absence, I will take your place and work with Tadek at the trailer. Let me check with Omlauf to see if he will approve your assignment—be ready in a few minutes."

After talking with Wiktor, SS Unterscharführer Omlauf told me to come with him to the old camp.

I quickly checked my clothes to make sure that all my numbers were properly displayed on my prisoner's uniform, in accordance with camp regulations. I waved good-bye to Tadek and Wiktor and in front of Omlauf I walked briskly towards the BIb camp gate. At the gate, as we were leaving the women's compound, I took off my hat and reported loudly to the SS man on duty who stood in front of the SS guard house, "*Schutzhäftling* 150302 requests permission to leave the camp." The SS man wrote my number in his roster book, looked me over, and nodded.

Outside the gate, we turned right and walked toward the main watchtower. In no time, accompanied by the SS Unterscharführer Omlauf as my escort, I was on my way to the old camp in Auschwitz, or "*Stammlager,*" as it was known among SS personnel. We walked along the new railroad ramp in Birkenau. The ramp was empty except for the prisoners from the "Canada" *Kommando* who were loading the leftover luggage from the recently arrived transport. Several SS men watching the working prisoners would occasionally shout at them.

"Faster, faster, you idiots, the new transport is coming in a few minutes."

Overworked men from the "Canada" *Kommando* frantically piled large suitcases on the hand-pushed roll-wagons parked in the middle of the platform. Some of the SS troopers standing across the railroad platform recognized Omlauf from the distance and shouted loud greetings and waved to him in very friendly manner. It was obvious that Omlauf was both well known and popular among his comrades.

Discreetly, I looked around. We passed under the main watchtower and left Birkenau behind us. The deserted country road on which we walked wound through cultivated farm fields. Then we crossed the main railroad line connecting Kraków and Vienna and approached the industrial complex of several brick and wooden barracks constructed outside of the old Auschwitz camp. The recently abandoned *Judenrampe* and railroad yards were on our right. In the distance I could already see the red brick administrative buildings. Closer on my left side was a wooden barrack housing the SS office responsible for "protective custody." Adjoining this office was the SS guardhouse. In front of me, I faced the famous Auschwitz entry gate with metal letters embossed above the entrance that declared, "*Arbeit Macht Frei.*"

I stopped in front of the SS guard, removed my hat and reported in German.

"*Schutzhäftling* 150302 request permission to enter the camp." Omlauf talked briefly to the SS Rottenführer standing in front of the guardhouse.

Omlauf told me to wait and showed me a place behind the entrance gate inside the camp. "Do not move until I come back"—he warned and then disappeared in the direction of a large, brick building. The imposing structure was partially hidden behind the administrative facilities and used as a storage for ammunition and disinfection supplies.

With my hat in my hand, I stood inside the camp near the main gate and looked around. It was early afternoon and traffic was light. The camp population, consisting of thousands of inmates, was working somewhere around the Auschwitz area. Until the *Kommandos* returned from work in the early evening for a meager meal and few hours of well-deserved rest, the main camp street was quiet and almost deserted.

Piepel, a young boy in crisp prisoner's uniform who served SS men in the guardhouse as a personal valet, came out from the barrack and waved to me. This was a good job. Young boys chosen by the SS men and functionary prisoners were assigned to clean the shoes, run errands, sweep floors, and keep their rooms in spotless condition.

SS Rottenführer, with a roster in his hand, stood across from me in front of the guardhouse and controlled the traffic. Occasionally, groups of prisoners went through the gate. All inmates, including functionaries identified by the color of the armbands as well as ordinary prisoners, were always accompanied by the SS guards and had to stop in front of the SS Rottenführer to report their business before passing the gate.

Across from me on the other side of the main entrance I noticed a stand for the camp orchestra. As in Birkenau, all work *Kommandos* marched twice a day through the gate, accompanied by the sound of music. Behind the stand, there was the blank wall of the kitchen barrack. I turned around and looked discreetly up and around me. Behind me stood a large, two-story, brick building with the number 24 painted above the entrance door. I remembered stories from Birkenau that Block 24 was well known to inmates from Auschwitz. On the second floor of this building, behind the closed curtains, was a camp brothel serving functionaries and other inmates who were camp officials. During my short stay outside the entrance gate I did not see anybody leaving or entering the premises.

Observing life around me in the old camp in Auschwitz, I had a strange impression that the huge, two-story, brick buildings, laid out in a symmetric pattern and extending from Block 24 into a labyrinth of deserted camp streets, were staring at me silently. I felt like an intruder in the strange

Stammlager surroundings. The temporary character of wooden buildings in Birkenau brought hope for an early conclusion to this nightmare, but the permanency of the brick blocks in Auschwitz overpowered me with despair. Silently, I deeply regretted that I had listened to Wiktor and agreed to visit the old camp in Auschwitz.

Now I looked eagerly to Omlauf's return. After almost two hours of waiting, he finally returned with a package under his arm, and he handed me the brown paper carton.

I looked curiously inside the package. There were two round, metal containers, similar to what we used to buy in a paint store before the war. On one side of each container there was a picture of a skull and crossbones. Below the picture some kind of explanation was written in German. Again, I glanced quickly inside the brown package and noticed that on each container in large letters was also printed the word *Zyklon B*.

Now I understood. Omlauf had picked up poisonous gas from SS Disinfections Depot in Auschwitz to delouse the women barracks by the *Desinfektionskommando* in Birkenau. As the SS SDG, Omlauf was authorized to handle poisonous gas for the purpose of disinfecting prisoners' barracks. Then I suddenly realized that this was the same gas that the SS used to gas Jews in the crematoria.

As I took the package with both containers from Omlauf, my hands were shaking. I could not believe that I was actually holding the instrument of death. Suddenly, I remembered thousands of Jews—men, women, and children—marching through the camp to the Birkenau crematoria. I also remembered seeing Red Cross ambulances delivering deadly packages from the Auschwitz warehouses.

Omlauf looked at me and smiled. "*Langer,* don't worry. Nothing will happen to you. Make sure that both containers are tightly closed and do not fall down with your package."

Carrying the package with gas containers under my arm, I walked slowly and carefully back to Birkenau. Walking behind me whistling popular German songs, SS Unterscharführer Omlauf was not concerned about my deadly cargo.

The walk back was long and frightening. I chose my steps carefully, carrying both containers very gently, as if they were full of highly explosive nitroglycerin. My hands were continuously sweating, making it more difficult to hold the package firmly and avoid any unexpected slippage.

Even Omlauf noticed my anxiety, and as we crossed BIb gate, he smiled and said, "*Langer*—relax. Nothing will happen to you. I have to carry this every day."

I was relieved that my journey was coming to an end. Of course, I could not expect he would understand my feelings. I was not so much concerned about my personal safety as I was tortured with guilt and rage that I was forced to carry this instrument of destruction and death. When Omlauf took the package with both containers from me, I felt a heavy load was lifted from my shoulders.

I went to the nearest washroom, and disregarding female inmates around me, scrubbed and washed my hands hard. Some of the women, engaged in their own cleaning chores, looked at me with curiosity and silently observed my erratic behavior. Slowly, I calmed down and returned to my work station at the disinfection trailer. I whispered to Wiktor. "Never again ask me to go with Omlauf to the old camp."

At the beginning of July, Wiktor told us that starting the following Monday, we would have to work night shifts. Apparently the decision was made by the Women's Camp Lagerführer to delouse some of the blocks in the evening. That meant that after spending ten hours working in the field, women prisoners were forced to spend sleepless nights in the bathhouse, and then in the morning, after a formal roll call, depart for their regular work. It was also intended that their blocks, including mattresses and blankets, would be treated with chemicals or disinfected by Zyklon B gasses while they were "processed" at the bathhouse. This was a murderous schedule, and I anticipated that many sick and elderly women would not be able to survive the hardship of working all day and the misery of delousing all night without a few hours of decent rest.

The following Monday after evening roll call, the three of us reported to the gate. Omlauf, on a bicycle, was already waiting for us outside the SS guard post. The SS Blockführer on duty noted our numbers in the log book and we left for the Women's Camp. In the evening the route looked somehow different. Thousands of electric lights mounted on concrete pylons illuminated long lines of barbed wire enclosing each camp. Bright reflectors on the top of watchtowers and additional huge antiaircraft searchlights mounted on the trucks rotated slowly, searching the perimeter of the Birkenau camp for potential escapees. A yellowish glow, reflecting the intensity of electrical installations surrounding the camp, hung above the barracks roofs. The streets were empty and quiet. Occasional duty calls from sentries stationed on the top of watchtowers interrupted the silence of the night. On the west side of the camp, closer to the Wisła River, tall, square, and dark chimney stacks discharged flames from the crematoria ovens. The bathhouse also looked different. Our trailer and work stations were all lighted. The space in front of the bathhouse was illuminated with several powerful reflectors, turning the dark, summer night into a luminous island.

In the bathhouse, hundreds of women were already waiting for their turn to be shaved, disinfected, and washed. They stood in long lines in front of Slovak girls who skillfully shaved their heads in not more than one minute per person. Pepi's *Kommando* girls were busy putting sacks in front of Tadek's work station. We all waited for SS Sturmmann Pherbinde, who was late. I saw Omlauf impatiently looking at his watch. It looked like our "electrical chief" was in some kind of trouble. Finally, he arrived, and after talking briefly to Omlauf, gave us the sign to start. The conveyor started moving toward me. Around midnight we all had a half hour break. Pepi's girls lay on the piles of disinfected clothes and rested, eating some of their saved bread rations. Omlauf, with his SS troopers and SS women supervisors, disappeared from the compound.

I sat with Olga by the trailer and we talked about everything but Birkenau. We both looked for an emotional escape from the misery of our camp existence, pretending to be normal. My German was getting better every evening, though it was ironic that both of us, victims of the Nazis, had to use our oppressor's language to communicate.

For a person born and raised in a respectable middle—class environment in Budapest, Olga had somehow managed to adjust to life in Birkenau. She still worried about the rest of her family in the transit camp. Every time we talked about their chances for survival at the ramp selection, she looked for my reassurances that they were still alive. Then we talked about our childhood, schools, friends, and the end of the war. I tried to calm her down. But regardless of how hard we tried, it was impossible to disregard the harsh realities of the present. In the darkness of the night, with all the security lights shining, the clearly visible red and sometimes yellow flames continuously coming out from the crematoria chimneys reminded us of our fellow prisoners' fate. Sometimes we stopped talking and looked silently at the fires. Behind Crematorium V, where SS Kommandant Höss ordered trenches dug, burned-out bodies under open air generated a yellowish glow of high intensity clearly visible from the bathhouse.

As soon as the SS men and SS women supervisors were back, Pherbinde called to the Women's Bathhouse Capo: "Let's start!" A new bunch of shaved, washed, and disinfected women came naked from the bathhouse and, in columns of five, waited in front of the trailer for their clothing. At 1 A.M., with reflectors flooding the yard with a yellow tint, the crowd of stark naked women of all ages and nationalities stood silently and watched us working around the trailer. They were trying desperately to snatch a moment of rest.

Working hours during the night shift seemed to drag on longer than normal day hours. The dark sky, the perimeter lights around us and reflectors above our heads, the crowd of naked women, silent and defiant in the middle

of the yard, all looked like an elaborate stage set during an evening performance in an open-air theater. I closed my eyes briefly as I imagined that the SS
troopers and the SS women supervisors played the main characters in this
sad human drama. The rest of us were part of the supporting cast. My fan-
tasy was rudely interrupted by Wiktor's irritated voice, "Janusz, watch out!
Sacks are piling up on your conveyer!" In no time, I suppressed my fantasies;
except for the noises coming from the bathhouse and occasional shots from
the crematoria, the rest of the camp was sleeping silently.

That night we finished our work about 4 A.M. By the time we walked
back to the Men's Camp, signs of life and intensive morning activities were
seen everywhere. There was the usual commotion and confusion among
newcomers who had a hard time identifying their own blocks in the dark.
After passing the main gate, we entered the camp and joined our Blockältester for a roll-call report. It took about an hour to find and count all inmates. When *Kommandos* were ready to leave the camp for work outside,
Tadek and I returned to our bunk for a few hours of well-deserved rest after
a long and exhausting night shift. Except for a few Stubendiensts cleaning
bunks and scrubbing floors, the block was very quiet.

There were, however, some advantages to working during the night in
the women's compound. Evening shifts at the disinfection site allowed us to
establish and maintain regular communication with our friends at the
Women's Camp. Every night we were able to share with them the latest information from the outside world, and at the same time, bring the good news
about the Allied forces' rapid advances on both fronts. The delousing
process usually started at the disinfection trailer one hour after the completion of the evening women's roll call. This late start made it possible for us to
meet secretly behind the bathhouse and at that time deliver notes and messages that we smuggled through the SS-guarded gates. As there were more
and more visible signs of the imminent liquidation of Auschwitz, the underground communication among inmates locked up in different camps increased considerably. Husbands, fathers, and brothers made every possible
effort to contact their loved ones prior to their deportation to other camps.
Since we were one of the very few *Kommandos* allowed to enter the Women's
Camp every evening, all of us were besieged with many requests from the
men in BIId to deliver their secret messages.

For the past several weeks, almost every evening I carried a letter from
Jan to his wife Irena. Both of them had been arrested in March 1943 and
after painful interrogations by the Gestapo in Pawiak prison sent to Birkenau. After arrival, they were separated and lost contact. Irena was assigned
to camp BIb and worked at the agricultural farm, while Jan was a mechanic.
After a short stay in Witek's *Kommando,* where I met him for the first time,

Jan ended up working as a fitter in *Zerlegebetriebskommando*. Hundreds of prisoners with mechanical skills like his were used for the dismantling of damaged German airplanes in search of reusable parts. The work was carried out in a nearby field close to the railroad tracks, but outside of the inner sentry lines. I was surprised by his assignment, since this was a favorable and almost exclusive *Kommando* of Russian prisoners of war. They searched the various parts of damaged airplanes for traces of alcohol, which they smuggled into the camp, drank themselves, or traded with others for gold or food. Occasionally, they could also find usable arms and ammunition that could be sold to *Sonderkommando* for gold or diamonds.

I recognized the risk involved in carrying letters every evening and watched nervously for any unusual signs of the SS inspections at the gate. My previously proven method of hiding letters in my cap behind a fake lining still worked for me. During each search I kept my cap high above my head in my outstretched hands, as the SS Blockführer at the gate inspected my pockets.

After my unhappy experience with Dr. Mengele, when I had met him in the middle of the Women's Camp, I was very careful not to be caught again by the SS officials. With so many selections being made on the unloading railroad ramps, contact with women was strictly forbidden, and every evening the SS women supervisors watched us very closely.

I was not very keen on serving as a messenger and risking the loss of my good job with the *Desinfektionskommando,* but I considered Jan to be my good friend and felt obligated to help him establish and maintain contact with his wife. They were both young, likable, a dedicated couple married just a few years ago in 1942, and still very much in love despite the Birkenau horrors and hardships of their everyday existence.

I talked to Jan every day in the Men's Camp, and I knew that he was terribly upset at not being able to help his wife. I could see in his eyes a feeling of frustration and bitterness. I tried to calm him down and talked him into a more rational and less emotional attitude. He listened to me, then with tears in his eyes said gently: "Janusz, it is very easy for you to be calm and pragmatic — but she is my love, my best friend, and my wife. I love her so much and may not ever see her again. I feel so helpless and worthless as never before."

Irena was a small and slender woman in her early twenties, with dark, large eyes and an angelic, radiant face. Her brown hair, cut very short after the last disinfection, was growing back in curls, making her look attractive in spite of her shapeless blue-white prison dress. Months of imprisonment made her "street smart" but still a very compassionate person. At her *Aussenkommando* she tried to help her older and less fortunate sisters and protected them against callous and vicious women functionaries. Her good knowledge of German helped her to deal with Capos and stay calm in the most difficult circumstances.

After getting to know her better, I treated her as if she was my own older sister, and I admired her composure. Most evenings, after the distribution of bread portions at the women's blocks, we met secretly behind the bathhouse's long, brick building in Camp BIb. Irena picked up Jan's letters and then we chatted for a few minutes, watching constantly for the SS wardresses who silently made rounds between blocks. In the darkness of the night and away from electric lights, dressed in dark capes and long boots, the wardresses looked like ghosts moving arrogantly among the doomed victims and relentlessly looking for new prey. They never missed the smallest opportunity to punish an inmate for breaking camp rules. Possessing an extra pair of underwear, talking to men, or hiding from work resulted in many hours of kneeling on the gravel with two bricks held in stretched arms over their heads.

One day I learned from Wiktor that Irena's block was selected for disinfection within the next few nights. When I told her about this, she was upset, terrified of the delousing process, and looked for any possible way to avoid it. "Irena," I said. " I don't understand you. For someone who is doing so well in this miserable existence, how can you be so upset about one night's disinfection routine. Sure it is a humiliating procedure but almost everybody survives it." Then I reassured her that I would try to help her as much as I could and nothing would happen to her.

She seemed calm and apologized for her hysterical outburst: "You are right—we all went through worse things than the delousing procedure." Then she added: "I am aware that people are dying every day on my *Kommando* and that nobody is getting killed during the disinfection process. I just hate to parade naked in front of the SS men." I looked at her and said: "Irena— Birkenau is not the place to worry about your modesty. This is the place to worry about your life."

She shook her head and said, "I know, you are right, and I should not make that much fuss about it." Then she told me that she had a few letters from Jan and their wedding photograph. Also, she had recently organized decent underwear and a couple of shirts and hated to lose all of these things during the delousing routine. I tried to sound encouraging, "Irena—you must go through this. If you worry about souvenirs and your underwear, give them to me for safekeeping. I will hide them in my trailer and return them back to you after you take the shower and pass the disinfection process."

The next day she brought me a small package. I realized that Wiktor would be terribly upset if he knew about this arrangement. Withholding personal belongings from the disinfection procedure was a violation of basic SS hygienic regulations. If this was discovered, Omlauf would most likely send me to the bunker in Auschwitz. Because of the 1942 typhus epidemic, in the SS men's eyes, a prisoner's attempt to avoid disinfection by hiding some clothing was one of the worst offenses in the camp. The SS strongly believed that the smuggling of personal effects defeated the purpose of disinfection and exposed prisoners and their own personnel to infectious diseases.

I took Irena's package with the letters and photographs to the trailer and asked Tadek to pack her personal clothing in one of his sacks, then run it on the conveyor toward me like any other sack of clothes packed by the girls for disinfection. In the late evening, Irena's block was lined up in front of the bathhouse. I gave her a victory sign from the distance, indicating that everything was under control. The long line of women started undressing at the command of the Blockältester, who was a middle-aged German woman with a black triangle. The story was going around the camp that she had been one of the Hamburg's prostitutes arrested before the war and sent to the concentration camp for rehabilitation. She was heavily built, tall, very muscular, with a large bosom and deep voice. Her language was full of filthy epithets and she cursed all the time.

I watched Irena from the distance. Even in the reflection of yellowish lights in front of the bathhouse, among hundreds of worn-out women, she looked attractive but nervous. Her short, brown, curly hair made her look even younger than twenty-two. Lost in the crowd of SS men and functionaries, she smiled shyly at me from the distance.

"Take it off"—called the Blockältester in her hoarse voice. "Faster, Faster"—she yelled, waving her stick and watching the undressing women. Since Irena had given me all her underwear and her shirt previously for safekeeping, she had nothing under her blue-white dress. The German woman was furious.

"Where is your underwear you Polish whore?" She shouted at the top of her voice. "Where did you hide your pants?"

Then she hit her hard with her fist. Irena tried to protect her face from the assaults. She screamed from pain and tried to hide behind the first line of the already undressed women, but the Blockältester would not slow down her attack. She kicked Irena in her stomach and yelled even louder, "Tell me where you hid your underwear or you will be really sorry." Helplessly, I watched what was going on from the distance.

The conveyor belt already started running fully loaded with sacks and I could not leave my position. Even if I could, it was unthinkable for male prisoners to publicly interfere with the official duties of women functionaries, especially in front of SS men and SS wardresses. I knew I had to do something drastic to stop the beating. Out of desperation, I turned to the SS Sturmmann

Pherbinde, who was sitting close to me at his control panels. I pointed my shaking finger at the Blockältester and said calmly, "Herr Sturmmann—this woman in front of the bathhouse is holding our flow. I am almost out of dirty sacks." Pherbinde looked at Tadek's table. Fortunately it was empty.

Pointing his finger, he yelled at the Blockältester. "Leave this woman alone and keep feeding the line."

One of the SS wardresses prodded the German woman with her cane, and said, "Can't you hear your orders. Stop beating this woman now." The beating stopped immediately. Irena sobbed uncontrollably, she was shaking and her face was covered with blood.

Olga who worked beside me sensed my pain and silently helped me to open the sack to recover Irena's personal belongings. My unexpected outburst and intervention surprised Tadek. This was the first time that I had ever said anything to SS Sturmmann Pherbinde. Fortunately neither Omlauf nor Wiktor were in close proximity of the trailer.

During the midnight break I went to look for Irena. She was now dressed, waiting with the rest of her inmates for the completion of the delousing process. We hid behind the first few rows of women and secretly I gave her back the photographs and letters and disinfected underwear. "Courage"—I whispered to her ear. With tears in her eyes, she responded: "Thanks Janusz. Please don't tell Jan what has happened." I promised I would not, and touched her face. It was bruised and her nose was still bleeding. I whispered again that she should try to stay calm, and returned to my trailer. Never did I mention this incident to Jan. "How is she doing?" He asked me the following day. "Just fine—Do not worry. She is a tough young lady and you should be proud of her."

Constantly witnessing the sufferings of thousands of women in Birkenau and being unable to do anything at all made me feel outraged.

I thought that my involvement with Irena was finished, but I was wrong. The next evening, Stenia, the Lagerältester or Camp Senior Prisoner in the Women's Camp came to see Wiktor. Stenia was a slender Polish woman, about forty years old. She had a civilian dress marked with red paint as required by the camp rules to prevent escapes, and she wore shiny black boots. Stenia projected an aura of cruelty and indifference to her less fortunate sisters. Her name was well known in Birkenau . I was told by women inmates that she frequently slapped prisoners without any reason and carried a long wooden cane, which she didn't hesitate to use on her subordinates.

I watched her from a short distance and heard as she talked to Wiktor. "I resent your worker's interference with my Blockältester."

Since Wiktor was not aware of yesterday's incident, he did not know what Stenia was talking about. He asked what was wrong. But Stenia lost her patience and raged hysterically: "Apparently, you don't even know what your people are doing. I will have to report this to Mandel." Wiktor did not want to make an issue, especially since he did not know what she was talking about. "I will look into this," he said. "Going to the Kommandant will not do either one of us any good. Remember that SS orderlies report to the chief SS doctor and not to the Kommandant. Your Lagerführer will not like it if we bring our internal quarrels in front of her bosses."

She shook her head. "Perhaps you are right. I hope this won't happen again." Then she turned around and left abruptly.

Wiktor called me to ask me what this was all about. After my explanation he was not too happy. "Janusz, don't do this again. All three of us may be in trouble. Irena may also be hurt since she lives all the time in the same barrack with the brutal German supervisor." I apologized and promised such a thing would not happen again, but Wiktor was not convinced. "Don't try to be a hero and a gentleman in the future. This is the wrong place and the wrong time."

Again he was right. I sulked in my thoughts for the rest of the shift. Only Olga tried to cheer me up and asked me half seriously: "Would you fight for me as well?" I could not help but smile. "Of course, Olga. You are much prettier than Irena and you are single."

She smiled, but when she looked across the railroad tracks and saw in the distance Crematorium III, with its tall chimneys from which yellow flames were shooting up with full force, she had tears in her eyes.

At the end of July, Tadek told me that Wiktor had received his first bonus. In the spring of 1943, the SS administration introduced compensation or a "bonus system" for prisoners, to encourage all inmates to increase their productivity. The monthly candidate's lists were submitted by each Lagerältester for the review and approval of the SS Lagerführer. Selected prisoners received very low bonuses of one to five German marks per person. With that money, they were allowed to purchase cigarettes or other items such as pickles, snails, mineral water, or shaving cream in the camp's canteen for prisoners. No other items were available.

As we walked to work through the main gate, one evening at the beginning of August, we noticed a long line of SS trucks lined up in front of the Gypsy Camp. As soon as we passed the gate, we could hear the sirens and loud calls behind us: "Lagersperre—all inside!"

On our way to the bathhouse, we passed a column of Polish doctors and nurses marching from the Gypsy Camp. The following day, after talking to his friends in the hospital, Wiktor told us that last night the whole Gypsy Camp had been sent to the gas chambers. The trucks we had seen had provided transportation. Prior to selection, all doctors and nurses were expelled from the camp and housed in Penal Company at Block 11 in the Men's Camp. Dr. Mengele's experimental twins were moved from Block 10 in the Gypsy Camp to the men's hospital compound in Birkenau.

Wiktor also learned from his underground contacts that the extermination of Hungarian Jews was slowly coming to an end, and because of this, Höss had left Auschwitz at the end of July. SS Sturmbannführer Baer assumed command of the total complex, including the old camp in Auschwitz, Birkenau, as well as all subcamps. The turmoil in accepting new transports from Slovakia, Poland, Italy, France, and other countries was still going on. As the trains with new deportees arrived at the railroad platform in Birkenau and after the Jewish transports were unloaded, hundreds of inmates with low numbers were packed into empty trains. They were then sent back to Germany to other concentration camps.

In August we witnessed the results of the liquidation of the Łódź ghetto. The young and healthy Jews were held in transit camps. Older men, women, and children under fourteen walked from the ramp to the gas chambers.

In the middle of the month, a strong rumor was circulating among inmates that one night an industrial complex in Monowice was damaged by American bombers. Since that day, we looked more often toward the blue sky and secretly hoped for another American attack. At the end of August, Wiktor told us that we were coming to the completion of our task. Almost all women in the camp were already deloused and several remaining blocks would be "processed" through regular channels using exclusively women's bathhouse facilities. The trailer installation would be dismantled and all equipment shipped to Germany. We suspected that the eastern front was rapidly moving closer and closer to Auschwitz, forcing the SS Camp Administration to evacuate more costly pieces of equipment for safekeeping in Germany. All three of us would be reassigned to the men's bathhouse located near the "Canada" barracks and adjoining Crematorium IV. As the news spread around the camp, Pepi's girls were upset; there was no indication of what was going to happen to them. Olga, on the surface, was calm, but I felt that she was tense and worried about her future, like all of us.

The war itself was approaching Auschwitz. We learned through illegal radio broadcasts picked up by inmates who worked in SS homes about the successes of the second front in France and the Polish Home Army uprising in Warsaw. During the day American planes bombed several adjoining camps. Camp records were continuously burned in the crematoria areas. As a result of the Warsaw uprising, the civilian population from Pruszków camp was brought to Birkenau and held in separate Men's and Women's Quarantine Camps. Mail and formal communication with families in Poland was disrupted. My food packages were not coming on a regular schedule since correspondence and shipment of packages had been stopped.

I had two concerns: my new assignment in the men's bathhouse and, more importantly, the end of my food packages. Without help from home, I would have to depend entirely on the meager Birkenau food rations. Continuous scheming and stealing by functionaries made the small portions even smaller and hardly sufficient to support the harsh physical work of prisoners. The tea or ersatz "coffee" in the morning was nothing but hot water. Soups served during lunchtime were tasteless, watery, and lacked any meat or protein. Evening portions of bread, approximately 300 grams per person with 25 grams of margarine or 25 grams of sausage, were hardly sufficient to provide energy for the starving inmates. I immediately started to ration the meager remains of my food parcels. I fully realized that in spite of encouraging signs of an Allied victory, I would be facing the toughest fight for survival from now on until the end of the war.

In the past I had watched helplessly as thousands of degraded and starving human beings, the Mussulmans, searched outside of the kitchen and food stores, begging for leftovers, licking the kettles, picking up trash full of rotten food and debris. The thought that I might be joining their ranks paralyzed my initiative and my will to survive. I was discouraged and very uncertain of my future. At the same time, my common sense was telling me that the end of the war was near. Although I might face tough and trying times, I was not prepared to give in to my oppressors; my will to survive was stronger than ever.

Our last night in the women's bathhouse, a warm and pleasant August night, was memorable in a depressing way. By the time we finished delousing the clothing for the last group of women, it was 3 A.M. The last group of women collected their articles of clothing and left for their barracks. Pepi's *Kommando* cleaned the yard, while Tadek and I closed the conveyor's opening. Olga was in good spirits. She had learned yesterday that Pepi had been appointed Blockältester and Olga would go with her as a Schreiber. Though she never found out what happened to her family, she was still hopeful, yet prepared for the worst. We kissed each other affectionately and we both cried.

Omlauf talked to Wiktor for a long time but none of us knew what they were discussing, since Wiktor did not share this conversation with us. As we left the women's bathhouse, old memories brought me back to my first day in the camp and Palitzsch's welcoming speech. The fear of the unknown had been strong, and one year later, as I marched with Wiktor and Tadek to the Men's Camp, the same fear was still hanging over my head. Omlauf and Charwin escorted us to the main gate and, after reporting to the SS Blockführer on duty, we marched with traditional *"Mutzen ab"* to our barrack. The camp was still asleep. With a heavy heart, I took my shoes off, stored them for safeguarding under my head as a pillow and tried to take a short nap before 4 A.M. morning roll call.

Two days later, Wiktor, Tadek, and I reported to a new *Entwesungskommando* at the men's bathhouse. As we passed the main gate of the Men's Camp, we turned left, walked between Crematorium IV and Crematorium V, and turned left again to the bathhouse. Wiktor, as an old hand, knew everybody and walked in the front row. Tadek and I marched at the end of the column wondering about our specific assignments. This was my fourth *Kommando* since my arrival in Birkenau the previous September.

The bathhouse was a one-story, brick, T-shaped building with four chimneys projecting high above the roof. Unlike the women's bathhouse, this building had all the facilities under one roof. The admission hall led to disrobing rooms with provisions to hang articles of clothing on small, movable trolleys. The trolleys were wheeled to specially constructed chambers where clothing was exposed to a high temperature, steamed, and chemically treated. The disrobing rooms adjoined several smaller rooms where the prisoners were shaved and received a medical examination before they entered the bathroom. The bathroom was equipped with showers and could accommodate approximately sixty people at one time. After the shower each prisoner was sprayed with carbolic acid and waited on the "clean side" for their disinfected clothes. The principal of delousing here was similar to the trailer approach except that it was easier for the prisoners to recover their own clothing after treatment.

The delousing squad, or *Entwesungskommando,* as it was called in German, was a good assignment. Since we were always under a roof, protected from the misty and chilly Birkenau weather, close to the Men's Camp, the *Kommando* offered reasonable conditions to survive the tough winter days ahead. There were quite a few people working in the bathhouse, the majority Polish and French Jews. Wiktor, who had previously worked there, dressed up every day in white overalls. He served as the coordinator and scheduler. Tadek and I stayed close together. We were assigned the task of pushing untreated and "dirty" clothing to the dry air chambers. There were very few new transports coming to the bathhouse, except for preselected young and healthy Jewish men who were registered, tattooed, and sent to one of the camps in Auschwitz or other subcamps in the area. These were the lucky survivors from Polish, French, or Slovak transports selected by SS Doctors Thilo or Mengele for work. Most of their families had perished in the gas chambers.

Since the complete ban on delivery of food parcels to prisoners from

Poland, the camp's food situation grew worse every day. The abundance of "Hungarian food" stolen or organized on the black market among the inmates was running out. New Jewish transports from other camps or ghettos brought with them limited food supplies. The price of bread rations soared on the camp's black market. The Birkenau food, which I used to treat with contempt, was now my only source of nourishment. Thus, the soup, still tasteless and watery, seemed to taste better every day. I tried to discipline myself, stretch my bread portions and leave some every night for the following morning. I knew I was losing weight. At every opportunity, I looked for "seconds" during lunch breaks in the bathhouse.

Fall weather was slowly coming to Birkenau, the nights getting cooler and longer. With a deep fear of the cold weather, we tried desperately to "organize" warm articles of clothing as we prepared for the wintry days ahead.

There were more visible signs of the SS Administration's desire to liquidate the camp and to destroy evidence of past atrocities by erasing all traces of their crimes. Previously buried corpses of gassed victims behind Crematorium V were now excavated by *Sonder* men and burned on a pyre. Ashes were disposed of in the Wisła River. Although the "Hungarian Action" was formally completed, new transports from Poland and other camps in Slovakia were still unloaded at the Birkenau platform. In spite of alarming news from both fronts about German defeats, the Nazi extermination process was still going on. Selections were carried out systematically as in the early years, and whole families of European Jews walked slowly and innocently to their death in the gas chambers.

By September, however, the number of prisoners departing to different locations in Germany exceeded the number of new arrivals. As the new transports were leaving for other camps, several hundred inmates, including part of the Penal Company, were assigned to the first SS Railroad Construction Brigade. They left Birkenau in a special train built by German contractors, their mission to repair bombed rail tracks and defuse unexploded bombs.

One day in the middle of September while I was working inside the bathhouse, I heard a sudden loud noise. It resembled an explosion of bombs and was coming from the direction of the old camp in Auschwitz. Later that day, I heard from the Schreiber of my block that Americans had bombed Auschwitz and two bombs also fell on Birkenau, killing several SS men and prisoners.

Because of renewed hope for the early defeat of Germany, the number of escapes from all camps in Auschwitz also increased. As usual, there was great secrecy surrounding such attempts. Only if there was a public execution, like the hanging of Edek and Mala, did we know anything about the success or failure of escapees. Unless one had good connections among the camp functionaries, access to false documents and contact with underground organizations outside the camp, it was almost impossible to cross SS sentry lines and to organize a successful escape. Under the circumstances, Edek Galinski's and Mala Zimetbaum's escape was quite a sensation in Birkenau. He was a low number, 531, and she was a runner and a favorite of the SS Rapportführerin Drechsel in Women's Camp BIa. They both walked out from Birkenau during the day. He was dressed up in an SS uniform and carried a revolver in his holster, pretending that he was escorting a female prisoner. The escape from the camp was successful, but they were captured by the border patrol, interrogated, then incarcerated in the bunker of Block 11 in the old camp in Auschwitz. After long and painful interrogations, they were hanged on the same day in September 1944 in their respective camps in Birkenau. As usual, after roll call, we were forced to form a large square around the gallows, close to the main entrance of the Men's Camp, and witness the execution. With a noose around his neck, Edek called in a choking voice, before the Lagercapo kicked away his stool, "Long live Poland." We stood numb and silent. After this execution, we spontaneously took off our hats out of respect to our dead comrade.

"Dismiss, dismiss" screamed the SS men and Lagerältester Franz Danisch, a German criminal, and Camp Senior Prisoner. He was concerned with a possible demonstration of solidarity and wanted to dismiss prisoners as soon as it was possible. The following day, a story was circulated in the Men's Camp that Mala was sentenced to hang the same day in the Women's Camp. But she heroically succeeded in preventing the execution. As the verdict was read, she slit both her wrists and assaulted one of her executioners. She was then taken to the infirmary to stop the bleeding but died on the way.

During the Höss regime, escapees who were caught and rearrested were hanged. Liebehenschel was more liberal, and unsuccessful escapees were sent to serve in the Penal Company. However, the risks in planning escapes during Baer's administration increased considerably. Baer ordered strict security measures, like changing forms and color of documents every day. He also introduced secret SS identification codes known only to SS guards. Baer also resumed the harsh treatment, and inmates caught trying to escape were hanged in front of their fellow prisoners to serve as an example and discourage future attempts.

I suspected that Wiktor had some connections with underground organizations because sometimes we learned from him about confidential details and circumstances surrounding successful escapes. He told me in great secrecy that he had delivered a pair of overalls to Mala for her escape with Edek Galinski.

With the reduced number of new prisoners admitted, registered, and tattooed, the *Entwesungskommando* was directed to disinfect piles of clothing from the "Canada" storage barracks. Every morning, a special *Kommando* brought all kinds of articles of clothing, from the most expensive, custom-made dresses to everyday work overalls. After disinfection, treated articles were returned to the "Canada" barracks, where a women's *Kommando* packed the quality dresses and suits for transfer to Germany. All furs were sent in special transports to the eastern front for the use of SS Fighting Formations.

Tadek and I worked closely together. We did not know any members of the *Kommando* and we recognized that if it were not for Wiktor we would never have been accepted in this group. We were also fully aware that a lot of organizing, stealing, and black-market activities were undertaken by low numbers in the bathhouse. Good quality suits, furs, expensive underwear, stockings, and other personal items carried high prices among the functionaries and senior prisoners. I suspected as well that some of the SS men were secretly dealing and exchanging food, alcohol, and cigarettes for fancy civilian wardrobes.

Tadek and I did not have enough experience to be directly involved in such transactions. But as part of the group we were allowed to share some of the successes of our fellow inmates. Occasionally we received additional portions of bread and sausages as a bonus for keeping quiet. Of course, any additional food was welcomed in our meager daily rations. I tried to adjust my eating habits to my new diet by practicing self-discipline and saving some of the bread for emergencies or possible transport, but the practical issue— where to keep saved rations—was never satisfactorily resolved. Although stealing from fellow inmates was a breach of the unwritten prisoners' honor code, it happened all the time. Stealing food from official camp stores was part of "organizing" ingenuity looked upon by other inmates as a highly commendable effort. Stealing food from friends, however, was a serious crime punishable by the inmates themselves with no mercy for the thief. Most were beaten to death by prisoners from the same block.

In the evening, lying side by side with Tadek on the top of our bunk before the "lights-out" gong, we talked about our work, our prewar experiences, and about our families. We analyzed our chances of survival and we both tried to decide the best course of action. Should we stay here and wait for the Red Army or should we make an effort to look for an assignment to one of the outgoing transports? There was no easy answer. I always remembered my old friend Bankier's comments about getting farther and farther from the crematoria. We also remembered a well-known SS habit of shooting all prisoners, regardless of religion, race, or nationality at the final liquidation of abandoned camps. This worried us a lot.

We even talked about camp politics. Because of his age, his prewar experience in Poland, and his earlier arrival to Auschwitz, Tadek was very familiar with some of the camp's underground activities and internal power struggles among various political factions. He even knew some of the Polish officers who had been arrested, interrogated, and murdered by the SS Political Department in October 1943. He was also aware of alliances among inmates representing many different nationalities and a multitude of political movements. The political structure of underground movements in all camps was complex and fluid. Continual arrests and executions of leaders by the SS required a high level of alertness and conspiracy among members of each underground organization, since informers working for the Political Department infiltrated many groups.

The communist underground movement reached across all nationalities, with ties particularly strong among German, Austrian, French, and Belgian communists. The prewar Polish Socialist Party also maintained close ties with the communist underground and since 1943 provided leadership in newly organized "Fighter Group Auschwitz." This organization was an umbrella for all left-wing movements in the camp. Russian prisoners of war, or what was left from the original group of twelve thousand people, were cooperating with the movement. By 1944, the independent Polish Home Army underground organization, established in 1940, also reached an understanding with the "Fighter Group." However, the communists viewed them with suspicion and distrust.

As the end of the war approached, and we were trying to assess our future, the murder of Jews was still going on. Transports from Theresienstadt were still marching from the railroad ramps to transit camps in Birkenau and some on to crematoria. After the mass gassing of Hungarian Jews and Höss's departure from Auschwitz, the number of incoming transports was reduced, but trains from different parts of central and eastern Europe were still arriving at the unloading platforms.

Every morning as we marched to work on the street between Crematoria IV and V, I watched with compassion *Sonderkommando* men working behind the barbed-wire fence guarded by machine pistol-toting SS guards. Although most of their work was performed inside, sometimes when the killing took place in the enclosed courtyard, the *Sonder* crew had to carry the blood-spattered bodies of victims to the ovens. We saw them through narrow openings in the fence as they loaded corpses on small dollies for transport to the main chambers. Low-number prisoners who worked with me in the bathhouse told me that the stress of the *Sonder* men's job was beyond anyone's imagination. On many occasions, they had to carry, and bury, members of their own families.

I also suspected some secret connection between inmates in the bathhouse and Crematorium IV. Some of the specialists and bricklayers who repaired the ovens worked also in the bathhouse making continuous improvements and alterations to the disinfection chambers. They always carried messages and packages between the bathhouse and *Sonder* crews. *Sonder* men had the first pick of the best clothing before it was sent to the "Canada" barracks for sorting. They also never used our facility since they had an elaborate shower and washroom in the crematorium building because the stench of burned bodies penetrated their clothes down to their bare skin. Their smell was so bad that even SS Kommandoführer encouraged *Sonder* men to take daily showers.

With gloomy fall weather around the corner, the prisoners felt restless. Every day seemed to be filled with expectation. *Sonder* men had a special reason to be nervous. It was a well-known SS policy to liquidate all witnesses to gassing people in crematoria and every few months replace them with new inmates. Gossip in the bathhouse was that the *Sonderkommando's* days were numbered.

In early October, I worked alone pushing trolleys with prisoners' clothing to the disinfection chamber for cleaning. The work was gruesome and the articles of clothing were wet, dirty, and heavy. After disinfecting, the clothing was to be picked up by "Canada" women for transportation to their barracks and subsequent sorting.

It was just after lunch when I heard the first shot. In itself, this was nothing unusual. We heard individual shots all the time coming from Crematorium IV. When there was not a sufficient number of victims sentenced to death to warrant operating the gas chambers, the victims were shot by SS guards on duty. If the sentences were executed in the courtyard, we could easily hear the screaming of victims and the sounds of firearms. Sometimes this was followed by a burst of rapid fire from machine guns, part of the normal crematorium routine. But this time shots were irregular and coming from more than one location. I looked through one of the windows. Behind a few trees and the barbed-wire fence, I could see the corner of the huge roof of Crematorium IV, with its solid, square, chimney stack in the middle. Surprisingly, the crematorium was not working and there was no black or yellow smoke hovering above the roof line. Since I did not notice anything unusual, I went back to work. Then I heard an explosion. I looked through the window again and this time the crematorium roof was on fire. A thick, dense cloud with red flames was coming through a huge hole in the roof structure. There were more shots, more explosions and then the camp's siren. Its shrieking noise was heard everywhere.

The door opened suddenly and an SS man holding a revolver burst into the room. "Hands up!" he screamed and pushed me with his pistol toward the adjoining room, used for the acceptance of new transports. He kicked me as I was crossing the threshold. As I fell down on my face, I saw the whole *Entwesungskommando* lying on the concrete floor. All men lay on their stomachs facing the floor with arms spread on each side. Several SS guards stood along the walls with machine guns in their hands and menacingly pointed them in our direction: "Anybody who moves or raises his head will be shot!" called the SS Unterscharführer in charge.

There were more shots from outside mixed with cries, grenade explosions, and the shrieking sound of truck brakes. There was a lot of screaming and a short burst of machine-gun fire. Then suddenly all was quiet.

With my head pressed against the concrete floor, I tried to turn sideways to see what was going on. The SS man standing right behind me put his heavy boot on my back: "Lie down or I will kill you!" he threatened. Then we heard new shots in the distance coming from the direction of Crematorium II, which was located on the outside of the Women's Camp. Rapid bursts of machine-gun fire followed by explosions of hand grenades intensified for a moment and then faded away. It sounded as if the action was quickly moving away from the camp grounds. We lay on the concrete floor wondering about our situation. Was this a general camp uprising, a crematorium revolt, or just a massive attempt to kill all of us before camp liquidation?

We were silent, expecting the worst. The SS Sauna Kommandoführer entered the room and called the Capo to form a column to return to the Men's Camp. I was relieved but still suspicious. Tadek whispered to me, "I don't trust them!" I shook my head silently in agreement. As we stood ready to march in a column of five, a large detachment of fully armed SS guards surrounded our *Kommando*. The camp siren wailed again, this time in the off-and-on pattern announcing an air raid at the very moment we were ready to march. "Back to the building and lie down on your bellies!" shouted the SS Unterscharführer, waving his revolver. At once, we were lying on the same concrete floor we had left a few minutes before. We silently listened for the sound of flying bombers. Every minute seemed like an hour, and this time I was too scared to raise my head.

Silence. There were no engine sounds, no falling bombs, and no explosions. It had been a false alarm! Again we formed our column in front of the bathhouse. SS guards were all around. The Capo called: "Forward march . . . left, right, left. . ." We started on our way to the Men's Camp. A large number of well-armed SS troopers with steel helmets and fixed bayonets walked with us on both sides of the column. As we walked back to camp, I saw on my right side the partially damaged Crematorium IV. Fire was still flickering in isolated places on the roof. The camp fire brigade, composed of inmates from Auschwitz, tried to control the fire and worked around the building. Through openings in the solid fence, I was able to see a number of people lying dead on the ground.

A large group of fully armed SS troops with steel helmets and full battle gear stood around the courtyard, surrounding the building on all sides. There were many military vehicles parked along the street heading to other camps. Additional SS troopers stood on the street with machine guns at the ready. They watched us with indifference.

In the evening after roll call, I learned from one of our Stubendienst what actually happened. After the mysterious disappearance of about 200 *Sonder* men in September, the *Sonderkommando* found out that there was a plan for liquidation of the whole group. This time they decided to mount resistance. Leaders who gathered for a meeting in Crematorium IV were surprised by a German informer whom they killed on the spot. In the early afternoon, in response to an SS roll call of individual names for a so-called transfer, the *Sonder* men attacked the guards, set Crematorium IV on fire and tried to escape by reaching a small wooded area. The *Sonder* men from Crematorium II, seeing the flames and hearing the shooting, believed that this was a signal for a general uprising and started action on their own. They beat to death several SS men, tore up the fences around the crematorium, and fled in the wrong direction, toward Rajsko. The SS troops responded swiftly by killing all the remaining inmates in Crematorium IV. They also surrounded and killed the *Sonder* men who escaped from Crematorium II in a little barn near Rajsko. In all, about 450 *Sonder* men were killed. The SS suffered 3 killed and had 12 wounded troopers. Crematorium IV was destroyed. There were several arrests in the Women's Camp and the SS Political Department conducted a very detailed investigation. The rumor circulated among the prisoners that many more inmates suspected of aiding the *Sonder* men might end up in the Bunker.

As we marched to work the following morning, we passed the gory ruins of Crematorium IV. I noted more SS guards escorting our *Kommando* to work. They were armed with machine guns and they had a few big Alsatian dogs with them. We all marched silently along the same route leading to the bathhouse between the two crematoria, the shadow of fear walking invisibly along with us.

The ongoing investigation and brutal attempts by the SS Political Department to find accomplices was excruciating. The SS investigators were searching for an answer to how weapons, firearms, and explosives were smuggled to *Sonder* men. Because of the bathhouse's close location to Crematorium IV, our *Kommando* was under suspicion. On the surface, it appeared that the camp was back to normal and routine operations. Meanwhile, selections of Jewish women were still carried out at various camps. Some of them were sent to work in Germany and some of them were led to the gas chambers. New transports from Theresienstadt were still coming. A story was going around the camp that all "green" criminal German nationals were leaving Auschwitz to join the SS Special Dirlewanger Brigade. The Police Summary Court of the Gestapo still functioned at Block 11 in the old camp in Auschwitz and large numbers of Poles were continuously executed in the crematoria. But below the surface many unusual activities, such as continuous destruction of records and increased deportation of inmates to women's concentration camps in Germany, indicated that Auschwitz was reaching the stage of final liquidation.

Tadek and I stayed close together. The weather was getting worse, but since I worked in the sorting and disinfection of clothing, I "organized" for myself a warm wool jacket and pants, decent underwear, and several pairs of socks. My leather shoes, which I had bought with my grandmother's onions and fruits a long time ago, served me well and were in excellent condition. A few weeks after the *Sonderkommando* uprising, the bathhouse Capo was told to reduce the number of workers in his group. Tadek and I expected to be the first to leave the *Kommando*. After all, we were newcomers and never able to really blend with the old crew. Wiktor tried to intervene on our behalf, but the order to reduce the number of inmates in the bathhouse came directly from the SS Kommandoführer and nobody could do anything about his decision. Suddenly, in the middle of the fall, on the verge of the liquidation of Auschwitz, we were left without work, which only made my personal situation worse. Except for Tadek and Wiktor, I had no friends left. My food parcels had stopped coming a long time ago. I did not have an important function in the camp's hierarchy and I did not know anybody important to help me obtain a good *Kommando* assignment.

Tadek had better luck. He met an old friend from his hometown who was a Schreiber and who offered him a job as a Stubendienst, and the same day Tadek moved to his new barrack.

After more than one year in Birkenau, I was alone. I was always hungry and thirsty; the hunger was painful, but the loneliness was even worse. With Tadek's departure, my bunk was full of strangers. There were Russian civilians evacuated from Minsk the previous year and assigned to dismantling of damaged German aircrafts. These men were tough, secretive, unfriendly; they stayed close together and were indifferent to their fellow inmates. I felt like crying in the darkness of the night, but I knew that this would not get me anywhere. I looked for a different *Kommando*, but this was a difficult task without friends. Since I did not have much luck in finding a place in a "good" work squad, I decided to go back to my old crew where I used to work with Witek.

The morning marching column still formed in the same place. The old Capo and Witek had left some time ago. I did not know the new Capo and his foreman, but I did know the type of work we used to do at "Mexico" camp. The *Kommando* still worked at the same location. This time, they were dismantling the same barracks we had built the year before. One of the old foremen recognized me and allowed me to join his squad. Part of "Mexico" camp was, until recently, occupied by thousands of young Jewish women. It served as a temporary transit location. Hardly dressed, not formally registered in the camp's records, starving and shivering from cold, they lived or "existed" in unfurnished blocks, without beds and mattresses and with very limited sanitary facilities. Blockältesters were mostly German or Czech women, who tried to organize these completely demoralized and starving women. They tried to bring some order and fairness to them.

In July of 1944, population in the camp reached its peak and the SS Administration was slowly reducing the number of women by sending them to Germany, transferring some to other camps in Birkenau, and selecting sick and feeble women for the gas chambers. By the time I joined the new *Kommando*, at the beginning of November, the remaining women in "Mexico" were already transferred to various camps in the area. As we started to dismantle barracks in "Mexico," for transfer of construction elements to Gross-Rossen, I found a few Greeks inmates who remembered me from the previous year. They were in bad shape. Starved and sick, they were slowly reaching the status of Mussulmans. The view of these struggling shadows surrounding me made me acutely aware of my chances to suffer the same fate. With a few weeks of work behind me in "Mexico," I was getting desperate and looked for other options. My jacket and pants became torn and dirty. My underwear was in pieces. Only my leather shoes were still holding up. Every night I put them under my jacket and used them as a pillow to protect them from being stolen.

Fall weather was getting foggy and cold. One evening a light snow began to fall gently, and by early morning the whole camp and adjoining areas were covered with a white, crisp powder. People without shoes had a hard time standing for long hours during roll calls. Frostbite and pneumonia took their toll among Mussulmans. Wild rumors were circulating among the inmates that Russian troops were around the corner, and liberation was expected within days. Meanwhile, on the surface, nothing changed.

In November 1944, the SS discontinued the gassing of Jewish transports and use of Zyklon B canisters. But the shooting and murdering of inmates still went on. Equipment in Crematoria II and III was dismantled for shipment to Germany. Crematorium IV was demolished. Only the ovens in Crematorium V were still working. In spite of many indications that the days of Auschwitz and Birkenau were coming to an end, we still marched every morning to dismantle the remaining wooden barracks in "Mexico" Camp. In the evening, we waited impatiently for our bread and margarine, nearly starved and exhausted after a full day of work. Most of all, we waited for news that the war was over and we were free. There were many rumors, but the iron discipline imposed by SS guards was still holding the inmates in a state of terror and submission. Executions were held every day. As I watched the SS men's frantic preparations to evacuate the camp, I realized that the massive Jewish train transports gradually ceased arriving at the railroad unloading ramp. Except for the hasty train departures with prisoners to other camps in Germany, the ramp was silent and deserted.

One Sunday in November, during prisoners' "free time," I went near the barbed-wire fence separating the Men's Camp from the ramps. When I looked across the wide, open area toward the women's compound, I could see clearly an empty platform and three distinctive rail tracks. The single railroad track originated at the old station in Auschwitz and entered the Birkenau grounds through the brick archway located under the main watchtower. The tower guarded the main entry to all camps in Birkenau. It had a glass observation deck above the roof line of adjoining buildings and it hovered high over the Birkenau landscape.

During my stay in the men's hospital, I had secretly watched the arrivals of Hungarian transports, but with so many people on the ramps and so many trains in the background, I never had a chance to comprehend the size and the scope of the unloading platform—the SS murderous installation. On this "peaceful" Sunday afternoon, I could see clearly shiny railroad tracks laid out straight from the main watchtower up to the entrances to Crematoria II and III. The junction switch box, located approximately a hundred meters from the entrance gate, allowed incoming trains to be switched from the main line to two side tracks encompassing the platform on both sides.

Looking at the silent unloading complex and what used to be a final destination stop for European Jewry, I was getting ready to face my own departure from the same ramps to an unknown future. It was strange, however, to reconcile my memories of the last summer's frantic and noisy selections of Jewish transports with the silence of the fall days. Although the ramp was now peaceful, the screaming of the SS men, shouting of Capos, and the crying and whisperings of confused victims were still vivid in my memory. The stillness was even more frightening in expectation of an unknown tomorrow.

I knew that it was only a question of days or perhaps weeks before I would also stand on the same platform and be loaded into the boxcars on my way to a mysterious destination. I tried to stay calm and get ready for the anticipated evacuation. Slowly, I got ready for my trip and traded one portion of my bread ration for a warm sweater, which I hid under my shirt. This should keep me warm wherever they were going to send me.

At the beginning of December, after evening roll call, the Schreiber called my number: "Don't go to work tomorrow," he told me. "Stay in the block and wait for further instructions." I was one of about fifty inmates told the same story. We all knew that this meant transport—but where?

Knowing that this was my last night in Birkenau, I felt strange. I was relieved that I was going away from this scene of mass murder and destruction of thousands of innocent people. At the same time, tomorrow's trip would take me further away from my homeland to a new terror in the heart of Germany. Without friends and surrounded by strangers, I tried to prepare myself for what would hopefully be the last stop on my journey. Memories of Lublin, Potoczek, Emmy, Zegota, and Czarnota faded away behind the shadows of Birkenau crematoria.

After the usual roll call and a bowl of ersatz coffee early in the morning, we marched under escort in a long column of five abreast to the railway ramp. A long string of boxcars and one passenger car for the SS and police escorts waited for us on the siding. I saw people marching from Auschwitz I, and also, a large number of inmates brought in Army trucks from Monowice camp joined us at the platform. After endless counting and checking of numbers, the SS Scharführer gave a signal and, in groups of one hundred, we climbed the steps of the boxcars. There was nothing inside, no mattresses, no blankets, no straw, and only a single bucket in the corner.

At the platform, before boarding the train, I saw Wiktor from a distance. Apparently the two of us were on the same transport. I waved to Wiktor from my car but he did not see me in the early morning mist that covered all of Birkenau. This was the last time I saw Wiktor. There was hardly any room to move around in the boxcar. We stood together, very close to each other, lost among strangers, lonely and scared.

"Where are we going?" somebody called. Nobody knew.

The SS train commander gave a signal. The train master whistled. I sensed a slow movement of the wheels, turning faster and faster away from the "factory of death" to our unknown future. I watched disappearing images of the camp through the small, barbed-wired window. There was dead silence in the car. Nobody felt like talking and wasting their energy.

As I closed my eyes, unforgettable scenes from the last year flashed in my mind: the brutal arrival and reception in the bathhouse; Mietek's cold-blooded murders; Dr. Thilo's selections; the loading of corpses in the hospital's mortuary; endless columns of people walking days and nights to the crematoria; and hundreds of naked women waiting for their clothing during the delousing routine. All this had happened against the everlasting background of solid, brick smokestacks with red and yellow flames floating high above Birkenau's barracks.

I also was leaving behind a place of suffering and murder of European Jews, Poles, and others. I could only speculate, on the basis of my personal observations from May to August 1944, that more than four hundred thousand Hungarian Jews alone perished in Birkenau. And what about the other victims? Will anybody remember the Gypsies sent to the gas? What about the thousands of Polish underground fighters detained in Katowice and adjoining prisons, sentenced by Nazi courts, then executed or gassed in Auschwitz? Would we ever know the killers' final count?

I looked at the fading view of the main watchtower above the main entrance to Birkenau, feeling relief, guilt, and deep sorrow. I was happy to still be alive, but I felt guilty because so many of my comrades were left behind. With their ashes scattered by the westerly winds, very soon there would be nothing left in Birkenau except for the melancholic landscape and our cry for revenge and justice. The jerking of the cattle cars and the sudden change in the sound of the wheels on the railroad tracks brought an abrupt end to my reflections. Exhausted by long hours of standing, some of the older or sick inmates tried to secure seating space on the floor. Squabbles and fights occurred everywhere, people cursing and calling each other names. Floor space was a precious commodity and carefully guarded by each occupant. Tempers were short and our fears of tomorrow made people irrational.

We passed lunch hour without stopping. The bucket in the corner was getting full and the floor around it was wet. Some of the urine was already splashed on the adjoining wall. Toward evening, after ten hours of travel, we were distraught. People moaned and begged for water, but there was nobody to listen to their pleas. The doors locked tightly the entire time and only the hypnotic rotation of the wheels made us aware that the train was running at full speed to our unknown destination. Two small, horizontal windows, protected by barbed wire, allowed some fresh air into the smelly and dusty boxcar enclosure.

The short December day was coming to an end, and with a sense of resignation and helplessness, we watched sparkling stars appear in the dark sky outside our windows.

Since we were not given any food in Birkenau, I expected a short journey, but I was wrong. The train was rolling faster and faster. Only the sound of wheels and the occasional screeching of brakes made us aware of our declining speed as we passed bridges, sleepy villages, and railroad junctions.

Without sleep, food, and water for two full days, I was losing control of my senses. Squatting on the floor, numb and breathing heavily, I was thirsty and hungry, and knew that I would not last for more than one more day. I looked occasionally at the growing pile of corpses in the corner and prayed silently for strength and encouragement. As the shining stars disappeared from the dark blue sky and a bright sun slowly rose from behind us, I noted that we had traveled west. We were in a mountainous terrain, with a small forest on both sides of the railroad tracks.

The wheels suddenly changed their beat. The train slowed down, whistled, and then stopped. At first there was complete silence outside. Then we heard the steps and cries of our escorts. Suddenly the door opened. "Out!" screamed an SS trooper with a big Alsatian dog on a leash. We all had a hard time moving after two days of standing or sitting in the most uncomfortable positions. It took time to stretch our legs. There were nine bodies left behind in the corner of our boxcar.

"Faster, you lousy bandits!" screamed the SS guard with the dog.

We hastily formed a column of five abreast on a long unloading railroad platform. We were at the very end of the railroad tracks. The concrete platform was surrounded by trees with a few wooden buildings standing on the opposite side of the railroad ramp. Light snow covered the trees and the ground. I had the impression that we were in the middle of an isolated and secluded forest. "Forward march!" barked the SS guard. A long column of prisoners left the platform and turned right toward the wide street surrounded on both sides by mostly one-story, brick buildings. On the left side was a huge garage with military vehicles parked in front. On the right side stood several office buildings, with SS personnel standing in front of the main entrance, looking us over with the usual cold indifference.

Some of the prisoners were unable to keep up the pace on the slightly inclined street, but the SS guards were merciless, pushing them forcefully with the butts of their rifles. "Faster, Faster, you dirty dogs!"

We passed a somewhat more imposing building on the left with a large sign above the front entrance, "*Kommandantur,*" and turned right. A long building with an observation tower over the main entrance and a large circular clock above the tower's roof was in front of us. Barbed-wire fences enclosed the areas on both sides of the building and a sign *Jedem Das Seine* was clearly visible on the iron entrance gate. Standing beside me, one of my fellow inmates looked at the sign and whispered: "It means: To each his due." Then he added, "We have arrived in Buchenwald."

CHAPTER NINE

Buchenwald-Ohrdruf

BUCHENWALD—the name sounded familiar. I had learned a lot about this place from my friend, Staszek, who worked with me in Witek's *Kommando*. Staszek was arrested in Bydgoszcz during the invasion of Poland by the German Army in September 1939. He and many other Polish citizens were accused by the SS Security Police of sniping at German soldiers. He was arrested, sent to Buchenwald, housed in tents and, in the summer of 1942, transported to Birkenau. After trying many difficult work details, he ended up working with us in the "Mexico." His memories of Buchenwald were not very happy.

Buchenwald was an old German concentration camp, organized in 1937. It was located in Thuringia on the top of a hill eight kilometers northwest of the city of Weimar. Inmates arrested by the Nazis after Hitler gained his political powers built the camp. It was later expanded to provide slave labor for adjoining armaments factories, agricultural enterprises, and stone quarries. The first prisoners were German criminals, Jehovah's Witnesses, social democrats, and communists. The first transport of German Jews was detained in Buchenwald in 1938. Although the acts of terror, beatings and cruelties by the sadistic SS guards applied to all inmates, Jews were usually selected for the most demeaning and humiliating treatment. After September 1939, with all the able-bodied men at the front lines, there was a shortage of laborers in Germany. More workers were needed to support the huge war-armament industry. An extensive network of subcamps was established to utilize slave labor for this purpose. All camps in Thuringia were put under the administration and jurisdiction of the SS Kommandant of Buchenwald.

At the beginning of the camp's existence, criminal prisoners held most of the important functions. As the base camp was expanded and the number of new inmates steadily grew, German political prisoners, mostly communists, climbed their way up in the camp's hierarchy. In a few years, the communists inherited the high administrative functions previously held by German criminals. The new officials were more compassionate in the treatment of their fellow inmates, providing they shared the same political views. The communists were, however, indifferent to prisoners who believed in other ideologies or supported strong national aspirations for their own countries.

Polish prewar intelligentsia, who were first imprisoned in Auschwitz and then transferred to Buchenwald, were treated by local functional senior prisoners with suspicion and contempt. Unless the new Auschwitz transferees were declared communists or socialists, they were accused of being Polish nationalists and chauvinists and had a difficult time being fully accepted by the "red" Buchenwald inmates.

As I vividly recalled Staszek's experiences from Buchenwald, I crossed the iron gate under the main entrance with great concern. The long, winding column of new arrivals was led through the *Appellplatz* toward the camp's transit facilities. The first step was registration, where I received a new Buchenwald number, 29272. Then we went through a delousing process similar to that in Birkenau. During my last months in Birkenau, I had avoided cutting my hair as much as possible, and it was now about one inch long. But this time, in the Buchenwald bathhouse, one of the barbers cut a swath of hair across my head from front to back. I looked terrible with short bunches of hair sticking out on both sides of my head above my ears. This special haircut was known in the inmates' language as "main street" and made us easily recognizable by any German authorities in case of escape. I was lucky to be able to find my own clothes and recover my own shoes in the bathhouse after the disinfecting process was completed. The shoes were in excellent condition and easily could have been stolen during the chaotic delousing procedure. After inspection of personal belongings, we were sent to one of the wooden barracks designated for new transports. This area was known in Buchenwald as the "Little Camp" and was used as a holding place for prisoners scheduled for relocation.

Many functional inmates from Buchenwald were easily recognized by their official armbands as they circulated among newcomers. I also noted a new group of functionaries walking around with the aura of authority and power. They carried armbands of *Lagerschutz* or camp police. In Buchenwald, the prisoners' camp police was in charge of maintaining discipline and order among inmates. They had tremendous influence on camp internal activities. All members were dedicated communists and mostly Germans. They were selected for the job by Buchenwald's secret Underground International Committee. One of the camp police functions as the self-appointed "people representatives" was to interview newly arrived transports and search for cruel, sadistic, or politically suspicious functionaries from other camps. The functionaries who were transferred from other locations and identified by their comrades as right-wing radicals or antisocials were separated by the camp police and locked up in a specially designated barrack. Their punishment was immediate transfer to other "death" camps, like Dora, where the work schedules were murderous and chances for survival very slim.

By now I felt completely lost among strangers and overwhelmed by the events of the last few days. At the same time, I was exhausted and almost indifferent to my new surroundings. I could hardly keep my eyes open as we waited for the evening meal. When the Stubendiensts distributed the evening bread portions with margarine, I ate all my bread at once. This was the first "regular" meal after many days of travel, and soon I felt cramps in my stomach. I also shared a bowl of hot ersatz tea with my new comrade on my bunk. He was from Warsaw and spent two years in Auschwitz. We talked briefly about our current situation but both of us were too tired for lengthy conversation. I climbed up on my assigned bunk desperate to rest after the long and exhausting journey.

The next morning, we were served a hasty breakfast of a strange tasting colored water. After a lengthy roll call outside our barrack, the Schreiber called my number in a loud voice. I was told to wait with a large group of about four hundred inmates in front of the "Little Camp" entrance. Camp police surrounded the group and led us to the main gate. We went through the checking and cross-checking of our numbers and verification of other personal data by the Lagercapo and his staff. Then, we were escorted from the gate by a heavily armed SS detachment. In a column of five, we marched to the large open area outside of the main gate and near the railroad terminal. A convoy of military vehicles, large green trucks covered with canvas roofs, waited for us. We were ordered to climb inside the trucks. Each vehicle accommodated approximately eighty inmates. We stood tightly together with hardly any air to breathe, and no space to turn around. At the sound of the SS Unterscharführer's whistle, all canvas covers were pulled down. We were left standing in complete darkness. I heard the roar of engines and the convoy started to move slowly. The uneven highway and a few potholes made the trucks sway from left to right, so we all had a hard time maintaining our balance.

The truck convoy and the complete darkness reminded me of the selection of Jewish transports at the Birkenau railroad ramp. Suddenly, I became suspicious. Since food rations were not distributed and even the routine "bucket" was not provided for each truck, I assumed this would be a short journey. My suspicion grew with every passing minute, though I tried to reason with myself. If we were going to be gassed, why did we go through the delousing process last night? More than half of the inmates in the transport were Jews. The rest of us were mostly political prisoners with red triangles. Is it possible that because of the changing fortunes of the war, the Nazi extermination policy had been suddenly expanded to include non-Jews? I could not see my fellow inmates' faces in the darkness, but I could feel agonizing fear creeping into everyone's heart. I could hear whispered speculations among the prisoners in many different languages. The secrecy of tightly covered trucks and an expectation of a short trip made us more and more suspicious about our fate and possible death. We discussed many different possibilities. Fear of gassing or execution weighed most heavily on everybody's mind. As I listened to all these speculations, I closed my eyes and felt a paralyzing numbness. Were we going to follow in the footsteps of the Jewish transports from the railroad platform in Birkenau to crematoria? Instinctively, we reached out to each other and held hands in the darkness. The whispering stopped and there was a deep silence in our truck. Moments passed; then the convoy reached the main highway and increased its speed.

I still argued silently with myself. It did not make sense to transfer us away from the camp for execution or even for gassing. There was an efficient crematorium in the camp at Buchenwald. The SS would not waste its precious gasoline to drive us for hours just to gas or even execute us in the forest, would they? I had no firm answer. In the complete darkness, I quietly shared my doubts with others. There were other voices of reason, and we tried to encourage each other. Then we all came to the conclusion that there must be another purpose for our trip. In many languages, words of faith, relief, and courage were expressed in the darkness of the truck. Gassing or mass execution seemed to be more remote with each and every mile taking us away from the camp. The journey, with occasional stops for the convenience of our SS escorts, took approximately two hours. A sudden jerking as brakes were applied and reduced speed made us realize that we were reaching our destination. The trucks slowed down on the unevenly paved city streets. I could sense when our truck crossed street intersections, turned right and passed through what could have been an entrance gate. All of us inside the truck were quiet. Some inmates continued to pray out loud. Finally, the trucks stopped. We could hear the SS escorts running around the parked vehicles. The sound of army boots marching on paved city streets and the clattering of the SS guards' equipment contrasted sharply with the silence in the trucks, interrupted only by the individual chanting of prayers.

The gray canvas truck covers were suddenly removed and the SS Unterscharführer ordered everybody out with a machine pistol pointed in our direction. "Do you want me to help you?" He made a menacing movement with his weapon. "Fast, fast, you dirty swines!" He kept calling us names. We jumped down and formed a column of five men abreast among the parked vehicles.

It was a cold and brisk December day. The convoy of military trucks was parked in the middle of a paved courtyard surrounded by large buildings on all four sides. The buildings facing the courtyard were at least three stories high. The massive, brick structures with many windows and doors at ground level blocked the cold winter sun and projected deep shadows across the entire area. The whole complex looked like a huge public-housing project or a military barracks with a parade ground in the middle. Internal entrances and the doors leading to the buildings were guarded by the SS sentries. Except for the long line of newly arrived inmates with SS escorts and a few high-level functional prisoners talking to the SS convoy leader, I did not see any other inmates.

After a half hour of roll-call procedures, we were divided into groups of one hundred and led by the Blockältesters to the buildings. A wide, concrete stairway with ample landing space provided entry to large dormitory rooms at each level. Looking around, I came to the conclusion that this was a complex of old military barracks and now part of it was designated for use by prisoners. Except for dirty mattresses half-filled with old straw, the large dormitory rooms were in deplorable condition. All windows were tightly closed, and the smell of urine and human excrement was in the air. Dirty walls looked at us as unwelcome intruders. Perhaps a few years ago, this was the home of a proud military formation, clean and neatly organized. Now it appeared to be an accommodation only for slave labor.

The Blockältester showed us one of the rooms on the second floor. "This is your new home, keep it clean and neat," he said. He was a German political prisoner with the red armband on his left arm. As all of us entered the room, he continued, "This is S III Sonderlager Ohrdruf. The work is about ten kilometers from here in the forest. Listen to your room orderlies and obey your Capos at work and you will be all right. Do you understand?"

"*Jawohl,* Herr Blockältester," we replied together. He was pleased with our response.

In a friendlier tone, he added, "Food is scarce, but don't try to steal from your comrades because you will be sorry. You may stay here until roll call."

Adjoining the landing was a lavatory and a washroom. The Scheissmeister in charge guarded this place and restricted the number of inmates who could use it at the same time. We had to wait in line in order to enter. I wondered what would happen in the morning when all of us had to use the bathroom before roll call. I picked out one of the least-worn, straw-filled mattresses in a corner next to the window. After checking for lice, I tried to rest for a few minutes and assess my new situation. Our previous fears about gassing were unfounded. Apparently this was a high-priority project since the SS administration was willing to commit their scarce resources, like gasoline, to get us here in a hurry, which made me curious about what kind of work awaited us in the forest.

The Blockältester, accompanied by several prisoners carrying notebooks and stacks of paper, arrived at the dormitory room. The Stubendiensts, or room orderlies, set up a line of portable tables across the room. One of them stood on a table and called as loudly as he could: "Attention! Form a line for registration. The Schreiber called our names and as we approached the table, each prisoner was given a new number, which was written in black pencil on a piece of white cloth. One of the clerks told me to attach it on my jacket as he gave me my new number, 111487. Since I had no way to sew this on my jacket, I memorized the number and looked among my fellow prisoners for somebody with a needle. When I realized I could not find anybody, I put my new "identity" in my pocket and tried to rest for a few more minutes on my mattress.

The Stubendienst appeared in the doorway and called out the magic word "soup." We quickly formed a line across the room. With the usual show of authority, he dispensed turnip soup into our metal bowls. I drank the whole portion in one gulp. Though the soup tasted terrible, it was warm and, to my surprise, I found a few solid pieces of turnip on the bottom.

My neighbor resting on the straw mattress was an older man in his forties, a schoolteacher from Kraków who had spent almost two years in the old camp in Auschwitz. On December 7 we both arrived in the same transport from Birkenau to Buchenwald. In spite of his age, he seemed to be in good physical condition. With a friendly smile amidst very unfriendly circumstances, he inspired confidence in his comrades. His name was Tomasz, and he used to be a Schreiber at the old camp in Auschwitz. He told me that he had a wife and son about my age in Kraków. Until the Warsaw uprising and before mailing privileges were canceled, he maintained regular correspondence with his family. Now, like the rest of us, he was completely isolated from any news of his hometown.

"Janusz," he reassured me, "you and I, we are old hands and we are going to make it." I wished I had the same faith as Tomasz.

In the late afternoon, I heard the sound of a marching column in the courtyard. Looking through the window I saw *"Aussenkommando,"* one of the field work details, entering the courtyard through the main entrance gate. In the usual rows of five men abreast, all formations walked to a previously designated space in the yard. As I looked more closely, I noted the appalling physical condition of the walking inmates. These were worn-out skeletons, struggling with every step. In striped uniforms, fighting the December cold wind and freezing temperatures, and obviously exhausted, they looked even worse than what I had previously seen in Birkenau. At the end of each work detail, they carried sick inmates and dead bodies. The courtyard was slowly filling with hundreds of these walking ghosts. Except for the sound of clogs—Dutch wooden shoes—reverberating on the hard surface of the paved areas, the columns were silent. With downcast eyes and struggling to make each step forward, inmates were holding each other in order not to break formation. I could not see a healthy face in the whole crowd. Without saying a word, I pointed out this frightening view to Tomasz. He said calmly,

"I told you we are going to make it. Courage, my friend."

I nodded, but could not take my eyes off the depressing sight.

"Roll call," called the Blockältester. "Everybody down! Fast! Fast!"

We all ran down the stairway and formed a column in front of the building. As soon as all work details arrived at the square, the SS guard closed the gate. Sick and dead prisoners carried by their comrades from the work details were laid together in one corner of the courtyard. The Lagercapo and his deputy then carefully counted heads and took down the numbers of the dead bodies. The rest of the inmates stood in long columns facing the main entrance gate. Ten men deep and divided into five groups, we waited for roll call to begin. I guessed that there were about five thousand men freezing in the cold December afternoon.

Apparently there was a problem. The SS Lagerführer called the Lagerältester for a conference. As we waited shivering for the resolution of a final head count, I glanced again at the prisoners. Their long, thin faces reminded me of ghosts floating slowly in the air as they struggled to look and act like human beings. And I wondered, if we were going to look like this after a few weeks in Ohrdruf.

The discrepancies with attendance numbers were finally resolved. *"Mutzen auf!"* The Lagerältester issued an order. "Dismissed," called the Blockältester. We broke ranks and I anxiously looked for a chance to talk to the "old" inmates who lived and worked in this camp for the past few months. I looked for information about the camp and work details. The prisoners who were transferred here before us sought news from the newcomers about the war and the progress of the Allied armies. This was the only time available when we could freely talk to each other.

The previously silent courtyard resounded now with the whispering of thousands of human voices, excited, despite their fatigue, by the good news coming through underground channels from both fronts. Glazed eyes began to sparkle with hope. I walked slowly across the yard looking for familiar faces from Birkenau, but I could not find anybody. People around me were talking in many foreign languages; finally I came across three inmates talking loudly in Polish.

I stopped and introduced myself, "I am Janusz from Birkenau. I just arrived. Can you tell me anything about this place, please?"

One of them, the youngest, turned to me and I saw that he was annoyed. The older man put his hand on the young man's shoulder and said: "Zbyszek, slow down. If we won't help him, who will?" Then he turned to me: "I am Adam, this is Zbyszek and Stach. What would you like to know?"

"I am sorry but I arrived this morning and had never heard about this place."

Adam talked slowly: "This is part of S III, Sonderlager Ohrdruf, one of the subcamps of Buchenwald. This is a new camp that opened only a few months ago. The SS Lagerführer and his Deputy SS Obersharführer Stiwitz, whom you may remember from Auschwitz, are cruel and demanding. Human life means very little to them. We all work on a special emergency project building in the Jonastal Mountains, an underground facility for the German Army Communication Center and an underground shelter for Hitler's headquarters train." Then he added that he had spent a few years in Auschwitz. "Believe me, this work is killing all of us slowly. It is far worse than *Königsgraben.*" *Königsgraben* was a tough penal *Kommando* in Birkenau excavating ditches for the drainage system where inmates worked submerged up to their waists in mud and water regardless of the season. Adam added that all three of them were working on the construction of a narrow-gauge railroad. The work was hard, and involved a long walk, but it was better than digging in the tunnels. He asked me to work with them and told me to meet the next day after roll call. Then he volunteered more information about another *Kommando* working closer to this camp on the extension of the railroad tracks from the Ohrdruf station to the military training grounds. Most of the inmates were Yugoslav prisoners of war and French and Hungarian Jews. They did not have to walk very far but the work was heavy and demanding. He stressed that I would be better off if I stayed with them.

I was grateful. Stach said that they had to go now to stand in line for evening rations, but they would see me the next day.

I returned to my dormitory in better spirits. The long line of inmates waiting for bread and marmalade had already formed in front of the entrance door. As each man entered the room, the Stubendienst dispensed food rations. After picking up a small piece of brown bread, a teaspoon of marmalade, and a metal bowl half filled with ersatz tea, I found my way to my mattress. Tomasz was already there, eating his bread. As soon as I settled next to him he informed me that he had met his friend from Auschwitz and he would work with him. He further explained: "My friend is a *Kommando* Schreiber and I will be a translator to the SS Kommandoführer, since I speak French, Russian and, of course, German. They are digging deep tunnels in the mountains. The work is dangerous but under roof." I was impressed with

Tomasz's organizational abilities. He had just arrived in a new camp and it sounded as if he already had a good job. Personally, I had some doubts about his new arrangements. Work in the tunnels was dangerous because of the use of dynamite to excavate them by exploding the large rocks. There were no safety precautions because the use of slave labor made life cheap and expendable. Being so close to the SS Kommandoführer could also be a risky job. Everything depended on what kind of a man you were dealing with. Tomasz added, "I will have to move to another room. The Capo wants all of the *Kommando* to stay together, but I will see you again. This is a small world behind barbed wire." I hardly got to know Tomasz and he was leaving already. I wondered how many people I had met without knowing their names. I remembered Moniek, Toni, Vera, Witek, and Olga's faces without even knowing their last names. I didn't even remember their numbers. I had spent much time with Wiktor, yet I knew hardly anything about him and his life before his arrest. Tadeusz was the only person I had a chance to know better in Birkenau. The Nazi dehumanizing system reduced all of us to a series of numbers, slave laborers without names or identities.

Our work day began very early. There was still dark night outside when lights went on in our blocks. "Get up, you lazy bastards!" The Blockältester screamed as he and his orderlies walked between the mattresses and occasionally kicked half-asleep prisoners mercilessly. "Get up and move faster, faster!" The latrine was already full of people trying to find a decent space for their most essential human needs. There was a lot of pushing and I had to fight my way to the bathroom. Once a neat and clean facility, it was now in a dilapidated condition, full of excrement on the floor and urine on the walls. The Scheissmeister, with a large stick, tried to maintain order among the hurrying inmates. After I gulped half of the bowl of warm tea, another yelling orderly pushed us out from the dormitory room for roll call. He banged his stick on the entrance door. Several hundreds inmates, half-asleep, were brutally pushed by the orderlies down the stairway to the roll-call area in the courtyard.

It was still dark outside so the courtyard was brightly lit by searchlights located on the roofs. We all stood shivering on this cold December morning somewhere in the heart of dying Nazi Germany. The Blockältester, with the help of his Stubendienst, counted us carefully. "Everything is fine. We are all accounted for," he greeted the Lagerältester as he emerged from the building. The crowd of SS Blockführers arrived at the entry gate and they split their ranks to inspect and count individual blocks. Then the Blockältester turned around and called *"Mutzen ab."* Automatically, I pulled my hat off with my right hand.

The SS man walked slowly, counting each row. The anxious Blockältester walked three steps behind him. The SS man nodded his head, "All in order." The Blockältester was happy and shouted, *"Mutzen auf."* We all put on our hats together at this command. "Dismissed! Report for work details," called the Lagercapo.

As previously agreed, after morning roll call, I met my three new friends in front of the entrance to Building number 2. This was the point of departure to work for the so-called *Kleinzugkommando,* a group of a hundred men assigned to the construction of the narrow-gauge railroad along the foothills of the limestone mountains of Jonastal Valley. The Capo was a naturalized German citizen from Prague. There were four foremen in charge of work details: two Germans, one French, and one Polish. My friends worked for the Polish foreman. His name was Louis, and although he was born in Poland, he had spent most of his adult life in France. Before the war, he took part in fighting with the International Brigade in Spain against Franco's dictatorship. After the Loyalists' defeat, he left Spain and settled in France as a dedicated communist. Together with many French Jews, he was arrested by the Gestapo in occupied France, identified as a Polish Jew, and sent to Drancy for transit to Buchenwald. Last September he arrived with the first group of prisoners to Ohrdruf and was forced to dig tunnels and work on the construction of the underground communication center for the German Army.

Louis was very friendly and welcomed me warmly to the group, "Another Polish boy from the old country. Do not give up. We Poles must stand together," he said half-seriously in heavily accented Polish. Then he added, "Do not worry. We will try to help you. Stay close to Adam. I hope that you don't mind that I will call you Jan; Janusz is too difficult for ordinary people." I shook his hand gratefully.

The yard was full of different work groups standing in marching formations in rows of five men abreast, awaiting orders. The shriek of the Lagercapo's whistle broke the silence. Each Capo led his group. As the marching column approached the SS officials, they bellowed once more, *"Mutzen ab!"* and we were on the city streets.

A large detachment of fully armed SS guards waited for us. Surrounded by soldiers on both sides of the column, we marched through the dark streets of Ohrdruf. A cold and penetrating wind blew in our faces from the west. The streets were covered with patches of snow, and slippery pavement made it difficult to maintain an even pace.

"Left, left, and left," called the Capo in his hoarse voice. I tried hard to hold my hat with both hands in order not to lose it. Discreetly, I looked around for signs of civilian life, but the city streets were deserted. Thousands of inmates' clogs, made a terrific noise that echoed across the city's cobblestone streets and markets. Even the SS guards, marching with us in their warm winter coats, gray field hats, and ear muffs, with rifles hanging loose across their shoulders, appeared to be as miserable as the rest of us. After we marched for an hour, the sun appeared on the horizon behind us, but the cold temperature held firm. My fingers were red, swollen, and frozen but I still held onto my hat. I said to Adam, who walked on my left side, "We won't have to work to die. This march will finish us."

Adam shook his head: "Don't talk. Save your breath. We have a long way to go."

We reached the outskirts of the city and now walked toward the gentle mountain peaks. After more than two hours of marching, we reached our destination. A huge construction depot with a large quantity of building equipment was in front of us. On the side of the wooded mountain, I could see many tunnels. We had arrived at Jonastal.

As we waited for the German civilian technicians to issue daily work orders to our Capo, Adam explained to me that the underground work in the Jonastal Valley tunnels was extremely tough and dangerous. Deep tunnels were drilled into the vertical slopes of the limestone mountains. Small tunnel openings, clearly visible from the distance, were located at regular intervals at the foothills of the mountain. The newly paved road and the railroad tracks, parallel to the existing winding country road from Crawinkel to Arnstadt, had been built to provide a vehicular entry to the recently excavated tunnels. Our task was to construct an embankment for the new rail line. The prisoners working inside the tunnels were guarded all the time by the SS sentries and were working directly under the technical supervision of German civilian experts in demolition. The inmates drilled deep holes in the existing tunnels and set explosives to enlarge the subterranean caverns. Another group of inmates removed the rocks and debris from the caverns and built new concrete floors. The newly excavated caverns provided temporary ammunition-storage space and an accommodation for the future permanent bunkers for the German Army Communication Center.

Adam pointed out one large opening in the side of the mountain and told me that this was a special secret construction project known as "Olga," built to provide an underground shelter for Hitler's train. For this work, every morning at roll-call time, the SS Kommandoführers selected healthy and strong-looking prisoners. This project was carried out twenty-four hours a day, by three shifts staffed by the selected inmates. The prisoners were given slightly larger food rations and were driven to work on military trucks. The work was extremely dangerous, with many fatal accidents and an unrealistic schedules for completion. As the front line was getting closer and closer, the working conditions and treatment of inmates grew worse every day. The SS Kommandoführers were brutal and vicious and drove the slave laborers to total physical and mental exhaustion. The reputation of the "Olga" project and its murderous working conditions were well known among the inmates. Nobody, if they could help it, wanted to be part of this *Kommando*. Every morning the selected victims were rounded up by the SS and after the roll call, guarded and beaten by the Capos with rubber truncheons; then they were forcibly loaded into military trucks. After several weeks of accelerated work, the prisoners became completely worn-out and sick, so they were classified as invalids, unfit for work, and hence doomed for the transports to the crematoria in Bergen-Belsen. Adam concluded his explanation with a stern warning: "Watch out every morning for the SS selection team, stay in the last row at the roll call, and avoid any confrontation with Capos."

Thousands of prisoners were already at work. Adam explained to me that some of the work squads lived here in the tunnels and some came from Crawinkel, a few kilometers from here, where they lived in tents. Thus, they didn't have to walk as far as we did. "Remember, work light. Save your strength for the march back home." I smiled when he said home, because it was strange to refer to our barracks in Ohrdruf as "home." We were lost souls in the heart of Germany, forgotten by the outside world and very far from our real homes.

Louis divided us into small work details. I was part of a team charged with leveling the ground and building up an embankment for installation of rails. As we worked, we all watched the SS Kommandoführer and his moves along the construction perimeter. If he came close to us, we labored hard. When he walked away, we took time to catch our breath. I understood from Adam that the SS Kommandoführer, a Bavarian corporal, had been ordered to join one of the SS regiments on the eastern front. Consequently, he had been very unhappy for the past few days, which made him change his attitude toward the inmates. Suddenly, he stopped beating prisoners with his cane and publicly displayed compassion for the men under his command. Adam cautioned, "I hope that we will have a decent replacement for this Bavarian hypocrite. He was a real bastard, but now he wants to make up for his sadistic behavior." Adam was really excited: "Do you know that last week he killed one young Frenchman for working too slow? Now he is worried about his own skin."

We stopped talking as the SS man turned around and came close. He asked Adam about how his work was going.

"Very well. We are making progress, Herr Underscharführer."

The SS man smiled ironically, "Keep going. It won't be long." Adam and I looked silently at each other as he walked away.

The soup for lunch arrived on army trucks. By the time we could stop working and form a long line in each *Kommando,* the soup was not only tasteless but cold. We sipped it slowly and looked for pieces of potatoes or turnips. As foreman, Louis was entitled to a second portion. He brought his extra bowl and offered to share half of it with me: "Jan, this soup is from the bottom of the kettle. It is still warm. Take half from me." I was grateful for every little piece of potato. I could see that the food situation here was really critical and getting worse every day. Now I understood why all the inmates looked like skeletons.

Most of the afternoon, we worked in silence to conserve our energy for the long walk back to camp. The afternoon sky was gray and cloudy. It looked and felt as if a snow storm was on its way. The damp air and cold wind penetrated our meager cotton uniforms and chilled us to the bones. By the time the Capo whistled the end of the day's work, I was totally exhausted. The march back to the camp was long and difficult. Weary as we were, we also had to carry the sick and wounded on makeshift stretchers back to the camp. All of the able-bodied prisoners rotated every few miles carrying five victims. One Yugoslav prisoner was injured by a heavy rail that smashed his foot. Two Russians were sick with pneumonia and could barely breathe. One German Jew died unexpectedly in the middle of the day. One Frenchman fainted and was still unconscious. Adam made a comment, "If our Bavarian had not changed his attitude, we would have ten more bodies to carry today." Apparently this was one of the better days for a *Kleinzugkommando*.

By the time we walked into the camp's courtyard, I could hardly feel my legs. The roll call was also unusually long. It took an extra hour to find a lost inmate in one of the bathrooms. He was sick and could hardly keep his balance. Two Capos found him on the bathroom floor and beat him unmercifully. Then his dead body was brought out from the building and laid on the courtyard to complete the count. I collected my meager bread portion and half a bowl of ersatz tea and lay down on my mattress wondering once again about my future. The work in bad weather was hard and demanding, but walking so many miles every day was far beyond my physical endurance. Clearly I had to make an effort to find another work detail. Perhaps I could stay at the camp and work some maintenance duties or perhaps I could clean the Blockältester's quarters. I would have to talk about this with Adam. The following day, after listening to my plans, Adam shook his head, "Janusz, you're wasting your time. They want you to work at the tunnels to save Germany. They do not want you to be a janitor at the camp." Then he added: "We all tried and it did not work. Don't give up and remember time is on our side."

I was discouraged, but I knew that he was right. I must find enough strong will and perseverance to survive a few more months. I knew that the end of the war was coming; what I did not know was whether I would have enough courage, strength, and luck to be able to witness its triumphant arrival. Each day was more difficult and more exhausting.

Except for Christmas Eve, when we did not go to work, Christmas 1944 passed unnoticed by the overworked and undernourished masses of slave laborers. On Christmas Eve, all the *Aussenkommandos* stayed inside the camp and the SS Blockführers and Blockältesters performed an official head count. We stood for hours at the roll call while the camp officials counted us endlessly. At the end of the day, I was told by one of the Schreibers that there were 5500 inmates identified and accounted for in the camp.

I did not even see signs of SS troopers celebrating the holiday. They seemed to be more vicious, cruel, and frustrated with the bad news for them that came from both fronts every day.

January brought more miserable and harsh weather, with snow and cold temperatures. Freezing rain and frequent snowstorms made our daily long marches to and from work more difficult. Under these conditions, every step forward on our way to the tunnels required an extra effort and full concentration that was often beyond our endurance. City streets were slippery and threatened our balance. The ground in the foothills of the mountains was frozen, and we had to perform strenuous digging with very primitive tools to build up the embankment for the narrow-gauge railroad. During work hours, we helped each other and, at the same time, kept an eye on the SS Kommandoführer. Sometimes during work hours he would stop and chat with our Capo on the side. I watched from a distance as these two Germans, representing two different worlds, talked quietly between themselves, and I often wondered how they felt about the changing fortunes of the war.

The Capo and Louis were very close, bound together by their communist ideology and fanatical allegiance to the Soviet Union. I noticed that the Capo was very partial to Louis and favored him at every opportunity. Louis and I were good friends. I liked his humor and perseverance. Although I did not share his political views, I respected the strength of his beliefs. He was a good and fair friend and treated everybody with respect, even the half-dying Mussulmans.

After a few months in Ohdruf, another enemy raised its ugly head: starvation. I was hungry all the time, from the early morning hours to the "lights out" call. Every day I thought less about liberation and more and more about food. Freedom was distant and uncertain, inching its way slowly to release us from this miserable existence; hunger was with us every day, and if it was going to stay with us much longer, nobody would be left to be liberated.

Continuous pain in an empty stomach intensified my despair each passing day. In the almost two months since my arrival in Ohrdruf, I had steadily lost weight. The dreadful vision of Mussulmans licking the kettles or searching for leftovers behind the kitchen barracks made me nervous about things to come. Because of our hunger, we were irritable, morose, and more depressed. If any energy was left after the day's work, it was committed to looking for ways to gain an extra bowl of soup or an additional piece of bread. There was not much "trading-in" among the inmates because most of us had nothing to trade. Cramps in my stomach even affected my attitude toward my closest friends. Adam, however, was upset with my depression and encouraged me daily to hold steady. He continually reminded me that according to the camp gossip, liberation was "around the corner."

In the middle of the winter, as the weather was getting worse every day, warm clothing also became a critical issue. Most of us from Auschwitz retained our clothing from the old camp. I was able to wear my previously "organized" sweater and underwear from the Birkenau Central Bathhouse. My shoes were still in good condition. But the prisoners in the new transports from Sachsenhausen and Flossenburg arrived in rough cotton striped uniforms and light coats. Some of them had wooden clogs but the majority had no shoes. They wrapped their feet with old rugs so they would not have to walk barefoot in the cold weather. In these shabby and light outfits, they were forced to march long distances every day, work outdoors, and stand long hours in the bitter cold during the never ending morning and evening roll calls.

One day, on our way to the job site, Adam told me in great secret that the "Bavarian" had already left and we would meet a new SS Kommandoführer that morning. He added: "Both Capos and Louis are concerned because this new fellow has a very bad reputation from Dora. His name is Koehler."

Dora used to be one of the subcamps of Buchenwald located about forty kilometers north of Weimar. A few years before, it was designated as the major camp Mittelbau-Dora, and connected with the Nordhausen concentration camp. Thousands of slave laborers under SS guards performed complex, very secret, and exhausting work in Dora's underground caverns. Every day and night, we saw on the horizon flashing lights and heard sounds of thunder. They came from the underground experimental facilities for testing V-1 and V-2 rockets in Dora. The sudden flares on the dark sky looked like powerful lightning with a deep sound of traveling thunder rolling over the Thuringian landscape. The inmates working under the supervision of German technicians lived, worked, and died in those deep underground tunnels. Their lives meant very little to desperate Germans who hoped that the fortunes of war could be changed in their favor by introducing new rocket weaponry systems.

The new SS Kommandoführer met us at the job site. After a report by the

Capo and the traditional routine of *"Mutzen ab"* we stood silently, holding our hats and listening to his speech. He was in his late twenties, tall and slim, with blue eyes and short, blond hair. His eyes were bright and energetic, but cold. His voice was loud and clear, although his unfamiliar accent made it difficult for some of us to understand him. In his field gray uniform with the SS Unterscharführer's black-and-silver insignia and a ribbon of the "Iron Cross" on the lapel of his tunic, the new SS Kommandoführer looked tough, confident, and dangerous.

Adam whispered to me: "I don't believe that the war will end soon enough because we must still work under the supervision of this dedicated and fanatic Nazi."

"Quiet!" I responded. "Don't take any chances. Let's not aggravate this son of a bitch."

The SS Kommandoführer's message was simple: "No more privileges. You must work hard and play an important part in the defense of Germany against the subhuman Bolshevik hordes. From now on, everybody will work twice as hard and at double speed. Laggards will be punished and saboteurs will be shot."

He concluded, "Every day I will establish a new goal to be accomplished in building the embankment. If my goals are not met, all of you will be punished." Then he turned and looked straight at the Capo: "Do you understand my orders?"

"Jahwohl, Herr Underscharführer!" The Capo stood at attention.

"Very well," the SS man nodded his head. "Dismiss and start working."

"Mutzen auf! Report to your work stations."

Our small group of about twenty inmates picked up the necessary tools and wheelbarrows and left the tool shack to start digging the frozen soil. Louis, who usually was very cheerful and optimistic, was visibly upset by our new leader. "Jan," he told me, "this man is dangerous. In Dora, he was a sadist and murderer. Watch your step!" Just before lunch break, I heard hysterical screaming coming from the embankment line a few hundred feet from our position. It sounded like the howling of a wounded dog and traveled fast above our heads, making all of us fearful. "What's going on?" I asked Louis.

"The new man is putting his theory into practice," he responded.

Adam came along: "Watch out and work faster. He is coming our way." Then he looked around and added, "He just mercilessly beat one of the Greeks. The poor soul is hardly alive."

That day, on the way back to the camp, we carried twice as many bodies as we had at the same time last week. Mussulmans were dying like flies because of the accelerated tempo of the work imposed by the new SS Kommandoführer. They were dying from exhaustion, apathy, hunger, complete resignation, and lack of will to hold onto the precious "joy" of living. In our case there was not much joy. Nor was there much living. Between the long marches and strenuous work, most of the inmates could not cope with the emotional and physical stress. An invisible shadow of gloom walked with us every evening on our way back to the camp.

The streets of Ohrdruf were empty and silent as usual. The staccato of wooden shoes marching on paved streets made our presence known to everyone. Yet, I could not see a single human face behind the closed windows with tightly drawn curtains. Where were the several thousand inhabitants of this town? Perhaps frequent Allied air raids on the valley of Jonastal and adjoining areas made the local population scared of any unusual sound. Or perhaps the clattering of our wooden shoes on the cobbled streets of Ohrdruf made the local citizens hide their faces as unwilling and ashamed witnesses to the concentration camps' horrors.

Marching twice a day along a Crawinkel street I wondered sometimes if anybody actually lived behind carefully protected windows in this ghost town. Small, two-story dwellings built closely together had their windows covered with crisscrossed paper strips as a protection against shattered glass from the explosions of bombs. From the distance the neatly glued paper strips on each window looked like installed iron bars that prevented inhabitants from leaving their quarters. The view from the street gave the passerby an impression of an enormous city jail that stretched for miles, with invisible prisoners hidden behind the silent walls. As I looked at the houses on both sides of the street, I silently wondered who the real prisoners were: They—invisible and solid citizens from the town of Ohrdruf, or we—visible and hungry skeletons from the Sonderlager III.

On cold winter days, with freezing rain or wet snow penetrating our light cotton garb, we marched twice a day through the ghostly city, shivering from cold and continuously trying to control our chattering teeth. In our white and blue, dirty and worn-out striped uniforms we blended inconspicuously with the grayness of the city landscape as we looked desperately for a friendly human face. Although we knew that the SS guards would not tolerate any visible sign of sympathy from the local population, we secretly hoped for the miracle of a friendly civilian soul appearing unexpectedly on an empty street corner to offer us a piece of bread or perhaps even a hot drink. It never happened. The sparse small trees planted on the outskirts of the city streets were the only friendly features in the landscape; They seemed to look at us silently with their lifeless and leafless branches. I noted that even the SS guards were affected by the strange and unfriendly city environment. They walked at both sides of our long column with their overcoat collars turned up, holding rifles in their stiff fingers and looking suspiciously at the empty streets and silent houses. As soon as we reached the city limit on the way to the camp, they prodded us more frequently with the butts of their rifles and shouted in high-pitched voices, "Faster, faster—you dirty bandits."

Adam, walking along on my left side whispered to me. "This is a strange place. Every time we walk through the city I have goose bumps on my skin and a fear of the empty streets. It looks as if these people pretend that we don't exist." I watched carefully around for the nearest SS guard and responded quietly. "Their strange behavior is because of their fear or perhaps because of their shame. But you and I will never know which one." As we passed the center of the town and turned right toward the large farm on the outskirts of the city, the entrance gate to the camp appeared in front of us. We marched through the main gate in front of the SS Rapportführer holding our hats in right hand and desperately trying to keep the even pace. "Left, left"—cried the Capo.

The army barracks where we lived were part of the Ohrdruf history from the beginning of the twentieth century. I was told by an old German prisoner that Kaiser Wilhelm II had ordered the construction of the military complex before the First World War. The Weimar Republic soldiers replaced the Kaiser's army in the late twenties. At the time of Hitler's assumption of power the place was designated for housing and training of SS elite troops. In the fall of 1944, part of this military complex was used as a temporary accommodation for concentration camp prisoners working on construction of Hitler's train underground shelter.

Late in the evening, Adam came to see me. He told me that Louis would be transferred to Buchenwald tomorrow. Apparently the SS Kommandant was bringing all communist prisoners back to the base camp. This was an unexpected move and made us suspicious. It was strange that at such a critical time, when Germany was fighting for survival, the SS and the Gestapo still had sufficient time to settle their political accounts. I knew that I was going to miss Louis. Not because of extra soup, but because he was a decent man, a warm human being with a difficult job in very unusual circumstances. He used his position of foreman to protect his fellow inmates and provide as much comfort as he could.

The next day on our way to work, I wondered who would be appointed to replace Louis. The Capo did not approach anybody and I presumed that he wanted the SS Kommandoführer's approval before making any change. Most of the morning, he stayed with our group and acted as foreman, directing the work of Louis's squad. The SS Kommandoführer suddenly arrived at our work station. He looked around and asked, "Where is the foreman?"

"He left for Buchenwald last night," the Capo responded after taking off his hat.

"Where is the new foreman?" The tone of his voice was not friendly. The Capo stood at attention and nervously responded: "I am doing the job today, but . . ."

The SS interrupted the Capo's explanation. His voice was furious: "You stupid idiot, you can't do two jobs. You can't even do one!" Full of anger, he hit the Capo across his back with the cane and barked louder and louder: "I will teach you how to lead your *Kommando!*" The Capo stood silent, awaiting more beating, but the SS man slowly regained his composure and he looked at the Capo, saying sarcastically, "Since you were unable to pick a new foreman, I will do this for you." He turned around and looked carefully at a few of us who were working in the vicinity. With my heart racing up to my throat, I concentrated on my work, trying to shovel frozen pieces of soil. The SS Kommandoführer turned toward me. Then he asked me a question: "Hey—you, do you speak German?"

I was not thinking clearly as I automatically pulled off my hat and said, "*Jawohl,* Herr Unterscharführer."

He looked at me with his critical, cold eyes. "From now on, you are the foreman."

I was surprised and fearful and responded in a stuttering voice, "*Ja, Jawohl,* Herr Unterscharführer."

Slowly, he said to me: "Make these idiots work. Otherwise they will carry you back to camp." Then he paused before he finished his sentence: "It's you versus them!" He swayed his finger and pointed to what was previously Louis's group. For the third time, in a meek voice, I responded: "*Jawohl,* Herr Unterscharführer." I was tired and hungry and hardly could hold my own as I desperately tried not to become one of the Mussulmans. However, I recognized at once that to refuse was out of the question. This would be sabotage and sabotage was punished by death. The SS man thrust his cane into my hands. "Use this! Otherwise I will use it on you." He turned abruptly and walked away from us toward another group of prisoners.

I was left alone with a large cane in my hand and twenty of my fellow inmates pretending that they were totally absorbed in their chores. As soon as the SS man left, the work slowed down. Already I knew I was in trouble. Adam was sympathetic: "Janusz, don't worry. Pretend that you are screaming, cursing, and threatening us. We will try to meet the day's norm." His reassuring voice gave me some confidence.

Russian and French inmates, hungry and tired, did not pay any attention to what was going on. They deliberately moved very slowly as they pushed their wheelbarrows and carried their tools around the job site. They worked with a sense of resignation and resentment. With no SS guards in sight, they stood still, watching every movement of the SS Kommandoführer. I tried my best French: "Please work harder before the SS man comes back." They looked at me with their sad eyes, but were not impressed with my words. As a matter of fact, they ignored my plea altogether, continuously watching the movements of the SS guards out of the corners of their eyes.

Before lunch, the Capo came to see me and asked how I was doing. I shook my head and responded: "Capo, I will not be able to make my norm." Scratching his head, the Capo offered unsolicited advice: "Push those bastards harder and watch out for the SS Kommandoführer."

I walked among my group, all the time pleading in German, French, and Polish: "Work faster before the SS man comes!" Looking at the faces of the prisoners, I knew that I was losing my battle with them.

The built-up embankment for support of the narrow-gauge rail track was slowly taking shape. Still, we had a long way to go to meet the daily objective established by the SS Kommandoführer. I could see that we would never meet our projected goal. In desperation, I left my cane on the ground and with a spade tried to dig the frozen soil and help the inmates to grade the embankment. Then I heard an angry voice behind me: "You stupid idiot, I told you to be a foreman, not to work side by side with these miserable creatures."

I could only say: "Herr ..." when the SS Kommandoführer picked up his wooden cane, which I had left on the ground, and struck me across the head. I tried to protect my face with both my hands. The SS man was furious: "You stupid idiot! I will teach you how to be a foreman. You will remember my lesson for a long time!" He hit me again and again. After the third strike, I lost my balance. I saw black circles floating in front of my eyes, which interfered with my vision, and I felt that my head was split. I tried to get up from the ground and, still holding my hat in my right hand, whispered: *"Jawohl,* Herr Unterscharführer. Then complete darkness surrounded me as I lost consciousness.

When I opened my eyes, I saw my squad working feverishly in complete silence. They were making a genuine effort to meet the assigned goal for today. Adam stood above me. He asked, "How do you feel?" I touched my head. My fingers were covered with blood. "It hurts," I whispered.

"We must bandage your head as soon as possible so you don't lose too much blood."

I pulled out the bottom of my shirt and tore off a large strip. "Use this," I told Adam.

With the top of my head covered with a colorful bandage, I walked slowly among my fellow workers. I was still concerned with the SS Kommandoführer's threats. "Please hurry up," I begged them in German. The prisoners looked at me with expressionless faces. Their eyes showed sympathy and compassion, but they had no energy left in their bodies. We were, however, slowly making progress toward our designated goal. My head hurt me every time I moved. As the Capo whistled for the end of the work day, we were still short of the goal set up by the SS Kommandoführer. I knew that he would be furious tomorrow and that the only solution to avoid future beatings was to change my *Kommando*.

That evening the march to the base camp was very painful and seemed extremely long. Adam helped me to walk and held my arm all the way to the front gate. My head was still bleeding and my temporary bandage was soaked with blood. I could hardly stand at the roll call as we waited to be counted by the SS Blockführer. The Blockältester called *"Mutzen ab!"* and the SS Unterscharführer approached the formation. This time I was standing in the first row. Usually, I tried to avoid this position since facing the SS Blockführer was always a risky proposition. The most practical approach was to hide behind the front row at the rear of the column and stay away from confrontation with SS men. With my hat in my right hand and the blood-soaked bandage on my head, I stood out in the crowd of my comrades. At first, the SS Unterscharführer passed my row as he counted the prisoners. Then he stopped and walked backward until he faced me: "What's wrong?" My heart beat faster from this unexpected confrontation.

The SS man looked at me and asked: *"Langer,* what are you doing here?" My first reaction was panic. I did not know what to say. Then I remembered that the only SS man in Birkenau who ever called me *Länger* was the SS Unterscharführer Omlauf. In a winter coat, with his field cap just above his eyebrows, I did not recognize him at first. The disinfection work in the Women's Camp at Birkenau flashed through my mind and then I realized that I was looking at my former SS Kommandoführer. Without thinking, I looked at him and whispered in an effort to talk. My head hurt every time I opened my mouth. I said, "I am dying, Herr Unterscharführer." Then I quickly realized that this sounded melodramatic; no SS man could accept this kind of answer from a prisoner.

Omlauf looked at me and my white bandage with red stains. "What's your number?" he asked me again. "111487," I whispered. I noted that he scribbled my number in his notebook, which he carried for the roll call. Abruptly, he turned around and continued with his head count as if nothing had happened. The whole incident lasted perhaps thirty seconds. *"Mutzen auf!"* called the Blockältester. "Dismissed!" repeated the Stubendienst. We broke ranks.

Adam came to see me: "What was that about?" he asked me. "I don't know," I said. "I used to work for him in Birkenau and he recognized me."

As soon as the evening portions of food were distributed, I went to see the nurse in a temporary clinic set up in one of the rooms on the ground floor. The French doctor, who worked as an orderly, looked at my split head and put a new paper bandage on the wound. The bleeding stopped.

"You have a nasty cut. Keep it clean. In a few days it will close up and you will feel much better," he told me as he gave me an extra bandage.

I found my way slowly up the steps to my dormitory, wondering about my unexpected confrontation with Omlauf. I was not too sure what to expect. Common sense and experience with Baretzki in Birkenau guided me to always stay away from SS troopers. Every confrontation usually evoked tragic circumstances for the prisoner. Today's beating confirmed my old theory. Why Omlauf took my number I had no idea, but I expected the worst. Soon the room orderly appeared in the doorway: "Number 111487, report to the Schreiber immediately!" he called loudly. I could hardly hear him among the many voices of socializing inmates. This was the only "free time," our moment of liberty before the "Lights out" whistles.

I struggled to walk across the room full of inmates visiting with their friends, getting ready to sleep, or engaged in the process of delousing: carefully checking their clothes and hunting for lice. One could hear a multitude of different languages. Some inmates, dead tired, lay on their straw mattresses resting and trying to recover their strength for tomorrow's chores. The Schreiber checked my number: "Tomorrow morning, do not go to work with your *Kommando*. You are being transferred to the North Camp," he said. I was both confused and relieved. Not facing my new SS Kommand-offührer at the *Kleinzugkommando* was a welcome surprise. But, at the same time, I was genuinely concerned about my future assignment.

"How come? What's going on?" I asked him. He told me, "Although there are still some working *Aussenkommandos* in the camp, the North Camp has been officially designated as a hospital for S III. You should be happy since you are assigned to work in the *Desinfektionskommando* and you will be housed with the hospital orderlies! You must have friends in high places." He smiled and patted me on the shoulder in a friendly way: "Good luck! It won't be long."

Now I understood. Omlauf arranged the transfer. As a SS SDG, he still had something to do with hygiene and hospitals. I was surprised because I never knew him well and hardly talked to him in Birkenau. Wiktor was always a middle man between the SS men and the prisoners. Perhaps it was Omlauf's conscience, or perhaps he wanted some insurance after the war when he and his comrades would be put on trial for their murderous behavior. I stopped speculating since I would never know the story behind his action. The most obvious and important thing for me was that I would not have to report to work tomorrow with my old "*Kleinzugkommando*." This was the best news I had had in a long time. I went to see Adam to share my good news with him. He was happy for me, but at the same time, concerned with his own future in the old work squad. The new SS Kommandoführer in a few short days had confirmed his murderous reputation from Dora and his fanatical commitment to the Nazi cause. At this stage of the war, that was a bad sign for all the prisoners working in his squad. He had demonstrated clearly that an inmate's life had no value to him and Adam expected many problems in the near future. Adam and I shook hands and promised each other that we would get together after the war. When he said, "Take care, big Janusz," Adam had tears in his eyes.

The next morning, after the roll call and departure of the *Aussenkommandos*, I was told to wait by the front gate. With a small group of about ten inmates, I waited. Then, led by the SS Unterscharführer and surrounded by an armed escort of several SS troopers, we left the barracks and walked toward the North Camp. I learned from one of the inmates walking by my side that Ohrdruf Concentration Camp or S III consisted of two camps, North and South, with approximately five thousand prisoners in each section. All of them worked at the railroad and tunnel installations. The North Camp, somehow hidden behind a gentle hill and away from the city, was constructed in the middle of an open field. Surrounded by barbed wire, the long lines of one-story, wooden barracks with rows of windows on each side looked harmless from a distance.

We passed through the gate and were ordered to wait in front of the administrative barracks. A large *Appellplatz* adjoining the long kitchen barracks was in front of us. The senior inmate with the armband of *Arbeitsdienst*, a labor official, looked at my number and checked his list. "Report to the hospital. You will work with the *Desinfektionskommando*," he said and showed me the way to the bathhouse. I left the group and walked alone to the disinfection barrack, which was constructed on a gentle slope and hidden from the rest of the camp.

The early March morning was bright and sunny, but still cold. Snow slowly disappeared from the unpaved streets between barracks, but open areas around the bathhouse were full of mud and dirt. The foreman expected my arrival. He gave me a curious look and said: "You will be working on the incoming site. Report to the SS Sturmmann who works there." I was surprised. In all my previous camp experience, I had never seen an SS man working alongside prisoners.

The disinfection area was a large room adjacent to the undressing area, which led to the shower room. In the middle of the acceptance area, an old man in the SS field camouflage uniform pushed trolleys full of clothing into a small disinfection chamber. He was at least sixty years old, small with a worn out face and sad eyes. I stood at full attention with my hat in my right hand. The SS man looked at me with his tired eyes.

"Do you speak German?" he asked.

"*Jawohl,* Herr Sturmmann."

He shrugged his shoulders. "Don't be so formal. You will work with me as my helper. Put your hat back on."

I felt more surprised and strange by the minute. After months of depravation, bullying, and beatings, I did not know what to make of this man. He did not act like a true and dedicated SS trooper. It took me a while to recover my composure. I put my hat back on, took off my jacket and started pushing loaded trolleys into the disinfection chamber. We hardly talked to each other for the rest of the day. Since I was familiar with the work, I did not need any instructions. The SS Sturmmann moved very quietly around the room and hardly paid any attention to my presence. In the late afternoon at the end of the workday, the foreman told me to join the work squad and attend the evening roll call. I was lucky. A small part of the hospital barrack was set aside for nursing orderlies and the disinfection squad. Straw-filled burlap mattresses lay close together on the concrete floor. There were few windows and the small room was almost dark. Only one electric bulb in the middle of the ceiling provided relief from complete darkness. As primitive as it was, this was still a luxury compared with the dilapidated and overcrowded barracks where field *Kommandos* were housed.

As we waited in front of our building for the beginning of the roll call, I watched work squads coming from the field. I was again shocked by their appearance and the poor condition of prisoners crossing the gate. By now, I should have been used to this view. From Birkenau through Buchenwald and now in Ohrdruf, it was the same story. Perhaps with the increased persecution and food shortages at the camp, the inmates were thinner, hungrier, and more desperate to survive each long day of slavery. I watched them silently as they formed their columns in front of the barracks. Each *Kommando,* as usual, carried their sick and dead comrades. The bodies were dumped unceremoniously on the ground. The callousness of human indifference among the prisoners was obvious. With the increased number of *Aussenkommandos,* or field squads, returning to the camp, the pile of dead bodies was growing with every passing minute. Although I considered myself to be a tough individual after many months of experience in the concentration camps, I looked with dismay at the human drama unfolding in front of my eyes. I could not get used to the misery of my fellow prisoners, regardless of how indifferent I wanted to be.

When would this end? As usual, I searched for an answer. The depressing picture of work squads gathering for roll call made me feel as small and insignificant as a raindrop lost in a deadly hurricane. *"Mutzen ab!"* The familiar order interrupted my thoughts. The SS Blockführer began to inspect and count the blocks. He walked briskly among the prisoners standing at attention with their hats held firmly in their right hand.

An anxious Blockältester who was concerned with making all the attendance numbers agree with the prisoners' roster followed each SS man. Pictures of different camps, blocks, barracks, and the people I had met and lost floated in my mind. Again, I felt lonely and abandoned. I did not know anybody and I was not anxious to meet new people.

My "next-door" neighbor in the barrack was a hospital orderly, a Belgian Jew. Except for a few words in French, we had no way to communicate. He did have a few friends in the *Desinfektionskommando* and spent all of his "free" time with them. They left me alone and, in a way, I appreciated my privacy. My battered head felt better and my wounds were healing. As I changed my paper dressings I could feel my split skin with my frozen fingers. At least the bleeding had stopped altogether. The Stubendienst distributed the evening bread portions. We all shared the metal bowls for drinking the ersatz tea. It smelled and tasted like the famous *Avo* tea in Birkenau.

The daily routine and the timetable was almost identical in all of the camps. The next morning, after the usual roll call, I left with my *Kommando* for work. The SS Sturmmann was already in the bathhouse. With a pipe between his teeth and in a camouflage army field uniform, he stood by the entrance door peacefully sucking his pipe. He looked like an ordinary worker since he was so different in temperament and attitude from the rest of his SS comrades.

He nodded his head: "Good morning." "What's your name?"

"Johann—Herr Sturmmann," I responded and tried to pull my cap off.

"Don't take your cap off when you talk to me," he reminded me quietly. "Where are you from?"

"Poland," I replied eagerly.

He nodded his head several times and puffed his pipe. "Long way from home," he muttered under his breath. Then he looked at his schedule for the day. "We expect about two hundred people today. It won't be too bad."

The prisoners from Crawinkel led by the Capo arrived late in the morning. Watching them undressing, I could see their skeletal bodies emerging from under their camp uniforms and their dirty and worn-out underwear. Their bodies were covered with scabs, full of sores and open wounds. Their limbs were thin and long. With sad and glassy eyes, they watched me in silence, with curiosity and indifference at the same time. One of the inmates used to be in Birkenau. While waiting for his disinfected clothes in the bathhouse, he talked to me briefly about his life in the Crawinkel tent camp. The camp was located about one kilometer from Crawinkel village. There were about three thousand inmates in that camp, all housed in tents. Three shifts of a thousand men each were forced every day to march through the village to work in a quarry in Jonastal Valley. They marched twelve kilometers every morning to the job site. The village of Crawinkel, like the town of Ohrdruf, was always deserted. Only the clapping of wooden shoes echoed through the silent streets of the village.

When the camp was extended in December 1944, the old underground bunkers constructed in 1934 for the storage of ammunition were now used to house the prisoners. Conditions in the new camp were abominable. There was no light, no water, and no heat. The prisoners slept on the concrete floor without blankets or straw mattresses. Some of the old underground bunkers were also used by the SS Political Department for imprisonment of arrested fugitives. Captured prisoners were hanged after a few days of cruel investigation. He also told me that because of the accelerated schedule and SS determination to complete the construction of the Communication Center as soon as possible, another new subcamp was recently established in the former Hitler Youth facility in Espenfeld. It was very close to the Jonastal construction site and the SS were merciless in driving the inmates to complete the construction of the tunnel works.

Our conversation was suddenly interrupted by the Capo who screamed: "Faster, faster" and waved his wooden stick. In a few minutes, after they hung their miserable prison clothes on the hangers mounted on trolleys, the whole group moved to the adjoining shower room. I pushed the trolleys inside the disinfection chamber and the SS man locked the door.

This was the only transport that day and I spent most of the afternoon cleaning the floor and collecting leftover uniforms and underwear. I discreetly observed, out of the corner of my eye, my "working partner." He hardly talked to me for the rest of the day, and I silently wondered how this old man with the SS insignia on his collar had ended up sharing this work with prisoners who, after all, were considered to be "the enemy of the Reich" and inferior creatures. With so many inmates available to do menial chores, I could not understand the need for an SS trooper to work alongside us. Since I could hardly ask him for an explanation, I kept quiet while I finished my chores for the day. The situation was strange; two of us working side by side in the shadow of the anticipated German defeat. However, it was far easier to push trolleys or wash concrete floors than to be working on an *Aussenkommando*, exposed to the cold winter weather and polluted air in the underground tunnels.

The sounds of explosions and bright flashes from V-2 test sites were more and more frequent. The tests were carried out both day and night. The occasional roaring of allied aircraft engines from hundreds of planes flying high in the sky made us aware of the deadly struggle going on around us.

"Americans!" whispered excited prisoners. We could almost sense some of the big changes at the front lines from the increased activity in the air high above our heads. The underground gossip anticipated liberation and the end of the war within a few weeks or perhaps sooner. Our SS guards, however, did not share the prisoners' hopes and expectations. They were as mean as ever. People were dying daily, and base camp routine was maintained with iron discipline. Although one could feel the nervousness and confusion among the SS troops, the SS Blockführers and SS Kommandoführers, on the surface, acted "normal" in their cruel and demeaning way. They continued to beat prisoners at the slightest provocation with the most meager excuses.

In spite of better spring weather, the everyday routine in the North Camp was bleak. The camp consisted of many single-story, wooden barracks. Barbed-wire fence, stretched on the rough wooden piles, surrounded the camp perimeter. The watchtowers were crudely constructed from unfinished lumber pieces. The "temporary" and "make-do" character of the camp was a far cry from the well constructed concrete piles and electrified fences of Birkenau.

My work in the bathhouse isolated me from the everyday cruelties inflicted by the SS guards and Capos upon inmates working at the tunnel sites. I almost felt safe and protected in the enclosure of the disinfection rooms. My head wounds were healing and after a few days I discarded the paper bandages. I was also able to exchange my striped white-blue uniform for a pair of civilian pants and a jacket with a red stripe painted on the back. There was, however, less and less work in the bathhouse. I noted during the roll calls that the number of inmates was gradually being reduced. Large groups of prisoners were taken every day by army trucks to the railroad station.

On the outskirts of the camp strange activities were taking place. Inmates assigned to a special *Kommando* were digging out previously buried corpses and cremating them on specially built pyres. The excavated bodies were laid in rows on the scaffoldings constructed from the railroad tracks and burned with the aid of wood and gasoline. The smell of burnt flesh was everywhere. People were still dying by the hundreds every day from sicknesses caused by the harsh life in the camp, hunger, and mistreatment by functionaries and SS guards. The last days of March brought more sunshine and the snow disappeared completely from the ground. The town's fields and shrubs were gradually turning green. We anxiously awaited April and our freedom.

CHAPTER TEN

Death March

THE APRIL MORNING roll call was extremely long. We stood for at least two hours, cold, thirsty, and, as always, hungry. We watched the sun slowly appearing on the horizon, bringing gentle light into the grayness of the dawn. The Blockältesters ran around the camp, checking empty buildings, looking for absentees, and counting prisoners at each block at least three times. Nursing orderlies were called to step forward. They were told by the Lagercapo to assist sick inmates in vacating hospital barracks. Because of the small size of the medical staff, the evacuation process was lengthy and painful. A majority of the patients were weak, undernourished, and unable to walk. After being dragged from hospital beds, they collapsed in front of the building and lay semiconscious on the grass under the open sky. The main entrance gate was closed. The field *Kommandos* were not allowed to leave the camp for their regular daily work assignments. We all suspected that something unusual was going on. None of us, though, had any idea what to expect. It appeared, however, that the camp was being prepared for evacuation.

Around 8 A.M., the *Desinfektionskommando* was also called to assist the nursing orderlies to transfer bed-ridden and terminally ill inmates from their beds to the open area at the *Appellplatz*. People unable to walk and half-conscious were carried out on makeshift stretchers and unceremoniously dumped in front of the barracks. The number of sick and suffering inmates lying helplessly on the ground increased with every hour. Half of them were slowly dying, some already dead. The remaining few, hungry and thirsty, continuously begged for a drop of water. As I helped to carry sick inmates from the barracks, on my return trips to pick up more patients, I smuggled with me a metal bowl full of water. Hiding my good intentions in front of the supervising Capo, I tried to share my meager supplies of precious water with a few inmates.

Meanwhile, a large group of heavily armed SS guards arrived at the outside of the main gate. The Lagercapo passed a new order among the standing prisoners to form one marching column. As soon as the first unit passed through the gate, they were surrounded by the SS guards. Very soon, a long, winding column of inmates dressed in their striped white-blues and surrounded by the armed SS guards, camouflaged in their green field uniforms, crisscrossed the peaceful Thuringian landscape. Nursing orderlies, working around me moving the sick inmates from their barracks, were told to join the marching column.

Suddenly, I was left alone in the middle of the *Appellplatz,* completely unnoticed by the camp functionaries. Piles of corpses and hundreds of slowly dying sick inmates lay in the open area in front of Block 4. The *Desinfektionskommando* was last to leave the camp as they marched at the very end of the departing column. The Capo noticed my absence, turned around and called me several times, urging me to join the ranks. I hesitated as I quickly looked around at hundreds of half-dead bodies lying on the ground. Many trembling inmates were still alive. They sat wrapped in old blankets, shivered and, with sad and dazed eyes, watched their departing comrades.

A few very sick inmates cupped their hands and begged for water. Wrapped in an assortment of rags, full of insects and lice, they whispered cautiously, "Water, water, water!"

I took a last look at the hospital barrack and the piles of corpses. I was ready to join my departing *Kommando,* but suddenly changed my mind. I was struck by a new idea. It was a bold, risky, but workable plan. By now, we all knew that the camp was being evacuated so that no prisoners were allowed to fall into American hands. The long march, probably to Buchenwald, would be deadly dangerous. If I could avoid this forceful evacuation and hide among the corpses, my chances for survival would be greatly improved. I found a narrow spot between two shivering bodies and, as I carefully lay down, I tried to pull my neighbor's blanket over my face. The idea was simple and exciting. I trembled with emotion as I was ready to play "dead." Except for the sound of marching feet, the camp was silent. From a distance, I could hear faraway explosions and see flashes across the sky. I knew that this time, they were not field tests of V-2 rockets, which we had become accustomed to during the past months in Ohrdruf. This was heavy artillery firing a long way from us, but steadily moving closer and closer toward the city.

I raised my head for a moment to see if the Capo was still looking for me. Then I heard shots behind me. I turned my head and was shocked. A long single line of SS guards led by the SS Scharführer walked slowly across the *Appellplatz* toward me. Occasionally, they stopped and carefully checked every body lying on the ground. First they kicked each person with their heavy army boots. Then, to be absolutely certain that they were not leaving any witnesses in the abandoned camp, they shot each prisoner in the head. The soldiers were very thorough in carrying out the executions. They were careful not to miss even a single body lying helplessly on the ground. Their passage was marked with piles of unburied corpses left to rot.

I was in a panic, not sure what to do. I had only two choices. First, I could stay in place and pretend that I was already dead. That would mean taking a chance of being shot in the head by one of the SS guards. Second, I could make an attempt to run, trying to join my *Kommando* which was just about to leave the camp. Again, I would be chancing a shot in the back by the same SS guard. I perspired, as they were only a few yards from me. Suddenly, I jumped to my feet and, with a wooden stick in my right hand, which I had picked up from the ground, I started screaming and cursing at the top of my voice. Also, I hit hard several of the dead bodies lying around me: "You dirty swines, lousy bastards! Get up! Get up! You are not sick enough to stay behind." The SS Scharführer heading the line of "shooters" stopped in front of me.

"What do you think you are doing?" he asked me calmly. He had a revolver in his hand.

"I am trying to force these bastards to join the column, Herr Scharführer," I responded, pounding heavily on one of the bodies. The SS man looked at me with an ironic smile. "You better run right now! We will take good care of your friends. Beat it, you crafty idiot!" he yelled at me, waving his revolver in front of my eyes. "*Jawohl*, Herr Scharführer," I whispered in a trembling voice. I was scared as I put my hat back on, threw away my wooden stick, turned around, and ran as fast as I could to join my departing *Desinfektionskommando*.

My heart pounded heavily and the distance seemed to be extremely long. Any second, I expected a bullet in my back. There were several rapid shots behind me. Halfway to the gate, I turned my head to see what was going on. The SS Scharführer and his squad had resumed shooting inmates as they searched for live bodies among the prisoners lying on the ground. I was out of breath when I caught up with my *Kommando*. The Capo looked at me, shook his head, but did not say anything. I hastily joined the last row of the marching column. The Capo, who walked right behind me, was the last prisoner to leave the camp.

The general mood of the SS guards was mean and grim. Every artillery shell exploding on the other side of the village was sweet music to the prisoners' ears. But it was a message of fear and defeat to our SS escort. They looked around curiously, watched the sky for enemy aircraft, and goaded us to march faster and faster. Weaker inmates, who could not keep the accelerated pace and lagged behind the marching column, were immediately shot. I looked behind me and I saw that the road from the camp, winding through the farm fields, was already marked with corpses of prisoners lying on both sides. For a short time, we were the only marchers, but as we crossed the first intersection with the major highway, we came across heavy pedestrian and vehicular traffic. Hundreds of military vehicles and thousands of pedestrians appeared suddenly on the congested highway. After we joined this huge exodus, the main highway was becoming more and more crowded with masses of civilian refugees carrying their personal belongings and walking on both sides of the road. They all tried hard to keep pace with the retreating military formations. There was hardly any room available for us to walk on the highway among the disorganized masses of civilians, soldiers, and horse-drawn wagons. The refugees walked silently on both sides of our column with expressions of contempt on their faces. The SS guards, using their dogs, tried to keep us together in a long column, winding through the sea of demoralized civilians.

"Why are they running away?" I asked my companion walking on my left.

"I think some of them are running away from the Americans," he responded. Then he added: "I was told by one of the Capos that many refugees are from East Prussia. They have been traveling for weeks trying to escape the Russians."

The traffic on the highway was getting more confused and congested with every mile. At the next intersection, I saw military police trying to bring some order among a bewildered crowd of soldiers and civilians. They held us back and told the SS Kommandoführer to stop the prisoners' column and wait by the adjoining farmhouse to make room for military traffic moving in the opposite direction toward the front lines. This decision to delay our march made our SS escorts very uncomfortable. From a distance, I saw the SS Untersturmführer in charge of our column arguing unsuccessfully with the military police Oberleutnant.

We were pushed aside from the main highway and ordered by the SS guards to move behind the large barn and lie down on our stomachs with our heads close to the ground. The soil was cold and muddy, but we welcomed this unexpected opportunity to rest and catch our breath after the long and exhausting morning march. "Keep your heads down!" I heard guards shouting at the top of their voices. I could also hear the sound of heavy tanks as they passed the farmhouse and headed north to face the enemy. After a few minutes the roar of engines faded away. "Get up and form the column!" yelled functional prisoners and SS guards. With much panic, we again formed a marching column. There was a lot of heavy beating and pushing by the Capos. Some of the SS guards fired shots in the air to accelerate our departure and frighten stragglers. Five men abreast in a long line, half-dead, we

were forced again to enter the highway's main stream of traffic. The road, including unpaved shoulders, was clogged with frantic refugees. Small groups
of civilians and formations of military detachments, all intermingled in complete chaos and fear, marched south toward Rudolfstadt. All were desperately trying to escape the advancing Americans. After we left the farm, the
field behind the barn was covered with scattered dead bodies of prisoners
who were unable to walk and were shot by the SS guards.

The terror and cruelties of war were not limited to inmates only. As we
passed the next intersection, I saw two corpses hanging from a big tree. They
wore the uniforms of German soldiers without military insignia. Each victim
had a sign around his neck whose large handwritten letters said in German "I
deserted my country."

The passing crowd of refugees looked in silence and with respect at the
hanging bodies. The conversation among civilians hushed as they walked
quietly by the large oak tree. The two corpses swung side by side on the low
branch and swayed in the gentle April breeze coming from the west. That
same breeze brought sounds of faraway explosions. One could feel the air of
gloom and defeat hanging above the highway. Intermingled with civilian and
military traffic and closely guarded by the SS escort, we walked slowly along
one side of the road. We were frequently forced to step aside into an adjoining ditch in order to allow military armored formations to move toward the
front lines. Pushed and squeezed together in the narrow ditch, we watched
whole families passing us slowly in the same direction. They pushed their
baby carriages or small carts or overloaded bicycles with their household belongings as they ran in fear from the danger of the front line.

I secretly enjoyed every minute of their visible suffering, knowing that
my own strength and ability to continue this deadly march was reaching its
limits. As we passed the small village near Rudolstadt with a few large farms
on the right side of the highway, I heard several shots from automatic rifles
behind me. The column suddenly stopped. An excited SS Unterscharführer at
the head of the convoy, with a pistol in his hand, screamed at the top of his
voice. "Stop—you damn Bolsheviks, or I will shoot all of you." He turned
around and ran toward the rear of the column. I looked around. Behind several rows of inmates, two SS guards stood on the shoulder of the highway
with their automatic rifles pointed at three prisoners lying on the ground,
across the ditch. I could see from the distance that two inmates were motionless on the rough surface of small stones. With their faces down on the
ground and buried in the gravel, and their arms spread, it looked like they
were shot suddenly from behind. The third inmate, lying on his back, was
just turned around by the towering SS man who still kept his right foot on the
chest of the victim. The inmate's eyes were wide open, but glazed and vacant.

A tiny stream of blood dripped from his twisted mouth. His dead face was white as snow.

"They tried to escape, Herr Unterscharführer," explained one of the SS guards. Then he smiled and said: "But they did not go too far."

The endless column of civilian refugees walking in the same direction on the opposite shoulder of the highway slowed down to watch the unfolding drama of a cold-blooded murder.

Somehow, as if from nowhere, on a bicycle a village policeman in his bluish uniform with dark brown collar appeared and stopped in front of the dead bodies. He was quite angry as he turned around and talked to the SS Unterscharführer: "Do not shoot people and leave them behind as you are running away from the Americans. I do not want to see any corpses in my village. I don't want to explain to Americans what you are doing to these people." I could not believe my ears as I listened to this unusual conversation. The SS man looked at the policeman with contempt and indifference and said: "You have nothing to say—this is a military matter." The policeman's face became red as he shouted, "I have a lot to say. This is my village and I am responsible for what happens here. You better take your corpses with you on your way to Buchenwald."

"Or what?" asked the SS man sarcastically. By now, a few civilians gathered around the policeman. They were dressed in the working field clothes of farm workers. Their faces were sunburned, weathered, and full of wrinkles but they had lively sparks in their eyes. They did not look like fleeing refugees. One of them said: "This is my land and this is my village. You have done enough destruction around here. Your time has gone. I suggest that you take your prisoners, alive and dead and leave this area as fast as you can. I do not want to be punished for your crimes." "Here, here," muttered other civilians standing nearby.

The SS Unterscharführer seemed to be confused. He looked at the long line of slowly moving civilian refugees and then he stared at the standing column of prisoners and measured up the group of militant farmers. They stood around the village policeman, defiant with their heads high, some of them holding hunting rifles in a menacing way. The SS Unterscharführer hesitated and turned around to one of his SS guards and said, "Assign people to carry the corpses and let's move on from here." The SS man called loudly, "Capo, pick strong muscles to carry this dirt."

The Capo, a German with a green triangle on his jacket and a large stick in his hand, selected twelve of the strongest-looking inmates from a row behind me to carry the corpses. "Fast you idiots. Pick up your comrades and move before somebody will carry you."

Four inmates picked up each of the three bodies and a small procession formed at the end of the column guarded by the SS men on both sides. "Forward march!" called the SS Unterscharführer as he was making his way to head the convoy. I discreetly looked behind me. We were on the move again. Struggling skeletons supporting one another walked slowly, carrying their fallen comrades. The policeman and his village friends looked at us silently as we left the village on our way toward Buchenwald.

When a marching group of prisoners was formed at the camp, I always preferred to walk in the middle row at the edge of the column. This position offered a better view of the highway and of course a better chance to escape. Exhausted after an all-day march, I watched with envy as hundreds of free civilians—men, women, and children—passed me by. They were so close that I could almost touch them. Only the SS guards, walking fifteen meters apart on both sides of the column separated us from the free world. The guards were also tired. I noted that when we left the camp, each sentry carried a large knapsack on his back with food supplies. I believed that all the food stolen from the prisoners' camp kitchen was generously divided and distributed among the SS guards. In addition to their weapons and heavy ammunition belts hanging across their chests, they had a real problem coping with the additional weight of knapsacks full of food supplies, which were their most valuable luggage. As we walked slowly up the hill on the widening highway, one of the guards untied his straps and suddenly put his heavy knapsack on the back of one of the inmates. The prisoner, who was already struggling trying to keep pace with the marching column, took a deep breath and almost collapsed under the heavy and unexpected load. "Keep going!" barked the SS man and added "Don't slow down, if you want to live." The drained inmate looked at the guard with his tired eyes and without one word made a desperate effort to stay in the ranks of the marching column. He was just in front of me and I could see him sweating and wobbling on his feet. His comrades on both sides held his arms to help him retain his balance as he was making a continuous effort to keep up with the brisk marching pace. The SS guard, relieved from the weight of his knapsack, walked along the prisoners' column, keeping his eye on his pricey possession. After a few kilometers, I could see that the inmate's steps were more uneven and uncertain. In spite of a fresh westerly wind, his face was red-hot. He wobbled occasionally as he tried to balance the heavy weight of the knapsack on his back.

I could sense from his behavior that the man was reaching the limit of his physical endurance. After another kilometer, he looked around, took a deep breath and fell down on his knees in the middle of the marching column. As he knelt in the center of the highway, the marching prisoners walked around him without slowing the pace. The SS guard was furious. He jumped to the middle of the column and pulled the poor soul to the shoulder strip on the side of the highway. Then he quickly untied the knapsack from the inmate's back. The prisoner, who was semiconscious by now, lay motionless on the asphalt surface. The guard looked carefully at the marching inmates. One of the prisoners was tall and well built, and appeared to be healthier than the others.

"Hey you!" The SS guard screamed. "Take this!"—and he quickly strapped the knapsack on the back of the new victim. After doing this, the SS guard turned his attention to the inmate lying on the ground. Without haste, he slowly loaded his rifle, and touched the forehead of the inmate with the long barrel. Suddenly, he pulled the trigger. The victim screamed in final agony. Blood and pieces of his brain splattered everywhere. The SS guard's black boots were covered with blood. He swore loudly and viciously kicked the dead body in the stomach. Then, he swung his rifle on his left arm and took his position among the marching SS guards. As he walked close to his new victim, who now carried his knapsack, he told the inmate with a sarcastic smile: "You better do a better job than your friend or you may join him very soon."

The idea of using inmates to carry SS knapsacks spread quickly among other guards. Very soon a large number of half-dead and exhausted prisoners were forced to carry the SS guards' food supplies on their backs. This was the first time that I regretted walking on the edge of the column. The exposure to the SS guards looking for help in carrying their supplies was exceptionally dangerous. I tried to keep my head down to make myself almost invisible. When I carefully watched the SS guards walking close to me, deep in my heart I silently prayed that they would not select me as their next victim. Long stretches of highway ahead of us were again marked by the corpses of prisoners who had been shot and left behind. Bodies of killed inmates were sometimes picked up by the trailing SS truck or when time permitted, buried in a makeshift grave on the side of the road. However, most of the time, corpses were left lying along the road, abandoned by the SS guards at the place of the execution. They lay everywhere on both sides of the highway, rotting under the open sky. This was a dramatic reminder of previous convoys who had preceded us by a few days in a desperate attempt to reach Buchenwald to escape the advancing Americans.

Civilian refugees, engrossed in their own fears, looked at the dead bodies without any sign of compassion. I tried to understand their feelings. After all, we were their enemy.

We were walking skeletons hardly able to keep our balance or drag our swollen feet. We struggled silently but were determined to survive this deadly and unbearable march. I could occasionally see a spark of sympathy in women's eyes, but in the confusion and chaos on the highway, it was impossible for us to beg for food or water from the masses of civilian refugees. It felt as if two different worlds walked side by side together, but separately, indifferent to and contemptuous of one another. At the intersection with the main road leading to Weimar, we passed a unit of *Volkssturm* veterans. Old men, some of them still in civilian garb with armbands on their jackets, each carried on his shoulders a *Panzerfaust,* a small personal antitank rocket. At this stage of the war, the civilian population, men and women of all ages, were mobilized across the country to make a last desperate attempt to stop the enemy. There was panic and despair among the older people. However, younger men were full of pathetic fervor and defiance, with unquestioning faith in their Führer.

In the evening, the SS Kommandant led the Ohrdruf convoy of prisoners to a small village, which consisted of not more than five farmhouses grouped together along a small country road adjoining the highway. We were divided into five groups and told to enter several large barns, half-filled with straw and agricultural equipment. Guards were posted outside. We were told to lie down and rest. There was no indication that any food would be distributed.

I looked for a well. But the guard would not let us do anything. "Lie down or I will shoot you!" he ranted, seeing our restlessness and desire to look for water. Sick people lying around me whispered: "Water, please comrade, water!" I knew that most of them would not last until tomorrow morning. I swallowed my saliva, but my throat was dry and sore. My neighbor was a French Jew whose name was Rubin. His German was not very good and, of course, my French was even worse. Rubin was in bad shape. His feet were swollen. He lay with his eyes closed and whispered every few minutes the only word he knew in German: "*Wasser, Wasser.*" Occasionally he opened his eyes and, with great effort, mumbled to me: "*Monsieur, c'est fini! Au revoir, mon ami.*"

I did not think he would last until morning. But he did. As we were pushed and prodded by Capos and SS guards to form a marching column the following morning, I told Rubin to stay close to me. He was grateful, but I could see that he was totally confused by the congestion, arguments, screams of inmates, and the sound of advancing tanks and military vehicles. They moved slowly against the human wave of civilians and prisoners, all mixed together, and crushed anything left standing in the middle of the highway. Since we left Ohrdruf, we had had nothing to eat or drink. Most of the inmates still alive were unable to walk any further. They slowly drifted behind the marching column, and as they were unable to keep up with the brisk pace of the marchers, were shot by the SS guards and left unburied. There was no time for any funeral at all. Our column of two thousand prisoners who had left Ohrdruf in the last phase of forceful evacuation was almost reduced by half. We were not even halfway to Buchenwald.

CHAPTER ELEVEN

White Stars

THE SECOND MORNING the thunder of big guns seemed to be getting closer and closer. Artillery shells were bursting in flashy explosions over the horizon. The occasional staccato of machine guns and single shots from the SS escort around the marching column telegraphed messages of fear and death. As the sun rose slowly from behind tall pine trees, it brought a new day brimming with fearful expectations. By then the march was a nightmare. As they had the day before, the SS escorts immediately shot anybody who strayed behind. Some inmates were so exhausted, thirsty, hungry, and indifferent to ongoing terror that they did not try to keep up. Early in the morning, long lines of dead bodies lying in the ditches on both sides of the road already marked our trail. There was no mercy and no explanation for the people staying behind—just one shot in the back.

The SS guards walked with us on both sides of the column with their rifles and machine guns ready. The fear of certain defeat, uncertainty of the future, hate, contempt, and desire for revenge made them real instruments of terror. Shots were heard continually along the full length of the marching column, and the shortage of food was felt everywhere. The watchdogs, barely fed the previous night, were vicious and mean. Big, black-brown Alsatian wolves led on long leashes terrified the prisoners. They chased stragglers, barking ferociously, and made escape from the column almost impossible.

Except for a bowl of watery soup served two days before, prior to our departure from Ohrdruf, we had had no food and no real rest. The world around us was in flames. The familiar scenes of yesterday came back to haunt us on the crowded highways. The country road in the heart of Thuringia, leading to Weimar, was full of refugees. Frightened by Nazi propaganda about American vengeance, with their knapsacks and few personal belongings, entire families marched with us in the same direction. German men and women of all ages walked slowly and silently, staring at us. I saw no dislike in their eyes, just resignation and fear. I smiled secretly inside. I thought, "At least we have something in common."

Convoys of army trucks and motorcycles passed us in the opposite direction. The trucks were full of *Volkssturm* volunteers on their way to the front lines. Old men, each holding his *Panzerfaust,* looked at us from the height of their trucks in contempt, as if we were the reason for their misfortune. Occasional armored cars, with young boys from Hitler-Jugend sitting outside the commander's turret with their machine guns across their knees and strings of heavy ammunition around their necks, sped across the highway. They disregarded pedestrian traffic and marching columns of prisoners. Many vehicles were abandoned on both sides of the overloaded highway. Burnt-out tanks and destroyed military trucks, pushed aside from the main road by the military police, cluttered the Thuringian landscape. Five abreast, long columns of walking skeletons were finding their way among the military and civilian traffic. Our shaved heads and striped uniforms made us stand out from the rest of the marchers. SS guards watched us closely all the time to make sure we stayed together and did not break ranks.

As we marched, I sensed that staying with the marching column could end my life. The SS guards were hysterical and out of control. The SS Untersturmführer leading the column was a sadistic murderer. Escape was the only way. In spite of the danger of being selected to carry the SS guards' knapsacks, I decided to walk in the outside row of the column. Escape was all the time on my mind. Next to me, on my left, walked Rubin. Since we could not communicate easily, we marched all day silently side by side. He was a worn-out young man, perhaps five years older than I. Without his glasses, which he had lost yesterday when he was hit by the SS guard, he could not see very well. In his Dutch wooden shoes every step was a struggle. His feet were swollen and bloody. It was obvious that he was having a hard time keeping up. With great effort I learned that he was arrested in Paris and sent to Auschwitz through Drancy in the summer of 1942. We discovered that we had arrived in the same transport from Auschwitz to Buchenwald on December 7, 1944.

Rubin labored for two years in Auschwitz, digging ditches to expand the existing sewer system. Work was difficult. Regardless of the season, he stood all day in the Birkenau mud and subsurface dirty water. Ohrdruf was even worse. For the past few months, he had been digging tunnels in the Thuringian Mountains to construct Hitler's underground command post and vast underground radio and telephone center. By now he was a half-dead, confused, hungry, and dehydrated Mussulman.

Since we started walking that morning, I held Rubin's right arm to help him to maintain his balance. He was grateful, and as we struggled together to keep up with the pace, he looked at me occasionally with his near-sighted eyes and whispered: *"Merci, Merci."* But, I knew I could not hold him for the rest of the day. As we began marching at the accelerated pace, I was slowly losing my strength. I was also observing the surrounding areas and assessing realistically the risks of an escape.

Suddenly, my friend pushed my arm away and without a sound fell down on the highway. It happened so fast that by the time I realized he was lying on the ground, the marching columns behind me split the ranks. Without stopping, they passed the fallen Frenchman. I could see Rubin lying in the middle of the road, protecting his head with both hands against the marching feet of his fellow inmates. I turned my head and hesitated, but I knew that I could not break the formation. In accordance with the camp's rules, as soon as there was an open space on my left, an inmate walking behind Rubin moved one row ahead to fill the void. We were again marching five men abreast. I turned my head again to see what happened to Rubin. As the last group of prisoners bypassed him lying on the ground, the SS guard walking at the very end of the column shot him twice in the head. At that moment, I knew that I must escape at the first opportunity.

One SS guard marched on the right side a few steps ahead of me. The next SS guard was approximately thirty meters behind on the same side. Fortunately, neither of them were accompanied by dogs. The highway started to turn gently to the left and a sparsely wooded area appeared on the right. For an hour I looked carefully for a suitable place to escape that would provide some protection against the anticipated barrage of bullets from the SS guards. As we were turning left and at the same time approaching a more densely wooded area, in a flash of a moment, I decided that this was an ideal place and opportunity to escape. Suddenly, I jumped the line and ran for the nearest bushes.

This was a life-and-death decision. Within a second, there was a rapid fire of shots from the automatic rifles. Bullets whistled around me. I ran as fast as I possibly could. My heart pounded. As I reached the line of tall trees, I gasped for air and dared to look back. One of the SS guards kneeled on the side of the road and fired rapid shots in my direction. I felt fear but at the same time I was relieved that I did not hear the barking of the dogs. I kept running until I was completely exhausted. My heart was now racing uncontrollably, my lips were completely dry, and I could scarcely see my way among the large pine trees. I staggered a few more steps and then collapsed in the nearby dense bushes. Trying to recover my strength and my breath, I listened to the sounds of the forest. I could still hear the rumbling of the big guns in the distance, but the trees were peaceful. As I rested on the ground, I tried desperately to collect my thoughts and make plans. I decided to keep walking northwest and look for food and water.

I moved carefully and silently, watching for German patrols crossing the forest. There was no sign of people or animals. Even birds somehow disappeared. The silence was unreal, until suddenly it was broken by the sound of an aircraft engine. I heard the noise of a low-flying airplane getting louder and louder. The shadow of the huge plane was gracefully floating among the tall pine trees above me. It flew very slowly, just above the treetops, and I thought that the sound of engines was heard for miles. Then, as the sound of noisy engines faded, there were one, two, three explosions. I heard a burst of rapid machine-gun fire, sporadic shots, and then silence.

"Americans!" That happy thought crossed my mind and I ran toward the sound of explosions. In a few minutes, I was at the edge of the forest. A paved and narrow country road leading to a small picturesque village was in front of me. I could see the colorful rooftops of houses on the horizon. Closer to me, a ball of black smoke rose toward the sky on one side of the road. I hesitated at first, but then, hiding behind smaller trees and bushes, I carefully approached the highway. In the ditch, with a rear wheel up in the air, was a motorcycle with a sidecar. The driver was leaning over the steering handles. He was in black uniform, his left arm was completely missing and his face was distorted beyond recognition. In the sidecar, another person was sitting silently. I moved closer, not knowing what to expect. A boy in Hitler-Jugend uniform, perhaps thirteen or fourteen years old, was sitting motionless in the sidecar, holding a revolver in his right hand. His eyes were wide open, but there was no movement. I moved even closer and noticed blood still dripping from the corner of his mouth.

I checked his pulse. He was dead. With blond hair, blue eyes, and a baby face, he reminded me of my thirteen-year-old cousin with whom I used to play soldiers or cowboys and Indians before the war. Only this was not play. This was a real and deadly struggle. I looked at the boy again and mumbled to myself, "The Germans must be in a real trouble when they are willing to sacrifice their children. There will be many crying and mourning mothers." I opened the boy's clenched fist and removed the revolver, then looked around for water or food in the motorcycle, but there was none. The road was empty, the village was silent; there was no life anywhere. I came to the conclusion that people must be hiding in their cellars. As each moment passed, I felt hungrier and thirstier. With a gun in my pocket I felt more secure and more willing to take a chance and look for food and water in the deserted houses.

I walked toward the village and knocked on the first door, carefully covering my head with a civilian hat to hide my prisoner's haircut. The house was isolated and close to the edge of the forest. There was no response. I knocked again. Slowly the front door was opened. An old man looked at me suspiciously and waved his hand: "Go away, we don't have any work."

I tried my best German, "Please let me in. I am a farm worker. We were bombed and dispersed. May I have some water, please?" The man tried to shut the door. I pushed my foot against the door and I touched my revolver in my pocket. Then I heard another voice behind the door. "Father, let him in, he needs help and food." A woman in her early thirties opened the door wide.

"Please don't mind my father," she said. "He lost his son in Stalingrad and my younger brother is fighting on the western front. Wait here for me."

She left me standing alone in front of the house and disappeared. In a few minutes, she was back with a large canister of water, a loaf of bread, and a large sausage.

"Take this with you. This is all we can share, but you can't stay here. It is too dangerous for both of us. Good luck and God bless you."

The old man was watching this in silence. I drank the water, hardly listening to my benefactress. I felt better already. I was moved as I left the house; and thankful that there were still decent people in Germany. She knew who I was, yet she was willing to risk her safety. As the woman was waving from her front door, I turned my head and called back, *"Danke Schön."*

After I left the village, I returned to the highway, passed the motorcycle with two dead soldiers, and walked north in the ditch along the main road. I looked up toward the blue sky. The April sun was shining brightly. It was warm and pleasant; war and the front lines seemed to be far removed from the tranquillity of "mother nature." I was tired but happy. With food and a gun in my pocket, my chances for survival looked better and better.

The clanking sound of moving metal parts interrupted my thoughts. I listened carefully. Tanks, but whose tanks? The sound was getting louder and closer. A huge tank painted with camouflage colors was slowly moving in the center of the highway. It was moving toward me. It had white stars painted on the green background. The tank's turret with the barrel of a long gun sticking forward moved slowly from left to right, searching for potential targets.

"Americans!" I was thrilled and excited. I jumped toward the middle of the road and waved my arms desperately. The tank stopped. The gun turret turned slowly in my direction. I could see the inside of the long barrel.

Are they going to shoot me? I frantically waved my arms and screamed in broken English and pidgin German. "Don't shoot. *Nicht Shissen*—prisoner, Auschwitz, Buchenwald, help!" As I looked at the menacing barrel in front of me, all my recent life experiences flashed before my eyes: September 1939, German occupation, the underground, my service with partisans, the Gestapo jail, my struggle for survival in Auschwitz, Buchenwald, and Ohrdruf. How is this going to end? How can one survive so much and end up as a casualty of friendly fire?

I waved and screamed at the top of my voice. Slowly, the hatch at the top of the turret opened. A soldier in a green uniform and leather helmet appeared above the gun barrel, waved to me and called; "Hands up! Get closer!" With my arms stretched as high as I could, eyes filled with tears, I slowly started walking toward the American tank with shiny, bright, white stars painted on the gun turret.

Epilogue

MEMORABLE DAYS of the Second World War, full of misery, destruction, atrocities, and death left many scars on the lives of the survivors. Entire families were wiped out, whole cities were destroyed, and the existence and future of many nations were profoundly affected. Six million Poles, including three million Polish Jews, lost their lives. Millions of other victims from all countries occupied by Nazi oppressors paid a heavy price for Hitler's warped dream of the "One-Thousand-Year Reich." Generations of European Jews were murdered in the ovens of Birkenau and other extermination camps. Their ashes, spread throughout the European continent, marked the places of mortal battles, cruel executions, and deadly crematoria sites.

As the tide of the war slowly changed, signaling the end of Nazi tyranny, German police started the forceful liquidation of Zaklików ghetto. They also carefully searched for Jewish families hiding in the forest along the Modliborzyce-Zaklików highway.

Jankiel Środek was killed by an SS man searching for escapees in *fabryka*—an industrial complex near the Lipa forest. His oldest daughter, Laika, was fatally shot on the same day by other German policemen in front of local peasants. Jankiel's younger daughter, Raisa, with blond hair and blue eyes, escaped to Lublin, pretended that she was a Christian, and volunteered to work in Germany. She never came back.

Szymsza Kuna, the storekeeper, disappeared with his family after the liquidation of the Jewish ghetto in Zaklików. They never returned to Potoczek. Their house in the middle of the village was taken over by the local peasants and still stands.

Wojciech Przanowski, the squire from Potoczek, died peacefully at his manor house before the end of the war and did not witness the demise of his estate or the exile of his children. The family left all their belongings behind and with a few suitcases escaped the Red Army. In the summer of 1944 they settled as refugees in Zakopane near Kraków.

With the Soviet Army's rapid advances across Poland, the Russian soldiers occupied the manor and the village. Local girls and young women were terrified of the soldiers' brutal behavior and stayed home behind closed doors. The wife of the distillery manager, Stanisław Kuryłło, jumped from the second-story window in her home to escape rape by drunken Russians. She broke both legs and had to be taken to the nearest local hospital in Janów. Later on, the Soviet troops established a warehouse in the distillery storage room, and when one of the soldiers tried to light his cigarette the whole distillery building exploded and was burnt down to the ground.

After the war, the Potoczek estate was taken over by the Polish communist government and a state farm was established. Some of the land was divided among the local peasants. The manor was turned over to the Communist Party and an agricultural school was established for the children of local peasants. The once graceful ballroom in the manor was divided into many classrooms to educate future farmers of Potoczek.

In order to avoid the Red Army's well-known rough treatment of wealthy Polish landowners, Ligowski and his wife quickly left their home in Matczyn to look for shelter among many other refugees in overcrowded Warsaw. They survived the 1944 city uprising but never returned to Matczyn. After the war the estate was divided among the local peasants and the state took over manor house and converted it into a home for mentally sick and retarded children.

In the fall of 1943, Lieutenant Spartanin, whose real name was Tadeusz Sowa, from Bychawa, near Lublin, led his platoon through many skirmishes with German police. In a shoot-out with a German patrol in December 1943, his unit suffered many losses and his platoon, "Spartanie," was temporarily disbanded. Recalled again in the spring of 1944, he fought Germans as the commander of the Special Security Unit protecting the Polish Home Army Regional Headquarters in Lublin. After Germany's defeat in Poland, he volunteered his services to the newly formed Russian-sponsored Polish People's Army.

Lieutenant Czarnota, who later assumed the code name of *Szaruga* and whose real name was Aleksander Sarkisow, was a Polish Army reserve officer. After the September defeat, he joined the underground ranks of the Polish Home Army. In 1942, he was appointed commandant of Jastków-Konopnica-Bełżyce Region. In the fall of 1943, he organized a special unit to accept air drops from the Polish Air force planes flying from Bari, Italy and supplying the Polish Home Army with weapons and equipment. His old friends Zegota and Gołąb left "Spartanie" and volunteered to join *Szaruga's* unit, which in the spring 1944 successfully accepted many air drops in the Lublin district and at the same time continuously fought Germans.

In July 1944, under his real name as the Captain Aleksander Sarkisow, he and his unit left the Polish Home Army and joined the newly formed Polish People's Army, where he was promoted to the rank of lieutenant colonel. After serving as the commanding officer of the Thirty-second Infantry Regiment, he was arrested by the Polish Communist Secret Police in October 1944. However, he was able to escape into hiding to avoid court-martial. Subsequent to his personal contact and interview with General Rola-Żymierski, at that time commander of the Polish People's Army, he was reinstated to his old rank and appointed commandant of the city of Łódź. Within one year, he was again rearrested, and after various interrogations and two years of imprisonment in the Polish Military Prison in Warsaw, he was finally released by the communists.

Zegota, whose real name was Apolinary Reps, served as a deputy commander of Szaruga's unit from the fall of 1943. In January of 1944, he was seriously wounded in a bloody fight with the German Army at Marysin near Lublin. Eighteen Polish Home Army soldiers were killed and many others were wounded. The unit lost many weapons and much of the equipment received from the air drops. After he recovered from his wounds, Zegota rejoined the Szaruga unit and with the whole group left the Polish Home Army and volunteered his services, in July 1944, to the newly organized Polish People's Army. Promoted to the rank of captain, he was assigned for a short period as an instructor to the Thirty-fourth Infantry Regiment. In December 1944 he was accused of treason by the Polish communists and in January 1945 was court-martialed and executed with seven of his colleagues from the Polish Home Army. His place of execution and the location of his grave were not made public for a long time.

Gołąb, in real life Józef Kasiak, an old soldier from the Spartanin and Szaruga units, took an active part in many battles with Germans in the Lublin district. In July 1944, as a second lieutenant under the Sarkisow command, he also volunteered his services and with the rest of the unit joined the Polish People's Army. Arrested in the fall, he spent several years in the Soviet detention camps, and then returned to Poland where he settled near his home village of Wierzchowiska.

Kommandants of Auschwitz-Birkenau Rudolf Höss, Arthur Liebehenschel, as well as Lagerführers Josef Kramer, Johann Schwarzhuber, Heinrich Schwarz, and the director of the crematoria in Birkenau, Otto Moll, stood trials as war criminals and were executed. Höss was hanged in Auschwitz in April 1947 near Crematorium I. Liebehenschel's successor Richard Baer died suddenly in prison, pending the investigation in Frankfurt-am-Main. Friederich Hartjenstein, Lagerführer of Birkenau, died in a French prison.

Dr. Eduard Wirths, SS Standortarzt and chief of all SS medical personnel, committed suicide after his arrest by the British Army. Dr. Heinz Thilo,

Lagerarzt of the Prisoners' Hospital in Birkenau, after his transfer to Gross-
Rosen died under unexplainable circumstances in May 1945. Dr. Josef Mengele, Lagerarzt of the Gypsy Camp in Birkenau, who was subject to the
"world hunt," disappeared in South America and presumably died in a
swimming accident.

Marie Mandel, SS Head-Supervisor of Women's Camp in Birkenau, "a
great music lover," was sentenced to death and executed in Poland.

Karl Kurpanik, SS Rapportführer from the Quarantine Camp in Birkenau, was arrested in July 1945 and sentenced to death by the Special
Tribunal in Katowice, Poland. Gerhardt Palitzsch, SS Rapportführer in
Auschwitz I, after being investigated and arrested by the SS Court of Inquiry,
was sent to fight partisans in Yugoslavia and presumably killed in action.
Stefan Baretzki, SS Blockführer from the Quarantine Camp in Birkenau,
was sentenced by the German court to life imprisonment on five counts of
murder.

Omlauf, Charvin, Charum, and Pherbinde, who served in the summer of
1944 as SS Sanitätsdienstgrade responsible for disinfection of the Women's
Camps, disappeared in the confusion of postwar activities. An attempt to
link Omlauf with the SS Unterscharführer Herman Umlauf, chief of the Penal
Company in Auschwitz in 1944, lacked clear and reliable documentation. It
appeared that both men with the same rank and almost the same name served
at the same time in Auschwitz-Birkenau. Omlauf was seen for the last time in
March 1945, in Ohrdruf, Sonderlager III, where he was assigned as SS Blockführer. SS Kommandoführer Richard Koehler, from *Aussenkommando*
Ohrdruf, was sentenced after the war to death by hanging.

Jurek Sucharzewski (No. 150304), my cellmate from Kielce jail, returned from Auschwitz and settled in Kraków, Poland.

Mietek Katarzyński (No. 8316), "The Bloody," Blockältester from the
Quarantine Men's Camp in Birkenau, was sentenced by the Polish court and
executed.

Franciszek Karasiewicz (No. 1825), Blockältester from the Quarantine
Men's Camp in Birkenau, was sentenced by the Polish court for a long-term
imprisonment.

Wiktor Sawik (No. 2861) survived Auschwitz, Buchenwald, and Litomierzyce and returned to Poland to settle in his native Warsaw.

Dr. Roman Zenkteller (No. 20497), chief prisoner-doctor in Birkenau
hospital, stood trial for persecution of prisoners and was found not guilty by
the Polish court.

Tadeusz Deperaszyński (No. 119694) disappeared after evacuation from
Auschwitz to Buchenwald.

Stenia or Stanisława Starostka (No. 6865), Lagerältester in the Women's

Camp, was accused after the war by the inmates of cruelty and sadistic behavior. She was sentenced by the British court to ten years of imprisonment.

Moniek and Icek disappeared from Birkenau in the midst of the early deportations to Germany.

Johann Mikas (No. 150284) was transported in May 1944 to Natzwiller.

Hans Bankier (No. 162692), left Birkenau in January 1945 with a railroad transport of prisoners scheduled for Gross-Rosen and Dachau.

The fate of Pepi and all her "girls" in the *Desinfektionskommando* is unknown.

Very few inmates from Ohrdruf, Sonderlager III, survived the war. Adam disappeared during the "death march" to Buchenwald.

After the liberation of Ohrdruf Concentration Camp by the American Army in April 1945, the commander of the United States Fourth Armored Division ordered all Ohrdruf officials and their wives to visit the camp and observe the atrocities committed by the SS troops before evacuation. The day after their visit, the Bürgermeister of Ohrdruf and his wife committed suicide.

The discovery of Ohrdruf atrocities and exposure of concentration camp horrors by the Allied soldiers generated a special interest among the press of all nations fighting the Nazis. General Eisenhower, accompanied by the Generals Patton and Bradley, toured the camp on April 12. After seeing the camp, he ordered every unit nearby to visit Ohrdruf in order for American soldiers to learn "what they are fighting against."

During the last days of war, the American troops, spearheaded by the General Patton's Third Army, moved rapidly east of Weimar. After my escape from German captivity during the forced "Death March" from Ohrdruf to Buchenwald, I returned to the liberated town of Gotha. There I volunteered to serve with the Guard Company. The American Military Government organized such units behind front lines to protect refugee centers, hospitals, and displaced persons' camps. The Guard Company units were staffed by liberated Polish and Yugoslav ex-prisoners of war. I was assigned to guard the international hospital in Gotha.

After Germany's unconditional surrender, I traveled south, crossed several international borders and joined the Polish Second Corps in Italy. Polish soldiers were part of the British Eighth Army, and after the Italian Campaign, were stationed along the Adriatic coast. In nine months I graduated from the Officers' Training School in Galipoli, Italy. I was one of many newly promoted officers in the Polish Second Corps whose future was bleak and uncertain.

The fighting was over. Germany was crushed. But in spite of the Allies' victory and a liberated Europe, my homeland was not free. The political decisions resulting from the Yalta agreement affected the lives and the future of the Polish Armed Forces in western Europe. Officers and soldiers who were not willing to return to the communist Poland were resettled in England.

The British government offered veterans of the British Eighth Army and their families a chance for permanent residence in England. There was also an option for younger people, willing to face the challenge of a new life in a new country, to begin higher education or to continue previously interrupted studies. English and Irish universities opened their doors to Polish soldiers.

During the following five years I studied architecture in London, and after graduation as a registered architect in the United Kingdom, I practiced my new profession in England.

In 1952 I met my future wife. We married two years later in a small church in Croydon, Surrey. In 1957 my wife and I arrived in the United States. New York's harbor looked huge, complex, and unfriendly, but New York's skyscrapers were awe-inspiring.

Another start in a new country required major adjustments and offered hope, new challenges, and opportunities. After a successful private practice of architecture in Philadelphia, Pennsylvania, I accepted a public-service appointment in Washington, D.C. We settled in our new home in Bethesda, Maryland, where we raised two sons, Christopher and Peter.

APPENDIX

GLOSSARY

BIBLIOGRAPHY

INDEX

Table of Military Ranks

Approximate Equivalence Between Armies
of the United States and Germany

SS	U.S. Army
Reichsführer-SS	
SS Oberstgruppenführer	General of the Army
SS Obergruppenführer	General
SS Gruppenführer	Lieutenant General
SS Brigadeführer	Major General
SS Oberführer	Brigadier General
SS Standartenführer	Colonel
SS Obersturmbannführer	Lieutenant Colonel
SS Sturmbannführer	Major
SS Hauptsturmführer	Captain
SS Obersturmführer	Lieutenant
SS Untersturmführer	Second Lieutenant
SS Sturmscharführer	Sergeant Major
SS Hauptscharführer	Master Sergeant
SS Oberscharführer	Technical Sergeant
SS Scharführer	Staff Sergeant
SS Unterscharführer	Sergeant
SS Rottenführer	Corporal
SS Sturmmann	Specialist
SS Oberschütze	Private First Class
SS Schütze	Private

Glossary of Camp Terms

Appellplatz: Roll call area.

Arbeitsdienst: Prisoner keeping records of work squad assignments.

Arbeitskommando: Squad of prisoners selected to perform special labor.

Aufräumungskommando: Cleaning-up detachment, known in camp slang as "Canada," symbol of unlimited abundance. Name "Canada" was quickly accepted by the inmates and became an official terminology of camp administration.

Aufseherin: SS woman supervisor in charge of women's blocks.

Aussenkommando: Work squad or group of prisoners that worked outside the camp.

Block: Brick or wood building that housed prisoners.

Blockältester: Block senior, a prisoner appointed by the SS.

Blockführer: An SS man who supervised prisoners in one or more blocks.

Blocksperre: Compulsory confinement of prisoners in the blocks.

Bunker: An underground basement in Block 11 in the main camp in Auschwitz. In the basement were cells in which prisoners were locked up for special punishment.

Bürgermeister: Mayor

Capo: A prisoner appointed by the SS to be in charge of a labor squad.

Dachdeckerkommando: Prisoners' work group responsible for installation and repairs of roofs.

DAW (Deutsche Ausrüstungswerke): German Armaments Works, Ltd., a commercial enterprise of the SS.

Desinfektionskommando: Prisoners' work group responsible for total disinfection process.

Dirlewanger Brigade: SS Penal Brigade composed of poachers, professional criminals and men under sentence of court martial commanded by the SS Oberführer Oskar Dirlewanger.

DM (Deutsche Mark): German currency.

Effektenlager: Part of the camp designated for sorting and storage of personal effects stolen by Nazis from the Jewish transports.

Entwesungskammer: Building, or area in the building, where delousing process of prisoners' clothes was carried out.

Entwesungskommando: Delousing squad. Prisoners' work group responsible for delousing processes of prisoners' clothes.

263

FKL (Frauenkonzentrationslager): Concentration camp for women.

Gestapo (Geheime Staatspolizei): Secret State Police of Nazi Germany.

Hitler-Jugend: Youth Organization in Nazi Germany

Judenrampe: Railroad platform in Auschwitz where newly arrived Jewish transports were unloaded and selected for work or for gassing before construction of new platform in Birkenau.

Kapellmeister: Bandmaster

Kesselkommando: Prisoners' work group responsible for delivery of food from men's camp kitchen to men's hospital.

KL (Konzentrationslager): Concentration camp.

Kommando: Labor squad of prisoners in the concentration camp.

Kommandoführer: An SS man in charge of labor squad of prisoners.

Königsgraben: The main drainage ditch in Birkenau, built by the prisoners.

Lager: Camp.

Lagerarzt: SS doctor in charge of the prisoners' hospital.

Lagerältester: A prisoner functionary appointed by the SS to be responsible for the camp internal administration.

Lagercapo: A prisoner appointed by the SS to be in charge of all labor squads working within the camp.

Lagerführer: SS man, chief of the camp.

Lagersperre: SS order prohibiting prisoners from leaving the camp.

Leichenkommando: Prisoners' work group responsible for transfer of prisoners' corpses from camp mortuaries to crematoria.

Leitenderarzt: Prisoner doctor in charge of hospital block.

"**Mexico**": Section BIII of Birkenau. This section of the camp was never completed.

Mussulmans: Prisoners who were in the final stage of physical and psychological exhaustion and lost their will to live. The weak, the inept, those doomed to selection.

Oberaufseherin: SS woman, chief superintendent of the women's camp.

Panzerfaust: Antitank rocket.

Penal Company: Prisoners in the Penal Company had to perform the heaviest work, were subject to cruel corporal punishment, and their meager food rations were smaller than those issued in the camp. They were not allowed to have any contact with other prisoners and were housed in separate barracks.

Pfleger: Prisoner male nurse.

Piepel: Young boy who served as a valet in the SS guardhouses or performed housekeeping services for Block Seniors and Capos.

Planierungskommando: Prisoners' work groups responsible for grading terrain in preparation for new construction.

Politische Abteilung: Political Department, the camp Gestapo office.

Polizeistandgericht: Police Summary Court. Sessions of Gestapo court-martial took place in Block 11 in the main camp. Prisoners were brutally tortured during interrogations and usually sentenced to death.

Quarantine: Newly arrived prisoners were kept in isolation for the purpose of preventing the spread of infectious diseases. However, the real purpose of isolation was to acquaint them with the harsh laws of the camp through endless drills and "sports," and to break their spirit and will to resist.

Rapportführer: SS man who was roll-call leader.

Reichsbank: German National Bank.

Sauna: Camp bathhouse.

Scheissmeister: Prisoner in charge of the lavatory.

Schreiber: Prisoner appointed by the SS to be responsible for maintaining prisoners' records.

Schutzhäftling: Prisoner in protective custody who was detained in the camp by the Gestapo for an indefinite period.

Sicherheitsdienst (SD): Security Service, part of the Gestapo.

Sanitätsdienstgrad (SDG): SS man—sanitary male orderly or disinfector.

Sonderkommando: Special squads of Jewish prisoners who were forced by the SS to work in the gas chambers removing the dead bodies and then loading them into the ovens of crematoria.

"Sport": Strenuous physical exercises and drills imposed on prisoners by the SS men.

Stammlager: Main camp (Auschwitz I)

Stubendienst: A prisoner appointed by the SS to be responsible for the housekeeping of the portion of the block. He reported to the Block senior.

Undercapo: A prisoner appointed by SS to be in charge of a portion of labor squad.

Volkssturm: German Peoples' Territorial Army

Vorarbeiter: Foreman.

Wehrmacht: German Army.

Zerlegebetriebskommando: Prisoners' work group for dismantling of damaged airplanes.

Zugang: New transport of prisoners.

Zugangsliste: List of newly arrived prisoners.

Zyklon B: A poisonous gas (hydrogen cyanide, whose pellets turned into a lethal gas when exposed to the air) used by the SS for disinfection of barracks and later on for mass exterminations of Jews and others in the gas chambers.

Bibliography

Abzug, Robert H. *Inside the Vicious Heart*. Oxford Univ. Press, 1985.

Caban, Ireneusz. *8 Pułk Piechoty Legionów Armii Krajowej*. Warsaw: Bellona, 1994.

———, i Zygmunt Mańkowski. *Związek Walki Zbrojnej i Armia Krajowa w Okręgu Lubelskim 1939–1944*. Tom Pierwszy i Drugi: Wydawnictwo Lubelskie, 1971.

Czech, Danuta. *Auschwitz Chronicle 1939–1945*. New York: Henry Holt and Company, Inc., 1990.

———. *Zeszyty Oświęcimskie No. 15—Rola Męskiego Obozu Szpitalnego w KL Auschwitz II*. Auschwitz: Państwowe Muzeum w Oświęcimiu, 1974.

Garliński, Józef. *Fighting Auschwitz*. New York: Fawcett Crest Book, 1975.

Hilberg, Raul. *Perpetrators Victims Bystanders*. New York: HarperCollins, 1992.

Höss, Rudolf, Pery Broad, and Johann Kramer, *KL Auschwitz Seen by the SS*. Auschwitz: Państwowe Muzeum w Oświęcimiu, 1978.

Höhne, Heinz. *The Order of the Death's Head*. New York: Ballantine Books, 1971.

Krzyżanowski, Jerzy. *U Szarugi*. Lublin: Norbertinum, 1995.

Lasik, Aleksander. *Zeszyty Oświęcimskie No. 20—Obsada Osobowa Służby Zdrowia SS w Obozie Koncentracyjnum Oświęcim-Brzezinka w Latach 1940–1945*. Auschwitz: Państwowe Muzeum w Oświęcimiu, 1993.

———. *Zeszyty Oświęcimskie No. 21— Ściganie, sądzenie i karanie członkow oświęcimskiej załogi SS*. Auschwitz: Państwowe Muzeum w Oświęcimiu, 1995.

Piper, Franciszek and others. *Auschwitz—Nazistowski Obóz Śmierci*. Edited by Franciszek Piper and Teresa Świebocka. Auschwitz: Państwowe Muzeum w Oświęcimiu, 1993.

Raschke, Helga. *S III bei Ohrdruf—Ausenlager des KL Buchenwald. Abh Ber.* Gotha: Haimatmuseum, 1968.

Remdt, Gerhard, and Gunter Wermusch. *Rätsel Jonastal (Die Geschichte des letsten "Führerhauptquartiers")*. Berlin: Ch. Links Verlag, 1992.

Smoleń, Kazimierz, and Świebocka Teresa. *Auschwitz-zbrodnia przeciwko ludzkości*. Auschwitz: Państwowe Muzeum Oświęcim-Brzezinka, 1990.

State Museum in Oświęcim. Archives and Protocols. Rozprawa główna Mieczysława Katarzyńskiego (Trial of Mieczysław Katarzyński), December 11, 1947. Prośba o łaskę Franciszka Karasiewicza do Prezydenta R. P. Ludowej, June 25, 1952

(Request for clemency to the president of the Polish People's Republic by Franciszek Karasiewicz). (Records of court cases, Regional Court of Poznan).

Strzelecka, Irena. *Zeszyty Oświęcimskie No. 19—Obóz Męski w Brzezince 1942–43*. Auschwitz: Państwowe Muzeum w Oświęcimiu, 1988.

———. *Zeszyty Oświęcimskie No. 20—Obóz kwarantanny dla więźniów mężczyzn w Brzezince (BIIa)*. Auschwitz: Państwowe Muzeum w Oświęcimiu, 1993.

Index

Arnstad, 219
Auschwitz-Birkenau, 49; Allied
  bombardment of, 193, 196; anti-
  Semitism in, 111, 133; barracks of, 100,
  118–19; camp orchestra in, 121–22;
  establishment and expansion of, 92–93;
  experimental gassing in, 92;
  extermination of Hungarian Jews in,
  155–60, 163, 193, 207; food rations in,
  194; gassing of Gypsies in, 192–93;
  international resistance groups in, 199;
  liquidation of, 164, 196, 203; murders
  in Quarantine Camp at, 101–3, 107–8;
  Police Summary Court at, 132, 203;
  Polish underground movement in, 129;
  power struggle among inmates in,
  110–11; prisoners' hospital in, 141–43;
  Quarantine Camp in, 96–98;
  registration of prisoners in, 91;
  Schillinger's death in, 133–35; selection
  of Jewish transports by SS at, 153–54;
  SS administrative structure in, 93; SS
  reorganization of, 138; Women's Camp
  in, 119–20, 122–23, 177, 181; Zyklon
  B and gassing of Jews in, 92, 160, 167,
  204–5. See also Concentration and
  extermination camps; Disinfection of
  prisoners; Höss, Rudolf; Judenrampe;
  Mengele, Josef, Dr., SS;
  Sonderkommando; Thilo, Heinz, Dr., SS

Babin, 73
Baer, Richard, SS, 163, 193, 197, 254
Bankier, Hans, 149–50, 155, 161, 165, 256

Baretzki, Stefan, SS, 99, 103, 105, 139,
  156, 230, 255
Beck, Captain, 15
Bełżyce, 36, 40–41, 48
Bergen-Belsen, 220
Berlin, 138, 157, 167
Bernacik, Józef, 149
Bielak, Captain, 4
Biernacki, General, 17
Biłograj, 66
Birkenau. See Auschwitz-Birkenau
Borów, 54–55
Bradley, General, 256
Buchenwald, 135; arrival to, 208;
  establishment of, 209; prisoners' self-
  government in, 210–11; transfer to
  Ohrdruf from, 211–12
Budapest, 158, 160, 170, 174, 186
Bug (river), 15
Buna, 93
Busko, 79
Bychawa, 36, 52, 66, 253
Bzura (river), 16

Charum, SS, 255
Charvin, SS, 171, 175–76, 255
Chołaj, Andrzej, 54. See also Jeleń
Chołaj, Bogdan, 54. See also Jelonek
Ciemięga (river), 60
Concentration and extermination camps,
  49; classification of inmates in, 94;
  prisoners' self-government in, 95;
  quarantine in, 103–4
Crawinkel, 219–20, 233–34

Crematoria in Birkenau, 92–93, 152,
159–60, 162, 199–200, 205
Croydon, 257
Czarnota, 47; air-drop unit and, 72, 253;
Motycz contact point and, 49–50;
Polish People's Army and, 254. *See also*
Sarkisow, Aleksander

Dachau, 13, 32, 256
Danish, Franz, 197
Deperaszyński, Tadeusz. *See* Tadek
Dirlewanger Brigade, 203
Disinfection of prisoners, 144; infectious
diseases and, 137–38; men's bathhouse
and, 195; SS hygienic regulations for,
190; trailer used for, 168; Women's
Camp and, 171–73, 181, 185; Zyklon B
and, 166–67
Dora, 211, 223–24, 231
Drancy, 123, 218, 247
Drechsel, SS, 197

Eichman, SS, 163
Eisenhower, General, 256
Emmerich, SS, 133–34
England, 75
Espenfeld, 234

Flossenburg, 223
France, 16, 218
Franek, 94, 98, 102, 107–8, 255
Frankfurt-am-Main, 254

Galant, 63
Galiński, Edek, 197
Gdańsk, 13
German Army, 13, 169
German police, 45
Germany, 3, 12, 14, 16
Gestapo, 17; arrest by, 75–76;
interrogations in Kielce by, 80–84;
murder in Potok Wielki by, 18;
selections in block 11 in Auschwitz by

Political Department and, 132; transfer
of political prisoners by, 226
Gleiwitz, 13
Gołąb, 51; ambush in Sieprawice and,
62–64; Jeleń detachment and, 53–56;
skirmish at Tuszówek and, 67–68;
Spartanie and, 70–73. *See also* Kasiak,
Józef
Gotha, 258
Gross-Rosen, 204, 255–56
Gruchot, Hans, 35–37, 40–41
Gypsy camp in Birkenau, 151

Hartjenstein, Friedrich, SS, 138, 163,
254
Himmler, SS, 17, 42, 47, 92
Hitler, 13, 31, 157, 216, 219, 226, 252
Höss, Rudolf, 92; camp inspections by,
138; execution of, 254; Hungarian Jews
and, 162–63, 186, 193; Shillinger's
death and, 134; transfer to SS
headquarters of, 138

Jankiel, 11–12, 45, 252
Janów, 12, 15, 30, 34
Jastków, 56, 253
Jawiszów, 93
Jeleń, 51–53, 57. *See also* Chołaj, Andrzej
Jelonek, 50–51, 53. *See also* Chołaj,
Bogdan
Jonastal, 216, 218–19, 234
Judenrampe, 182; Birkenau expansion of,
132, 153, 205; SS distribution of Jewish
property at, 157; work of "Canada"
Kommando on, 122, 154, 156, 158,
160

Kabuszkin, Senior Lieutenant, 58
Karasiewicz, Franciszek. *See* Franek
Karlicz, Jan, 23
Kasiak, Józef, 254. *See also* Gołąb
Katarzyński, Mietek. *See* Mietek
Katowice, 38, 132, 207, 255
Kawka, 58

Kielce, 72–73, 78, 84–85, 101
Klocek, Władysław, 143
Koehler, Richard, SS, 223, 255
Konopnica, 52, 253
Kowal, 25
Kowalski, Stanisław, 83
Kowno, 171
Kozłowiecka Forest, 58
Kraków, 17, 75, 255
Kramer, Josef, SS, 163, 254
Kraśnik, 34, 71
Kruk, Jurek, 54
Kuna, Szymsza. *See* Szymsza
Kurpanik, Karl, SS, 98, 112, 139, 255
Kuryłło, Stanisław, 253
Kutrzeba, General, 16

Liebehenschel, Arthur, SS, 138, 163, 197, 254
Ligowski, Jan, 35, 37, 39, 253
Lipa, 13, 22, 27
Lipa Forest: Jews and winter in, 45; partisans of, 19, 22; SS "pacification raids" at, 27–29
Liquidation of Łódź Ghetto, 193
Lisowski, Piotr, 166
Lisowski-Palone, Tadeusz, 129
Lithuania, 171
Litomierzyce, 255
Łódź, 193, 254
London, 19
Lublin, 3, 35, 46, 49, 62, 66, 69, 82, 253–54
Lublin Castle, 30, 49
Łukasik, Olek, 64
Lwów, 20; defense of, 16; life in prewar, 5; Military Academy in, 3
Łysa Góra, 27
Łysaków, 21–23

Majdan, 59–60, 62
Majdanek, 49, 171
Mandel, Marie, SS, 121, 178, 192, 255
Marysin, 254
Matczyn: hiding of Rosa Maria in, 36–40;

Jewish labor camps near, 36; Ligowski's escape from, 253; manor house in, 35
Mauthausen, 163, 165
Mengele, Josef, Dr., SS, 144; anthropological experiments by, 151; death of, 255; encounter with, 179–80; gassing of Jews from Theresienstadt and, 175; selection of Jewish transports by, 195
"Mexico" camp in Birkenau, 115, 136, 204
Mietek, 94, 96, 98–99, 101–3, 107–8, 255
Mikas, Johann, 149, 256
Mildner, SS, 132
Miłocin, 62
Mittelbau-Dora, 223
Modliborzyce, 12, 18, 45, 252
Moll, Otto, SS, 163, 254
Monowice, 93, 138, 163, 193
Moszna, 56, 62
Motycz, 47–48, 78, 92
Murnau, 16, 75
Mussulmans, 94, 117, 125, 137–38, 194, 223–24, 227

Nagórski, Józef, 23, 25
Nałęczów, 62–63
Natzwiller, 256
Niedrzwica, 66
Nordhausen, 223

Ohrdruf, 213; disinfection in, 231–32, 234–35; escape during march from, 248; evacuation from, 236–37; history of SS barracks at, 226; *Kleinzugkommando* in, 218–21, 230–31; liberation of, 256; special project "Olga" in, 219–20; streets of, 225–26
Omlauf, SS, 167; disinfection process and, 169–70, 172–74, 177–78, 185; SS hygienic regulations and, 189–90; tour of duty in Ohrdruf of, 229–30; unknown fate of, 255; Zyklon B and, 184–85

Palitzsch, Gerhard, SS, 93, 110, 139, 255
Paris, 114, 247
Patosz, Jan, 6, 17
Patton, General, 256
People's Guard, 19, 22
Pherbinde, SS, 169, 171, 174, 176, 255
Philadephia, 257
Piłsudski, Józef, 12
Plicha, Hans, 92
Podole, 52
Poland, 17
Polish government, 12; defeat of, 17; Hitler's invasion of Poland and, 13; Soviet attack on Poland and, 14
Polish Home Army: ambush in Sieprawice by, 62–65; celebration in Majdan by, 59–62; Jeleń detachment of, 51–52, 59; Lublin district commander of, 47; political diversity of military units and, 19; skirmish at Tuszówek and, 66–68; Soviet partisans and, 43–44, 58; Spartanie platoon of, 59, 69–71, 253; underground secret code names in, 48; Warsaw uprising (1944) by, 193
Polish Peasant Army, 57
Potoczek, 3; eviction of owners from, 252; Jews in, 11–12, 152; social structure in, 8; Soviet occupation of, 253; summer vacations in, 5; village of, 10
Potok Wielki, 10, 18, 27, 46
Prague, 218
Prawiedniki, 66
Propad, 125
Przanowski, Halina, 11
Przanowski, Helena, 9
Przanowski, Michał, 11, 23
Przanowski, Wojciech, 5, 12, 252
Przemyśl, 5

Quakernack, SS, 134

Radom, 73, 75, 95, 166–67
Ravensbruck, 175, 179
Reps, Apolinary, 254. See also Zegota

Rola-Żymierski, General, 254
Romania, 16
Rudy, Oskar, SS, 30–31
Rudolstadt, 240

Sachsenhausen, 110, 223
Sadurki, 63
Saloniki, 116
Sarkisow, Aleksander, 253–54. See also Czarnota
Sawik, Wiktor. See Wiktor
Schillinger, Josef, SS, 133–34
Schuster, Dr., 146–47
Schwarz, Heinrich, SS, 138, 163, 254
Schwarzhuber, Johann, SS, 134, 254
Sieprawice, 62
Skrzypek, Aleksander, 22
Skrzypek, Bronek, 22–23
Skrzypek, Jan, 22
Skrzypek, Stanisław, 22–23, 42
Sobieski, Jan, 48
Soła (river), 132
Sonderkommando: destruction of, 202; Jewish transports and, 152; October uprising by, 200–201; recruitment and work of, 148
Sosnowiec, 123
Sowa, Dr., 21, 23, 25, 29
Sowa, Tadeusz, 253. See also Spartanin
Spartanin, 59, 69–71. See also Sowa, Tadeusz
Środek, Jankiel. See Jankiel
SS Railroad Construction Brigade, 196
Stalin, 31
Stalingrad, 43, 45
Starostka, Stanisława, 255. See also Stenia
Stenia, 191
Stiwitz, SS, 216
Stojeszyn, 21, 23, 25
Strojnowski, Janusz, 46, 73, 76. See also Strzemię
Strzemię, 48, 50–51, 55, 58, 60, 62, 73. See also Strojnowski, Janusz
Sucharzewski, Jurek, 255
Suryn, Aleksander, 35
Szymsza, 11, 98, 255

Tadek, 166, 255; disinfection work and, 167–68, 195, 198; search for wife by, 175
Tarnów, 129
Theresienstadt, 112, 123, 203
Theresienstadt family camp in Birkenau, 112
Thilo, Heinz, Dr., SS, 134; death of, 254; disinfection process and, 164; inmates' hospital and, 146; selection of Jewish transports by, 156, 158–60, 195
Tomaszów, 17
Treblinka, 37, 41
Tuszówek, 66, 69

Umlauf, Hermann, SS, 255

Von Taub, Lieutenant, 30–31

Wannsee confernece, 92
Warsaw, 13, 19, 35, 193, 253–54

Warsaw Ghetto uprising (1943), 59
Washington, D.C., 257
Weimar, 31, 209, 223
Wierzchowiska, 52, 254
Wiktor, 255; disinfection work and, 164, 167, 192, 206; Mala and, 197; Sonderkommando and, 147–48
Wirths, Eduard, SS, 167, 254
Wisła (river), 13, 17, 132, 196

Zaklików, 6, 10, 18, 45, 252
Zakopane, 252
Zakrzówek, 8, 13, 16
Zamość, 42
Zawiercie, 98, 123
Zegota, 48; ambush at Marysin and, 254; court-martial and death of, 254; Jeleń detachment and, 52, 56, 60, 62, 67, 70; Spartanie and, 71. See also Reps, Apolinary
Zenkteller, Roman, 147, 255
Zimetbaum, Mala, 197